W9-BNL-107

WASHINGTON, D.C., AND
NORTHERN VIRGINIA

Part of the Ulysses S. Grant Memorial, with the U.S. Capitol in the background. Photo by Nathan Borchelt.

FIRST EDITION

Washington, D.C., and Northern Virginia

Debbie K. Hardin
and Nathan Borchelt

 The Countryman Press
Woodstock, Vermont

*For my daughter Juliane and my husband Jon, for their unflagging support
and encouragement throughout a long year of research and writing.*

—DKH

*For my parents Gregg and Kathy, for bringing me to D.C. in the first place,
and to my sister Gretchen for making staying here so easy.*

—NB

First Edition

ISBN 978-1-58157-076-2

Cover photo by Debbie K. Hardin
Interior photos by the authors unless otherwise specified
Book design by Bodenweber Design
Composition by Chelsea Cloeter
Maps by Mapping Specialists Ltd., Madison, WI © The Countryman Press

Published by The Countryman Press, P.O. Box 748, Woodstock, Vermont 05091

Distributed by W. W. Norton & Company, Inc., 500 Fifth Avenue, New York, NY 10110

Manufactured in the United States of America

10 9 8 7 6 5 4 3 2 1

GREAT DESTINATIONS TRAVEL GUIDEBOOK SERIES

Recommended by *National Geographic Traveler* and *Travel + Leisure* magazines.

[A] CRISP AND CRITICAL APPROACH, FOR TRAVELERS WHO WANT TO LIVE LIKE LOCALS.
— *USA Today*

Great Destinations™ guidebooks are known for their comprehensive, critical coverage of regions of extraordinary cultural interest and natural beauty. The authors in this series are professional travel writers who have lived for many years in the regions they describe. Each title in this series is continuously updated with each printing to ensure accurate and timely information. All the books contain more than 100 photographs and maps.

Current titles available:

The Adirondack Book

Atlanta

Austin, San Antonio
& the Texas Hill Country

The Berkshire Book

Bermuda

Big Sur, Monterey Bay
& Gold Coast Wine Country

Cape Canaveral, Cocoa Beach
& Florida's Space Coast

The Charleston, Savannah
& Coastal Islands Book

The Chesapeake Bay Book

The Coast of Maine Book

Colorado's Classic Mountain Towns:
Great Destinations

The Finger Lakes Book

The Four Corners Region

Galveston, South Padre Island
& the Texas Gulf Coast

The Hamptons Book

Honolulu & Oahu:
Great Destinations Hawaii

The Hudson Valley Book

The Jersey Shore: Atlantic City to
Cape May (includes the Wildwoods)

Los Cabos & Baja California Sur:
Great Destinations Mexico

Michigan's Upper Peninsula

Montreal & Quebec City:
Great Destinations Canada

The Nantucket Book

The Napa & Sonoma Book

North Carolina's Outer Banks
& the Crystal Coast

Palm Beach, Miami & the Florida Keys

Phoenix, Scottsdale, Sedona
& Central Arizona

Playa del Carmen, Tulum & the Riviera
Maya: Great Destinations Mexico

Salt Lake City, Park City, Provo
& Utah's High Country Resorts

San Diego & Tijuana

San Juan, Vieques & Culebra:
Great Destinations Puerto Rico

The Santa Fe & Taos Book

The Sarasota, Sanibel Island
& Naples Book

The Seattle & Vancouver Book: Includes
the Olympic Peninsula, Victoria & More

The Shenandoah Valley Book

Touring East Coast Wine Country

Washington, D.C., and Northern Virginia

Yellowstone & Grand Teton National Parks
and Jackson Hole

Yosemite & the Southern Sierra Nevada

If you are traveling to, moving to, residing in, or just interested in any (or all!) of these enchanting regions, a Great Destinations guidebook is a superior companion. Honest and painstakingly critical, full of information only a local can provide, Great Destinations guidebooks give you all the practical knowledge you need to enjoy the best of each region. Why not own them all?

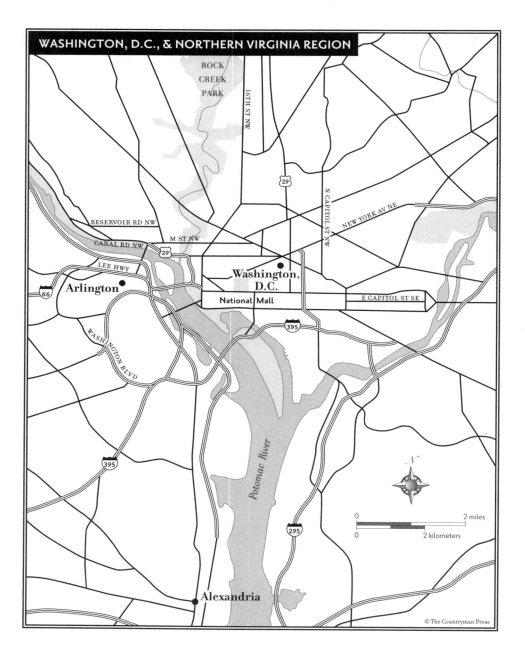

WASHINGTON, D.C., & NORTHERN VIRGINIA REGION

ROCK
CREEK
PARK

16TH ST NW

29

N CAPITOL ST NW

NEW YORK AV NE

RESERVOIR RD NW

M ST NW

CANAL RD NW

29

LEE HWY

66

Arlington

Washington,
D.C.

National Mall

E CAPITOL ST SE

395

WASHINGTON BLVD

395

Potomac River

N

0   2 miles
0   2 kilometers

295

Alexandria

© The Countryman Press

Contents

I

HISTORY
"The City of Magnificent Intentions"
26

2

TRANSPORTATION
Getting from Here to There
42

3

LODGING
A Room of One's Own
60

4

THE NATIONAL MALL
America's Attic and More
94

Acknowledgments

A book like this requires the cooperation and help of myriad public relations professionals, and we were lucky to find some of the best in the business in the Capital area. For their willingness to go above and beyond the call of duty, we extend our thanks to Amanda Abrell, Beth Amedeo, Megan Bailey, Sallie Buben, Danielle Burgos, Anaïs de Viel Castel, Carla Berry-Austin, Sarah Crocker, Carrie Foster, Heather Freeman, Meredith Goldberg, Wendy Gordon, Carl Halverson, Anthony Hesselius, Maureen Hirsch, Joan Hisaoka, Katherine Hoving, Bill Hurd, Lori Isaac, Bronwyn Elizabeth Jacoby, Virginia Lee, Aileen de Luna, Meagan Nicholas, Rebecca Pawlowski, Amber Pfau, Katie Rackoff, Simone Rathle, Emily Samuel, Camille Santry, Heather Shaw, Chrissy Sutphin, Danielle Tergis, Lindley Thornburg, Laura Trevino, Melissa Wood, and Lisa Zusman.

For entrusting us with this project, we thank our kind and nurturing editors, Kim Grant and Kermit Hummel, as well as the fabulously efficient and cheerful production staff at The Countryman Press: Chelsea Cloeter, Fred Lee, Julie Nelson, Jennifer Thompson, and Doug Yeager. Finally, the book benefited greatly from the efforts of our good-humored and meticulous copy editor, Kathryn Flynn.

—DKH and NB

We also called on family and friends to share their favorites in Washington, D.C., and northern Virginia, and we dragged these folks to venues across the region to help us uncover the best the area has to offer. For their advice and good humor, I especially thank Ann and Tony Davies, Kerry Kern, Anne Scott, Cindy Simpson, and Rosi and River Weiss. Finally, special thanks go to my husband Jon Preimesberger and our daughter Juliane, for helping with research, keeping me company on countless reviews, and offering new adjectives when mine grew stale.

—DKH

I'd like to thank everyone around me for dealing with the endless "so what about..." queries, but want to give special thanks to Molly Apter, Julie Farnen, Zoey Rawlins, and my sis Gretchen for pointing me toward all the stores they love. I'd also like to thank Pawan Batia, Toby Gohn, Craig Falls, Inge Dewulf, Pete Mohan, and Alistair Wearmouth for joining me on several outings—and to their wives and girlfriends for putting up with me in the process.

—NB

INTRODUCTION

The first time I saw Washington, D.C., as an adult, I was on an escalator, riding up alone from the underground Metro that had carried me from a friend's apartment in Arlington, Virginia, to the Smithsonian Institution station, which ultimately spills out on to the National Mall. As I traveled up slowly into the daylight, my heart pounded as I caught my first glimpse of the city: the classical and unmistakably powerful Washington Monument, the cornucopia of museums that make up the Smithsonian Institution, and the stately U.S. Capitol, which overlooks it all from a hilltop vantage point. I hadn't expected that exiting a subway would elicit much emotion, but by the time I stepped off the escalator, I was overwhelmed. It was as if I were coming home. Americans are introduced to this city with our *ABCs*, and we are reminded of its face on almost every nightly news broadcast. It is every American's hometown, and the imposing monuments and stately buildings are legacies that remind visitors that Americans are heirs to great ideals, steely purpose, and a bounty of good fortune—no matter how much we may or may not agree with our current national political figures. A few years after this first encounter, I moved to D.C., where I stayed happily for a decade. In the hundreds of times I've returned to the heart of the city with friends and family in tow and once again see the places I've seemingly always known, I never fail to feel a catch in my throat.

But the memorials to long-dead leaders, museums full of historic documents, and august buildings housing important people doing serious work are only part of the picture. The area is not just about the past; it is a vibrant and exciting place to visit and to live, offering unparalleled cultural experiences, recreational activities, and world-class entertainment. Within a city block you can snack on Ethiopian *injera,* East Indian *naan,* and French croissants. You can see the greatest ballets performed by the most famous dancers in the world; catch Broadway-quality theater; and stroll through miles of galleries that house Vermeers, Monets, and Picassos. You can skull across the Potomac alongside the Georgetown University team, jog beside presidents at the Tidal Basin, or play a game of touch football in the shadows of the Lincoln Memorial.

There is a seemingly endless amount to do—although folks who live here don't always have the time to enjoy the riches, because careers are made and broken in D.C. (A local television station used to say viewers should watch its newscasts because it was the only station in town that realized that in D.C. "it's not who you are but what you *do.*") At heart this is a company town. The biggest employer in the area is also the main tourist draw: The federal government throws open the doors of its institutions so that visitors can witness democracy firsthand—anyone who wants to can observe a congressional debate in the chamber galleries or tour the home of the president of the United States, security conditions permitting. Since the tragedy of 9/11, visitors face additional security checks on entering federal buildings, and tours and visiting hours can be canceled without warning; but curators of these buildings remain adamant that they be available as much as is practical to the people who own them: the American taxpayers. And you're likely to see important people inside these important buildings, too. In fact, you're probably more likely to spot someone famous here than you might in Hollywood, although you'll have to follow politics to recognize the luminaries. I once spotted a Supreme Court justice in the local library thumbing through gardening books; and nearly ran down a one-time presidential candidate with a shopping cart (by accident) as he browsed the soup aisle in my neighborhood grocery store.

Many first-time visitors are surprised to find that the area also has incredible beauty. More than 200 years ago, Pierre L'Enfant designed the city layout to inspire and impress, and the wide boulevards flanked with mature trees and the expansive empty spaces between monuments make a grand, almost royal impression. But it's not just the neoclassical architecture, the bewildering array of statuary, and the Palladian outdoor spaces that make the area stunning: Natural beauty is abundant. Springtime brings lemon-colored daffodils in dizzying profusion, in large part thanks to Lady Bird Johnson, who as first lady oversaw the planting of millions of bulbs along roadways and in parks in her effort to beautify the area. Other show-stoppers include cream and salmon dogwoods; giant azalea bushes in every shade of pink, red, purple, and white; and the famous pale pink cherry blossoms that surround the Jefferson Memorial and the Tidal Basin. Summer brings humid, hot weather and noticeably increased smog—but it also brings a tropical lushness, as trees turn an impossibly deep green and regular afternoon rain and thunderstorms keep vegetation thick. In fall the abundant trees put on a fireworks show of changing colors, and public gardens brim over with plum and caramel mums and purple and white ornamental kale. And when the occasional winter snowstorm blankets the area, turning the serious and important city into a storybook illustration, day-to-day activities nearly come to a standstill—and not *just* because the public works departments are notoriously slow about plowing.

Washington, D.C., and Northern Virginia are rich with history, and visitors here not only get a peek into the past, but have the chance to be among those working to protect and secure the future. I lived and worked in Washington, D.C., and Northern Virginia for a decade. My early years in the city were spent on the West End, near stately old Georgetown. During mild weather, I spent my lunchtimes walking through centuries-old neighborhoods to admire the restored town house fronts and strolling through nearby Oak Hill Cemetery to read the historic tombstones. A few years later I had the great honor to be appointed to a political position in the White House working as a writer and editor for President Bill Clinton, where I witnessed state arrival ceremonies on the South Lawn and guided friends and family through the West Wing after hours to see the Oval Office. It was a busy time, but I tried whenever possible to stop and smell the Rose Garden.

My coauthor, Nathan Borchelt, has lived in D.C. for more than 10 years, first as a graduate student and then as an editor and writer for various associations. He now works as the managing editor for an online travel company based in the city. His relationship with D.C. has relatively little to do with the political identity of the city—he brushed elbows with Tim Russert at a downtown Starbucks once, but he's more liable to recognize one of the District's underground musicians or artists than members of the House of Representatives. He's got a voracious cultural appetite and spends most waking hours taking advantage of D.C.'s ample green spaces (save for days swathed in the infamous swampland humidity).

Together, we offer expertise on both the official city as a cultural and tourist destination as well as the lesser known heart of the city, which is a vital, exciting home to more than a half million people. We both know and love this area, and it is our pleasure to share it with you. Let us guide you through the best the city and its environs have to offer, and with the help of this book, we'll make sure you don't miss a thing.

—Debbie K. Hardin

About the Authors

Debbie K. Hardin moved to Washington, D.C., in the early 1990s to pursue career opportunities, and she lived and worked as a writer and editor in the city for 10 years. In addition to working for several top-rate publishing houses, she had the honor of working for President Bill Clinton in the White House as a department director, editor, and writer. She authored another travel guide in Countryman's Great Destinations series (*Great Destinations: San Diego and Tijuana*, 2008), a book on international travel and cooking (*A Taste for Travel*); more than 100 book chapters on travel, history, art, and politics in a dozen anthologies; and numerous reviews of travel, books, films, and restaurants in local and national newspapers and magazines. She has been a book editor for more than 20 years.

Nathan Borchelt moved to the D.C. region during high school and has stayed in and around the city ever since. He's lived in the District itself for a decade, and has worked both in Virginia and within the city limits. He has been an editor and writer for more than 10 years, and is currently the managing editor for The Away Network, a series of online travel resources that includes Away.com, Orbitz, and the online edition of *Outside* magazine. In addition to publishing travel articles on mountain biking, hiking, scuba diving, skiing, culture, and food for the Network's Web sites, he's had travel articles appear in such publications as the *Washington Post, Backpacker,* and *Outside.*

THE WAY THIS BOOK WORKS

In this book we recommend those places that are quintessentially D.C., rather than providing cursory coverage of everything the area has to offer. This region is rich with possibilities, and we've opted to be selective rather than encyclopedic. Each entry offers an in-depth profile that delves into the history, culture, and atmosphere of each establishment. We've vetted cultural offerings, dining and nightlife choices, lodging options, and recreation possibilities carefully so you can be sure that we've included the best of what the area has to offer.

Organization

To orient you to the area quickly and to help you narrow your focus we've separated this book into 10 chapters, each with its own overview. Chapter 1 provides an introduction to the geography, history, and politics of Washington, D.C. Chapter 2 offers information about transportation both to and within the area, along with a couple of suggestions for extending your visit beyond the D.C. area. Chapter 3 provides an overview of accommodation options in the District as well as Northern Virginia and includes a thorough listing of independent hotels and B&Bs. Chapter 4 is dedicated exclusively to the National Mall—the well-known chunk of real estate that is demarcated by the U.S. Capitol to the east, the Lincoln Memorial to the west, and the White House to the north. Within this chapter you'll find comprehensive coverage of the museums, memorials, gardens, and important federal buildings. We've also included a handy table (see pages 112–113) that will help you find the most famous artifacts housed within these important buildings. Chapter 5 explores the many cultural opportunities beyond the Mall, including theaters, gardens, and myriad historically significant sights. Chapter 6 offers a handy compendium of fine dining restaurants, inexpensive quick bites (cafés, burger joints, pizza shops), and bakeries and ice cream shops, along with a list of farmer's markets and wine stores, should you wish to pull together a picnic in one of the many scenic parks throughout the region. This chapter also reviews some of the most exciting, cutting-edge nightclubs the Capital metropolitan area has to offer, along with a healthy dose of iconic old favorites. Chapter 7 offers a guide to the best outdoor recreation available, including places where you can bike, boat, and golf, as well as details on where you can watch some of the best professional athletes in the world. We've also included a "Family Fun" section in this chapter; Washington, D.C., offers limitless possibilities for folks traveling with children, and in this section we've pointed out some particularly kid-pleasing options. Chapter 8 provides a guide to the diverse shopping available in the District and beyond, including antiques, political memorabilia, books and music, and a section on clothing that will satisfy just about every fashion sense. We've also included a section on the best spots to buy cosmetics and beauty products, along with a brief listing of some day spas in the area. Chapter 9 offers a handy collection of addresses, telephone numbers, and Web sites for services you might need while in D.C., along with a brief bibliography of books and films about the region, should you be interested in delving into the Capital city before you even arrive. Finally, in Chapter 10 we've pinpointed our absolute favorite cultural options, hotels, night spots, and restaurants; if you're only in D.C. for a short while, be sure to check out what we've termed the "best of the best."

Within these chapters, big-ticket considerations like accommodations, restaurants, and nightlife have then been subdivided by neighborhood, while other interests like shopping, culture, and museums have been cordoned into thematic groups so that your particular interests can guide you. Entries are presented in alphabetical order, and we've provided an information block that includes addresses, contact names, and information about handicap accessibility for each. Throughout we've included insider tips (look for the italicized text set off with rules above and below) to give you insight into how locals think and to help you get the most out of your visit. Finally, we've included useful indexes that list hotels by price and dining options by cuisine and price, along with a general index that covers everything in the book. Use these in conjunction with the geographical listings in the body of the text to help you find exactly what you need.

Pricing

Rather than provide exact prices for hotels and restaurants that quickly become outdated, we've offered price range categories to help you gauge the costs.

Dining

(per person, including appetizer, entrée, dessert, tax, and tip, but excluding drinks)
    Inexpensive: Up to $15
    Moderate: $15–30
    Expensive: $30–75
    Very Expensive: $75 and up

Lodging

(per night, standard room in high season, standard view; taxes and parking excluded)
    Inexpensive: Up to $125
    Moderate: $125–250
    Expensive: $250–400
    Very Expensive: $400 and up

Credit cards are abbreviated as follows:
    AE—American Express
    D—Discover Card
    DC—Diner's Club
    MC—MasterCard
    V—Visa

Neighborhoods

Because of its proximity to that big, white-domed building, Capitol Hill attracts a mixture of politicians, journalists, lobbyists, interns, and young professionals. The Northwest quadrant of the city encompasses several different neighborhoods, most central being the vicinity of the National Mall, the hub of tourist activity and home to many of the most famous sites in the city; and Foggy Bottom, a quickly evolving neighborhood that comprises the quiet, slightly residential West End and The George Washington University close to Washington Circle. Heading east you'll find Chinatown/Penn Quarter, a neighborhood enjoying a recent and stunning revitalization; it's now defined by exciting restaurants and

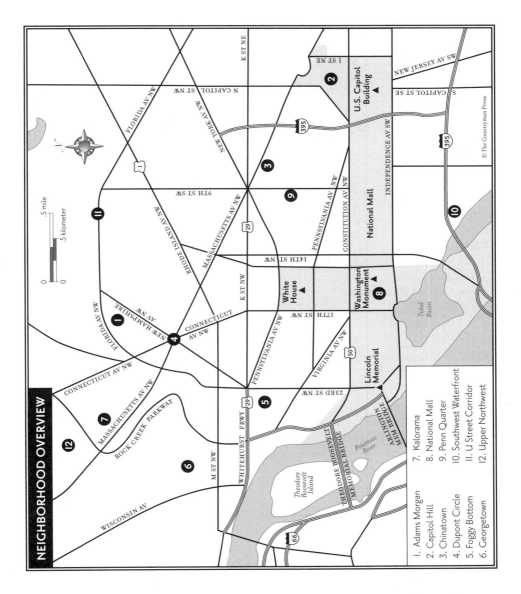

nightlife, new residence and office complexes, and a burgeoning shopping district that mimics the glittery excess of NYC's Times Square, anchored by the Verizon Center and a fantastic group of theaters. Dupont Circle, meanwhile, has long been established as one of the *it* neighborhoods, thanks in large part to a vibrant and active gay and lesbian community (the country's largest after San Francisco). You'll also find Embassy Row to the northwest, which boasts a collection of some of the most breathtaking mansions in the area. North (and slightly east) of Dupont lies Adams Morgan, a melting pot of Columbian and

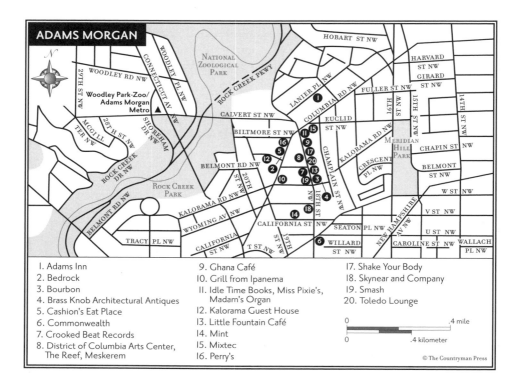

ADAMS MORGAN

1. Adams Inn
2. Bedrock
3. Bourbon
4. Brass Knob Architectural Antiques
5. Cashion's Eat Place
6. Commonwealth
7. Crooked Beat Records
8. District of Columbia Arts Center,
   The Reef, Meskerem

9. Ghana Café
10. Grill from Ipanema
11. Idle Time Books, Miss Pixie's,
    Madam's Organ
12. Kalorama Guest House
13. Little Fountain Café
14. Mint
15. Mixtec
16. Perry's

17. Shake Your Body
18. Skynear and Company
19. Smash
20. Toledo Lounge

0   .4 mile

0   .4 kilometer

© The Countryman Press

Ethiopian immigrants intermingled with young professionals who together have created one of the city's most diverse, interesting neighborhoods. The college crowds and suburbanites transform the streets into a madhouse on the weekends.

The U Street Corridor, meanwhile, branches off of the southernmost region of Adams Morgan, stretching down U Street all the way to Seventh Street, and down the length of 14th Street. This neighborhood has also recently undergone a great renaissance, blending live jazz with global cuisine alongside a crop of hip, fashionable shops. To the far west of the city, Georgetown, isolated from a Metro stop by either the Key Bridge or a substantial hike from Foggy Bottom, still reigns supreme as D.C.'s most elite neighborhood. Expect cobblestone streets, couture shopping, and a crowded nightlife dominated mostly by college students from nearby Georgetown and American Universities; the quaint Chesapeake and Ohio Canal tucked between the southern reaches of Georgetown and the harbor offers pastoral respite. Upper Northwest—near the zoo and the impressive National Cathedral—boasts more enviable real estate and provides a calmer vibe that many visitors miss because it is less central than some other city neighborhoods.

Separated by the slow-flow Potomac River, the Virginia suburbs of Alexandria and Arlington sway to a slightly slower rhythm than the District. Arlington city comprises about a half dozen neighborhoods that have sprung up along the Metro's Orange and Blue lines. Home to the Pentagon, the Iwo Jima statue, and Arlington National Cemetery, Arlington remains rooted in the national character of the District while its multicultural population provides a unique local flavor of its own.

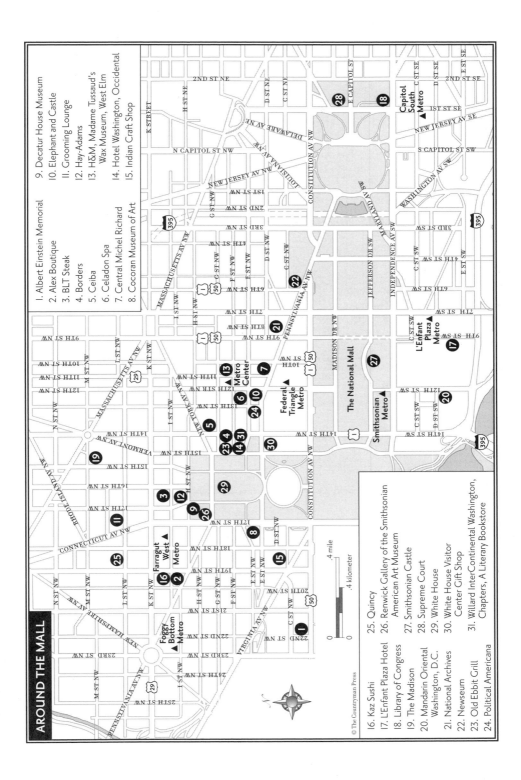

AROUND THE MALL

1. Albert Einstein Memorial
2. Alex Boutique
3. BLT Steak
4. Borders
5. Ceiba
6. Celadon Spa
7. Central Michel Richard
8. Cocoran Museum of Art
9. Decatur House Museum
10. Elephant and Castle
11. Grooming Lounge
12. Hay-Adams
13. H&M, Madame Tussaud's Wax Museum, West Elm
14. Hotel Washington, Occidental
15. Indian Craft Shop
16. Kaz Sushi
17. L'Enfant Plaza Hotel
18. Library of Congress
19. The Madison
20. Mandarin Oriental Washington, D.C.
21. National Archives
22. Newseum
23. Old Ebbit Grill
24. Political Americana
25. Quincy
26. Renwick Gallery of the Smithsonian American Art Museum
27. Smithsonian Castle
28. Supreme Court
29. White House
30. White House Visitor Center Gift Shop
31. Willard InterContinental Washington, Chapters, A Literary Bookstore

© The Countryman Press

.4 mile
.4 kilometer

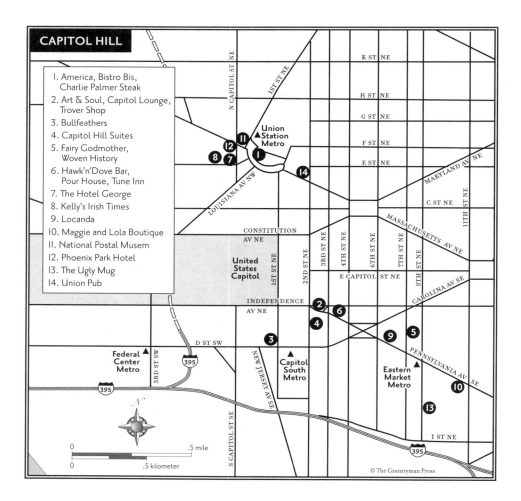

CAPITOL HILL

1. America, Bistro Bis, Charlie Palmer Steak
2. Art & Soul, Capitol Lounge, Trover Shop
3. Bullfeathers
4. Capitol Hill Suites
5. Fairy Godmother, Woven History
6. Hawk'n'Dove Bar, Pour House, Tune Inn
7. The Hotel George
8. Kelly's Irish Times
9. Locanda
10. Maggie and Lola Boutique
11. National Postal Musem
12. Phoenix Park Hotel
13. The Ugly Mug
14. Union Pub

© The Countryman Press

Lining the western banks of the Potomac River, the postcard-perfect town of Alexandria, meanwhile, draws much of its identity from the city's centuries-long history. With George Washington's home at Mount Vernon nearby, much of the buildings in the historic Old Town section date to the founding of the U.S. But Old Town has more to offer than history, and today its streets are lined with shops, restaurants, art galleries, and nightlife venues, along with expansive waterfront parkland and plenty of boat access.

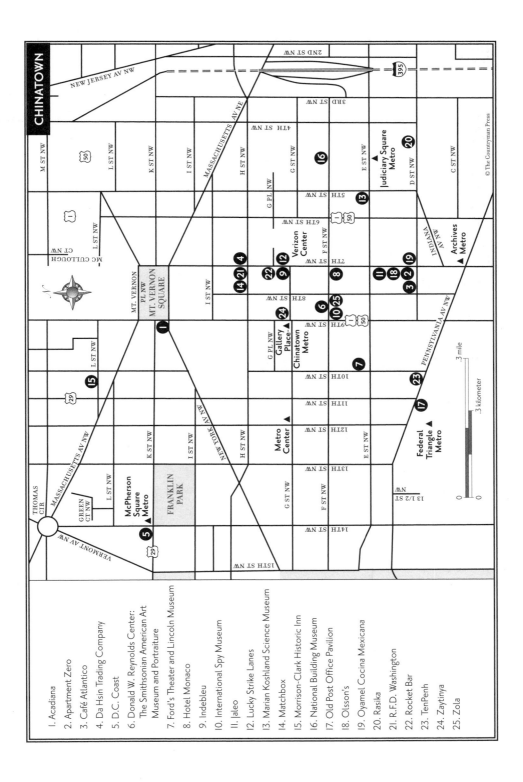

CHINATOWN

1. Acadiana
2. Apartment Zero
3. Café Atlantico
4. Da Hsin Trading Company
5. D.C. Coast
6. Donald W. Reynolds Center:
   The Smithsonian American Art
   Museum and Portraiture
7. Ford's Theater and Lincoln Museum
8. Hotel Monaco
9. Indebleu
10. International Spy Museum
11. Jaleo
12. Lucky Strike Lanes
13. Marian Koshland Science Museum
14. Matchbox
15. Morrison-Clark Historic Inn
16. National Building Museum
17. Old Post Office Pavilion
18. Olsson's
19. Oyamel Cocina Mexicana
20. Rasika
21. R.F.D. Washington
22. Rocket Bar
23. TenPenh
24. Zaytinya
25. Zola

© The Countryman Press

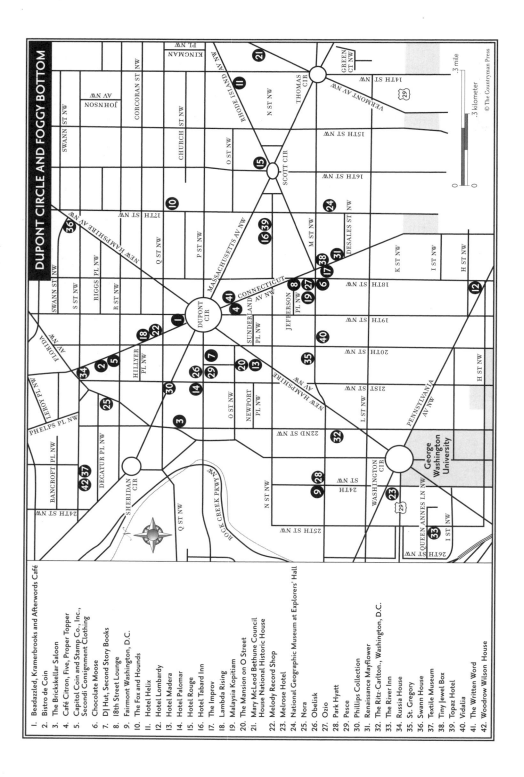

DUPONT CIRCLE AND FOGGY BOTTOM

© The Countryman Press

.3 mile

.3 kilometer

1. Beadazzled, Kramerbrooks and Afterwords Café
2. Bistro de Coin
3. The Brickskellar Saloon
4. Café Citron, Five, Proper Topper
5. Capitol Coin and Stamp Co., Inc., Secondi Consignment Clothing
6. Chocolate Moose
7. DJ Hut, Second Story Books
8. 18th Street Lounge
9. Fairmont Washington, D.C.
10. The Fox and Hounds
11. Hotel Helix
12. Hotel Lombardy
13. Hotel Madera
14. Hotel Palomar
15. Hotel Rouge
16. Hotel Tabard Inn
17. The Improv
18. Lambda Rising
19. Malaysia Kopitiam
20. The Mansion on O Street
21. Mary McLeod Bethune Council House National Historic House
22. Melody Record Shop
23. The Ritz-Carlton., Washington, D.C.
24. National Geographic Museum at Explorers' Hall
25. Nora
26. Obelisk
27. Ozio
28. Park Hyatt
29. Pesce
30. Phillips Collection
31. Renaissance Mayflower
32. The Ritz-Carlton, Washington, D.C.
33. The River Inn
34. Russia House
35. St. Gregory
36. Swann House
37. Textile Museum
38. Tiny Jewel Box
39. Topaz Hotel
40. Vidalia
41. The Written Word
42. Woodrow Wilson House

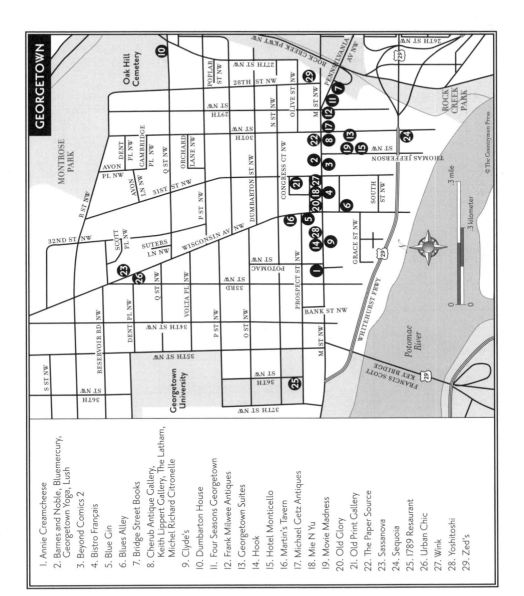

GEORGETOWN

1. Annie Creamcheese
2. Barnes and Noble, Bluemercury, Georgetown Yoga, Lush
3. Beyond Comics 2
4. Bistro Français
5. Blue Gin
6. Blues Alley
7. Bridge Street Books
8. Cherub Antique Gallery, Keith Lippert Gallery, The Latham, Michel Richard Citronelle
9. Clyde's
10. Dumbarton House
11. Four Seasons Georgetown
12. Frank Milwee Antiques
13. Georgetown Suites
14. Hook
15. Hotel Monticello
16. Martin's Tavern
17. Michael Getz Antiques
18. Mie N Yu
19. Movie Madness
20. Old Glory
21. Old Print Gallery
22. The Paper Source
23. Sassanova
24. Sequoia
25. 1789 Resaurant
26. Urban Chic
27. Wink
28. Yoshitoshi
29. Zed's

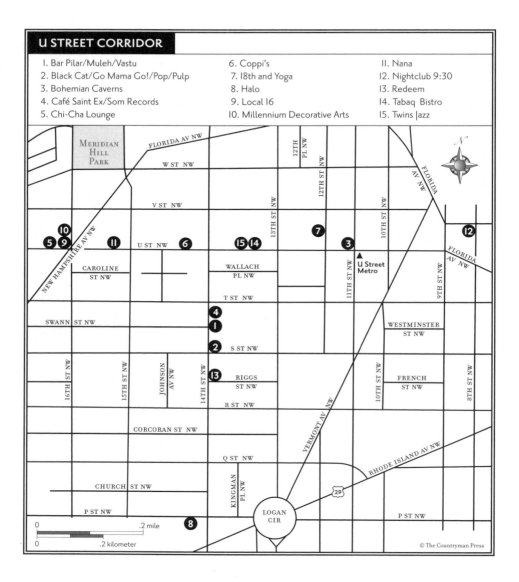

U STREET CORRIDOR

1. Bar Pilar/Muleh/Vastu
2. Black Cat/Go Mama Go!/Pop/Pulp
3. Bohemian Caverns
4. Café Saint Ex/Som Records
5. Chi-Cha Lounge
6. Coppi's
7. 18th and Yoga
8. Halo
9. Local 16
10. Millennium Decorative Arts
11. Nana
12. Nightclub 9:30
13. Redeem
14. Tabaq Bistro
15. Twins Jazz

© The Countryman Press

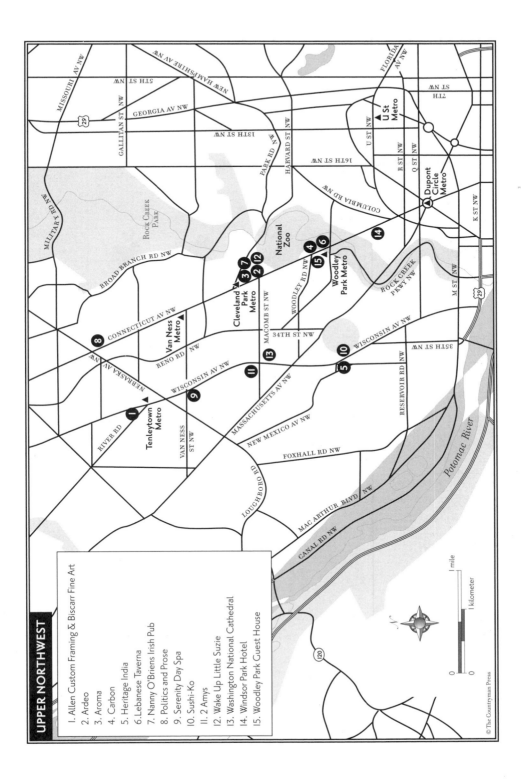

UPPER NORTHWEST

1. Allen Custom Framing & Biscarr Fine Art
2. Ardeo
3. Aroma
4. Carbon
5. Heritage India
6. Lebanese Taverna
7. Nanny O'Briens Irish Pub
8. Politics and Prose
9. Serenity Day Spa
10. Sushi-Ko
11. 2 Amys
12. Wake Up Little Suzie
13. Washington National Cathedral
14. Windsor Park Hotel
15. Woodley Park Guest House

© The Countryman Press

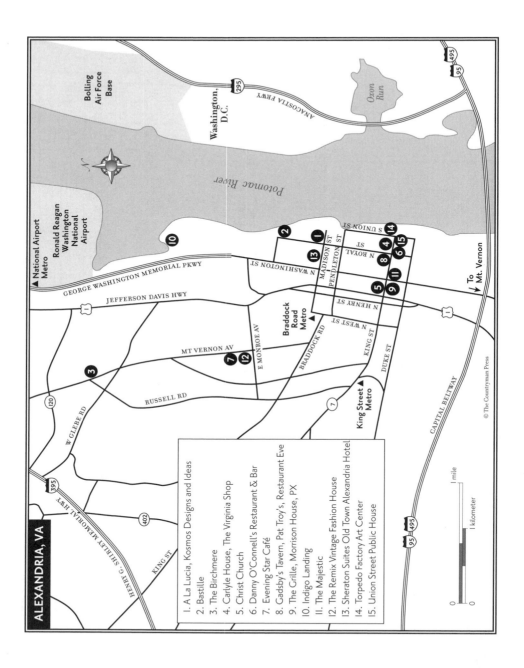

ALEXANDRIA, VA

1. A La Lucia, Kosmos Designs and Ideas
2. Bastille
3. The Birchmere
4. Cartyle House, The Virginia Shop
5. Christ Church
6. Danny O'Connell's Restaurant & Bar
7. Evening Star Café
8. Gadsby's Tavern, Pat Troy's, Restaurant Eve
9. The Grille, Morrison House, PX
10. Indigo Landing
11. The Majestic
12. The Remix Vintage Fashion House
13. Sheraton Suites Old Town Alexandria Hotel
14. Torpedo Factory Art Center
15. Union Street Public House

© The Countryman Press

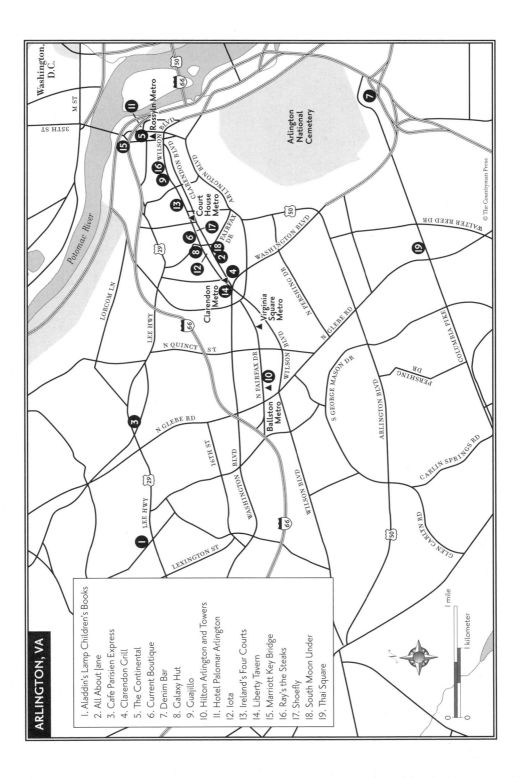

ARLINGTON, VA

1. Aladdin's Lamp Children's Books
2. All About Jane
3. Cafe Parisien Express
4. Clarendon Grill
5. The Continental
6. Current Boutique
7. Denim Bar
8. Galaxy Hut
9. Guajillo
10. Hilton Arlington and Towers
11. Hotel Palomar Arlington
12. Iota
13. Ireland's Four Courts
14. Liberty Tavern
15. Marriott Key Bridge
16. Ray's the Steaks
17. Shoefly
18. South Moon Under
19. Thai Square

Washington, D.C.

Arlington National Cemetery

Rosslyn Metro

Court House Metro

Clarendon Metro

Virginia Square Metro

Ballston Metro

Potomac River

© The Countryman Press

1 mile

1 kilometer

The striking U.S. Supreme Court Building was designed to resemble a Greek temple. Photo by Debbie K. Hardin.

History

"The City of Magnificent Intentions"

"It is sometimes called the City of Magnificent Distances, but it might with greater propriety be termed the City of Magnificent Intentions; for it is only on taking a bird's-eye view of it from the top of the Capitol that one can at all comprehend the vast designs of its projector, an aspiring Frenchman."

—Charles Dickens on Washington, D.C. (1849)

Washington, D.C., sits on the Atlantic coastal plain, tucked between the Chesapeake Bay and the Blue Ridge Mountains and bound by Virginia and Maryland.

The major river running through the District, the Potomac, rises and falls with the Chesapeake Bay—and as a result, portions of the city were little more than swampland before the federal government decided to call this patch of marsh home. Other tributaries in the region include the Anacostia River, which runs south through the eastern part of the city, and Rock Creek—a much smaller stream—which runs through the northwestern portion of the city. An underground stream called Tiber Creek flows mostly beneath the city (it was covered over when Constitution Avenue was paved in the 1800s). The city's highest point is 410 feet above sea level (in Tenleytown, a neighborhood in the northwest part of the city); the city's lowest points are the Tidal Basin, along with the Anacostia and Potomac River shorelines, which sit at sea level.

In addition to being home to the three branches of the U.S. federal government, more than a half million people call the District home—and more than 5 million live in the greater Washington Metropolitan area that extends into the Maryland and Virginia suburbs. In addition to being the capital city of the United States, D.C. is an international center, housing the headquarters of the International Monetary Fund and the World Bank; it also hosts more than 150 foreign embassies.

The federal government provides more than a quarter of the jobs in the District, and many related businesses such as federal contractors, law firms, lobbying groups, and nonprofit and nongovernmental organizations make up another significant source of employment in the city. Washington is a favorite tourist destination for Americans, as well as for those who live abroad, and thus tourism is an important resource for the local economy, too.

PISCATAWAY INDIANS AND THE EARLY SETTLERS

Indigenous peoples were living in the Washington, D.C., area as long ago as 11,000 B.C. By the 16th century, the Piscataway were well established in settlements near the Potomac and

Anacostia Rivers. The Piscataway were part of the Algonquian group of natives who occupied a great deal of the East Coast before the colonists arrived in America. They lived in small communal villages and subsisted by cultivating vegetables and fishing in the nearby rivers. Although the Piscataway were peaceful people, they were often forced to fight off their more aggressive neighbors, the Iroquois and Susquehannocks, who lived in the north.

By the time the first wave of English settlers arrived in what is now Washington, D.C., in early 1634, Piscataway warriors were weakened from fighting off attacks and raids by the Susquehannocks, and they had few resources and little energy to resist the newcomers. The Piscataway instead tried to befriend the settlers, but most were quickly rebuked. Within the first year after the colonists arrived, thousands of indigenous people had died from exposure to small pox, known by the natives as "white man's disease." By 1680, almost all of the Piscataway who had lived in the region were either dead or had been driven out.

The new colonists formed England's Maryland Colony, which was run by George Calvert, an English nobleman who was also known as Lord Baltimore. Well before, in 1607, Captain John Smith and cohorts had founded the first European settlement in nearby Jamestown, Virginia. To support themselves, both colonies grew tobacco on large plantations. Although the crop was lucrative, it was also labor-intensive, and the wealthy plantation owners soon began to import slaves to harvest and maintain the tobacco.

In 1751, Georgetown was founded, and it soon became an important, prosperous port town. Because it was situated directly on the Potomac River, it provided easy access for tobacco farmers to ship their crops to the Chesapeake Bay and through to the Atlantic, then on to the lucrative markets in Europe. The majority of land throughout the Maryland and Virginia colonies was farmed until the late 18th century, and as the plantations grew, so did the demand for labor in the form of African slaves.

REVOLUTIONARY WAR AND THE NEW FEDERAL CITY

After being governed from abroad by British royalty for more than 100 years, many colonists—who thought of themselves first and foremost as Americans—began to chafe under colonial rule. In 1775, these Revolutionaries took control of the 13 American colonies, including Maryland and Virginia, formed a Continental Army, and created the Continental Congress. The next year in the Declaration of Independence, Thomas Jefferson and other Founders articulated Americans' desire for self-government and their determination to become a free and independent nation:

> We hold these truths to be self-evident, that all men are created equal, that they are endowed by their Creator with certain unalienable Rights, that among these are Life, Liberty and the pursuit of Happiness.

With this the colonies proclaimed their independence from England once and for all, and a bitter war soon ensued. Although British forces were better equipped and better funded, the Revolutionary army was augmented by French forces, and it wasn't long before the war became an international endeavor, with the Spanish and Dutch joining against the British as well. African Americans—both slaves and free men—were recruited by the British, and Revolutionary leader General George Washington also called on blacks to fight for the Continental Army. More than 25,000 American soldiers were killed during the

The District was named after the first president, of course, but George Washington never referred to the city as "Washington," preferring instead to call it the "Federal City." Photo courtesy of the Library of Congress.

drawn-out war, and as many as 25,000 more were seriously injured and later died from their wounds. In 1781, the final land battle of the war was fought in nearby Yorktown, Virginia, when nearly 20,000 American and French soldiers forced British General Charles Cornwallis to surrender. The war continued at sea for several more years, and the formal end of the war came with the Treaty of Paris, signed on September 3, 1783, and ratified by the Continental Congress on January 14, 1784.

The new country began to look for a suitable capital city; within just a few years the national government had moved from Philadelphia to Baltimore to New York, before finally settling on what is now Washington, D.C. The site was chosen in large measure because it was midway between the established states, so that lawmakers from afar could split the traveling distance. In addition, by this time there was already a growing schism between the North and the South, and the leaders of the new country tried to find common ground. Proximity to the Potomac River, the already thriving port city of Georgetown, and George Washington's home in nearby Mount Vernon were added bonuses.

Washington, D.C., was officially founded on July 16, 1790, as a federal district, which allowed the U.S. Congress to maintain ruling authority over the city. In 1791, Virginia and Maryland ceded a total of 100 square miles of land to the government to create the District. At the commonwealth's request, in 1846, Congress retroceded the Virginia portion back (now these bits make up Arlington and Alexandria, Virginia). Today what is Washington, D.C., is composed entirely of land that originally belonged to Maryland.

PIERRE L'ENFANT'S GRAND PLAN

French-born Pierre Charles L'Enfant (1755–1825) was a one-time art student from Paris who had volunteered to fight with the Americans during the Revolutionary War. When he learned about the plans for the new capital city, he contacted George Washington directly to ask if he could help with its design. Washington was impressed with his enthusiasm, and appointed him architect of the new Federal City under the supervision of three commissioners who were to oversee the details.

Pierre L'Enfant died in 1825 in relative poverty. Today he is buried at Arlington National Cemetery, overlooking the city that still very much resembles his dream. Photo by Debbie K. Hardin.

Along with surveyors Andrew Ellicott and Benjamin Banneker (a self-taught, freed African American slave), L'Enfant put together his dream for the city in a matter of months. His design was quintessentially Baroque and included grand buildings set on wide boulevards; expansive vistas of both green space and monuments and memorials, which were part of the city plan from the very beginning; and a central Capitol Building, from which all other parts of the District would radiate.

For a young country that had just finished a bloody war against aristocracy, L'Enfant's regal plans—which called for Pennsylvania Avenue to be 400 feet wide and envisioned the president's residence to be much like the royal palaces in Europe— seemed *too* grand. To make matters worse, L'Enfant ?didn't get along well with the commissioners overseeing the city design—he even tussled with Washington a few times. Above all, L'Enfant was stubborn about making suggested changes.

The writing was on the wall: As his last official act, L'Enfant ordered that a house owned by an influential, wealthy citizen be torn down because it was in his way. Washington had little choice but to fire him. L'Enfant left D.C. in a huff—and he took the plans for the city with him. Luckily, Banneker remembered them well enough to re-create them from memory, and although alterations were made over the years, the city plan remains very much as L'Enfant envisioned it. To compensate him, Congress offered to pay L'Enfant the then-kingly sum of $2,500 for services rendered, but he proudly refused.

An early depiction of the U.S. Capitol dome under construction
Photo courtesy of the Library of Congress.

Progress on the capital city was slow. In fact, the early city was a mess; dirt roads were choked with dust in dry weather and mired in mud in wet weather. Cattle and pigs wandered the city without rein. Raw sewage and garbage were dumped into the streets, and the water system was horribly polluted. But despite such challenges, building progressed. In 1793 Washington laid the cornerstone of the Capitol building—the first major federal structure to be completed in the city.

In 1792 James Hoban won a national contest to design the White House, then known as the President's Mansion. The Georgian building was begun in 1793, and it took more than

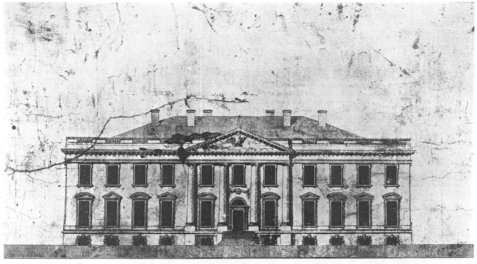

ORIGINAL DESIGN FOR THE WHITE HOUSE, BY JAMES HOBAN, 1792.
From the collection of Mr. Glenn Brown, F. A. I. A.

James Hoban's original design for the White House. Photo courtesy of the Library of Congress.

seven years to complete. In 1800, John Adams became the first president to live in the White House; it was still under construction when he and Abigail moved in. Abigail was appalled by the living conditions in the early President's Mansion; she found it difficult to get wood for fuel and water for baths in the city. She is said to have used the now stately East Room as a place to hang her laundry because it was too dirty and dusty to hang it outside.

THE WAR OF 1812: A CITY IN FLAMES

The plaster was not dry on the federal buildings—what few existed—before the new country went to war again with Britain, this time over trans-Atlantic shipping rights (among other issues). On August 24, 1814, British soldiers occupied D.C. and burned large swaths of the city, including the Capitol, the bridge over the Potomac River, and the President's Mansion. (Smoke stains are *still* visible in the basement kitchen of the White House.) The Washington Navy Yard was also lost to fire—but this time it was set by American sailors to keep the ships and weaponry housed there out of British hands. Fires likely would have completely destroyed the entire city if not for a providential hurricane with heavy rain that extinguished the flames the next day.

During the siege, President James Madison fled the city well before the occupying troops arrived, but his feisty wife, Dolley, remained behind in the White House until the very last possible moment, when she loaded a cart with personal belongs, official papers, and—famously—the Gilbert Stuart portrait of George Washington. Legend has it that she had the canvas cut from the frame in her haste, but in fact she merely unscrewed the frame from the wall and rolled up the canvas for transport.

In the wake of the devastating destruction caused by the fire, Washington, D.C., was rebuilt in an even grander style than L'Enfant proposed, because in the aftermath of the

British invasion, citizens throughout the country invested great pride in showing that the capital—and the country—could rebound. The Capitol and Presidential Mansion were completely rebuilt by the end of the 1820s. Many history books write that during the rehabilitation process, the stone façade of the Presidential Mansion was so sooty that it had to be painted white, a task that was undertaken in a day. Neighbors were said to be so startled to find the freshly painted mansion that they exclaimed, "What is that white house?" However, the more likely reason the Presidential Mansion was painted was to prevent water from seeping into the porous limestone and cracking it. Whitewash was the least expensive paint available to cover the large structure. The name "The White House" was later made official when Theodore Roosevelt had it printed on his presidential stationery.

CIVIL WAR
AND A CAPITAL DIVIDED

From the earliest days, D.C. was a hub of the slave trade. In a shameful chapter of Washington, D.C., history, human beings were actually auctioned on the National Mall and numerous other sites throughout the city. Passionate protests against slavery

Dolley Madison fled the White House in such haste to avoid invading British troops during the War of 1812 that she left behind a dining table full of food. British soldiers devoured the still-warm food, looted the mansion for souvenirs, and then set it on fire.
Photo courtesy of the Library of Congress.

throughout the country finally brought about the Compromise of 1850, whereby the slave trade was abolished in the District even as slavery was allowed to continue.

The issue of slavery remained divisive throughout the U.S., and along with traditional regional rivalries between the North and South, the moral question of human bondage ultimately led to the outbreak of the Civil War. In 1860, the Southern states—whose agrarian legacy was built on the backs of slaves—seceded from the Union. War between the states was, by then, inevitable.

In 1861, in the first few months of conflict, nearby Manassas, Virginia, saw one of the bloodiest battles of the war. In the First Battle of Bull Run—a fight the North ultimately lost—more than 450 Union soldiers were killed, and Confederate casualties were almost as high. Another decisive Civil War battle took place in the District itself in what is known as the Battle of Fort Stevens. The fort (which is now partially restored at 13th and Quackenbos Streets, N.W.) was built to defend Seventh Street Pike (now Georgia Avenue), the main thoroughfare from the north into D.C. In the summer of 1864, there were approximately

9,000 troops defending the District—down from nearly 25,000 a few months earlier. Confederate General Robert E. Lee learned that the city was vulnerable, so he sent General Jubal Early with 20,000 troops to attack the city. Early came to the region by way of nearby Frederick, Maryland, in early July, where he demanded and received $200,000 to spare that city. When Union General Ulysses Grant heard of the large number of forces so near to the District, he sent reinforcements from around the country to help defend the capital. When Early and his forces arrived on July 12, they found the fort well guarded and heavily armed. Early abandoned his plan to invade D.C. as a result, but the general ?couldn't resist a good fight. President Abraham Lincoln heard of the impending battle and brought his wife and other officers to the scene to watch—much as if it were a sporting event! Officers were said to instruct the president to duck during incoming volleys. The rebel forces were quickly outmanned and outgunned, and they retreated by midnight. Fort Stevens became the only battle in which a sitting president was actually present and under fire.

Abraham Lincoln died in the Peterson House, across the street from Ford's Theatre, in the very building that his murderer, John Wilkes Booth, occupied the night before. Photo courtesy of the Library of Congress.

So many wounded soldiers filed into the District during the war that the existing hospitals couldn't hold them, and other municipal buildings, as well as private homes, were converted into makeshift hospitals. At the same time, the war resulted in expansion of the federal government, bringing additional workers into the city. From 1860 to 1870, the city's population nearly doubled from 75,000 to nearly 135,000. Basic necessities like food and water were in short supply, and dysentery was epidemic. The Union army struggled to maintain its men as well. Washingtonian Frederick Douglass, a former slave and passionate champion for equality for African Americans and women, argued for the use of black troops in the Union army. He personally recruited more than 100 African American soldiers, including two of his sons. In 1863 Douglass appealed to President Lincoln directly to treat these soldiers the same as their white counterparts in terms of rank and pay. By the end of the war, more than 180,000 African Americans had joined the fight, and nearly a third of them lost their lives as a result.

The Civil War was a bloody, destructive campaign. In some 10,000 battles more than a million were killed, nearly two-thirds of whom died from disease or infection. The war finally ended on April 9, 1865, when General Lee surrendered to General Grant in Appomattox, Virginia, and the Confederacy collapsed. Less than a week after Lee's surrender, on April 14, 1865, Lincoln was shot and killed by John Wilkes Booth at Ford's Theatre, just a few blocks from the White House.

After the war, the Confederate states were incorporated into the Union and slavery was made illegal throughout the U.S. Shortly after, thousands of freed African Americans left their old homes in the South and moved North, many of them settling in Washington, D.C. African American influence in the city quickly increased as a result of the growing numbers of black citizens, and African Americans began to take an important role in local politics.

In 1871, D.C. was declared a municipal corporation and given the authority to construct a territorial government. Alexander Shepherd—remembered as an influential political boss—was appointed to the D.C. Board of Public Works. It was his job to finally make the struggling city a livable, vibrant place to exist. He oversaw the paving of roads, planting of parklands, and construction of sewers. But he was the first of many ineffective financial managers the city would see, and in a few years he had overspent to the tune of nearly $20 million. In 1874, ostensibly because of city debt but also in part because many Southern congressional representatives resented the power that African Americans in city government had acquired, Congress took away D.C. citizens' right to vote. The president appointed three commissioners to oversee the running of the capital.

THE MODERN ERA

World War I caused another spike in population in the District, and the 1920s saw a building boom. It was during this period that many of the earliest monuments and federal buildings were completed. (The Lincoln Memorial, for example, was finished in 1922.) But not

FDR's New Deal projects around the city include the Jefferson Memorial (shown here amid cherry blossoms) and the Supreme Court Building. Photo by Debbie K. Hardin.

long after, the Great Depression hit D.C., and the entire country, hard—perhaps no one harder than the District's African Americans, who were already limited by law in their employment opportunities. During the Depression, millions of out-of-work folks, both black and white, flocked to D.C. looking for jobs. President Franklin Roosevelt's economic recovery programs, under the banner of the New Deal, were designed to benefit both unemployed individuals and the country at large. Under this far-reaching governmental program thousands of men repaired roads and trails throughout national parks, replanted national forests, and helped with major construction projects across the country. As part of this program, members of the Civilian Conservation Corps built more than 70 scenic over-looks and cleared 500 miles of trails in nearby Shenandoah National Park in Virginia (see page 252).

By the time the U.S. entered World War II in 1941, the black population in D.C. was increasing steadily. In 1944, Mississippi Senator Theodore Bilbo was appointed chair of the committee that oversaw the management of the District. Bilbo was a segregationalist and widely acknowledged racist, and did little to hide his disdain for the black citizens of the District. Many believe that Bilbo denied the city needed funds because of his bigotry. He was soon replaced by John L. McMillan, who served as committee chairman for more than 20 years. Better known as "Johnny Mack," McMillan refused to even call for hearings to *consider* the notion of self-government in the District.

In 1961, when the 23rd Amendment to the U.S. Constitution was ratified, finally allow-ing residents of D.C. to vote for president and to have their votes counted in the Electoral College, the D.C. population was 54 percent African American. The only catch to the new amendment: The District was not to have more electoral votes than the states with the smallest populations

The Civil Rights Movement in the District

On August 28, 1963, during the historic March on Washington—an enormous political rally to support the Civil Rights legislation introduced by President John F. Kennedy's adminis-tration—Martin Luther King Jr. delivered his "I Have a Dream" speech on the steps of the Lincoln Memorial, with participants spilling throughout the expansive National Mall. The well-recognized strip of grassland surrounded by monuments was then firmly established as *the* place for political demonstrations. The largest known rally was the Vietnam War Moratorium Rally in 1969, where an estimated 500,000 people gathered; thereafter, National Park Service officials stopped releasing crowd counts.

Washington, D.C., and its citizens played an enormous role in the Civil Rights move-ment, and many in the area were devastated when Dr. King was assassinated in 1968. Shortly after his death, horrific riots broke out in traditionally black sections of town, including the historic Shaw neighborhood and Columbia Heights. Deeply distraught people and lawless mischief-makers set fires, broke into stores, and looted or vandalized prop-erty. President Lyndon Johnson sent in more than 13,000 federal troops in an effort to con-trol the chaos. Marines mounted machine guns on the steps of the U.S. Capitol, and armed soldiers were brought in to guard the White House. Over the course of four days (April 4–8), 12 people were killed and more than 1,000 injured. More than 6,000 people were arrested, at least 1,200 buildings were damaged or destroyed, and financial losses were estimated at nearly $30 million.

The March on Washington attracted approximately 250,000 people to the National Mall. Photo courtesy of the Library of Congress.

But the greatest destruction might have been to the city's image: The legacy of the riots was an inner-city ghetto where there had once been a thriving community, and although many businesses in the riot zone were rebuilt within a few years, the neighborhoods and their residents suffered for decades. Many affluent white citizens fled the city and settled into the Maryland and Virginia suburbs, deflating the District's tax base and perpetuating the city's financial woes. It is worth noting that similar riots broke out in more than 100 other cities around the country after King's assassination (although most were significantly less destructive).

ALL POLITICS ARE LOCAL

In 1970 D.C. was allowed by Congress to elect one nonvoting delegate to the House of Representatives. A few years later, in 1973, home rule was instituted by way of the District of Columbia Self-Rule and Government Reorganization Act, which allowed D.C. voters to elect their own mayor and city council. Walter Washington was elected the first home-rule mayor of D.C. and took office in 1975. He served one term.

In 1979, Marion Barry became the second mayor of Washington, D.C. Barry began his career as a civil rights activist, organizing peaceful street demonstrations in the mid-1960s; he went on to serve on the local school board and was elected to the D.C. city council in 1974. Initially Barry was a popular politician throughout the city, especially among the African American community, despite poor financial management and charges of nepotism

The Tragedy of September 11

On September 11, 2001, a series of coordinated terrorist attacks were made against the U.S. by al Qaeda, an Islamic extremist terrorist organization. Nineteen individuals hijacked four commercial airplanes and determined to crash them into important U.S. buildings. In a scenario that is by now well-known to all Americans, the first two planes struck the twin towers of the World Trade Center in New York City, causing both buildings to collapse. A third airliner was crashed into the Pentagon in Arlington, Virginia; the plane struck the western section of the building, which housed the Naval Command Center as well as other offices. The crash and subsequent explosion caused a fire that spread through the three outer rings of the western side of the structure. The outermost section was almost completely destroyed, and a segment of the building collapsed completely. One hundred twenty-five people working in the building were killed, along with all onboard the aircraft. A fourth aircraft, which many believe was headed to the White House or U.S. Capitol, crashed in Somerset County, Pennsylvania, after passengers overtook the hijackers. In total, close to 3,000 people were killed as a result of these senseless attacks.

The physical damage to the D.C. area was repaired quickly, and visitors today will not see the destruction sustained at the Pentagon. When the Pentagon was rebuilt, a private chapel and indoor memorial were incorporated into the design. As this book went to press, an outdoor memorial was being built on the site as well, which will include a park with 184 benches facing the Pentagon, to memorialize the 184 people who perished during the attacks, including the hijackers.

The emotional effects of the tragedy are harder to erase. Although these terrorist acts have profoundly affected U.S. citizens throughout the country, as the site of the federal government, Washington, D.C., has felt the full brunt of new security measures designed to protect the city and its citizens from future attacks. These measures affect the tourism industry as well, and include physical alterations to federal buildings and memorials, increased security at the three airports that serve the capital area, and numerous restrictions to public buildings. This means long lines to get through bag checks at museums and memorials on the National Mall and decreased access to federal buildings. The White House and U.S. Capitol, particularly, are much more difficult to visit, and access inside the buildings has been significantly curtailed. The FBI no longer allows the public inside for tours, and because of security concerns, even the Bureau of Engraving and Printing is closed to tourists more often than not.

throughout his reign. After three tumultuous terms, Barry was caught on video smoking crack cocaine in an FBI sting operation, and in 1990 he was convicted of illegal drug possession and perjury. He served six months in prison.

When Barry was forced to bow out of the mayoral race because of his legal troubles, Sharon Pratt Kelly ran for and was elected mayor in 1990, becoming the first African American woman to hold such a position in a major U.S. city, and only the third elected mayor in D.C. history. Astonishingly, once Barry was released from prison, he jumped right back into city politics, and in 1992 he won a city council seat. With one post-prison election success under his belt, Barry ran for a fourth mayoral term in 1994 and defeated incumbent Kelly, returning once again as mayor of the District. During his contentious fourth term, the city nearly went bankrupt, and as a result was forced to relinquish some of its home rule. In 1995, President Bill Clinton created a control board to oversee the city's finances, which stripped Barry and his successors of much of their power. Mayor Anthony Williams was elected mayor in 1998, and is widely credited for leading the city to fiscal solvency.

Today the city is run by the elected major (currently Adrian Fenty) and 13 city council members, one from each ward and five members elected at large. In addition, there are 37 elected Advisory Neighborhood Commissions. But the U.S. Congress still has the ultimate authority. Although the D.C. mayor and council pass a budget, Congress reserves the right to make any changes it sees fit. The federal government is most concerned with fiduciary control, but the Congress sometimes steps in to countermand local decisions made about such topics as District schools and gun control policies.

Washingtonians have no voting representation in Congress. Eleanor Holmes Norton is currently D.C.'s nonvoting delegate to the U.S. House of Representatives, but there is no representation in the Senate, despite repeated calls for reform. In recent years D.C. license plates have featured the sardonic motto "Taxation Without Representation" (plates that were even sported on the presidential limo when Bill Clinton was in office).

The perennially popular Barry continues to be a force in local D.C. politics; since 2004 he has been a D.C. council member representing Ward 8—a seat he won by an overwhelming majority in the predominately African American southeast portion of the District.

THE NEW RENAISSANCE

In the late 1980s and early 1990s, the aging city was in bad shape, with a crumbling infrastructure and serious financial difficulties. Crime and poverty were rampant in portions of the city, and all but the most affluent neighborhoods were suffering. Crime in the city reached a zenith in the early 1990s, when the District was known as the "Murder Capital of the United States." (There were 479 homicides in 1991.) However, concerted effort on the part of law enforcement and citizens determined to take back their city helped turn this tide of crime, and by the mid-1990s, violent crime in the District had decreased drastically.

Today Washington, D.C., has largely lived down its reputation as a high-crime metropolis. Although portions of the city remain unsafe, as is the case with any major urban area in the U.S., District crime these days is largely the result of drug trafficking and gang activity. This is generally confined to small portions of the city, and not usually encountered by tourists, provided they exercise good judgment and a modicum of street smarts (see page 292).

The District's economy has rebounded in recent years as well, and the city has enjoyed a remarkable renaissance. New buildings are popping up throughout the city and in the popular suburbs of Arlington and Alexandria, and throughout the region formerly blighted neighborhoods are enjoying revitalization. For example, the historic U Street neighborhood—heir to a proud musical legacy and host to luminaries like native Duke Ellington, as well as Louis Armstrong, Ella Fitzgerald, Billie Holliday, and Sarah Vaughn—was left in rubble after the 1968 riots. In 1999, the U Street/African American Civil War Memorial/Cardoza Metro stop came to the neighborhood, bringing with it renewed business interests, and renovation hasn't slowed since. The historic Lincoln Theater and the Bohemian Caverns jazz club (see page 233) are once again going strong, along with many other popular nightclubs in the area. In addition, hip new restaurants have sprung up throughout the neighborhood, making this a local favorite for eclectic dining. The Penn Quarter has flourished in the past decade as well, enjoying a renaissance that began with the 1997 opening of the Verizon Center (home of the Washington Wizards and the WNBA Mystics; see page 257).

The Friendship Gate in Chinatown, near the Verizon Center. Photo courtesy of Jon Preimesberger. Used with permission.

This area has also attracted a number of boutique hotels, fine restaurants, and the new International Spy Museum (see page 153) has brought in visitors by the busloads.

LOOKING FORWARD

Numerous problems face the Washington, D.C., area in the future. The recent housing boom the District has enjoyed has sent local real estate prices skyrocketing, filling the tax coffers but at the same time making it increasingly difficult for low- and middle-income individuals to secure affordable housing in the District and Northern Virginia. In addition, after years of neglect, the city's deteriorating infrastructure demands attention. Crumbling public school buildings, an aging public transportation system, and the untenable combination of high poverty paired with the exorbitant operating costs of a capital city promise to stretch thin even a fiscally solvent District. In addition, the racial inequality that has marked the District from its earliest days continues to be an underlying source of discord. Another demoralizing issue with which Washingtonians are forced to contend is the ironic position of living in the nation's capital city without the right to full self-governance, a sore spot with just about everyone who calls the city home.

Despite these challenges, Washington, D.C., remains among the most vibrant, exciting cities in the world, with unparalleled cultural and recreational opportunities and myriad multicultural influences that enrich the lives of both citizens and visitors. Thanks to the heavy presence of the federal government—which generally operates no matter what—the economy is virtually recession-proof, if only political leaders maintain the will to manage the wealth responsibly. Inevitably, the most valuable natural resources in the region are the people from around the globe who call Washington, D.C., home, and these determined folks are sure to keep working to improve their communities for themselves and for those who visit.

Typical congestion on Capitol Hill, with the stunning U.S. Capitol as a backdrop.

Photo courtesy of the Washington, D.C., Convention and Visitors Corporation. Used with permission.

2

Transportation

Getting from Here to There

Washington, D.C., is a compact city—just under 70 square miles. And thanks to Metrorail, the efficient public transportation system in the area, Alexandria and Arlington are within easy reach by subway as well. Although there are sights worth seeing throughout the region, most visitors find themselves spending the majority of their time in the Northwest Quadrant of the city, the portion of Arlington that runs along the Orange Metro line from the Rosslyn station to the Ballston station, and Old Town Alexandria. This means the distance an average visitor covers is even smaller. The District is a thriving metropolis with busy streets and plenty of congestion, but thanks to the tight, well-planned city design, it is surprisingly accessible for newcomers. Familiarize yourself with the street layout, learn the basics of the subway system, and you'll be ready to dive in and navigate the area like a native.

Getting to Washington, D.C., Alexandria, and Arlington

By Air

The Washington, D.C., area is served by three major airports. **Ronald Reagan Washington National Airport** (abbreviated DCA; 703-417-8000) is closest to the city—just across the Potomac River in Virginia and directly on the Metro subway line. If you aren't lugging too many bags, the subway is an inexpensive and easy way to get to the city from Reagan National. Use the enclosed walkway that runs from the airport to the concourse-level Metro station to catch the Blue or Yellow line. One-way fares are a few dollars per person (depending on distance traveled and time of day; rush hour is more expensive). A taxi ride into D.C. will cost about $20.

Most international flights—and many long-range national flights—are served by **Washington Dulles International Airport** (abbreviated IAD; 703-572-2700). Dulles is nearly 30 miles outside the city limits, in Chantilly, Virginia, and is not connected by subway line (yet—there have been plans in the works for decades to extend the Metro, and imminent construction has been promised for years). You can catch the Washington Flyer Express Bus that runs between Dulles and the West Falls Church Metro station (on the Orange line), and from there catch a subway into the city. Buses run about every half hour and one-way fares are about $10. A taxi ride for the 40-minute trip into D.C. will cost close to $60. Note that Dulles is configured so that you must take a shuttle to and from the terminals before and after arrivals. For years, visitors moved between the terminals via the euphemistically

Planes into Reagan National Airport come in fast and low over the Potomac River. Photo by Debbie K. Hardin.

named "mobile lounges," but construction is under way to replace these oversized buses with an underground train system, which promises to be more efficient.

Finally, **Baltimore-Washington International Thurgood Marshall Airport** (abbreviated BWI; 1-800-435-9294) is just outside Baltimore, nearly 45 miles from the center of D.C. Although its slightly far-flung location makes it less convenient than the other two airports, it is often the least expensive option thanks to a number of bargain airlines that serve BWI. Guests can catch an Express Metro Bus that runs from BWI to the Metro Greenbelt station (on the Green line) for about $3. Buses leave every 40 minutes, and the ride will take about 30 minutes, without traffic. A taxi ride for the 50-minute trip into D.C. will cost about $70.

Supershuttle (1-800-258-3826; www.supershuttle.com) is a less expensive transportation option from all three airports. Service is first-come, first-served, and the shuttle—which is likely to be full—will probably make numerous stops before yours. Note that if you arrive at any of the airports after midnight, you'll have to call for a shuttle (1-888-826-2700). Fares are calculated on distance, and range from $15 to $32. Families traveling together enjoy significant discounts. Although you cannot reserve a seat on a Supershuttle leaving *from* the airports, you must make a reservation at least 24 hours in advance to take a shuttle *to* the airports.

By Bus

Arrive by bus into the city (or surrounding Virginia and Maryland suburbs) via **Greyhound** (1-800-231-2222; 1005 First St., N.E., Washington). Taxis are generally waiting outside the District bus station, and the Union Station Metro stop (on the Red line) is nearby. D.C. also sits on the southernmost stop of the famed Chinatown buses that run between New York City, Philadelphia, Baltimore, and Boston. The departure times are typically in the middle of the day or late at night, and the ride is generally crowded with customers from all walks of life. However, for $35 round-trip bus rides to Manhattan, the experience may be worth enduring. Greyhound has also recently started to match the Chinatown bus fares, provided you've got a reservation a week in advance.

By Car

Rental cars are readily available from Washington's three airports. Some agencies have rental car offices in Reagan National itself; for these, follow the pedestrian walkway on the concourse level to Garage A. Otherwise, catch the rental agencies' shuttles outside the terminal (just past the baggage claim areas). From Dulles, walk past baggage claim to the outside curb and watch for shuttle buses serving individual rental agencies. For BWI, travelers will catch a free shuttle bus on the lower level to the central BWI Car Rental Facility (7432 New Ridge Rd., Hanover) 10 minutes away that houses all rental agencies.

A new approach to car rentals has recently come to the Washington, D.C., area: Cars are for rent by the hour, and included in the rate are fuel, insurance, and preassigned (and reserved) parking spots. These services are membership-based (e.g., Flexcars, www.flexcar.com; Zipcar, www.zipcar.com) and require a yearly fee; patrons can reserve autos online, walk to a predesignated car, and take off. Both services offer cars in a variety of low-emission, fuel-efficient, sporty makes and models. Although daily rates for these cars are generally more expensive than daily rates for traditional auto rental agencies, if you just need a car for a few hours, this is the way to go. And given these services provide gas and parking fees—and reserve precious parking spots around town strictly for their vehicles—they can't be beat for convenience.

If you drive your own car into Washington, D.C., you are likely to arrive from the north or south via I-95. Major highways into the area are I-270 (which connects with I-70 to the north), US 50 from the east, and I-66 from the west. Note that I-66 designates nearly 20 miles as an HOV (high-occupancy vehicle) road starting in Northern Virginia and flowing into D.C. during weekday morning rush hours and from D.C. into Northern Virginia during afternoon weekday rush hours. During these periods you must have at least two people in a vehicle to drive any of the lanes along this route.

Throughout the region, traffic into the city in the mornings and out of the city in the afternoons during weekdays is generally very heavy, and gridlock within the District can be nightmarish at all times of the day (especially if there is a special event or a governmental motorcade—neither unlikely events in this city). Many national surveys rank the D.C. area as having the third worst traffic in the country. This is compounded by frequent roadwork—especially during the spring and summer months, to repair the damage done to the roads due to the winter freeze-thaw cycle—and numerous one-way streets. Other challenges while driving include the ubiquitous traffic circles that can disorient even natives and the many narrow roads that crisscross the residential sections of the city. Add to this the annoying habit of delivery trucks double-parking and a local affinity for "blocking the box" at intersections (forcing oncoming traffic to wait through a signal light to pass) and you have a recipe for frustration. Indeed, for those who drive in the city, tempers are quick to flare; expect plenty of horn honking, yelling, and impolite gestures.

Another sure source of traffic is the infamous Beltway, also known as I-495, which rings the city. The Beltway connects to I-66 in the west, I-95/395 in the south, I-95 in the north, and I-270 in the northwest. The Beltway can be extremely confusing—with exit lanes on the far right *and* the far left—and it is important to know the exact exit you'll need in advance, as road signs offer few clues. Expect construction somewhere on the Beltway any time you visit. To minimize delays, be sure to contact the Virginia Department of Transportation (dial 511 or visit www.virginiadot.org) and the Maryland Department of Transportation (www.mdot.state.md.us) to check out possible delays.

Parking is also a challenge in the District, and paid lots are few and far between in particularly populous areas. But with that said, if you love your wheels and are determined to drive, D.C. is a relatively easy city in which to get one's bearings, thanks to the grid system described on pages 54–55.

By Train

Near Capitol Hill you'll find **Union Station** (202-289-1908; www.unionstationdc.com; 50 Massachusetts Ave., N.E.), a stunning Beaux-arts train depot designed in 1908 by Daniel Burnham to resemble the Roman Baths of Diocletian. **Amtrak** (1-800-872-7245) runs trains into and out of Union Station from major cities throughout the country. In addition, an express **Metroliner** train runs between Washington, D.C., and New York City, and an even faster option is the **Acela Express**, a high-speed train line that runs hourly during rush hours between D.C. and Boston, with stops in Philadelphia and New York. These full-service trains travel at up to 150 mph, offer electrical outlets at every seat for laptops or music players, and have conference tables on board. Regardless of your mode of transport, you'll find a Metro stop on-site at Union Station, which makes getting to and from D.C. extremely convenient. There is always a long line of taxis waiting outside the front entrance of Union Station, too.

INSIDER TIP: *If you find yourself with some time to kill before your train leaves, be sure to wander around Union Station. The lovely building was restored and rejuvenated in the 1980s, and in addition to transportation services you'll find a three-level shopping mall, an expansive food court, and a few decent sit-down restaurants.*

GETTING AROUND THE AREA

By Bus

The District offers two reliable bus systems: the red, white, and blue Metrobuses that connect with the Metrorail line stops and beyond, and the new bright red Circulator buses, which help tourists and locals alike navigate those areas not as well served by the Metro system.

D.C. Circulator

As noted, the D.C. Circulator (202-962-1423; www.dccirculator.com) is a convenient new bus service that serves the center city, with routes that link business, cultural, and entertainment hot spots more directly than the Metro. The brightly colored, easy-on, easy-off vehicles have been a hit with both locals and tourists, because the routes are generally faster for short trips through the city than the Metro buses—and the system is easier to understand as well. Circulator buses run every 10 minutes, and the fare is $1 (for now), regardless of destination. (You must have exact change.) Several routes are available, including a much-needed loop that serves Georgetown (the Metro train does not); a route that runs along the National Mall, with stops at most museums and monuments along the way; and a route that serves the D.C. Convention Center. The Smithsonian loop runs starting at 10 AM (when the museums open), and the other routes begin running at 7 AM. Please refer to page 48 for existing routes, but note that because of the popularity of the Circulator system, new routes are added regularly.

Metrobus

The Metrobus system is meant to cover whatever ground the subway system (see below) does not. Look for well-marked stops around the city and into the Virginia and Maryland suburbs. Fares are less than $2 in D.C. Children aged 4 and younger are free, and seniors and riders with disabilities (who have the proper I.D. card, which can be obtained from WMATA Headquarters; 202-637-7000; www.wmata.com; 600 Fifth St., N.W., Washington) ride at a discount. Riders must have exact change. A one-week unlimited pass is available for about $11 and can be purchased at Metro Center (12th and F Sts., N.W.) and online (www.wmata.com). Buses run frequently during peak hours.

By Subway

The subway system in Washington, D.C., known as the Metrorail—Metro for short—is clean, safe, efficient, easy to use, and can even be fun. A system of tunneled rails runs beneath the District and the immediate suburbs, and eventually aboveground farther out into Virginia and Maryland, with stops conveniently located throughout.

Start by purchasing a computerized fare card at one of the many ticket vending machines at the entrance of each station (just beyond the escalators in the subterranean stops). You can add the minimum fare (about $1.50 as this book went to press) or as much as $20 to the fare card, and it can be used until it runs out of money—or recycled into another fare card when the total drops below the minimum fare. The vending machines will accept cash, coins, and credit cards. You can also buy a Seven-Day Fast Pass, which allows unlimited travel during a one-week period. One-Day Fast Passes are also available for unlimited travel during a one-day period; note that the one-day passes are only valid after 9:30 AM on weekdays and all day on

The D.C. Circulator is a fast, direct way to reach points in Georgetown and along the National Mall that are not easily accessed via other public transportation. Photo by Nathan Borchelt.

Many visitors to the District are surprised to find the Metro subway system easy to use, clean, and safe.
Photo courtesy of the Washington, D.C., Convention and Visitors Corporation. Used with permission.

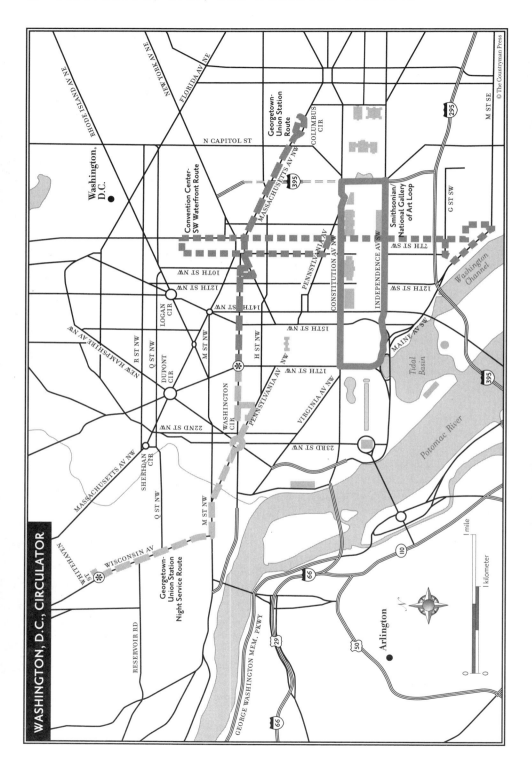

WASHINGTON, D.C., CIRCULATOR

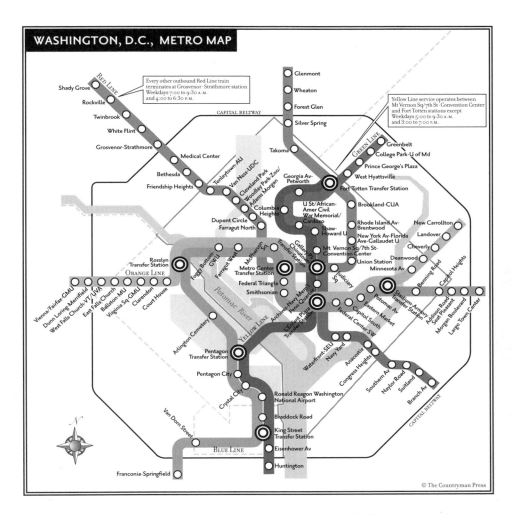

WASHINGTON, D.C., METRO MAP

Every other outbound Red Line train terminates at Grosvenor-Strathmore station Weekdays 7:00 to 9:30 A.M. and 4:00 to 6:30 P.M.

Yellow Line service operates between Mt Vernon Sq/7th St-Convention Center and Fort Totten stations except Weekdays 5:00 to 9:30 A.M. and 3:00 to 7:00 P.M.

© The Countryman Press

weekends. You can purchase these passes at all stations, at WMATA Headquarters (202-637-7000; 600 Fifth St., N.W., Washington), at Metro Center (12th and F Sts., N.W., Washington), local grocery stores, and online (www.wmata.com).

Fares are calculated based on distance and time of the ride. During peak hours (5–9:30 AM and 3–7 PM weekdays) the minimum fare will take you 3 miles. During nonpeak hours, the same fare will take you 7 miles. The maximum fare is a little more than $4 one way.

Once you have your fare card in hand, proceed to the electronic turnstile and place it in the slot above the lighted green arrow (red minus signs indicate the turnstile is going the other direction). The fare card will be sucked in momentarily and then shoot out of an opening at the top of the turnstile; pull out the card and the turnstile will open. No money will be deducted from your fare card until you exit the system, so be sure to have your ticket handy on the other end, where you'll repeat the process to pass through the turnstiles and out of your destination station. If you miscalculate and don't have enough money on your fare card, there are machines to allow you to add the fare you owe to your card before exiting. Each Metro station offers a wheelchair-accessible turnstile; in these wider venues the card sometimes shoots back out via the same slot in which it was inserted. (These turnstiles are useful when traveling with large suitcases.)

To figure out which side of the track you need, locate your stop marked on vertical brown posts found just beyond the turnstiles. Getting to your destination requires little more than knowing where you are and where you're going. Study the metro map on page 49 (or better yet, pick up a colorized version at the information kiosk at any Metro station). Determine the train line your starting point serves (designated by colors) and the line your destination requires, and then plan to change stations as necessary at the line intersections (Metro Center, for example, is an interchange for the Blue, Orange, and Red lines; Gallery Place/Chinatown is an interchange for the Red, Yellow, and Green lines; L'Enfant Plaza is an interchange for the Green, Yellow, Orange, and Blue lines). You can find out in advance which Metro lines and bus routes service particular street addresses by visiting www.wmata.com.

Trains have an electronic screen on the front of the first car that designates the line and on the sides of all cars that identifies the line and the direction of the train, which is called out by the last stop in the direction the train is heading. So imagine you are at the Dupont Circle Metro station (served only by the Red line) and want to visit Arlington Cemetery (served only by the Blue line). From Dupont Circle, you would first board the Red line heading to Glenmont; get out a few stops later at Metro Center and transfer to a Blue line train heading to Franconia-Springfield; and then exit this train at the Arlington National Cemetery station. Drivers announce stops in advance, but the audio system is horrible and almost always inaudible. It's a good idea to know the stop *before* the one you want, so that you can be ready to exit. Stops are also marked with small signs in the tunnels.

Metro trains get jammed during rush hour, and it is often difficult to find a seat during these periods. There are grab bars on the top of every bench and overhead, and there are poles near the exits, so if you have to stand, try to hang on, or the herky-jerky motion of the train might send you stumbling into someone's lap. Also note that during heavy traffic you might want to make your way toward the exit doors before the train comes to a complete stop, because stops are brief and it can be hard to elbow through crowds to the doors.

Platform lights that run parallel to the tracks will begin flashing about 60 seconds before the train arrives. You'll also find electronic boards in most stations that will provide the schedule of upcoming trains, including the direction, line, and number of minutes before the train arrives, as well as the number of cars.

Brown information posts like this one can be found in every Metro station; they list stops, in order, for incoming trains. In this example, dots after "Metro Center" and "Pentagon" indicate stations where a transfer to another line can be made.

Photo by Debbie K. Hardin.

The Christopher Columbus Memorial Fountain greets visitors to Union Station. Photo by Debbie K. Hardin.

The Metrorail system opens at 5:30 AM weekdays and 7 AM weekends, and closes at midnight Sunday through Thursday and 3 AM Friday and Saturday. Holiday hours are generally shorter, and the schedule is often extended for large-scale events like inaugurations and Fourth of July celebrations.

INSIDER TIP: *Stand to the right on Metro escalators so that riders in a hurry can walk past on the left. If you fail to extend this courtesy, expect locals to get testy.*

By Taxi

It is easy to hail a cab in the city, except during inclement weather and exceptionally heavy traffic. If you can't get a taxi to stop for you on the street, walk to the nearest large hotel, and there is bound to be a line of taxis waiting for fares. You'll also be sure to find cabs traveling the major tourist corridors along the Mall (Constitution and Independence Avenues), outside large Metrorail stops, and in popular restaurant and theater districts in the evenings. Venture outside of the tourist-frequented areas of the city, however—in other words, anything too far beyond the Northwest Quadrant or Capitol Hill—and it's another story because cabs are reluctant to visit dicier neighborhoods.

Taxis operating within the District used to run on a zone system. However, because of repeated complaints from cabbies and tourists, District taxis have now switched to meters. Per-mile charges are more during rush hour. Expect to be charged extra for additional passengers and luggage handling; fuel surcharges may be assessed as well.

Note that taxi drivers are allowed to stop for other passengers, even while already carrying people—and unrelated passengers pay full fare. Also take heed: In the worst of the summer swelter, it is rare to find a District cab whose air conditioning is in good repair (despite cabbie protestations to the contrary).

Fares for District taxis that cross into Maryland or Virginia—as well as cabs operating outside of D.C.—are also based on mileage. It will cost $3.25 for the first half mile and 90 cents for each additional half mile (or fraction thereof). If you are traveling outside of the District, always get a verbal estimate before you board the cab. Beware rogue cab drivers operating throughout the region. Look for a cab driver's license inside the car to make sure you are dealing with a certified driver. For more information on taxis, visit the **D.C. Taxicab Commission** at www.dctaxi.dc.gov.

TOURS

Tours can be an efficient, fun way to see a new city, and are especially helpful in D.C. if your visit is brief. For those visitors wishing to get an inexpensive overview of the major sites, both **Old Town Trolley Tours** (202-832-9800; www.oldtowntrolley.com) and **Tourmobile** (202-554-5100; www.tourmobile.com) are good options. Both have on and off privileges at numerous stops along the National Mall and at Arlington Cemetery. In addition, a number of specialty tours offer insight into the city that even locals will appreciate, and novelty transportation can add to the fun.

Bike the Sights (202-842-2453; www.bikethesights.com; 1100 Pennsylvania Ave., N.W., Washington). Tour D.C. on two wheels in organized bike tours that include pedaling adventures for children aged 4–9 and adults, as well as nighttime bike tours for just the grown-ups; there are also seasonal tours that include biking through the cherry blossoms in early spring and a ghost bike tour the last week in October. Reserve online or call for availability and prices.

Capital Segway Tours (202-682-1980; www.capitalsegway.com; 1350 I St., N.W., Washington). With this mode of transportation, getting there truly is half the fun. Glide past monuments, museums, and all the rest of the famous city sites on the latest Segway model, all the while attracting more than a little attention from the poor saps who are hoofing it. You'll start your tour onboard the ultra-cool Segways with a brief lesson in maneuvering, and then you'll head out for a 2?-hour tour along the open sidewalks and walkways of D.C. Adults 16 years and older only; $65.

DC Ducks Tour (1-800-213-2474; www.dcducks.com; tour desk in Union Station). Climb aboard a genuine 1942 World War II amphibious vehicle (nicknamed the Duck) for a humorous 90-minute tour that runs from Union Station past the Capitol, Washington Monument, and White House, with commentary about D.C. trivia along the way. Then splash down into the Potomac River and continue your trip on the water. Knowledgeable and friendly guides are a little hard to hear over the loud, aging vehicles, but it's worth putting up with the poor audio system to see the looks on the faces of passers-by as the extremely odd-looking Duck rolls past. Each guest receives a duck whistle, suitable for annoying friends or family—or for ensuring that fellow travelers respect your space on the crowded Metrorail system. Buy tickets in advance online or purchase them the day of the tour at the Old Town Trolley Tour desk in Union Station. Runs mid-March through September, 10–4 (on the half hour). Adults $30, children $14.

The DC Ducks tour hits the major sights in the city—and then heads out to open water for even better views.
Photo courtesy of Old Town Trolley Tours and DC Ducks. Used with permission.

D.C. Movie and TV Sites Tour (212-209-3370; www.screentours.com). This three-hour bus tour takes you past more than 30 sites used in the filming of movies and TV programs, including the house featured in *The Exorcist,* the bar used in *St. Elmo's Fire,* and various shooting locales for *Forrest Gump, The West Wing,* and *The X-Files.* The tour is led by actors from D.C., includes onboard video screens showing film clips, and stops for shopping. Catch the tour near Union Station (boarding locations vary, so verify when booking). Friday–Sunday beginning at 2 PM. Adults $34.

Ghosts and Graveyard Tour (703-519-1749; www.alexcolonialtours.com; Ramsay House, 221 King St., Alexandria). Tour the cobblestone streets of old Alexandria by lantern light with an 18th-century costumed guide who will regale you with stories of unrequited love and vengeful ghosts. Hour-long tours begin at the Ramsay House in Old Town. Schedules vary by season so call ahead for specifics. Adults $10, children $5.

Half Had Not Been Told to Me (408-794-0812). Use your cell phone to learn about the African American history of Lafayette Square, across the street from the White House. Pick up a tour map at the **Decatur House** (see page 148), call the prerecorded tour at the telephone contact above, and punch in the numbers that correspond to the map. This free tour begins with an introduction by D.C. Mayor Adrian M. Fenty; along the way you'll learn about sit-ins at the White House, enslaved African Americans married at nearby St. John's Church, and how a slave helped create the statue of Andrew Jackson that sits in the heart of Lafayette Square.

Scandal Tours (202-783-7212; www.gnpcomedy.com/ScandalTours.html). Led by a comedy group that calls itself the Gross National Product, Scandal Tours takes guests on an irreverent tour of the seamier side of the nation's capital. Visit the site where stripper Fanny Fox cavorted with Congressman Wilbur Mills; drive past Gary Hart's town house, where Donna Rice made her memorable escape out the back door; and be regaled with the latest shenanigans going on in the White House. Catch tours at the Willard Hotel (1401 Pennsylvania Ave., N.W.). Preregistration is required, either by phone or via the Web. Although children aren't prohibited, the tour is strictly PG-13. Tours operate at 1 PM Saturday, April–early September. Adults $30, seniors $25, students $20.

Spies of Washington Tour (703-569-1875; www.spiesofwashingtontour.com). Visit some of the most notorious sites in Washington, D.C., including the suburban park where FBI counterintelligence agent Robert Hanssen was arrested and sites in Georgetown frequented by World War II Allied agent Betty Pack, and learn about Russian intrigue in the shadows of the White House. Four- and eight-hour bus tours are available, as well as two-hour walking tours, all of which are conducted by a retired Air Force officer and former president of the National Military Intelligence Association. Schedules and prices vary by season and by tour. Call ahead for reservations and meeting locations.

Washington Walks (www.washingtonwalks.com). In business since 1999, this organization offers a number of walking tours through the city's cultural and historical districts, including a tour of "haunted" spots in the city such as the Octagon House, memorials by moonlight, and what is billed as the White House "Un-Tour" for those who didn't get tickets to see the President's Mansion.

STREET LAYOUT AND QUADRANTS IN WASHINGTON, D.C.

With the exception of ubiquitous one-way streets and ever-increasing traffic, Washington, D.C., is remarkably easy to navigate. This is because it is one of the first planned communities in the world, thanks to French-born Pierre L'Enfant, who was appointed by his former Revolutionary War commander, President George Washington, to design the new capital city. L'Enfant's original and extremely detailed plan specified exactly where major federal buildings and monuments were to be placed, and he included vast expanses of green space to keep what he believed was a properly grand scale.

The city was originally carved from 10 square miles taken from Maryland and Virginia, crossing the Potomac River (the Virginia portion was later given back at the request of the

Why There Is No J Street in Washington, D.C.

A portion of the east–west streets in the District are named after letters of the alphabet. Savvy visitors will notice, however, that there is no J Street in the city. Legend has it that city architect Pierre L'Enfant hated John Jay, the first chief justice of the Supreme Court, and that he refused to name a street after him. However entertaining this urban myth, it is unlikely: L'Enfant was forced to submit each detail of his plan to a board of planning commissioners who were unlikely to allow such a petty personal indulgence. Although no one knows for sure, it is likely that there is no J Street in D.C. because the handwritten letters J and I in 18th-century script were nearly indistinguishable; thus using both letters would have been too confusing for postal carriers.

commonwealth). L'Enfant divided this land into four quadrants (Northwest, Northeast, Southwest, and Southeast), with the Capitol at the center, placed on a high point in the city (hence the term Capitol *Hill*). North–south roads are designated as numbered streets, beginning with First Street in each quadrant. East–west streets are named for letters, up to the letter *W* (with one exception; see the sidebar on page 54). After W Street, the east–west streets have names in alphabetical order, arranged first with two-syllable names, then three-syllable names, and then finally with the names of flowers and trees. Avenues named after states radiate out from the White House and the Capitol and converge in traffic circles, which as noted earlier can be disorienting even for locals.

INSIDER TIP: *Be sure to ascertain the quadrant when using any address; asking a cabbie to drive to the corner of Third and E is virtually meaningless without adding "Northwest," "Southeast," etc.*

PICKING A HOME BASE IN WASHINGTON, D.C., AND NORTHERN VIRGINIA

Centrality Is Key

Washington, D.C., is a relatively compact area, and thanks to excellent public transportation, visitors to the city are never far away from the major sites. Even hotels along the Metro line in Alexandria and Arlington are within a 15-minute drive to the heart of downtown.

The Gallery Place/Chinatown neighborhood makes for an interesting, exciting home base while visiting Washington, D.C. Photo by Nathan Borchelt.

When choosing a hotel, the major determining factor will probably be cost. Although guests can save a little money lodging in Arlington and Alexandria, price generally has less to do with location than amenities. There are relative bargains to be had in pricey neighborhoods like Georgetown and Capitol Hill, just as there are pricier options for traditionally less expensive neighborhoods like Chinatown.

Visitors will note, however, that tourist-grade hotels are clustered in certain neighborhoods and not available in others. The bulk of accommodations in this book can be found in the Northwest Quadrant of D.C., in Old Town Alexandria, and along the Metro Orange line in Arlington (see Chapter 3). This corresponds both to the availability of public transportation and to business centers within the city and its suburbs.

EASY SIDE TRIPS

Should you wish to expand on your visit to the Washington, D.C., area, there are a number of historic, scenic cities and small towns within a few hours of downtown. Below we outline two of our favorites.

Colonial Williamsburg, Virginia

Approximately 150 miles south of Washington, on a peninsula off the east coast of Virginia, Colonial Williamsburg is accessed by car via a bucolic drive along I-95. The venerable city dates to 1699, when Virginia established Williamsburg as the capital of the colony. The lovely tidewater city was already home to the College of William and Mary, the second oldest university in the nation and the eventual alma mater of Thomas Jefferson and James Monroe. Throughout the 1700s, Williamsburg prospered as a site of trade and politics, and came to play a crucial role in the American Revolution as both a center of political debate and the very backdrop of history; for example, in 1781 George Washington assembled the Continental Army in Williamsburg for the siege of Yorktown, the last major land battle of the Revolutionary War.

In the late 18th century, the capital of Virginia was moved to Richmond, and Williamsburg's prominence faded quickly. The city transformed into a sleepy college town, and many of its historic buildings were left to decay. In 1926, John D. Rockefeller Jr. rediscovered the city and undertook the massive restoration and reconstruction of more than 300 acres in order to celebrate the early history of America and its first patriots. The result of his efforts is the vital, living historical park that has become one of the most beloved tourist attractions in the eastern United States.

An entrance ticket (adult daily passes start at $36, children $18) is required to tour the nearly 40 original and reconstructed public buildings, private homes, taverns, and shops, as well as 90 acres of historically accurate gardens. Visitors can drop in on "historical re-enactors"—costumed docents—and watch as they perform traditional tasks such as blacksmithing nails, printing political pamphlets, and curling and powdering wigs; take a turn themselves at spinning yarn or grinding spices in a traditional kitchen; tour meticulously accurate historic homes to see how Colonial families cooked, taught their children, and entertained their family and friends; and visit public buildings such as the grand Governor's Mansion and the Capitol Building. Shop in a dozen re-created Colonial markets for 18th-century toys like bilbo catchers and clay marbles; decorative home and garden items like glazed bird bottles and marbled slipware pie plates; and even traditional snacks like bracingly strong ginger beer and blackberry preserves. Scattered throughout the historic area are daytime programs that include interactive discussions with "Founding Fathers" such as Thomas Jefferson and Patrick Henry; re-enactments of trials in the courthouse building; and political debates held on street corners and in taverns. Check the daily printed guide available in Colonial Williamsburg or call 1-800-HISTORY for exact times and locations. Although the historic buildings close their doors at dusk, there are also evening programs throughout the city that include a well-attended witch trial, lantern-lighted ghost tours, and elaborate demonstrations of Colonial music and dance.

Dining in Colonial Williamsburg offers a chance to try dishes based on original recipes from the colony in authentic surroundings, although the meals are prepared in a modern kitchen and served with luxuries like forks and napkins, which were not available to the average Colonial citizen. On the main thoroughfare of Duke of Gloucester Street, **King's**

The Governor's Mansion and gardens are a highlight of Colonial Williamsburg. Photo by Debbie K. Hardin.

Arms Tavern (757-229-2141), an 18th-century chop house, serves up rich, creamy peanut soup and a refreshing berry shrub, a nonalcoholic cocktail made from cranberry juice, raspberry sorbet, and fresh mint; or try more substantial offerings like fried chicken served with salty Virginia ham and pickled vegetables. On Waller Street, near the Capitol Building, **Christiana Campbell's Tavern** (757-229-2141) specializes in seafood, offering authentic lump crab cakes, oyster fritters served with sour cream and bacon, and pan-fried rainbow trout. All Colonial restaurants are extremely popular dining options and require reservations several weeks in advance for dinner; it is first-come, first-served at lunch, and long waits are typical. To avoid the worst of the lines, opt for a quick snack like a soft gingerbread cookie or a ham and cheese biscuit available at the **Raleigh Tavern Bakery** just off of Duke of Gloucester Street (703-229-2141).

The **Woodlands Hotel and Suites** (757-229-1000; 105 Visitor Center Dr., Williamsburg) and the **Williamsburg Lodge** (757-229-1000; 310 S. England St., Williamsburg) offer comfortable, moderately priced accommodations within a half mile of Colonial Williamsburg. But for a real treat—and one that will require a significant financial investment—book an overnight stay in an authentic colonial house (757-229-1000; 306B East Francis St., Williamsburg); the number of these tiny homes is limited and they require reservations as much as six months in advance.

Baltimore, Maryland

The beautiful, historic city of Baltimore (pronounced something like "Ballmer" by locals) is about 45 miles from the center of D.C. on Maryland's picturesque Chesapeake Bay. Many visitors to D.C. fly into the Baltimore airport, which often offers the best airfares into the region. Thus if you're looking to extend your travels while in the vicinity of the District, it makes sense to add this pretty city on the water to your itinerary.

"Charm City," as Baltimore is nicknamed, began life as a port town in the 17th century shuttling tobacco to foreign locales, and later the city was home to one of the country's primary granaries. The city and its citizens served an important role in history by rebuking the British during the War of 1812. After the British tried to burn down the District in 1814, they headed to Baltimore, attacking by land and by sea. Baltimore was better prepared than Washington, D.C., however. During the infamous Battle of Baltimore, soldiers at Fort McHenry and North Point tenaciously fought off the attackers with guns and cannons, and citizens threw anything they could get their hands on at the invading forces—pots, pans, rocks—ultimately forcing the British to withdraw.

Despite its storied past, Baltimore fell on hard times in the 1960s and early 1970s when urban flight virtually emptied the downtown, and the Inner Harbor became a haven for homeless folks and little more than a collection of abandoned warehouses. In the late 1970s, the city undertook one of the most remarkable inner-city revitalizations in the country. Business and civic leaders spearheaded Harborplace, an appealing shopping and restaurant complex directly on the waterfront that opened in 1980. The world-famous **National Aquarium in Baltimore** (410-576-3800; www.aqua.org; 501 E. Pratt St., Baltimore) opened on the harbor shortly thereafter, and ever since, the Inner Harbor has attracted tourists and locals in droves to shop, dine, and just soak up the casual ambiance. Other charming neighborhoods in the city include the gentrified Fells Point and Little Italy, *the* place to find authentic Italian restaurants.

If you're looking for culture, try the **Baltimore Museum of Art** (443-573-1700; www.artbma.org; 10 Art Museum Dr., Baltimore). With 90,000 pieces in the permanent collection, including the largest Henri Matisse collection in the world as well as pieces by Picasso, van Gogh, and Cezanne, this museum takes a backseat to none. Open 11–5 Wednesday–Sunday. Admission is free.

If high culture isn't your thing, try the quirky **National Museum of Dentistry** (410-706-0600; www.dentalmuseum.umaryland.edu; 31 S. Greene St., Baltimore), which houses everything related to dental hygiene, including a pair of George Washington's dentures (ivory—not wooden!), gilded dental tools used on Queen Victoria, and a "tooth jukebox" that plays TV jingles about dental products. Catch up on your history at the **National Great Blacks in Wax Museum** (410-563-3404; www.ngbiwm.com; 1601 E. North Ave., Baltimore), which features lifelike castings of historic figures like W. E. B. DuBois, Harriet Tubman, and Nat Turner, as well as more contemporary individuals like Nelson Mandela, Thurgood Marshall, and Martin Luther King Jr.

Baltimore is also the home of **Oriole Park at Camden Yards** (1-888-848-BIRD; www.mlb.com/bal/ballpark; 333 W. Camden St., Baltimore), a beautiful, relatively new baseball stadium designed to remind visitors of the ballparks of the past. New ballparks throughout the country imitate this stadium's intimate design.

You don't have to go far to find myriad fine dining in Baltimore—often at prices significantly less than at comparable restaurants in the District. Although there is an international variety of foods to be tried here, come for the seafood, especially the famous

Maryland blue crab. On the Inner Harbor waterfront, **Phillips Harborplace Restaurant** (410-685-6600; 301 Light St., Baltimore) offers water views and impeccably fresh fish. Or, if you're near the airport, **G&M Restaurant** (410-636-1777; 1-877-554-3723; 804 N. Hammonds Ferry Rd., Linthicum) is home to possibly the largest crab cakes you'll ever see—roughly the size of half a grapefruit.

Thanks to a large Italian American community, there are also endless possibilities for Italian cuisine in the Little Italy section of town. Among the best are **Amicci's** (410-528-1096; 231 S. High St., Baltimore), a longtime favorite housed in a century-old row house, and **Boccaccio** (410-234-1322; 925 Eastern Ave., Baltimore), a romantic space serving imaginative, artistically plated meals.

Stay at the chic boutique **Pier 5 Hotel** (410-539-2000; 711 Eastern Ave., Baltimore), a high-style, vibrant lodging option right on the waterfront, or the cozy and historic **Admiral Fell Inn** (410-522-7380; 888 S. Broadway, Baltimore), a European-style hotel with Old World charm, 18th-century furnishings, and a few resident ghosts.

The Mary Livingston Ripley Garden, just east of the Arts and Industries Building on the National Mall. Photo by Debbie K. Hardin.

3

LODGING

A Room of One's Own

Washington, D.C., and the surrounding Virginia suburbs comprise some of the most expensive real estate in the country, and the lodging rates reflect this. Budget options are few and far between during high season; the good news is that supply and demand drives the hotel industry, and bargains can be found if you're willing to visit during the less popular months (see below for specifics). It also pays to check for Web site specials; many independent lodging options in the city offer packages online that include room and dinner, or room and passes to cultural events, which can be real money savers—and a good way to secure tickets at the last minute.

As with any major city, the area is well populated by chain accommodations, many of which provide good value and convenient locations. These large, cookie-cutter hotels, however, are often generic, and so we've focused instead on options that are unique to the Washington, D.C., area—either because of their amenities, their historical significance, or their prime location. The renaissance that has swept through D.C. in the past decade has brought with it many stylish new lodging options, and a few are even relative bargains. In response, many formerly stodgy or plain-Jane accommodations have spruced up to compete. In addition, several well-respected independent lodging options are currently undergoing renovation or have just completed extensive remodels. These include the members-only **Club Quarters** (212-575-0006; www.clubquarters.com; 839 17th St., N.W., Washington), the **St. Regis** (202-638-2626; www.starwoodhotels.com/stregis; 923 16th St., N.W., Washington) near the White House, the high-style **Hotel Ralph Pucci** (1-888-587-2388; www.hotelralphpucci.com; 1310 Wisconsin Ave., N.W., Washington) in Georgetown (formerly known as The Georgetown Inn), and the historic **The Jefferson** (202-347-2200; www.thejeffersonwashingtondc.com; 1200 16th St., N.W., Washington) in the heart of downtown. These expensive revamps equate to the best in updated amenities and decor. And every season brings a new crop of boutique hotels. For example, in late 2007 the **Hotel Monaco Alexandria** (703-549-6080; 480 King Street, Alexandria) opened its doors in the heart of Old Town Alexandria and is a favorite choice with stylish travelers. There are still few independent lodging options in Arlington, Virginia, and for this reason we've highlighted some of the nicest of the chains there.

For convenience, lodging is broken down by location, but understand that hotels are not distributed evenly throughout the city. Recently revitalized neighborhoods like the Penn Quarter and the U Street Corridor offer a number of exciting dining and entertainment options (see Chapter 6), but lodging is less plentiful. The bulk of the hotels in Washington,

D.C., can be found north of the National Mall and just northwest, in the Dupont Circle and Foggy Bottom neighborhoods. Capitol Hill has its fair share of interesting accommodations as well, and Georgetown, in the westernmost reaches of the District, is a perennial favorite with out-of-town guests, even though it is a little less convenient because there is no Metro station. There are also a handful of lovely options in the upper northwest corner of the city. In Alexandria, we've concentrated on hotels in historic Old Town; and in Arlington, we've focused on hotels easily accessible via the Metro Orange line, from the Rosslyn station, just across the Potomac River, extending west to Ballston.

LODGING NOTES

Washington, D.C., has three free hotel booking services. Although they won't necessarily help guests find deals, they are excellent resources if you are planning a last-minute trip and are having a hard time securing lodging (not unusual during the busy season of spring). **Capitol Reservations** (www.hotelsdc.com) and **D.C. Accommodations** (www.dc accommodations.com) are particularly good if you find yourself in a pinch and can't find a room. The **Washington, D.C., Convention and Tourism Corporation** also operates a hotel booking service (1-800-422-8644; www.washington.org) that offers exclusive packages that sometimes include hard-to-get event tickets.

Rates

High-season rates apply in Washington, D.C., and Northern Virginia during the springtime months, thanks in large measure to the city's beloved cherry blossoms, which generally bloom the first week in April. Hotels (and city attractions) are also busy when Congress is in session (mid-September until Thanksgiving and then again from mid-January through June). Highest rates will apply from mid-March through June. Although costs are calculated on a supply-and-demand basis, and conventions can fill up vacant rooms any time of the year, highest vacancy—and thus the lowest rates—in the city will generally be found July (after the big Independence Day celebrations) through early September and December through early January.

Because prices change quickly—and vary widely by season—we've avoided specific pricing information on hotels and instead designate a category that indicates a range of prices (see below). Note that the stated price category reflects the average rate for a standard room (without view) on a weekday during high season. Rates are almost always lower on weekends, and be aware that even inexpensive and moderate lodging can have larger, fancier suites that drift into the very expensive category. Note that on the high end of the "very expensive" category there are standard rooms that go for more than $1,000 a night.

Prices

Inexpensive: $125 or less
Moderate: $125–250
Expensive: $250–400
Very expensive: $400 and up

Minimum Stay

During high season, and at some smaller establishments all year long, it isn't unusual for hotels to insist on a minimum stay of two or even three nights for advance bookings. However, if you reserve accommodations at the last minute (not really recommended, because you could find yourself out of luck), you can often bypass these requirements.

INSIDER TIP: *Rooms on higher floors are generally quieter and offer better views. Although hotels won't guarantee specific rooms (aside from Presidential Suites), you have a better chance of getting what you want if you specify preferences at the time you book your room; reiterate your requests 24 hours before arriving; and arrive in the early afternoon, as close as possible to the hotel's check-in time.*

Deposit/Cancellation

You'll be expected to provide one night's security deposit, which may be charged to your account at the time of your booking or may be charged the day you are due to arrive. Most hotels will allow cancellations and rescheduling up to 72 hours in advance without penalties, but expect as much as a full night's charge if you cancel within 24 hours. Make sure you understand the hotel policies *before* you book.

Handicap Access

With the exception of smaller historic properties and some B&Bs, the majority of lodging options in the area meet the ADA specifications for handicap accessibility—providing grab bars in bathrooms, shower stalls wide enough to accommodate wheelchairs, and so forth. If this is an issue for you, be sure to call ahead to verify that the hotel you've chosen can accommodate your particular needs. It's also a good idea to ask about construction in the immediate area; pockets of downtown D.C. are being rebuilt at a remarkable rate, and the detours and inconveniences that go along with this might be a problem for folks with mobility issues.

Other Options

As noted, hotels in this area can be pricey, and when traveling with a family or staying for an extended period, they can be exorbitant. But because D.C. is a transient region, with lots of people coming in on business for a few weeks or a few months, there are long-term options that can be cost-effective and more spacious than traditional hotels.

House Swaps

House swaps are one-to-one exchanges between individuals from different cities who are willing to lend out their private homes in exchange for the use of a home in a preferred locale. For a yearly membership fee, online services (for example, Digsville, www.digsville.com; Homelink, www.homelink.org; Intervacus, www.intervacus.com) match up individuals with similar needs, and the parties involved are left to make their arrangements online. Although it requires a leap of faith, such home swaps can save thousands of dollars—and can be a fun way to experience a city the way locals do. The only catch is that the swap has to be mutual—so you have a better chance of finding someone willing to lend you their home in D.C. if you have a home, say, on a beach or in another attractive city to exchange. There are several hundred apartments, town houses, and single-family homes in the Washington, D.C., and Northern Virginia area that participate in such programs, so if this kind of arrangement interests you there are plenty of possibilities.

House swaps are possible throughout the region, even in tony neighborhoods like this one in Georgetown.
Photo by Debbie K. Hardin.

Short-Term Rentals

Corporate and short-term furnished apartments are readily available throughout the city, and are generally much homier, more spacious, and less expensive on a daily basis than hotels, with fully stocked kitchens, laundry facilities, linens, and usually housekeeping services as well. All utilities (generally including cable TV and high-speed Internet) are included, and parking is sometimes available as well—though for an additional fee. Expect to pay from $120–200 per day for a one-bedroom unit, and note that most properties have 30-day minimum stays. Companies that can assist visitors in finding short-term rentals in the city include **Attaché Property Management** (202-787-1885), which brokers individually owned town homes and apartments; **Bridgestreet Corporate Housing** (1-800-278-7338), which owns and manages properties throughout the city; and **Interim Housing Solutions** (1-866-279-4471), an agency that coordinates with a network of short-term and corporate rental agencies. A high-style temporary option near the White House is the newly opened **AKA** (1-888-KORMAN1; www.stayaka.com; 1710 H St., N.W., Washington), which rents one- and two-bedroom furnished apartments by the month; these sleek residences offer gourmet kitchens with stainless steel appliances, chic interior designs, and regular housekeeping. Similarly, the smaller **La Maison Vert** (1-866-246-1958; www.lamaisonde-tre.com; 328 Massachusetts Ave., N.E., Washington) offers stylish furnished apartments for rent by the week or month in a historic Victorian town house near Capitol Hill, just east of Union Station.

ACCOMMODATIONS

ADAMS MORGAN
ADAM'S INN
Innkeeper: Anne Owens
202-745-3600 or 1-800-578-6807
www.adamsinn.com
1746 Lanier Place, N.W., Washington, D.C.
20009
Price: Inexpensive
Credit Cards: AE, MC, V
Handicap Access: No
Nearest Metro Station: Woodley Park, Red
line

This quaint Victorian B&B is one of the best
antidotes to the profusion of chain hotels
throughout the city. The property is made
up of three converted, three-story row
houses nestled on a quiet residential street
that is within easy walking distance of the
perpetually buzzing neighborhood nightlife.
The inn boasts a total of 26 guest rooms (16
with private baths), along with amenities
like high-speed Internet access and a stunning continental breakfast. Beyond the
immediate proximity of the Adams Morgan
strip, the Woodley Park Metro station is a
15-minute walk away, and Rock Creek
National Park and the back entrance to the
National Zoo are both a pleasant stroll away.
The staff is friendly and can point you
toward D.C. attractions, both mainstream
and off the beaten path. If you want to sample what it feels like to live in a bona fide
D.C. neighborhood, this is the place.

KALORAMA GUEST HOUSE
Manager: Kurt Haroldsen
202-667-6369 or 1-800-974-6450; fax
202-319-1262
www.kaloramaguesthouse.com
1854 Mintwood Pl., N.W., Washington, D.C.
20009
Price: Inexpensive
Credit Cards: AE, D, DC, MC, V
Handicap Access: No
Nearest Metro Station: Woodley Park, Red
line

This homey B&B offers 30 units, half with
private baths. A large variety of options are
available, ranging from a studio apartment
with a tiny kitchen to two-bedroom suites.
Accommodations are comfortable and cozy,
filled with antique furniture and country
design, with quilts on the beds and doilies
on the eclectic tag-sale tables. A complimentary cold breakfast is provided every
morning, and lemonade and cookies are
offered every afternoon. Guests have access
to laundry facilities, a much welcome benefit for families (although note that very
young children are not allowed). The owners have a second location near the zoo with
similar amenities (**Kalorama Guest House
at Woodley Park;** 202-328-0860 or 1-800-
974-9101; 2700 Cathedral Ave., N.W.,
Washington).

AROUND THE MALL
HAY-ADAMS
Manager: Kay Enokido
202-638-6600 or 1-800-853-6807; fax
202-638-2716
www.hayadams.com
800 16th St., N.W., Washington, D.C. 20006
Price: Very Expensive
Credit Cards: AE, D, DC, MC, V
Handicap Access: Yes
Nearest Metro Station: McPherson Square,
Blue and Orange lines

This sumptuous historic property dating to
1928 has hosted the cream of American
society and letters, including Charles Lindbergh, Ethel Barrymore, and Sinclair Lewis,
and it remains among the top choices for
VIPs visiting the city today. This is thanks in
part to the fact that the Hay-Adams has *the*
most elite address in Washington, D.C.: It
sits off Lafayette Square, directly across
from the White House, and extremely
pricey rooms offer unparalleled views of the
president's mansion, as well as the Wash-

The pricey and opulent suites in the historic Hay-Adams offer refinement and elegance second only to that of its neighbor, the White House. Photo by Debbie K. Hardin.

ington Monument in the background. The small lobby is a study in opulence, with original walnut wainscoting, enormous brass chandeliers, marble floors covered with fine Asian carpets, ornate archways, and Tudor- and Italian-inspired gilded plasterwork on the ceilings. Guest rooms are layered in luxurious, neutral-toned fabrics in shades of cream and sage and are rich with sophisticated patterns, and each boasts canopied beds that give the space a palatial feeling. Bathrooms are small, as is typical for a historic property, but they are swathed in marble and offer upscale bath products. Suites are worthy of a queen (or president), with a commodious sitting area, many with fireplaces, comfortable couches, and plenty of room to host—and impress—friends or colleagues. Service is impeccable and professional, and employees are friendly and accessible.

INSIDER TIP: *Reserve a (relatively!) less expensive Lafayette Room at the Hay-Adams if you are visiting in the late fall or winter, when trees that obscure the view of the White House during other seasons have dropped their leaves. You'll get the premier view without paying the princely rates of a designated view room.*

HOTEL WASHINGTON

Manager: Craig Scott
202-638-5900 or 1-800-424-9540; fax 202-638-5900
www.hotelwashington.com
515 15th St., N.W., Washington, D.C. 20004
Price: Moderate
Credit Cards: AE, D, DC, MC, V
Handicap Access: Yes
Nearest Metro Station: Metro Center, Blue, Orange, and Red lines

This grand, Italianate structure was designed in 1917 by the same architects who dreamed up the Senate and House buildings on Capitol Hill, but the regal Hotel Washington is instead more reminiscent of the White House, which is just a block away. The cavernous, high-ceilinged lobby arrayed with massive arched columns and oversized crystal chandeliers and festooned with American flags looks to be straight out of the presidential mansion. Opulent guest rooms are decorated with Federal reproduction pieces in dark woods and beds are covered with sophisticated floral fabrics. Bathrooms are small here and clad in marble. Some deluxe rooms have fine views of the Washington Monument. But without a doubt the best view of the National Mall, especially when the sun goes down and the lights transform the monuments, is from the hotel's famous rooftop **Sky Terrace Restaurant** (see page 225), open from April through October. This lounge is a relaxing place for a late-night drink, and is popular with both locals and out-of-towners. Note that this lovely bar, as well as the storied hotel, has drawn its fair share of celebrities—both Hollywood stars of the past like John Wayne and Will Rogers, as well as current political heavyweights like Bill Clinton and Al Gore. It also has attracted some turkeys: To be precise, the august Hotel Washington is the official temporary home of the "National Turkey" every year before it receives its traditional presidential pardon the week of Thanksgiving. Note that this property recently changed ownership and is slated to close for renovation in 2008.

L'ENFANT PLAZA HOTEL
Manager: Yussef Radquane
202-484-1000; fax 202-646-4456
www.lenfantplazahotel.com
480 L'Enfant Plaza, S.W., Washington, D.C. 20024
Price: Moderate
Credit Cards: AE, D, MC, V
Handicap Access: Yes
Nearest Metro Station: L'Enfant Plaza, Blue, Green, Orange, and Yellow lines

Location is everything at this family-friendly hotel, which is the closest available lodging to the Smithsonian Institution Castle—and about a 5- to 10-minute walk from the National Air and Space Museum. The structure is connected to the large underground L'Enfant Plaza complex, which has a plethora of fast-food options, shopping, and its own Metro stop. The hotel's large lobby is neutral and somewhat devoid of personality, but the clean lines and muted colors are soothing. Rooms are smallish and slightly dated, with light fabrics, reproduction furnishings, and comfortable beds. The interior design matters less if you secure a view room; because of the close proximity to the National Mall, some guest accommodations boast premier vistas of the monuments. There is a year-round rooftop pool, as well as small fitness and business centers. Rooms are equipped with Wi-Fi (which comes at an additional cost), and the hotel welcomes pets.

THE MADISON
Manager: James Lobosco
202-862-1600; fax 202-785-1255
www.madisonhoteldc.com
1177 15th St., N.W., Washington, D.C. 20005
Price: Moderate
Credit Cards: AE, D, DC, MC, V
Handicap Access: Yes
Nearest Metro Station: Farragut North, Red line

An elegant option in the heart of downtown, The Madison is particularly popular with business travelers, offering in-room high-speed Internet access and a full range of services at its on-site business center. Public spaces are grand, with Old World flourishes like extravagant moldings and ornate chandeliers. Guest rooms are predictable and comfortable, with monochromatic, neutral walls and carpets, light fabrics, and

Feng shui experts were consulted on the interior design of public and private spaces at the Mandarin Oriental; the results are guest rooms that offer total relaxation. Photo by Debbie K. Hardin.

dark wood furniture. Bathrooms have large showers with heated towel racks, and guests are treated to Bloom bath products, which are made with all-natural herb extracts. There is a well-equipped fitness center available 24/7. The hotel is pet- and child-friendly, offering treats for the former and a lending library of games for the latter. The modern and chic **Palette Bar** is a quiet place to unwind in the evenings. Front desk folks seem to be a little overwhelmed, however, and service can be slow.

MANDARIN ORIENTAL WASHINGTON, D.C.

Manager: Jan Goessing
202-554-8588 or 1-888-888-1778;
fax 202-554-8999
www.mandarinoriental.com/washington
1330 Maryland Ave., S.W., Washington, D.C.
20001

Price: Very Expensive
Credit Cards: AE, D, DC, MC, V
Handicap Access: Yes
Nearest Metro Station: Smithsonian, Blue and Orange lines

Considered among the finest properties in the country, the Mandarin Oriental came to D.C. a few years ago, anticipating the Renaissance along the waterfront, which is expected to explode thanks to the new baseball park in Anacostia (see page 256). The luxurious property is near the Jefferson Memorial, in a quiet area several blocks south of the National Mall and overlooking the river. The sophisticated round lobby features oversized floral arrangements and soft background music. Step down into the lovely sunken lobby bar, which overlooks an expansive, secluded courtyard. Throughout are Asian-inspired design elements, including two magnificent beaded kimonos hanging behind the check-in desk and vases of orchids scattered about on Chinese-style lacquered tables. Guest rooms are elegant and comfortable and feature richly patterned fabrics and carpets, beds piled high with pillows, and walls adorned with tapestries and Asian prints. Each room features a flat-screen plasma TV, Wi-Fi, a DVD player, and surround sound. Suites offer large sitting areas with a table and chairs and a comfortable sofa, and baths are luxurious and commodious, with extensive marble, deep soaking tubs, and multihead showers in glass enclosures. Many rooms offer stunning views of Arlington National Cemetery, monuments, and the waterfront.

If you have the means to indulge, visit the pricey **Spa at the Mandarin Oriental**, a dimly lighted haven of relaxation decorated with natural elements like a small garden of bamboo and an enormous backlit slab of jade granite. Treatments are said to be a blend of ancient techniques and modern practices, and evolve from Asian, Mediterranean, and Middle Eastern traditions. Log too many miles in the museums? Soothe tired feet with a hot stone treatment, or strengthen your immune system with a cherry blossom scrub (a concoction made with cherry tea leaves, sugar, and aromatic oils) that is rich in antioxidants. Do not miss the Amethyst Crystal Room, a spectacularly lovely setting for moist aromatherapy. Also on site is **CityZen** (see page 170), a gorgeous, expensive restaurant under the direction of Eric Ziebold, one of the most acclaimed chefs in D.C.

QUINCY

Manager: Charles Honnaker
202-223-4320 or 1-800-424-2970; fax
202-293-4977
www.quincysuites.com
1823 L St., N.W., Washington, D.C. 20036
Price: Moderate

Each roomy suite at the adorable Quincy hotel offers a sink-down comfy sectional sofa piled with colorful pillows. Photo by Debbie K. Hardin.

Credit Cards: AE, D, DC, MC, V
Handicap Access: Yes
Nearest Metro Station: Farragut North, Red line

In the epicenter of downtown D.C. but still within easy access of the National Mall, the Quincy is a hip boutique hotel designed for comfort *and* style. The small lobby is sleek and spare, and guest rooms are plush and homey. The recently renovated suites feature wooden blinds, a 7-foot work desk, and a luxurious pillow-top mattress dressed in earth-toned fabrics and modern geometric patterns. There is also an oversized sitting area that makes rooms feel particularly residential. Bathrooms offer showerheads the size of dinner plates, as well as upscale bath products. Each room features free high-speed Internet access, and working travelers will appreciate the complimentary business center on site. Service is exceptionally friendly and efficient, and guests will be happy to learn that the popular **Mackey's Pub** next door is on call for the Quincy's in-room dining. The price at this hotel fluctuates with the seasons; during off months and on weekends, rooms can be an incredible value (starting as low as $150), especially given the central location and the urbane decor.

INSIDER TIP: *If the Willard Hotel prices are beyond your means, drop by for a visit anyhow. Daily afternoon tea is served in Peacock Alley, just beyond the famous lobby, so you don't have to be a hotel guest to enjoy the Willard's legendary service.*

WILLARD INTERCONTINENTAL WASHINGTON

Manager: Herve Houdre
202-628-9100 or 1-800-827-1747; fax 202-628-9100
www.washington.intercontinental.com
1401 Pennsylvania Ave., N.W., Washington, D.C. 20004

Price: Very expensive
Credit Cards: AE, D, DC, MC, V
Handicap Access: Yes
Nearest Metro Station: Metro Center, Blue, Orange, and Red lines

Since opening its doors in 1850, this spectacular grand dame has hosted some of the most influential and powerful people in U.S. history, including every president since Zachary Taylor. Abraham Lincoln lived in the Willard Hotel with his family for several weeks before his inauguration, as did Calvin Coolidge while he waited for President Warren Harding's widow to move out of the White House. President U.S. Grant used to sneak away from the White House to enjoy a brandy and cigar in the Willard so often that folks soon flocked to the lobby in an effort to plead their personal causes to him. Grant branded these favor-seekers "lobbyists," and the name stuck.

Once inside the regal Beaux-Arts structure, everything about the place screams privilege and power: Opulent marble floors, sparkling crystal chandeliers, gilded lamps and mirrors, and elegant damask sofas and chairs in various shades of gold remind guests that they are VIPs. Public spaces are perfumed with fresh flowers, and guest rooms feature divinely comfortable beds piled high with down comforters and pillows. Amenities include a luxurious waffle robe to enjoy during your stay, marble bathrooms with fine bath products, and fresh apples delivered at check-in. During your visit, pamper yourself with at least one room-service meal, because the impeccable presentation alone is worth the hefty price. Service is unobtrusive, professional, and precise: Housekeepers maintain the rooms in perfect order, and in-room dining service is promised to the minute. Fine dining is available at the **Willard Grill**, and the new on-site French bistro, **Café du Parc**, serves moderately priced meals all day. The regal **Round Robin** (see page 225) bar is an

Inspiration for the term "lobbyists," the famous Willard Hotel lobby draws hundreds of tourists a week who come to snap a photo or just drink in the ambiance. Photo by Debbie K. Hardin.

elegant place for a nightcap. Or unwind from a long day of power-brokering at **The Spa at the Willard** (202-942-2700), which features a jet-lag bathtub infused with lemon, orange, and rosemary.

CAPITOL HILL SUITES

Manager: Hans Eckert
202-543-6000 or 1-800-424-9165; fax
202-547-2608
www.capitolhillsuites.com

200 C St., S.E., Washington, D.C. 20003
Price: Inexpensive to moderate
Credit Cards: AE, D, DC, MC, V
Handicap Access: Yes
Nearest Metro Station: Capitol South, Blue and Orange lines

The Capitol Hill Suites is near the Library of Congress and within easy walking distance of the U.S. Capitol. So close, in fact, this is said to be popular with House representatives, who lease rooms for extended stays when Congress is in session. The clubby lobby is masculine and warm, with comfortable leather chairs and sofas and a big, inviting fireplace. Cold breakfast and coffee are served here daily as part of the standard rate. Guest rooms are painted deep blue, slightly worn bed coverings are sky blue, and basic wood furniture is honey-toned. Each unit is equipped with a kitchenette, an ergonomic desk chair, and a large work table. Bathrooms are small, and pedestal sinks offer little counter space, but given the low rates and unbeatably convenient location, this hotel is a terrific value.

THE HOTEL GEORGE

Manager: Jennifer Harris
202-347-4200 or 1-800-576-8331; fax 202-347-4213
www.hotelgeorge.com
15 E St., N.W., Washington, D.C. 20001
Price: Expensive to very expensive
Credit Cards: AE, D, DC, MC, V
Handicap Access: Yes
Nearest Metro Station: Union Station, Red line

The small Hotel George near Union Station, several blocks from the U.S. Capitol, falls in a transitional neighborhood that is convenient if not completely appealing. The diminutive lobby is covered in rough fossilized coral stone, and a gleaming baby grand piano adds elegance and grace. Guest rooms are calm and comfortable and are wrapped in creams and beige neutral tones. The hotel's personality is subdued, but a little quirkiness shines through with a brightly colored throw on an armchair and the signature oversized print of a dollar bill with namesake George's face washed with rainbow hues. Beds are thick with comforters and pillows, and each room features a flat-screen plasma TV, DVD player, clock radio with CD player, work desk with ergonomic chair, and free Wi-Fi. Bathrooms are spacious, although not luxurious.

Guests will be thrilled to find one of the best restaurants in the city on site: **Bistro Bis** (see page 177) serves both hotel guests and a loyal local following as well.

PHOENIX PARK HOTEL

Owner: Daniel Coleman
202-638-6900
www.warwickhotels.com
520 N. Capitol St., N.W., Washington, D.C. 20001
Price: Moderate
Credit Cards: AE, D, DC, MC, V
Handicap Access: Yes
Nearest Metro Station: Union Station, Red line

Recently renovated on Capitol Hill, the Phoenix Park Hotel is a small property with European style. Rooms are compact and elegantly furnished, with elaborately carved headboards, rich fabrics in shades of green, patterned wallpapers, and luxurious carpets. Beds are dressed in fine Irish linens, and each comes with a comfy neck-roll pillow. Wood furniture is a pleasing mix of dark warm tones and country-style whitewashed pieces, giving the rooms a collected, homey feeling. Each guest room offers a flat-screen TV, and there is a small fitness center on site. Two-level suites with lofts offer more space for families. The property is an easy walk from the U.S. Capitol and Union Station, and represents a good value in this neighborhood. Note, however, that parts of Capitol Hill are transitional; streets are generally safe during daytime hours but less so in the evenings.

CHINATOWN/PENN QUARTER

HOTEL MONACO

Manager: Ed Virtue
202-628-7177 or 1-800-649-1202; fax 202-628-7277
www.monaco-dc.com
700 F St., N.W., Washington, D.C. 20004
Price: Very expensive
Credit Cards: AE, D, MC, V

Brilliant colors, bold design, and a dash of historic importance make the whimsical Hotel Monaco stand out from the crowd. Photo by Debbie K. Hardin.

Handicap Access: Yes
Nearest Metro Station: Gallery Place,
Green, Yellow, and Red lines

Step into this stylish, high-end boutique hotel and find a whimsical lobby painted vibrant green, with deep-backed, red-velvet sofas; playful accessories like the puzzle-piece mirror that hangs over a traditional marble fireplace; and emerald-green chandeliers that look to be straight out of Oz. This chic and fun sensibility is juxtaposed with the history of the 1839 structure that houses it: Known for years as the Tariff Building, it also served as the General Post Office, the Patent Office, and a hospital during the Civil War. The Kimpton Hotel group leased the aging beauty several years ago and revitalized and repurposed it; the results are quintessentially Washington—a seamless blending of high style, classic elegance, and historical relevance. Some of the public spaces—particularly the wide corridors tiled in gray and white marble worn smooth from generations of footsteps and trimmed in ornate moldings—remind visitors of other federal buildings that were built in similarly opulent style in the early 19th century. Guest rooms are shallow—they used to be offices, after all—but have extremely high ceilings and original moldings, as well as bold, fresh decor. An 8-foot-high padded headboard extends almost the full width of the room; bright colors and modern, geometric patterns blend harmoniously; and Asian-inspired black end tables and armoires add a Zen-like air. Well-lighted baths have granite countertops and sleek modern faucets and come supplied with high-end French bath products. Service is personalized, and employees are enthusiastic and truly engaged with their customers. A high-tech fitness center with individual plasma screens is available 24 hours a day, and the hotel provides morning coffee and an evening wine hour. And to make your stay as homey as possible, the hotel invites guests to adopt a resident goldfish to enjoy during their stay. **Poste Moderne** is the gorgeous on-site restaurant, offering a popular bar lounge, creatively presented dishes, and a charming courtyard dining space. Perhaps best of all, the hotel is brilliantly located in the hip, revitalized Penn Quarter, just blocks from several Metro stops; it's literally across the street from the Verizon Center, International Spy Museum, and National Portrait Gallery. The only minor complaint we have of this near-perfect accommodation is that the late-night room service carts clattering down the long marble hallways can be disturbing to light sleepers.

MORRISON-CLARK HISTORIC INN
Manager: Joe Jennings
202-898-1200; fax 202-371-0377
www.morrisonclark.com
1015 L St., N.W., Washington, D.C. 20001
Price: Moderate
Credit Cards: AE, D, DC, MC, V
Handicap Access: Yes
Nearest Metro Station: Metro Center, Blue, Orange, and Red lines

This historic inn is housed in two beautifully restored Victorian mansions that date to the mid-19th century; the properties are located near the Washington Convention Center and are close to Metro access. Public spaces are historically correct and feature over-the-top Victoriana, patterned wallpapers, brightly colored upholstery, ornately detailed wood, and Italian Carrera marble fireplaces. Private spaces are more subdued, with lighter colors and fewer patterns. Standard guest rooms have oversized French armoires and neutral fabrics; Victorian guest rooms offer a bit more pomp and circumstance, with richer colors and period furniture, and many boast balconies and decorative fireplaces. Larger Parlor suites have a separate sleeping and living area. The property is 100 percent nonsmoking and offers free Wi-Fi. The much-lauded **Morrison-Clark Inn Restaurant** on site features contemporary American cuisine and is increasingly popular with locals. This property offers a good value year-round, but in the slower seasons look for especially good bargains, with numerous package deals that include tickets to plays, area attractions like the International Spy Museum, and dining packages.

DUPONT CIRCLE AND FOGGY BOTTOM
FAIRMONT WASHINGTON, D.C.
Manager: George Terpilowski
202-429-2400 or 1-800-441-1414; fax 202-457-5010
www.fairmont.com
2401 M St., N.W., Washington, D.C. 20037
Price: Expensive
Credit Cards: AE, D, MC, V
Handicap Access: Yes
Nearest Metro Station: Foggy Bottom, Blue and Orange lines

The Fairmont (formerly the Monarch Hotel) is in a peaceful corner of the West End, sandwiched midway between the Dupont Circle and Foggy Bottom Metro stations and within easy walking distance of Georgetown. The serene marble lobby is dominated by a massive, Italian-inspired atrium with a skylight roof. Standard rooms,

The Fairmont's light-filled atrium looks out onto peaceful views of a lovely interior courtyard overflowing with flowers and blooming trees. Photo by Debbie K. Hardin.

although nondescript, are quite large for the city, and are decorated with muted, neutral tones. The hotel features one of the most expansive hotel health clubs in the area, with a lap pool, racquetball and squash courts, and state-of-the-art fitness equipment. Service is respectful and efficient, and concierge services are especially helpful in securing hard-to-get restaurant reservations and last-minute event tickets. The hotel has two restaurants on site—**The Bistro** and **The Colonnade**—and is within minutes of dozens more. There are especially good deals to be had when the convention season falls off in the summer.

HOTEL HELIX

Manager: Mike Damion
202-462-9001 or 1-800-706-1202; fax
202-332-3519
www.hotelhelix.com
1430 Rhode Island Ave., N.W., Washington,
D.C. 20036
Price: Moderate
Credit Cards: AE, D, DC, MC, V
Handicap Access: Yes
Nearest Metro Station: Dupont Circle, Red
line

Equal measures Andy Warhol and groovy neon glam, this eclectic, slightly over-the-top Kimpton property aims to amuse. Massive portraits of Jackie Kennedy grace the public walls, and ultramod private spaces feature Day-Glo decor, brightly colored Euro furniture, and flat-screen TVs with DVD players. Guests will enjoy Wi-Fi access throughout the property. There are 178 colorful rooms available, in addition to 18 suites and 12 specialty rooms, like the Eats Room, which comes with an Italian-style kitchenette, or the Bunk Room, which comes with a bunk bed, Nintendo, and a king-sized bed in the same room—perfect for the hip family on the go. The manager hosts a special champagne-fueled Bubbly Hour each evening in the "living room"; in addition, the adjoining lounge and off-street patio embrace a '60s-era, predominately white aesthetic—popular with the rank and file of D.C.'s hipster scene, who swill colorful specialty cocktails until last call at 1 AM. Burgers and beer are half price daily from 5 to 7, and during the warm months a special Friday happy hour from 5–8 includes inexpensive grilled hot dogs and burgers and half-price beers.

HOTEL LOMBARDY

Manager: Sherane Berkeley
202-828-2600 or 1-800-424-5486; fax
202-872-0503
www.hotellombardy.com
2019 Pennsylvania Ave., N.W., Washington,
D.C. 20006
Price: Moderate
Credit Cards: AE, MC, V
Handicap Access: No
Nearest Metro Station: Farragut West, Blue
and Orange lines

This small boutique hotel on busy Pennsylvania Avenue, a few blocks from the White House, is cozy and residential, and staying here will probably remind you of visiting an aunt—if your aunt has a big, old house a few blocks down from the president's place. The front doors open to a small parlor, and check-in is in a separate, tiny room to the

left, big enough only for two blood-red velvet Queen Anne chairs and a small sideboard with a big bowl of apples. The diminutive elevators are antiques and must be hand-operated by hotel staff—a cheery, friendly bunch who treat guests like family. Rooms are large and airy, with high ceilings, bleached-white bed linens, old-fashioned metal headboards, and a well-worn ambiance. You'll find a small wet bar with a refrigerator, and many rooms have a separate breakfast nook with table and chairs. Bathrooms are very small, with pedestal sinks that don't allow much room for grooming products. This hotel is especially popular with European travelers who appreciate the multilingual staff. The quaint **Café Lombardy** is on site.

HOTEL MADERA

Manager: Marco Scherer
202-296-7600 or 1-800-368-5691; fax
202-293-2476
www.hotelmadera.com
1310 New Hampshire Ave., N.W.,
Washington, D.C. 20036
Price: Moderate
Credit Cards: AE, D, DC, MC, V
Handicap Access: Yes
Nearest Metro Station: Dupont Circle, Red
line

The miniscule lobby and narrow corridors of the Hotel Madera are testament to the roots of this structure, which started out life as a 1940s-era apartment building. It is tucked into a quiet, residential-ish stretch of New Hampshire Avenue between the Dupont Circle and Foggy Bottom Metro stations, and it still retains a homey atmosphere. Standard guest rooms are elegant and designed with subdued colors, while flashes of leopard print, brightly colored contemporary art, and eclectic lighting remind guests that this is a hip boutique hotel. The Madera offers specialty rooms such as the Cardio Room, with a separate gym space and state-of-the-art exercise equipment, or the Entertainment Room, with an extra-comfy lounge chair and ottoman in front of a flat-screen TV with surround sound. The hotel hosts a complimentary wine hour from 5–6 each evening, and from 10–11 guests can indulge in Oreo cookies and a glass of milk. In addition to creating a home away from home, the Madera has an environmental conscience: Patrons with hybrid cars get free parking, each room has a recycling bin, the hotel provides environmentally friendly Aveda bath products, and lamps are equipped with energy-efficient light bulbs. On site is the lovely **Firefly Bistro,** popular with the local crowd for its inventive cocktails and small-plate meals in the evenings, as well as the "firefly tree" that sprouts from the floor.

HOTEL PALOMAR

Manager: Brett Orlando
202-448-1800 or 1-877-866-3070; fax 202-448-1839
www.hotelpalomar.dc.com
2121 P St., N.W., Washington, D.C. 20037
Price: Expensive
Credit Cards: AE, D, DC, MC, V
Handicap Access: Yes
Nearest Metro Station: Dupont Circle, Red line

On a busy street near Dupont Circle, this Kimpton property exudes an urban vibe with dark, moody colors; oversized contemporary artwork; and pulsing music in the public spaces. Guest rooms are more subdued, with floor-to-ceiling padded headboards, glowing bedside tables that are lighted from within, and faux mink throws on beds layered with pillows and fine linens. Bathrooms are spacious and offer beautiful granite vanities and modern basin sinks; some rooms feature waist-deep whirlpool tubs that are big enough for two. There are a number of specialty rooms on the property, including a few with tiny sep-

arate rooms meant for yoga or that are stocked with fitness equipment. Bunheads will want to check out the ballet room, decorated with the help of Washington Ballet Artistic Director Septime Webre, who incorporated dance company memorabilia into the design; the room has its own dance studio with ballet barre, floor-to-ceiling mirrors, and dance DVDs. The hotel offers a 24-hour fitness facility, a pool, and an on-site restaurant called **Urbana.** Be aware that this relatively new hotel is still working out the kinks in its service, and the front desk staff are often frantic and sometimes inaccessible.

HOTEL ROUGE

Manager: Don Anderson
202-232-8000; fax 202-667-9827
www.rougehotel.com
1315 16th St., N.W., Washington, D.C. 20036
Price: Moderate
Credit Cards: AE, D, MC, V
Handicap Access: Yes
Nearest Metro Station: Dupont Circle, Red line

The campy lobby of the Hotel Rouge near Embassy Row boasts satiny black floors, white leather furniture, the omnipresent splashes of scarlet red for which the hotel is famous, and amusing accents like a plaster nude draped in a red feather boa. Guest rooms are equally whimsical and cheerful, offering oversized red padded headboards, red dust ruffles, red carpets, red lampshades, red ottomans, etc., as well as modern furniture and large art prints. Amenities include free Wi-Fi, an impressive fitness center that is open 24 hours a day, and exceptionally personalized service. Every evening the hotel offers complimentary red wine and red beer in the lobby. On-site is the **Bar Rouge,** a mod, seductive lounge space that also offers small plates of French-inspired food.

The quirky Hotel Rouge offers a Bloody Mary bar and cold pizza in its eclectic lobby every weekend.
Photo by Debbie K. Hardin.

HOTEL TABARD INN

Manager: Cindy Miller
202-785-1277; fax 202-785-6173
www.tabardinn.com
1739 N St., N.W., Washington, D.C. 20036
Price: Moderate
Credit Cards: AE, D, DC, MC, V
Handicap Access: No
Nearest Metro Station: Dupont Circle, Red line

Staying at the Hotel Tabard Inn feels like a visit to an eccentric relative with the good fortune of living in four joined, 19th-century row houses. The name originates from the hotel in Geoffrey Chaucer's *The Canterbury Tales,* and the property succeeds in creating a hip, literary vibe. Pass through the small lobby cluttered with artwork and you find yourself in a maze of lounge rooms with chipped Victorian furniture, working fireplaces, and low lights, crowded by both guests and locals in love with the cozy, shabby-chic decor. From mango- to mahogany-colored walls, none of the 40 guest rooms are the same, whether you opt for an in-suite or shared bathroom. Expect four-poster beds; cushioned love seats; plush rugs and carpets; and a lived-in, old-school sensibility that's essential to Tabard's identity—which is why no elevator has been installed to navigate its four floors. The ground-level dining room, bar, and brick-lined, vine-enshrouded outdoor patio serve delicious contemporary American cuisine and offer homemade donuts as part of their sumptuous breakfasts. Service across the board is attentive and friendly without treading into overblown pomp. The hotel has high-speed wireless Internet access and free passes to the nearby YMCA National Capital. All rates include a continental breakfast.

THE MANSION ON O STREET

Owner: H. H. Leonards-Spero
202-496-2000; fax 202-833-8333
www.omansion.com
2020 O St., N.W., Washington, D.C. 20036
Price: Very expensive
Credit Cards: AE, MC, V
Handicap Access: No
Nearest Metro Station: Dupont Circle, Red line

The labyrinthine, vaguely gothic Mansion on O Street defies description, and no amount of prose can do it justice. With that said, we'll try, anyhow: Imagine a stately mansion on a quiet street near Dupont Circle stuffed from floor to ceiling with bohemian chic antiques, exquisite inlaid-wood tables, charming French writing desks, fine art, massive quantities of crystal and cut glass, layers of Persian and Turkish rugs, hundreds of guitars signed by world-famous rock stars, literally tens of thousands of books, enormous state-of-the-art flat-screen TVs, and kitschy pop-culture treasures. The Mansion has 100 rooms, many of which are accessed through more than 30 secret doors hidden behind bookshelves or mirrors. Part museum, part private club, part hotel, part tag-sale extravaganza (the management boasts that everything in the place is for sale), the pub-

Each room in The Mansion on O Street is brimming with artwork and books, and most have a guitar, should musical inspiration strike. Photo by Debbie K. Hardin.

lic rooms in the mansion are the site of private functions such as weddings and exclusive parties; small business conferences and retreats; and a decadent brunch on Sunday and Monday. Visitors can also make advance reservations to tour what is designated as the museum portion of the mansion (adults $5). Perhaps most fantastical are the 26 hotel rooms, each one unlike any other in the mansion—or anywhere else, for that matter. The campy Log Cabin room has an oversized fish tank mounted over the headboard, boasts one of the largest flat-screen TVs we've ever seen, and has a loft with kitchen, games, food, drinks, barware, toys, art, music, and more; its bathroom features a sauna and steam shower. The small and charming Octagon Room is an eight-sided gem with Prussian blue walls and ceiling, an antique crystal chandelier, rich Indian silks on the cozy bed, and a fire-escape balcony that leads to the top floor. This peaceful space was home to Civil Rights activist Rosa Parks for several years before her death. The Presidential Suite has an Empire-style bed made for a king and is filled with original artwork; most impressive, however, is the bathroom, which is decked out with a teak soaking tub, twin teak sinks, and a kitchen-table-sized chess set made of etched glass and cast metal and valued at more than $20,000. Our favorite space is the John Lennon Room, with a canopied ceiling, a priceless Asian armoire whose every inch is inlaid with mother-of-pearl, and Indian artwork and artifacts throughout. In the bathroom there is a projected-light photo of Lennon on the floor, and hung on the wall there's a pissy note written in his own hand complaining that Yoko Ono's laundry was not done properly. Guests of the hotel can use public rooms like a communal kitchen stocked with breakfast items; homey, cluttered sitting rooms with TVs, audio equipment, books, and games; and the stunning Billiards Room with an enormous pool table Teddy

Roosevelt once enjoyed. An air of mystery pervades the place; staff members are scrupulous about maintaining absolute privacy for their guests, and one has the sense that fabulously famous, artistic, and eccentric folks are lurking behind the hidden passageways.

PARK HYATT

Manager: Michael Morauw
202-789-1234; fax 202-419-6795
www.parkwashington.hyatt.com
1201 24th St., N.W., Washington, D.C. 20037
Price: Expensive
Credit Cards: AE, D, MC, V
Handicap Access: Yes
Nearest Metro Station: Foggy Bottom, Blue and Orange lines

Reopened in 2007 after a $24 million renovation by famed New York designer Tony Chi, the Park Hyatt has undergone a surprising transformation into a luxury boutique hotel. Conveniently located in the West End (near Georgetown and downtown), the newly designed accommodations offer a peaceful haven for city-weary guests. The Zen-inspired lobby is dominated by an enormous glass sculpture etched with images of the city's beloved cherry blossoms. The minimalist design is carried through in the spacious guest rooms with a soothing color palate, extensive use of natural materials, and clean lines—accented with quirky folk art pieces like antique checkerboards and duck decoys. Theatrical lighting and modern furniture are luxurious, although storage space is limited. Each room has a flat-screen TV, an ergonomic work desk, and a collection of art books. Spalike bathrooms are palatial: Ensconced in moody gray and taupe limestone with rain showers and oversized soaking tubs, the bathrooms take up a full third of the room space. The hotel offers its own line of upscale bath products, scented with its signature fragrance designed by Blaise Mautin

The Park Hyatt's Tea Cellar is a peaceful, high-style oasis popular with some local business people as an alternative to "power lunches." Photo by Debbie K. Hardin.

(an "artisinal perfumer" from Paris). On-site dining is available at the acclaimed **Blue Duck Tavern**, which boasts a gleaming open kitchen and Chef Brian McBride's showcase of fresh, regional ingredients. Also on site is the pretty **Tea Cellar**, walled off with glass just beyond the lobby, which offers more than 50 rare teas, including the most expensive handpicked teas in the world (priced at up to $850 a pound!) and vintage Pu-Erh tea from Yunnan, China, which has been aged in caves for hundreds of years. The hotel also offers a nice perk: Two complimentary chauffeur-driven Audi A8 L sedans, available to guests traveling within the District.

INSIDER TIP: *If you have allergies or sensitivity to strong smells, request in advance an unscented room at the Park Hyatt; otherwise, housekeepers will perfume the space before you check in.*

RENAISSANCE MAYFLOWER

Manager: Joseph Cardowe
202-347-3000 or 1-800-228-7697; fax 202-776-9182
www.renaissancehotels.com/WASSH
1127 Connecticut Ave., N.W., Washington, D.C. 20036
Price: Expensive
Credit Cards: AE, D, DC, MC, V

Handicap Access: Yes
Nearest Metro Station: Farragut North, Red line

Since opening its doors in 1925, this venerable D.C. institution has been a favorite with Washington's movers and shakers. Franklin Roosevelt wrote his inaugural address in Room 776 and proclaimed that the nation had "nothing to fear but fear itself." FBI head J. Edgar Hoover is said to have eaten in the hotel's **Café Promenade** at the same table every day for 20 years. And President Nixon favored the Mayflower to put up visiting dignitaries; in the early

The Ritz-Carlton, Washington, D.C., offers several intimate nooks like this one, where guests can relax with the morning paper or enjoy a nightcap. Photo by Debbie K. Hardin.

1970s he took over the entire sixth floor for the employees of the Chinese Embassy while their offices were being renovated. Now the hotel is popular with visiting families as well as businesspeople wanting to be close to the downtown action. Walk into the famous lobby today and you'll find three parts Old World elegance and one part Las Vegas glitz: The wide, deep "grand promenade" houses several thousand pounds of crystal chandeliers, along with neon lights in the **Lobby Court** bar and a massive quantity of gilded ornate Corinthian columns and moldings. Private spaces are subtler and inviting. Large bedroom suites have plenty of natural light and feature deep blue and gold fabrics; some even offer original (ornamental) fireplaces. Standard rooms are equally spacious and decorated in neutral tones, with splashes of bright accent color in throws and pillows. Bathrooms are average sized but well appointed with marble accents, large shower heads, and premier bath products. The on-site, clubby **Town and Country Lounge** has been a favorite watering hole for elite Washingtonians for decades, thanks in part to martini glasses the size of bathtubs. Note that the hotel is 100 percent nonsmoking.

THE RITZ-CARLTON, WASHINGTON, D.C.

Manager: Adrian Ratter
202-835-0500 or 1-800-241-3333; fax 202-835-1588
www.ritzcarlton.com/en/properties/washingtondc
1150 22nd St., N.W., Washington, D.C. 20037
Price: Very expensive
Credit Cards: AE, D, DC, MC, V
Handicap Access: Yes
Nearest Metro Station: Foggy Bottom, Blue and Orange lines

The Ritz-Carlton brand is synonymous with luxury and premier service, and this outlet near the Foggy Bottom Metro station is considered among the finest accommodations in the city. Public spaces are paneled with warm woods and adorned with fine artwork, enormous brass and crystal chandeliers, and oversized arrangements of exotic fresh flowers. Gleaming marble floors are softened with fine Asian and European carpets, and intimate lounges are tucked into private corners. Visitors know they've stepped into rarified air, because the superior acoustics completely obliterate the outside traffic and construction noise from this growing neighborhood. Guest rooms are large and traditionally furnished, and comfortable beds are dressed with fine Frette linens and 100 percent goose down pillows. Oversized marble bathrooms offer soaking tubs, upscale personal products, and thoughtful extras—like a crystal bowl full of cotton balls and pots of fresh orchids. Guests have access to the 100,000-square-foot **Sports Club/LA**, which offers classes in martial arts, yoga, and nutritional services. This fully equipped fitness center also has a large pool, basketball and volleyball courts, steam rooms and saunas, and personal trainers to help guests maneuver through the circuit of cardio and strength-training equipment. In 2008, Eric Ripert of New York's famed Le Bernadin opened **Weekend Bistro** on site, drawing guests from around the city.

THE RIVER INN

Manager: Janine Heath
202-337-7600 or 1-800-424-2741; fax 202-337-6520
www.theriverinn.com
924 25th St., N.W., Washington, D.C. 20037
Price: Moderate
Credit Cards: AE, D, MC, V
Handicap Access: Yes
Nearest Metro Station: Foggy Bottom, Blue and Orange lines

This pretty and homey hotel is tucked into a quiet residential enclave midway between the Foggy Bottom Metro station and Georgetown, on a charming and peaceful tree-lined street full of old row houses. The small lobby boasts a cozy fireplace and chic, Asian-inspired decor in apple greens and deep browns, and colorful modern art hangs behind the reception desk. This all-suites hotel offers a fully equipped efficiency kitchen in each unit, complete with grinders and fresh coffee beans. Corporate suites (as standard rooms are called) are wrapped in bright, contemporary fabrics in shades of caramel and pumpkin, with dark, clean-lined wood furniture; a huge work desk; and a full-sized sofa. Accents include inviting bed throws and beautiful black and white photography. Windows are enormous, and many overlook the Watergate complex and the Potomac River beyond. Bathrooms are standard size and adjoin a dressing area with a large granite vanity and mirrors all around. For about $50 more, guests can enjoy a Potomac Suite, which offers a separate bedroom; an expansive sitting room with a large sectional, another full-sized couch, and several large tables that can be used as work space; and a small dining area with table and chairs. A fully equipped, newly renovated fitness facility is on site, as are laundry facilities. Guests are close to dozens of fine dining options, but the hotel's **Dish** makes it tempting to stay put for the evening, thanks to inventive recipes like ginger and cilantro cured salmon served with a mango slaw and traditional Louisiana gumbo. This hotel is also convenient to the Kennedy Center, which is an easy 10-minute walk away; in fact, visiting musicians performing at the Kennedy Center often stay here. Week-long and month-long rates are available at a discount, but even at full price, The River Inn is one of the best values in the area, and an extraordinarily efficient and friendly staff make this feel like home away from home.

Clean lines, fresh design, and ample space make the River Inn one of the most intriguing, affordable lodging options in the District. Photo by Debbie K. Hardin.

ST. GREGORY

Manager: Jay Haddock
202-223-0200; fax 202-466-6770
www.stgregoryhotelwdc.com
2033 M St., N.W., Washington, D.C. 20036
Price: Moderate
Credit Cards: AE, MC, V
Handicap Access: Yes
Nearest Metro Station: Foggy Bottom, Blue and Orange lines

This completely remodeled and redesigned hotel on the West End, close to the Foggy Bottom Metro station, is most remarkable because of its price, which fluctuates by season but can be a real value when occupancy is low. The new lobby is decked out in elegant beige marble floors and neutral colors, but the first thing you're likely to notice is a life-size sculpture of Marilyn Monroe with her dress blowing up beneath her. Guest rooms are commodious, and all feature new flat-screen TVs. Decor is comfortable and monochromatic, with beige- and gold-toned walls and fabrics and honey-colored woods. Suites offer a cozy sitting area with a full-size sofa and comfortable chairs. The small **M Street Bar and Grill** just off the lobby offers intimate dining spaces near a fireplace or tucked into a corner—and because of this hotel's central location, guests are close to lots of fine dining choices off site.

SWANN HOUSE

Manager: Rick Berkler
202-265-4414; fax 202-265-6755
www.swannhouse.com
1808 New Hampshire Ave., N.W., Washington, D.C. 20009
Price: Moderate to expensive
Credit Cards: AE, D, MC, V
Handicap Access: No
Nearest Metro Station: Dupont Circle, Red line

A romantic B&B housed in a gorgeous Victorian mansion near Dupont Circle, Swann House is an elegant, peaceful retreat from the busy outside world. Guests will be treated to fresh brownies and lemonade or iced tea in the afternoons and sherry cordials in the evenings. Weekday breakfasts are beautifully displayed and feature seasonal fruits, house-made granola, pastries, coffee, and a variety of teas. Weekend breakfasts offer hot treats like frittatas, creamy soufflés, and French toast. Each guest room is individually decorated in warm colors, most in neutral tones—although there are a few frillier, more traditionally Victorian designs. All rooms have private baths, antique headboards, and featherbeds with down pillows; pricier rooms have whirlpool tubs, fireplaces, and balconies as well. The inn boasts a lovely small courtyard pool (in season). Children 12 and older are welcome, but note that this is really designed to be a couples retreat.

TOPAZ HOTEL

Manager: Mike Sutter
202-393-3000 or 1-800-424-2950; fax 202-785-9581
www.topazhotel.com
1733 N St., N.W., Washington, D.C. 20036
Price: Expensive
Credit Cards: AE, D, DC, MC, V
Handicap Access: Yes
Nearest Metro Station: Dupont Circle, Red line

If staying in anonymous hotel rooms drains you of your travel sanity, Topaz may be your panacea. Each of the 99 rooms at this Kimpton property is imbued with a soothing New Age vibe. Bold, colorful stripes on the walls; sleek wooden surfaces; flat-screen TVs with a special all-yoga channel; Wi-Fi access; dim lights; tasteful explosions of colorful upholstery; and luxurious carpets and rugs make your room feel more like a home and less like a cookie cutter hotel room. Add to that details like by-request gratis yoga mats, daily morning energy drinks, specialty rooms with exercise equipment, and candied ginger at the front desk, and Topaz's personality shines. Public rooms are Asian tempered with contemporary sensibilities, as evidenced by the doormen's blue Nehru jackets. The bar/lounge off the main lobby, complete with shifting mood lights and furniture draped with animal prints, may strike some as a bit too hip for its own good, but the expertly blended seasonal cocktails and inventive, if small, food menu justify repeated visits.

GEORGETOWN
FOUR SEASONS GEORGETOWN

Manager: Christopher Huntsberger
202-342-0444 or 1-800-332-3442; fax 202-944-2076
www.fourseasons.com/washington
2800 Pennsylvania Ave., N.W., Washington, D.C. 20037
Price: Very expensive
Credit Cards: AE, D, DC, MC, V
Handicap Access: Yes
Nearest Metro Station: Foggy Bottom, Blue and Orange lines

This sophisticated brick structure backs up to the historic C&O Canal (see page 247) and is tucked into the westernmost edge of

Georgetown (a tad bit of a hike from the heart of the restaurant and shopping district). Throughout the subdued and elegant lobby you'll find oversized vases of fragrant cut flowers; elsewhere there is a rock and bamboo garden that demarcates a lobby bar and eclectic original artwork. As with any Four Seasons property, expect premier service from the moment you arrive, including well-informed front desk staff and housekeepers who uphold the highest standards. Guest rooms are lushly decorated with thick patterned carpets; sumptuous bedding; and rich, fresh colors. A three-level fitness facility offers a variety of cardiovascular equipment, each arrayed with its own TV, DVD player, and CD player. The indoor lap pool, which was recently converted from chlorine to a salt system, provides both a hygienic swimming environment and a greener operation that eliminates the need for smelly chemicals. It's worth noting that the hotel's dry cleaning is run with an environmentally friendly system that does not use harmful chemicals. A full-service spa offers massages, scrubs, facials, and a steam shower, and on-site dining is available at the gardenlike **Seasons,** a fine-dining restaurant that highlights fresh, local ingredients. Children will enjoy their own indulgences at the Four Seasons, including child-sized robes, age-appropriate books and magazines, a chocolate chip cookie delivered to her or his guest room, and bowls of candy scattered throughout the public rooms.

GEORGETOWN SUITES

Manager: Crystal Sullivan
202-298-7800 or 1-800-348-7203; fax
202-333-2019
www.georgetownsuites.com
1111 30th St., N.W., Washington, D.C. 20007
Price: Moderate
Credit Cards: AE, MC, V
Handicap Access: Yes
No Metro access

If you have your heart set on staying in stylish Georgetown while visiting D.C. and you're traveling on a budget, the Georgetown Suites might just be the place for you. The somewhat anonymous red brick structure is located near numerous fine dining and shopping opportunities, yet it's just off the main drag of busy M Street, and is therefore relatively quiet. Accommodations are surprisingly spacious and clean but a tad style-impaired. Fabrics are dated and the furniture is generic and a little worn. The good news is that the handy kitchens come fully equipped. If you aren't planning to spend much time in your hotel or don't expect your hotel to be too cool for school, this well-located property presents a true value, and depending on the season, rooms can even fall into the "inexpensive" category. Note that continental breakfast is included and laundry facilities are on site. The hotel also offers free Wi-Fi and HBO.

HOTEL MONTICELLO

Manager: Albert Brito
202-337-0900; fax 202-333-6526
www.monticellohotel.com
1075 Thomas Jefferson St., N.W., Washington, D.C. 20007
Price: Moderate
Credit Cards: AE, D, DC, MC, V
Handicap Access: Yes
No Metro access

On a side street near the picturesque C&O Canal and within easy walking distance of the Potomac waterfront, this small hotel offers another great value in Georgetown, one that is especially appealing for families. The tiny lobby is welcoming and pretty, although short on glitz. The traditionally decorated guest rooms are a bit dated and dark, but they are enormous—easily commodious enough for a family of four or five. The all-suite accommodations include a separate sleeping room and a full-sized living space with a refrigerator, microwave,

Expect world-class service in a friendly, intimate atmosphere at The Latham, a well-kept secret in Georgetown. Photo by Debbie K. Hardin.

and wet bar. Each room also offers a generous work space and a large bathroom. Thomas Jefferson, who once lived on the street where the hotel is located, is represented in oil paintings throughout the property, and the friendly staff at this unassuming property try hard to evoke the hospitality for which the former president was famous at his own Monticello.

THE LATHAM

Manager: John Cairns
202-726-5000 or 1-888-587-2377;
fax 202-337-4250
www.georgetowncollection.com/latham_hotel
3000 M St., N.W., Washington, D.C. 20007
Price: Moderate

Credit Cards: AE, D, MC, V
Handicap Access: Yes
No Metro access

Set back slightly from busy M Street, in the heart of fashionable Georgetown, The Latham is an often overlooked gem close to myriad opportunities for fine dining and shopping, and is an easy stroll from the charming C&O Canal. The European ambiance and service that goes the extra mile are worthy of a much more expensive hotel; happily, rates here are reasonable, and during slow seasons there are even bargains to be had. Rooms are spacious and furnished elegantly; bathrooms are small but charming, with brightly patterned wallpaper and granite throughout. Each accommodation includes a bed piled high with fine linens, a commodious work desk, Wi-Fi, and bathrooms with upscale bath products. In addition to a number of standard and deluxe room choices, the hotel offers lovely suites on two levels. These include a loft space above that overlooks a comfortable sitting area and two bathrooms—perfect for families. The hotel boasts the only rooftop pool in Georgetown (open seasonally), and guests can make preferential reservations at the on-site **Michel Richard Citronelle** (see page 193), the finest dining option in the city—and one of the hardest tables to secure in the District as well.

INSIDER TIP: *Many D.C. hotels, including The Latham, offer special package rates in the summer, when business is typically slower—and there are even greater discounts on weekends. Look for deals that include breakfasts, attraction tickets, and even public transportation passes.*

MELROSE HOTEL

Manager: Terry Ryan
202-955-6400; fax 202-955-5765
www.melrosehotelwashingtondc.com
2430 Pennsylvania Ave., N.W., Washington, D.C. 20037
Price: Moderate
Credit Cards: AE, D, DC, MC, V
Handicap Access: Yes
Nearest Metro Station: Foggy Bottom, Blue and Orange lines

Located on the most famous street in Washington, D.C., the Melrose Hotel on Pennsylvania Avenue isn't really close to the White House, but it is conveniently located midway between Georgetown and the Foggy Bottom Metro station—and location is the main attraction of this lodging option. The small, utilitarian lobby offers a few chairs and tables but little luxury, although the friendly bellmen and front desk staff make up for the lack of glamour. Guest rooms have recently been renovated and offer

four-poster beds, ornately patterned fabrics, and traditional style. There's a small in-house fitness center for guests, Wi-Fi, 24-hour room service, and on-site dining. The neighborhood is a little noisy, so light sleepers will want to book an upper floor.

UPPER NORTHWEST
THE INTOWN UPTOWN INN

Innkeeper: David Handy
202-541-9400; fax 202-318-8361
www.iuinn.com
4907 14th St., N.W., Washington, D.C. 20011
Price: Moderate
Credit Cards: AE, D, DC, MC, V
Handicap Access: No
No Metro access

This elegant, well-designed B&B is housed in a 1908 Victorian home in an old northwest neighborhood. Although far-flung—the Metro station is beyond a comfortable walk—there is local bus service nearby, and street parking is possible if you're willing to search for it. Service is friendly and relaxed, and staying here is more like visiting with relatives than staying at a hotel—not unusual for B&Bs in general, but The Intown Uptown seems to connect especially well with its guests. Individually decorated rooms are unique and imaginative, and manage to be both graceful and fun. Lovely bathrooms are tranquil, and some feature Jacuzzis. There is a well-tended garden on the property with two decks and an outdoor Jacuzzi. But the best part of this place could be the three-course hot breakfasts—a huge step up from the standard continental fare available in many hotels. The meal is served on fine china in a home-style setting that encourages guests to get to know each other. The chef is happy to accommodate special requests, but be sure to ask about this in advance.

WINDSOR PARK HOTEL

Manager: Sam Najjar
202-483-7700 or 1-800-247-3064; fax

Living with Scandal: The Watergate

The Watergate is a complex of gently curving steel-and-glass midrises that house expensive apartments and office buildings; it is strategically located on the Potomac River, next door to the Kennedy Center and near the State Department. The luxurious buildings and killer views, however, take a backseat to the Watergate's reputation: This was the site of the infamous 1972 break-in at the Democratic National Committee headquarters, the subsequent cover-up of which led to the resignation of President Richard Nixon. Despite its brush with scandal, high-end apartments on site have been home to the likes of Monica Lewinsky, Bob and Elizabeth Dole, and more recently Condoleezza Rice. The Watergate also houses a high-end hotel, with 250 guest rooms, many of which enjoy spectacular views. If you have a penchant for mischief and intrigue—or if the Watergate's historical significance appeals—this could be an ideal lodging choice (202-965-2300 or 1-800-289-1555; fax 202-337-7915; www .watergatehotel.com; 2650 Virginia Ave., N.W., Washington). But you'll have to be patient: The hotel closed its doors in 2007 for an extensive remodel and won't reopen again until 2009.

Although the name is synonymous with scandal throughout the world, Beltway insiders know the Watergate is one of the best addresses in town. Photo by Debbie K. Hardin.

202-332-4547
www.windsorparkhotel.com
2116 Kalorama Rd., N.W., Washington, D.C. 20008
Price: Moderate
Credit Cards: AE, D, MC, V
Handicap Access: Yes
Nearest Metro Station: Woodley Park, Red line

Part B&B, part modest boutique hotel, the Windsor Park Hotel, which dates to 1926, is an economic option in the upper northwest area of D.C. The property is near Rock Creek Park and within relatively easy access to the zoo. The basic decor of the small rooms includes country fabrics, traditional dark-wood furniture, and clean bathrooms. The hotel offers a cold breakfast of pastries, fruit, bagels, juice, and coffee, and there are two computers with Wi-Fi that guests may use. There is no on-site parking available. Although this property is not luxurious, service is helpful and the hotel is family friendly.

WOODLEY PARK GUEST HOUSE
Owner: Courtney Lodico
202-667-0218 or 1-866-667-0218; fax

202-667-1080
www.woodleyparkguesthouse.com
2647 Woodley Rd., N.W., Washington, D.C.
20008
Price: Inexpensive to Moderate
Credit Cards: AE, MC, V
Handicap Access: No
Nearest Metro Station: Woodley Park, Red
line

An 18-room B&B in a stately old home near the zoo, this is a quiet and peaceful alternative to large hotels, yet guests are still within easy access to the Metro and numerous dining and shopping opportunities. The cozy front porch is lined with white wicker furniture and pillows, giving guests ideal access to the fresh evening air in the moderate seasons. The structure of this recently restored home is charming, and guest rooms feature interesting sloped ceilings, bay windows, and small window nooks that are perfect for curling up with a good book. Each room is different, and some offer shared baths, but all accommodations are light and bright, with neutral tones on the walls, extensive hardwood floors, and old-fashioned bedspreads. Furnishings are antiques or reproductions, and are comfortable rather than fussy. A breakfast of scones, croissants, yogurt, fruit, and coffee is included in the room rate, and the inn offers free Wi-Fi. Note that parking is limited and must be reserved in advance; if secured, it will cost nearly $20 more a night. There are no TVs or radios on the property—and also no smoking, no children, and no pets. The inn requires a two-night minimum stay.

ARLINGTON, VIRGINIA
HILTON ARLINGTON AND TOWERS
Manager: Mark Driscoll
703-528-6000; fax 703-812-5127
www.hiltonarlington.com
950 N. Stafford St., Arlington, VA 22203
Price: Moderate
Credit Cards: AE, D, MC, V

Handicap Access: Yes
Nearest Metro Station: Ballston, Orange
line

You can't find a hotel in Arlington closer to a subway stop than this one: You literally walk out the front door and onto the escalator that takes you to the Ballston Metro station. The hotel is also connected via an enclosed elevated walkway to Ballston Common Mall, a retail shopping center with restaurants and a multiplex cinema. The small lobby has comfortable chairs and a large-screen plasma TV. Recently redecorated guest rooms are large and comfortable—albeit unexciting—with beige fabrics and dark woods. Each room is equipped with a large work table with data ports and Wi-Fi, and there is ample light for reading. Nicely appointed bathrooms offer Crabtree and Evelyn products. The hotel is 100 percent nonsmoking—not an easy find in the state that used to be the hub of the tobacco economy.

HOTEL PALOMAR ARLINGTON AT WATERVIEW
Manager: Sholeh Kia
703-351-9170 or 1-866-936-1001;
fax 703-351-9175
www.hotelpalomar-arlington.com
1121 N. 19th St., Arlington, VA 22209
Price: Very expensive
Credit Cards: AE, D, DC, MC, V
Handicap Access: Yes
Nearest Metro Station: Rosslyn, Orange line

This new Kimpton property (opened in early 2008) just across the Potomac River from Georgetown and near the Rosslyn Metro station is a pricey—but well worth it—alternative to the myriad plain-vanilla chain hotels throughout Northern Virginia. Accommodations run from the 4th through the 15th floors of the contemporary Waterview highrise and offer stellar views of the river and Washington, D.C.; the hotel even provides mini binoculars so that guests can make the most of these fabulous vistas. Public spaces are filled with original artwork and offer interesting, homey niches in which to relax over a glass of wine during the complimentary cocktail hour or linger over coffee and the newspaper in the morning. Private spaces are wrapped in chocolate browns and café au lait tones, with a hit of mango in accent pieces like cozy woolen bed throws. Amenities include an ergonomic desk chair at an oversized work table, flatscreen plasma TVs, iPod docking stations, and free Wi-Fi. Luxurious baths feature modern basin sinks and ultracool lighting fixtures and come stocked with upscale French toiletries. The hotel is nonsmoking and pet-friendly. On-site dining is available at **Domasoteca Moderna Taverna,** which serves Italian specialties in a high-style atmosphere.

MARRIOTT KEY BRIDGE

Manager: Sharon Lockwood
703-524-6400; fax 703-524-8964
www.marriott.com/waskb
1401 Lee Hwy., Arlington, VA 22209
Price: Moderate
Credit Cards: AE, D, MC, V
Handicap Access: Yes
Nearest Metro Station: Rosslyn, Orange line

Cross over the Key Bridge adjacent to this well-placed riverfront Marriott and you're in the heart of Georgetown—or hop on the nearby Rosslyn Station Metro for easy access to the National Mall and Smithsonian museums. This 100 percent nonsmoking hotel recently renovated its guest rooms, which feature neutral decor, 300-thread-count linens and down pillows on the comfy beds, and a large work space with bright task lighting. Although the property is somewhat lacking in personality, it does offer killer views of the city from the higher floors, and amenities include both an indoor and outdoor pool and a nice in-house fitness center. The hotel allows its

guests a later checkout than most: You can kick back here until 1 PM.

INSIDER TIP: *If you are visiting the D.C. area over the Fourth of July but don't want to hassle with the crowds at the National Mall, the Marriot Key Bridge hotel offers rooms with a view of the fireworks; they also have a rooftop lounge that hosts a Fourth cocktail hour (reservations and a stiff additional fee are required).*

ALEXANDRIA, VIRGINIA
MORRISON HOUSE

Manager: Nick Gregory
703-838-8000; fax 703-684-6283
www.morrisonhouse.com
116 S. Alfred St., Alexandria, VA 22314
Price: Expensive
Credit Cards: AE, DC, MC, V
Handicap Access: Yes
Nearest Metro Station: King Street, Blue and Yellow lines

George Washington never slept here, but if he had, he would have felt right at home in the elegant neo-Colonial decor. This small hotel a few blocks from the heart of Old Town Alexandria isn't a historic property, but it has the ambiance of a refined 18th-century mansion. Expect impeccable personal attention from staff here, Father of the country or not. Off the tiny lobby, the plush period-designed parlor glitters with a heavy crystal chandelier and cozy fireplace, and the next room over is a manly wood-clad library—the perfect place to curl up with a good book or engage in a game of chess. Standard guest rooms are smallish, but not prohibitively so—with period reproduction four-poster beds, side tables, elegantly upholstered side chairs, and commodious armoires, all lighted romantically with brass chandeliers on dimmer switches. Fabrics and wallpapers are traditional and rich in color and design, and supremely comfortable beds are piled high with down pillows, Frette linens, thick

Enjoy a nightly wine hour in this pristine Alexandria parlor, courtesy of Morrison House.
Photo by Debbie K. Hardin.

comforters, and a soft throw blanket. Bathrooms are also on the smaller side, but include two sinks, wall-to-wall marble, enormous Turkish bath towels, and fine French bath products. Suites offer a large sitting room furnished with reproduction antique sofas, a desk, a table, and several side chairs. You won't need to leave the property for fine dining; **The Grille** (see page 208) is one of the most innovative restaurants in Alexandria. And once you're ready to call it a night, the thoughtful staff will even tuck you in with a bedtime story, a copy of which is left during turn-down service, along with a few chocolates on the pillow. If you plan to arrive by car, keep a keen eye out or you'll drive right by the place: The pretty façade of the building—with a curving marble double staircase and a soothing water fountain in front—is oriented toward the side alley instead of the street.

SHERATON OLD TOWN ALEXANDRIA SUITES
Manager: Leon Cox
703-836-4700 or 1-800-325-3535; fax 703-548-4514
www.sheraton.com
801 N. Saint Asaph St., Alexandria, VA 22314
Price: Expensive

Credit Cards: AE, D, DC, MC, V
Handicap Access: Yes
Nearest Metro Station: King Street, Blue
and Yellow lines

This midrise brick structure blends in reasonably well with its historic setting in the heart of Old Town Alexandria. Guest rooms are designed to be soothingly neutral, using deep blue fabrics and clean-lined furnishings, and bathrooms are commodious and well-appointed with upscale bath products and fine towels. Beds here, as with all Sheraton properties, are extra luxurious, with a plush pillow-top mattress, down pillows, and cozy comforters. Amenities include high-speed Internet access and a well-equipped fitness center with an indoor swimming pool. There is nothing Revolutionary about this chain hotel, but it is conveniently located near Alexandria's nicest shopping and dining, and is within walking distance of the waterfront.

THE NATIONAL MALL

America's Attic and More

For many visitors, the National Mall *is* Washington, D.C., and some surveys indicate that, aside from traveling to and from their lodging, as many as 50 percent of tourists never stray beyond its perimeters. This isn't hard to understand. The National Mall—the nearly 2 miles of acreage running from the Lincoln Monument east to the U.S. Capitol, and for the purposes of this chapter including the White House just north of the Washington Monument and the Jefferson Memorial just south—houses a wealth of historical and cultural treasures.

Newcomers are often fooled by the deceptive scale of the National Mall. The towering monuments, federal buildings, and enormous Smithsonian museums make the distances between them seem closer than they actually are. It is certainly possible to walk from one end of the Mall to the other in one visit, with stops at major points along the way, but it makes for a long, tiring day—and can make for a rushed experience, especially if you try to hit the museums, too. A more practical way to navigate the Mall is to divide it into manageable chunks. Explore, say, the west end of the Mall one day: Take in the Tidal Basin and the Lincoln, Jefferson, Roosevelt, Korean War, and Vietnam Memorials. Then, on a second day, tackle the World War II Memorial, the Washington Monument, and one or two of the Smithsonian museums. On yet another day, focus on the east end, exploring the U.S. Capitol, the Library of Congress, the U.S. Supreme Court Building, and a few more museums. Of course, if your time is limited, by all means see as much as you can: Get an early start, wear comfortable shoes, and plan a meal break!

For up-to-date information regarding the National Mall—especially important during one of the massive events regularly held here (major parades, inaugural activities, etc.)— tune to the National Park Service's radio station, which offers its own broadcasts of visiting hours, traffic updates, and news. You'll find this 10-watt signal at 1670 AM—but note that you'll only be able to pick up the signal if you are within 3 miles of the Mall.

GARDENS ON THE MALL

In addition to being a treasure trove of history and culture, the National Mall is also an indescribably beautiful place, with immense expanses of green grass, old-growth trees— many of which flower profusely in springtime—and flower beds that burst with color in all but the harshest winter months. Visitors will delight in discovering more than a dozen gardens as well, tucked in and around the museums and monuments. Spring is the most

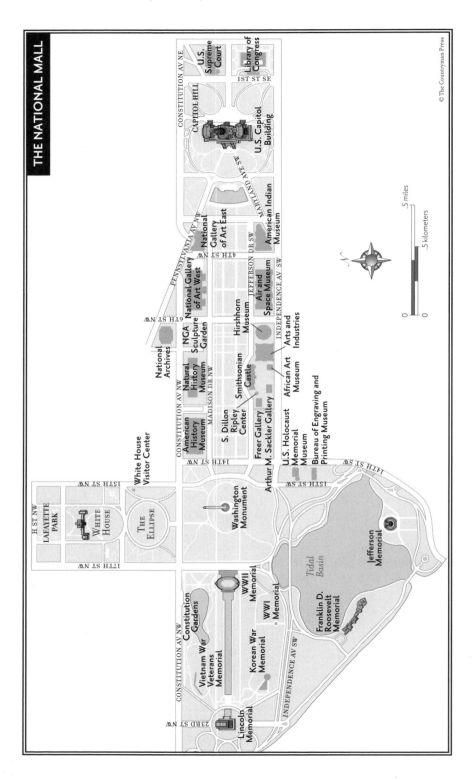

THE NATIONAL MALL

© The Countryman Press

rewarding time to visit these oases, and summertime also brings heavy blooms and deeply colored foliage. However, fall and winter offer their own rewards, which include frost-resistant pansies, decorative grasses, and surprisingly colorful ornamental kale.

Butterfly Habitat Garden (east side of the Natural History Museum at Ninth St., N.W., between Constitution Ave. and the National Mall; nearest Metro: Smithsonian, Blue and Orange lines). This urban garden features plants and flowers that are particularly attractive to butterflies, often seen in abundance throughout the spring and summer, along with plenty of bees. The garden highlights a number of habitats, including a wetland area with a small pond, a meadow area that features wildflowers and ornamental grasses, and a shady woodland area featuring birch and ash trees and shade-loving plants like nettles and ferns.

Constitution Gardens (www.nps.gov/coga; west end of the Mall, on Constitution Ave.; nearest Metro: Smithsonian, Blue and Orange lines). This lushly treed 50-acre park near the Vietnam Veterans Memorial features a pond with a small island that is popular with ducks and geese. During the Bicentennial in 1976 a memorial to the 56 signers of the U.S. Constitution was dedicated on the island, and every year the National Park Service holds a naturalization ceremony for new U.S. citizens here. Year-round it is a peaceful, uncrowded place to spend a few moments, and children will enjoy watching the wildlife.

Enid A. Haupt Garden (1050 Independence Ave., S.W.; nearest Metro: Smithsonian, Blue and Orange lines). This quiet oasis just beyond the crowds on the National Mall is tucked behind the Smithsonian Castle—and rests on top of the subterranean African Art

Spring blossoms in the Enid A. Haupt Garden frame the back of the Smithsonian Castle. Photo by Debbie K. Hardin.

Museum. The 4.2 acres of formal gardens and walkways center on a formal parterre garden flanked by Hawthorn trees, black sour gums, weeping cherry blossoms, and spectacular saucer magnolias. The garden is punctuated with ornate 19th-century wrought-iron benches, several pretty water features, and standing urns and hanging baskets brimming with seasonal blooms. Look for the Chinese Moon Gate sculpture on the west end that leads to a shallow pool. Free tours are available in the summer.

Heirloom Garden (on the east end of the American History Museum, facing Madison Ave., N.W.; nearest Metro: Smithsonian, Blue and Orange lines). These nostalgic beds, which surround the American History Museum, highlight plants and flowers that have been cultivated in American gardens for more than 50 years, including columbine, cone flowers, dianthus, digitalis, and hollyhocks—many species of which were grown by George Washington and Thomas Jefferson in their ornamental gardens.

Katherine Dulin Folger Rose Garden (on Jefferson Dr., near the Smithsonian Castle; nearest Metro: Smithsonian, Blue and Orange lines). In front of the Arts and Industries Building, just east of the Smithsonian Castle, this charming rose garden boasts several dozen varieties of colorful, fragrant roses. Blooms are most prodigious in late spring and early summer. The garden also features bulbs, cool-season annuals, and hollies, which provide interest during the other seasons. The cast-iron fountain that sits in the center of the garden is an original 19th-century piece restored for the site.

Mary Livingston Ripley Garden (between Independence Ave. and Jefferson Dr., N.W.; nearest Metro: Smithsonian, Blue and Orange lines). Tucked between the Arts and Industries Building and the Hirshhorn Museum is a lovely, small garden of raised beds that features a fanciful wrought-iron fountain, colorful birdhouses, and an overflowing cottage-style design that buzzes with bees and butterflies, especially during the summer months. Autumn colors are also particularly showy here. Despite being in one of the busiest sections of the National Mall, this garden is relatively undiscovered, and it is a perfect place to enjoy a respite from the crowds.

National Museum of the American Indian Gardens (202-633-1000; www.nmai.si.edu; Fourth St. and Independence Ave., S.W.; nearest Metro: Capitol South, Blue and

The colorful Katherine Dulin Folger Rose Garden offsets the fanciful Arts and Industries Building. Photo by Debbie K. Hardin.

Yoshino cherry trees reflect morning light on the Tidal Basin. Photo courtesy of Jon Preimesberger. Used with permission.

Orange lines). The grounds of this museum honor local American Indians by featuring four environments indigenous to the Chesapeake Bay area: hardwood forest, wetlands, cropland, and meadows. More than 40 so-called Grandfather Rocks represent the longevity of the Native people's relationship with the environment.

Surrounding the sand-colored structure are gardens that include—in season—corn, beans, tomatoes, and peppers growing in a cropland area and a meadow area full of wildflowers. In all there are more than 33,000 indigenous plants representing 150 species, including 25 native trees like red maple and white oak. Organic-appearing waterfalls cascade over large boulders, and you'll find water lilies and cattails in a nearby wetland area.

Tidal Basin (www.nps.gov/thje; southwest of the National Mall; nearest Metro: Smithsonian, Blue and Orange lines). In early spring, hundreds of thousands of visitors descend on the Tidal Basin in front of the Jefferson Memorial to see the famous Washington, D.C., cherry blossoms at their peak. There are close to 3,700 cherry trees representing 11 different species scattered throughout East Potomac Park and along the grounds of the Washington Monument, but the most famous are the more than 1,600 Yoshino variety that ring the peaceful, duck-filled Basin. Most of the mature trees were a gift from Japan in 1912. The ethereal blossoms range from pure white to pale pink, and dark gray branches arch gracefully over the concrete walkway and dip close to the water. The

National Park Service monitors their blooming cycle as early as February and makes annual (and generally quite accurate) blooming predictions on its Web site (www.nps.gov/nacc/cherry). Although peak blossom time varies yearly—and a big rainstorm can wash them all away in a matter of hours—expect them in very late March and the first week in April.

INSIDER TIP: *The walkway rimming the Tidal Basin is one of the loveliest places in the city to see the famous cherry blossoms during the short blooming season. It is also the most crowded. To avoid the congestion, come early enough to watch the sun rise over the Jefferson Monument. You'll have the walkway to yourself, and you'll even find coveted parking right on the Basin. First-morning light is also one of the best times to snap photos of the blossoms.*

United States Botanic Garden (202-225-8333; www.usbg.gov; 100 Maryland Ave., S.W., Washington; nearest Metro: Capitol South, Blue and Orange lines). Adjacent to the Capitol, the U.S. Botanic Garden exhibits more than 25,000 plants, including hundreds of endangered species, as well as historic specimens that date to the original 1842 founding collection. The centerpiece of the garden, a storybook conservatory, is a tropical paradise housing full-sized palm trees, luxuriant ferns, babbling brooks, and more than 200 blooming orchids. (The collection actually includes more than 5,000 specimens of orchids, but only a fraction are on display at any one time.) When inside the conservatory, be sure to climb up to the catwalk to get a treetop view. Also on-site are a children's garden, a succulent garden, and a collection of medicinal plants. Visit the conservatory during cool months or in early hours during the summer because the humid, windless environment inside is oppressive when outside temperatures soar. **The National Garden** to the west of the conservatory (at Third St. and Independence Ave.) features a regional garden highlighting native plants of the Mid-Atlantic region, a

Bartholdi Park, just southwest of the U.S. Capitol, is a pleasant surprise for those who venture a few blocks beyond the Capitol. Photo by Debbie K. Hardin.

butterfly garden, a rose garden, and a pond accented with a bold, colorful glass sculpture by Dale Chihuly. **Bartholdi Park** (open from dawn to dusk) is behind the conservatory, triangulated between Washington Street, First Street, and Independence Avenue. This portion of the U.S. Botanic Garden is little known, and thus is often a retreat from the chaos of the surrounding city. There are numerous quiet spots to sit, including a delightful pergola with a half-dozen wooden rocking chairs. The garden serves as an outlet for landscape demonstrations on the latest techniques in American horticulture. Be sure to visit in the fall for a spectacular show of color.

Museums on the Mall

When most visitors think of the National Mall, they think of the incredibly diverse Smithsonian Institution—often called "America's Attic" because of its myriad collections. Although it is represented by the iconic Castle—the fanciful red brick structure visible just as one emerges from the north exit of the Smithsonian Metro station—the institution is really a collection of museums, a few of which lie beyond the parameters of the Mall and some of which aren't even in D.C. (See Chapter 5 for additional museum coverage.) However, not all museums on the Mall are part of the Smithsonian; many folks are surprised to learn that the National Gallery of Art is not a Smithsonian museum.

One of the great benefits of D.C. culture is its accessibility: All Smithsonian museums are free to the public (although in these times of lean political support, donations are always welcome), as are both the East and West Wings of the National Gallery. Most museums on the Mall are open 10–5:30 daily (closed on Christmas Day), although hours can vary seasonally. Exceptions are noted below.

INSIDER TIP: *Although Smithsonian museums are free, Smithsonian members enjoy 10 percent savings on all gift shop purchases and in museum restaurants, along with significant discounts on Smithsonian lectures and popular day camps for children. Members also receive a subscription to the* Smithsonian Magazine. *Call 202-357-3030 or go online to www.smithsonian.org/membership for more information—or visit the membership desk inside the Smithsonian Castle.*

Arts and Industries Building (202-633-1000; www.si.edu.ai; 900 Jefferson Dr., S.W., Washington; nearest Metro: Smithsonian, Blue and Orange lines). Sadly, the Arts and Industries Building is closed indefinitely in anticipation of a major renovation. This whimsical red brick and sandstone building—just east of the Smithsonian Castle and resembling it in style and building materials—was completed in 1881 and served as the first U.S. National Museum. For years before it closed, it housed exhibits from the 1876 International Exposition, which showcased the latest in technology and industry.

Freer Gallery of Art and Arthur M. Sackler Gallery (202-633-1000; www.asia.si.edu; 1050 Independence Ave., S.W., Washington; nearest Metro: Smithsonian, Blue and Orange lines). The Freer Gallery and the Sackler Gallery collectively represent the finest collection of Asian art in the nation. Access both subterranean galleries from a lovely pavilion on the Mall just west of the Smithsonian Castle, and don't miss the two entertaining 14th-century Kongorikishi warriors at either end of the shared entrance corridor.

Arguably the more important of the two museums, the **Freer Gallery** is named after Charles Lang Freer, a Detroit industrialist who amassed an extensive collection of fine

Don't miss the relaxing courtyard at the Freer Gallery, where in warm months you'll find chairs from which to enjoy the peaceful setting. Photo by Debbie K. Hardin.

Asian art throughout his life. In 1906 Freer donated the collection to the Smithsonian, along with considerable funds to endow it, and the gallery opened its doors in 1923. The collection spans 6,000 years and myriad cultures. Among the many treasures, visitors will find an exquisite collection of tiny Egyptian glass vessels dating to 1550 B.C.; ancient Iranian manuscripts; gilded and enameled 14th-century glassware from Syria; Near Eastern metalware; and Chinese and Japanese sculpture. Besides Asian art, the Freer also has a collection of 19th- and 20th-century American art, including the largest collection of work by James McNeill Whistler in the world. (See the sidebar on "The Peacock Room," opposite). The small Gallery Shop has unusual gift items from Asia, including Chinese brush painting kits, Japanese puzzle books, and hand-painted silk scarves and fans. The **Sackler Gallery** was founded to extend the coverage of Asian art to include contemporary art and works in various media. The museum opened in 1987 and originally housed more than 1,000 works donated by benefactor Arthur Sackler, a physician and medical publisher whose collection included early Chinese jades, ancient Near Eastern ceramics, and sculpture from Southeast Asia. The Sackler's collection has since expanded to include Persian books from the 12th century, Khmer ceramics, contemporary Japanese porcelain, and modern paintings and sculptures from India, Korea, and China. An extensive gift and book shop offers quirky Asian bath products, pottery and ceramics, and handmade jewelry. Open 10–5:30, with extended hours in the summer.

Hirshhorn Museum and Sculpture Garden (202-633-1000; www.hirshhorn.si.edu;
Independence Ave. and Seventh St., N.W., Washington; nearest Metro: Smithsonian,
Blue and Orange lines). Dedicated to modern and contemporary art, this dramatic
museum opened in 1974 thanks to philanthropist Joseph Hirshhorn, who donated his
massive collection of artwork to the Smithsonian Institution. Today the permanent collection of more than 11,000 pieces includes paintings, sculpture, and mixed media representing the most important modern and contemporary artists from around the world,
including Alexander Calder, Alberto Giacometti, Willem de Kooning, Henri Matisse,
Henry Moore, Nam June Paik, and Andy Warhol. The striking building is a modern art
statement itself, designed by architect Gordon Bunshaft in the form of a hollow cylinder
82 feet high and 231 feet wide, with a large, round fountain slightly off-center inside.
Across the street is the restful **Sculpture Garden**—including Calder's *Six Dots over a
Mountain* and August Rodin's *Burghers of Calais*—a peaceful oasis with plentiful benches
to allow for quiet contemplation. The museum sponsors educational programs year-
round, including a "meet the artist" series, lectures by artists and art historians, children's programs, and art-making workshops. Its well-respected film series focuses on
independent cinema and highlights documentaries, experimental features, and shorts.
Don't miss the exceptional museum store, which offers jewelry designed by artists, chic
purses made from gum wrappers and pop tops, book bags fashioned from seat belts, and
Eames-inspired dollhouse furniture, among hundreds of other items. Open 10—5:30.

The Peacock Room

One of the highlights of the Freer Gallery is the Peacock Room, the one-time London dining room of
wealthy shipping magnate Frederick R. Leyland. The room, decorated with an intricate lattice of
shelving and covered with leather, was designed by architect Thomas Jeckyll and was created to provide display space for Leyland's extensive collection of Chinese porcelain. On its completion, Leyland consulted artist James McNeill Whistler—whose painting *The Princess* was meant to be hung in
the dining room—about the colors used in the room, lest they clash with his beloved artwork.
Whistler offered to make adjustments to the room's color scheme accordingly, and Leyland agreed to
let him. However, Whistler got carried away, and while Leyland was out of the country Whistler covered the ceiling with imitation gold leaf and then painted on peacock feathers; gilded Jeckyll's lat-
ticework shelving; and painted extravagant peacocks directly on the room's wooden shutters.
Whistler then called in the press to show off his new masterpiece—all without consulting Leyland.
When it came time to pay the bill, Leyland was furious with Whistler for his overreaching, and after
much wrangling agreed to only half of Whistler's requested fee. In retaliation, Whistler painted over
the pricey leather walls with a green-blue paint and added a huge mural depicting a pair of gold and
silver peacocks in angry confrontation; one of the peacocks was said to resemble Leyland. At the feet
of the birds Whistler painted silver coins, and to make sure his one-time client understood the alle-
gory, Whistler named the mural *Art or Money; or, The Story of the Room.* Surprisingly, afterward Leyland kept the room exactly as Whistler had designed it. More than a decade later, after Leyland's
death, Charles Freer acquired the room, and after living with it himself for many years, had it moved
to the Freer Gallery and reassembled. Now the room is filled with examples of Chinese blue and
white porcelain, much like the pieces Leyland built the room to exhibit.

The sunken Hirshhorn Sculpture Garden is open dawn to dusk, making it a good spot to relax if you arrive on the Mall before most museums open at 10 AM. Photo by Debbie K. Hardin.

National Air and Space Museum (202-633-1000; www.nasm.si.edu; Independence Ave. and Seventh St., S.W., Washington; nearest Metro: L'Enfant Plaza, Blue, Green, Orange, and Yellow lines). Since opening in 1976, the National Air and Space Museum has been among the most visited museums in the world—and the ubiquitous crowds show no signs of shrinking. The museum boasts the world's largest collection of historic air and spacecraft, with more than 50,000 artifacts that encompass the earliest attempts at flight through the current space age. The main floor of the museum houses some of the most important pieces in the collection, including the *Spirit of St. Louis,* the plane in which Charles Lindbergh made the first nonstop solo trans-Atlantic flight; the Apollo 11 command module *Columbia,* which brought home the astronauts from the first moon landing; and *SpaceShipOne,* the first privately piloted ship to enter outer space. Don't miss the touchable moon rock displayed just beyond the security checkpoint near the front door. Delve deeper into this cavernous museum and you'll encounter the original 1903 Wright Brothers *Flyer;* the kid-friendly "How Things Fly" exhibit, with more than 50 interactive learning toys to demonstrate the principles of flight; and a walk-through mock-up of the Skylab that illustrates the cramped quarters in which astronauts live. To orient yourself, remember that airplanes and aviation are on the west end of the building and rockets and spacecraft are on the east end. Near the entrance is an IMAX theater, which features a rotating collection of movies about flight and space specially created to be projected onto a dome-shaped screen. These 40- to 50-minute films give viewers the sensation of being a *part* of the action—and most of the films give the feeling of flight itself. Tickets are required for IMAX movies, as well as for the Albert Einstein Planetarium upstairs, which also shows films about space on a 70-foot dome and offers lectures on the night sky as well as multimedia presentations on astronomy. Note that significant discounts are available if you purchase tickets for more than one show. But if these aren't thrilling enough for you, check out the flight simulators scattered throughout the museum, which give guests the chance to experience simulated dogfights, blast-offs into outer space, and explorations of distant planets. A well-visited gift shop sells ever-popular freeze-dried ice cream (and even full astronaut meals), a plethora of kites, and a wide variety of model spacecraft. There's also an enormous McDonald's on site, which offers the standard fast-food grub in a surprisingly lovely atrium setting. Some of the cafeteria-style tables even offer premier views of the Capitol. Open 10–5:30.

Despite the seemingly overwhelming collection at the Mall location, because of space limitations only 10 percent of the museum's artifacts are actually on display. To remedy this, the **Steve F. Udvar-Hazy Center** (202-633-1000; www.nasm.si.edu/museum/udvarhazy; 14390 Air and Space Museum Pkwy., Chantilly, VA) opened in late 2003 to house the overflow. The Udvar-Hazy is spacious enough to allow for even larger scale exhibits of aircraft that include an Air France Concorde, one of the supersonic jets that

The National Air and Space Museum is massive in scale and allows curators to display hundreds of full-sized space- and aircraft. Photo by Debbie K. Hardin.

until recently made trans-Atlantic flights in half the time of conventional aircraft; the *Enola Gay,* the airplane from which the atomic bomb was dropped on Hiroshima; and the first American space shuttle *Enterprise.* A bus runs four times a day between the National Air and Space Museum on the Mall and the Chantilly site. Purchase round-trip tickets at the IMAX box office at the Mall location for $12 per person. (If you drive yourself, you'll pay $12 for parking.) Open 10–5:30.

INSIDER TIP: *IMAX movies at the Air and Space Museum are not to be missed, but they sell out quickly. Head to the box office as soon as you arrive to buy tickets, and then plan your museum visit around the ticket time. You can also purchase your tickets online 24 hours in advance.*

National Archives (866-272-6272; www.archives.gov; 700 Pennsylvania Ave., N.W., Washington; nearest Metro: Archives, Green and Yellow lines). This repository of documents is home to the most important papers in the history of the United States: Inside the Rotunda, guests can view the Constitution, the Bill of Rights, and the Declaration of Independence. Although the three documents are heavily guarded and kept within immense glass cases, it is still possible to get a good look at these historic papers—especially if the Rotunda isn't too busy and you can take your time. Other exhibits include the "Public Vaults" exhibit, which displays original Indian treaties, formerly classified audio recordings of presidents, and rare film footage from the earliest days of movies. Most of these exhibits are multimedia presentations and many are interactive. In addition to the artifacts on display, the Archives catalogs and stores the country's most extensive collection of census figures, federal documents, birth and death records, and military service records, which are available to any adult wishing to do genealogical research. The Archives shop, **The National Archives Experience,** is a great place to find books on genealogy and political science, prints of historic documents, luxurious stationery and old-fashioned fountain pens, and beautifully bound journals. Unfortunately, the crowds at the National Archives can be overwhelming, and without reservations, average waits to enter the building are an hour or two. To avoid a *long* line (most of which is outside and exposed to the elements), secure tickets by e-mailing visitorservices@nara.gov at least six weeks in advance to reserve space in a self-guided tour group, or call 202-357-5450 for a spot on a guided tour. Spring crowds are oppressive, especially in March and April when thousands of school groups descend on the city—and almost all of them make a stop at the National Archives. Avoid the museum during the spring and instead come in what Archives officials claim are the best months to visit: between June and February (not counting the days immediately surrounding the Fourth of July). Whenever you visit, it's best to leave purses and bags at home to make the thorough security check quicker; no backpacks are allowed. Open 10–5:30 Monday through Saturday, with extended hours in the spring and summer; closed Sundays and all federal holidays. The last admission is 30 minutes before closing.

National Gallery of Art (202-737-4215; www.nga.gov; Fourth St. and Constitution Ave., N.W., Washington; nearest Metro: Archives, Green and Yellow lines). The National Gallery of Art is one of the finest art museums in the world and comprises more than 100,000 paintings, sculptures, and mixed-media pieces dating from the Middle Ages to the present. The museum is divided into two distinct wings: the original West Wing and the newer East Wing. The museum was conceived (and first funded) by philanthropist and art collector Andrew Mellon in 1937, and the founding collection was housed in a

The Greek-revival façade of the National Archives building, which is both a museum and the nation's largest repository of documents. Photo by Debbie K. Hardin.

magnificent neoclassical structure designed by famed architect John Russell Pope (who designed many of the other imposing marble buildings on the National Mall, including the National Archives). The original building now designated as the West Wing features old-school display space, with traditional roomlike galleries; high ceilings; expansive corridors; highly polished wooden plank floors that cry in protest when sneakers walk on them; and restful atria filled with ferns, sculptures, and fountains. This portion of the museum specializes in European art from the 13th through the 19th centuries, as well as American art that dates from colonial days to the early 20th century. Wander among the innumerable galleries and discover treasures that include Raphael's luminous *Madonna and Child,* one of the most extensive collections of Vermeer's tiny paintings outside of Holland, the only Leonardo da Vinci painting permanently displayed in the U.S. (*Ginevra de'Benci,* 1474), and a lovely collection of Impressionistic and post-Impressionistic paintings by artists such as Monet, Van Gogh, Cezanne, Mary Cassatt, Pissaro, and Degas.

The newer East Wing is dedicated to modern and contemporary art, and is accessed via a separate entrance to the I. M. Pei-designed structure east of the original building

I. M. Pei's pyramids sit between the East Wing of the National Gallery (shown) and the West Wing.
Photo by Nathan Borchelt.

or through an underground passageway between the buildings, which passes beneath Pei's signature glass pyramids. These sculptural pyramids separate the East and West Wings above ground and act as skylights for the passageway beneath. Once inside the East Wing, it is immediately clear you've crossed over to the modern era; the expansive, angular space soars with high ceilings, glass and steel interior features, and an abundance of natural light. Dominating the entrance is an enormous Alexander Calder mobile hanging overhead, commissioned for the museum shortly before the artist's death. A nearby ground-level gallery houses a captivating collection of Calder's works; other artists on permanent display in the East Wing include Jasper Johns, Miró, Picasso, Pollack, and Rothko. The Tower Gallery upstairs offers a whimsical display of Matisse "cutouts." (Note that the Tower Gallery has limited hours: 10–2 Monday through Saturday, 11–3 Sunday.)

The **National Gallery of Art Sculpture Garden** is located across from the West Wing on Seventh Street, and encompasses two city blocks displaying 17 large-scale sculptures set amid a mature garden. Pieces include a lyrical, oversized typewriter eraser by Claes Oldenburg and Coosje van Bruggen; a leaning tower of blue chairs by Lucas Samaras;

THE NATIONAL MALL **109**

and a cartoonesque playhouse by Roy Lichtenstein that seems to defy perspective. A beautiful central fountain is transformed into an ice skating rink from mid-November through mid-March (see page 259).

The National Gallery has an engrossing, extensive bookstore housed on the concourse level between the two wings, as well as a nice cafeteria (**The Cascade Café**) where it's possible to secure a table directly beneath Pei's skylights. An even lovelier option for a light lunch or afternoon snack is the **Garden Café** on the ground floor of the West Wing, which serves fruit and cheese plates, sandwiches, and salads. The museum is the site of numerous free lectures, film series, and the very popular live jazz performances held on Friday nights (5–8) in the summer at the Sculpture Garden. Open 10–5 Monday through Saturday, 11–6 Sunday (with extended hours Memorial Day through Labor Day).

National Museum of African Art (202-633-1000; www.africa.si.edu; 950 Independence Ave., S.W., Washington; nearest Metro: Smithsonian, Blue and Orange lines). Accessed from the serene Enid A. Haupt Garden, just behind the Smithsonian Castle, the subterranean National Museum of African Art celebrates the rich cultural and artistic heritage of Africans and African Americans. The permanent collection includes beautiful examples of intricately carved wood, ivory, and stone; fine historic masks from nations throughout the African continent; and astonishing textiles and pottery. The extraordinarily well-designed display space is bright and cheerful, and artifacts are often displayed in freestanding glass cases, which makes it possible to wander among the art pieces in a way that traditional against-the-wall displays don't allow. This is not a heavily trafficked museum, and thus it is a nice place to escape the crowds during busy seasons. The museum sponsors regular family activities such as storytelling, musical performances, and hands-on art workshops.

National Museum of American History (202-633-1000; www.americanhistory.si.edu; 14th St. and Constitution Ave., N.W., Washington; nearest Metro: Smithsonian, Blue and Orange lines). The exhibitions of the National Museum of American History focus on the history and culture of the U.S., from the Revolutionary War to the present day. Visitors will find otherwise mundane items that hold special significance because of their historical, political, or cultural importance—objects like Thomas Edison's light bulb, Abraham Lincoln's top hat, Jacqueline Kennedy's inaugural gown, and Archie Bunker's chair from the TV show *All in the Family*. The 3 million-plus artifact collection is mind-boggling, and visitors of all ages and interests are sure to find something appealing. In fact, it's easy to spend a full day exploring the museum and still walk away feeling that there is much more to see. In addition to its massive collection, the museum also hosts an array of public lectures, demonstrations, and festivals, as well as performances by chamber music ensembles, jazz orchestras, and gospel choirs.

In late 2006, this beloved museum closed its doors for a major renovation that is set to be complete by the end of 2008. The refurbished museum will provide a new gallery for the Star-Spangled Banner, the enormous flag that inspired Francis Scott Key to write the national anthem; a soaring central atrium with a massive skylight; and various infrastructure upgrades. Until the museum reopens its doors, some of the most famous pieces have been relocated. The exhibit "Treasures of the American History Museum," housed on the second floor of the National Air and Space Museum, includes Dorothy's ruby slippers from *The Wizard of Oz* and an original script of the film; Thomas Jefferson's Bible; the original Kermit the Frog; an example of the first Barbie sold in the U.S., along with her extensive wardrobe; the "puffy shirt" from TV's *Seinfeld;* and the lunch counter

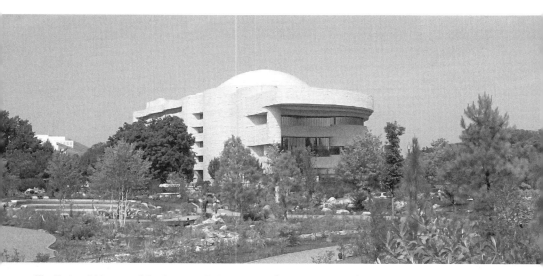

The National Museum of the American Indian, as seen from the grounds of the U.S. Botanic Garden.
Photo by Debbie K. Hardin.

from Greensboro, North Carolina, where four black students staged a six-month sit-in during the 1960s Civil Rights movement. In addition, portions of the collection have been touring the country.

National Museum of the American Indian (202-633-1000; www.nmai.si.edu; Fourth St. and Independence Ave., S.W., Washington; nearest Metro: Capitol South, Blue and Orange lines). The architecture of the National Museum of the American Indian, the newest museum on the National Mall (opened in 2004), stands apart from that of its older siblings. The rough Kasota limestone exterior the color of sand curves organically, seemingly wind-carved, and derives from ancient places like Chaco Canyon and Mesa Verde. The main entrance faces the rising sun (and the Capitol) in the east. The structure was designed by Douglas Cardinal, a Blackfoot who worked with a team of Native American architects and artists to make sure the building respected its natural surroundings, and the grounds are surrounded by extensive gardens (see page 98). The interior is also much different from traditional museum spaces; exhibit walls undulate and twist, imbuing the exhibits with movement and life while breaking up the cavernous space into intimate venues. The permanent collection offers more than 800,000 works of aesthetic, cultural, historical, and spiritual significance to Native Americans, including a dizzying array of gold coins, tomahawks and other weaponry; fine examples of basketry and beading; elaborate feather bonnets; wood and stone carvings; and spiritual artifacts. Start your visit with the 13-minute film, *Who We Are,* in the Lelawi Theater on the fourth floor, to gain insight into Native American life today. Also be sure to stop by the Welcome Desk on the way in to pick up a free *Family Activity Guide* for kids. The **Chesapeake Museum Store** sells hard-to-find Native-made objects from around the country, including turquoise jewelry, pottery, beaded headbands, dolls, and a nice collection of books. The museum also houses what is likely the most popular eatery on the Mall these days: the **Mitsitam Native Foods Café,** which serves indigenous foods like buffalo chili, fry bread, and sweet plantain empanadas in vanilla sauce. Open 10–5:30.

National Museum of Natural History (202-633-1000; www.mnh.si.edu; 10th St. and Constitution Ave., N.W., Washington; nearest Metro: Smithsonian, Blue and Orange lines). Opened in 1910, the lovely Beaux-Arts National Museum of Natural History houses extensive specimens of gems and minerals, fossils, and insects. The enormous exhibition hall encompasses more than 325,000 square feet of public space—it is large enough to fit 18 football fields inside!—and houses 126 million natural science specimens and artifacts. The museum's unofficial mascot, an African bush elephant that stands 13 feet 2 inches at the shoulder and weighs nearly 12 tons, greets visitors in the massive rotunda at the entrance, and from there exhibits radiate outward and upward. This museum is extremely popular with children, likely because of the extensive first-floor collection of dinosaur bones that include woolly mammoths and a 65-million-year old *Tyrannosaurus rex*, among the thousands of other ancient species represented. Another favorite is the Geology, Gems, and Minerals Hall on the second floor, which boasts the famous Hope Diamond, now displayed in a freestanding glass case, the interior of which rotates 90 degrees every few seconds. Unfortunately, this portion of the gems collection is often so crowded it is sometimes hard to get a good look at the impressive blue diamond. In the same gallery and also worth a peek are diamond earrings once owned by Marie Antoinette and a gem-encrusted crown that belonged to Napoleon. Also on the second floor, visitors will find the world's largest meteorite collection (20,000 examples), some of which

Expect long lines in the mornings at the National Museum of Natural History, the first stop for many tour buses. Photo by Debbie K. Hardin.

Where Are They Now? A Guide to the Nation's Most Famous Artifacts

Artifact	Description	Museum
Apollo 11 Command Module *Columbia*	The command module from the first lunar landing mission in 1969	National Air and Space Museum
The Burghers of Calais	August Rodin's sculptural ensemble, dating to 1884–1889	Hirshhorn Museum
Declaration of Independence, U.S. Constitution, Bill of Rights	The three most important documents in the nation	National Archives
Diplodocus	80-foot-long dinosaur skeleton—one of the largest animals to have roamed Earth	National Museum of Natural History
Dorothy's ruby slippers	The red-sequined shoes worn by Judy Garland in the 1939 Hollywood classic *The Wizard of Oz*	National Museum of American History
First ladies' gowns	A collection of inaugural gowns worn by first ladies through the years	National Museum of American History
Fonzie's jacket	The leather jacket worn by actor Henry Winkler in the popular TV sitcom *Happy Days*	National Museum of American History
George Catlin's Indian Gallery	More than 250 of George Catlin's 19th-century paintings of Native Americans	Renwick Gallery
Hope Diamond	45.52-carat blue diamond set in a necklace	National Museum of Natural History
Jenny airmail stamp	24-cent inverted airmail stamp from 1918; likely the most famous U.S. stamp	National Postal Museum
Julia Child's kitchen	The complete contents of cooking legend Julia Child's Cambridge, Massachusetts, kitchen, which was used as the set for Child's three TV shows	National Museum of American History
Leonardo da Vinci's *Ginevra de'Benci*	Oil painting	National Gallery
Lincoln's life mask	A cast of the president's face months before he was killed	Library of Congress
Mars Exploration Rover	A full-scale mock-up for *Spirit* and *Opportunity*, rovers that landed on Mars in 2004	National Air and Space Museum
Moon rock	Collected from the lunar surface by Apollo 17 astronauts	National Air and Space Museum
Nam June Paik's *Video Flag*	Video installation	Hirshhorn
Portrait of George Washington	Gilbert Stuart's "Lansdowne" portrait of George Washington	National Portrait Gallery
Raven Steals the Sun	A blown- and sand-carved glass sculpture by Preston Singletary	National Museum of the American Indian
Spirit of St. Louis	Charles Lindbergh's airplane, used to make the first nonstop solo trans-Atlantic flight in 1927	National Air and Space Museum
Tyrannosaurus rex	One of the oldest and largest fossils on display	National Museum of Natural History
Wright *Flyer*	The 1903 aircraft the Wright Brothers flew at Kitty Hawk, North Carolina; the first heavier-than-air craft to make a sustained flight	National Air and Space Museum

Floor and gallery	Notes
Gallery 100, ground level	
Sculpture Garden	
Rotunda exhibit	
Reptiles: Masters of the Land gallery, downstairs	
Icons of American Popular Culture, Music, and Sports	Housed within "Treasures of American History" exhibit upstairs in the National Air and Space Museum until the National Museum of American History is reopened in late 2008
First ladies' Political Role and Public Image	Available once the National Museum of American History reopens in late 2008
Icons of American Popular Culture, Music, and Sports	Housed within "Treasures of American History" exhibit upstairs in the National Air and Space Museum until the National Museum of American History is reopened in late 2008
Grand Salon	Other Native American studies by Catlin are on display at the National Portrait Gallery
Janet Annenberg Hooker Hall of Geology, Gems, and Minerals, Harry Winston Gallery, second floor	Housed in a glass exhibit case that rotates 90 degrees every few seconds
Philatelic Gallery	Part of a rotating exhibit, so not always on display
Julia Child Gallery	Available once the National Museum of American History reopens in late 2008
West Building	Look for a second da Vinci painting on the back, which is visible thanks to a see-through case patrons can walk behind
Varies	Not always on display
Gallery 207, upstairs	Look for a piece of Mars nearby that came via a meteorite found in Antarctica
Gallery 100, ground level	In a glass case just past the main security checkpoint; you can actually touch a piece of the moon!
Second floor	
Hall of Presidents	
Fourth level	
Gallery 100, ground level	Suspended from the ceiling near the entrance; look up!
Ground floor	
Gallery 100, ground level	

visitors can touch for themselves. The Discovery Room has hands-on exhibits that allow young visitors to explore the natural world using museum objects (open noon–2:30 Monday through Thursday, 10:30–3:30 Friday through Sunday; passes—distributed at the room's entrance—are required for busy days, and one adult must accompany each child). The Orkin Insect Zoo houses live spiders, centipedes, ants, and hundreds of other arthropods, and is another favorite with children (and an exceedingly noisy exhibit space). The museum has an IMAX theater downstairs that boasts a six-story screen designed to show both two- and three-dimensional movies (pick up tickets early in the day). Don't miss the **Smithsonian Jazz Café** (6–10 Friday), which offers live jazz, food, drinks, and IMAX movies for a $10 cover charge. Open 10–5:30, until 7:30 in the summer.

INSIDER TIP: *Be sure to keep a couple of quarters with you at all times. Many museums and government buildings do not allow bags inside. Security guards will direct guests to store their gear in coin-operated storage lockers that accept only quarters. Coins also come in handy if you're driving, as most parking in the vicinity of the National Mall is metered.*

The iconic Smithsonian "Castle" was designed by James Renwick Jr. and completed in 1855.
Photo by Debbie K. Hardin.

Smithsonian Institution Building (a.k.a. The Castle) (202-633-1000; 1000 Jefferson Dr., S.W., Washington; nearest Metro: Smithsonian, Blue and Orange lines). The Smithsonian Institution was named after James Smithson, a wealthy English scientist who never set foot in the U.S. when he was alive. He died during the 19th century and bequeathed a large portion of his considerable estate to the U.S. for the purposes of establishing a museum. He also donated a vast collection of minerals and a significant scientific library.

When people outside of D.C. think of the beloved Smithsonian, they often think of the fanciful red-brick structure adorned with romantic spires, leaded glass windows, and soaring towers that was designed by James Renwick Jr. and completed in 1855. The extravagant building, nicknamed "The Castle," is actually only the figurehead of the museum collection, which now comprises 19 museums (some outside of Washington). The Castle currently houses Smithson's crypt, as well as the Smithsonian membership desk—a good place to pick up maps and brochures; guests can also catch an informative orientation video here. In the east wing of the building you'll find an exhibit hall offering a preview of the Smithsonian museums in D.C., with a handful of items on display from each one. A video monitor shows live coverage of the pandas at the National Zoo. The **Castle Café and Coffee Bar** sells sandwiches, salads, soups, and pastries. The Castle opens at 8:30, well before the rest of the buildings on the National Mall (which open at 10), thus it's a good place to come if you arrive early. Open 8:30–5:30.

INSIDER TIP: *If the security lines are long at the front Castle entrance, walk around back and try the entrance from the Enid A. Haupt Garden. It's generally much shorter.*

United States Holocaust Memorial Museum (202-488-0400; www.ushmm.org; 100 Raoul Wallenberg Pl., S.W., Washington; nearest Metro: Smithsonian, Blue and Orange lines). This is arguably the most important museum in Washington, D.C., and undeniably the most difficult to visit. The United States Holocaust Memorial Museum was founded to document, interpret, and study Holocaust history, and serves as a testament to the millions of people who were killed during the most far-reaching genocide of the modern era. The exhibits encourage visitors to reflect on this unfathomable atrocity as well as on the tragic legacy of both Holocaust victims and survivors. Begin your visit to the solemn permanent exhibit by picking up an identification pass that tells the story of a real person during the Holocaust; most of the individuals profiled in these small pamphlets perished by the end of World War II. Take the elevator to the top floor to begin a chronological review of the events that led to the Holocaust. In addition to scores of photographs depicting victims, TV screens scattered throughout show news reels of the day, and there are moving collections of everyday items that were lost to those who were shipped to the concentration camps—photographs, personal letters and mementos, including a particularly disturbing pit full of tens of thousands of shoes that were left behind. Visitors will walk through a Karlsruh freight car that was actually used to transport thousands of victims to the concentration camps; pass by bunks taken from Auschwitz II-Birkenau; and view a horrifying diorama of a gas chamber. There are also private video stations where visitors may watch films on Nazi book burnings and the 1936 Berlin Olympics, as well as larger theaters that show films of Holocaust survivors recounting their memories.

Another gallery, "Remember the Children: Daniel's Story," is intended for children. The display begins with a film about "Daniel," a typical Jewish boy who enjoyed a comfortable, middle-class existence in Germany before the Nazis came to power. Visitors can peek into a kitchen of the era, hear the sounds of a happy family going about their daily lives, and even walk through Daniel's bedroom, which is filled with toys and books. The exhibit then shifts to life in the Jewish ghettos, where hundreds of thousands of Jews in Germany and elsewhere were relocated. Guests will see the NO JEWS ALLOWED signs and walk through a squalid ghetto apartment. The exhibit ends with a room full of desks and pens, so that children can write down their thoughts and feelings on postcards and mail them to "Daniel." If visiting with kids, please be forewarned: There are numerous graphic images and audio descriptions displayed throughout the museum that are quite disturbing. Although this exhibit provides a powerful introduction to the Holocaust in a way that enables children to reflect on the horror without being overwhelmed by it, we don't recommend this museum for children younger than 12.

Downstairs is the "Hall of Remembrance" where an eternal flame burns in memory of the more than 6 million people who were murdered during the Holocaust. Guests may

Voyage Model of the Solar System

Washington, D.C., can be an overwhelming place to visitors, who often underestimate its size and end up wandering the National Mall in a state of exhaustion. To put the seemingly large city into universal perspective, check out the Voyage Model of the Solar System, running along the southern sidewalk of Jefferson Drive. This model is presented on a 1-to-10 billion scale, demonstrating the vast distances between planets and their relative sizes: The sun is shown roughly the size of a large grapefruit, and Earth is depicted as a small circle the size of a pin head, orbited by a tiny moon with a circumference about equal to that of a strand of human hair. The exhibit is made up of 8-foot columns, each with an informational plaque that provides scientific data, and three-dimensional scaled representations of the bodies set at eye level. Start by checking out the sun at the east end of Jefferson Drive near Fourth Street, just in front of the National Air and Space Museum, and follow the pathway a third of a mile to Pluto, in front of the Smithsonian Castle. Although the International Astronomical Union demoted Pluto to dwarf planet status in 2006, there are no current plans to rearrange the Voyage Model. But you might see flowers and condolence cards at the base of the Pluto model, a tongue-in-cheek homage from visitors to what used to be considered the ninth planet in our solar system.

The inner planets are depicted in close proximity in the Voyage Model of the Solar System: the models of the outer planets stretch a third of a mile from the model of the sun. Photo by Debbie K. Hardin.

The Holocaust Museum sits a few blocks to the south of the National Mall, and is best accessed via the Smithsonian Metro station's Independence Avenue exit. Photo by Debbie K. Hardin.

also light candles. In addition, the "Wall of Remembrance" is a tribute to the 1.5 million children killed during the Holocaust. American schoolchildren designed and painted the more than 3,000 ceramic tiles that make up the memorial. Also downstairs is the Wexner Learning Center, where visitors can research various aspects of the Holocaust through literature, photographs, and films; there is an extensive library and photo archive (on the fifth floor), too, for those wishing to do in-depth research. The Meed Registry of Holocaust Survivors on the second floor encourages individuals who survived the Nazi terror to register and preserve their history.

Timed passes are required to visit the permanent exhibit. Reserve up to 10 tickets online at www.tickets.com or call 1-800-400-9373. Same-day tickets are also available at 10 AM at the information desk inside the museum, but availability is limited, and lines begin as much as two hours in advance during busy seasons. Open 10–5:30.

NATIONAL MONUMENTS AND MEMORIALS

The National Mall is famous for its memorials, but critics from the earliest days of the Republic have worried that this precious real estate will someday become choked with too many statues, walls, and edifices. As anyone who's walked this expanse of acreage can attest, however, the Mall is an awfully big place, and it'll be a long time before it is overcrowded. This is good news for folks who welcome greater diversity among those memori-

A bronze, larger-than-life statue of Franklin Roosevelt with his beloved dog, Fala, is rubbed shiny in spots by visitors to the FDR Memorial. Photo by Debbie K. Hardin.

alized here. As this book went to press, fund raising and planning were well under way for a Martin Luther King Jr. Memorial, which will be built on the Tidal Basin, aligned perfectly with the Lincoln and FDR Memorials.

Albert Einstein Memorial (Constitution Ave. and 22nd St., N.W.; nearest Metro: Smithsonian, Blue and Orange lines). Across the street from the National Mall, the Albert Einstein Memorial sits on the southwest corner of the grounds of the National Academy of Sciences. The 12-foot bronze statue of the great physicist—rendered by Robert Berks based on a bust of Einstein he sculpted from life in the 1950s—is dressed in sandals and holds a piece of paper inscribed with his most famous formulas. At the base of the statue, more than 2,700 metal studs are embedded in a field of granite—each representing the planets, stars, and other celestial bodies—arranged by astronomers from the U.S. Naval Observatory as they appeared from Earth on the day the statue of Einstein was dedicated. The scale of the statue is just right for kids, who like to climb in Einstein's lap.

Franklin Delano Roosevelt Memorial (202-426-6841; www.nps.gov/fdrm; West Basin Dr.; nearest Metro: Smithsonian, Blue and Orange lines). Just off the Tidal Basin, the Franklin Delano Roosevelt Memorial is an outdoor garden that stretches across 7.5

acres, with cherry blossom trees, extensive water features (including a roaring waterfall made from granite blocks), and statuary displayed in four "rooms." Each room represents one of FDR's terms in office and is demarcated by granite walls, many of which are engraved with quotations from the eloquent president. In addition to a large statue of a seated FDR, guests will also encounter a sculpture grouping depicting a bread line from the Great Depression; a man hunkered close to an old-fashioned radio, presumably listening to a "fireside chat"; and a statue of the president's wife, Eleanor Roosevelt (the first such memorial to a first lady). Shortly after the memorial was complete, outcry by citizen groups who were unhappy that Roosevelt's disability (incurred as a result of polio) was not represented anywhere in the memorial prompted President Bill Clinton and the Congress to secure funding to add an additional sculpture that shows the former president in a wheelchair. Visitors can find this small addition at the front of the memorial.

Jefferson Memorial (202-426-6841; www.nps.gov/thje; East Basin Dr., S.W.; nearest Metro: Smithsonian, Blue and Orange lines). Located directly on the cherry-tree studded Tidal Basin, the Jefferson Memorial is a colonnaded white-marble rotunda that was built to honor the nation's third president, Thomas Jefferson. The memorial was modeled after the Pantheon in Rome, and the neoclassical structure also mimics the architecture of Monticello (Jefferson's home in Charlottesville, Virginia) as well as the University of Virginia—both of which Jefferson designed himself. Original architect John Russell Pope began the exterior of the memorial, but died before he was able to complete it; Daniel P. Higgins and Otto R. Eggers took over in 1937. Franklin Roosevelt laid the cornerstone in 1939 and ordered that all the trees between the memorial and the White House be cut down so that the view between the two was unobstructed—FDR was a great admirer of Jefferson, and he wanted to be able to look out his window and see

Because of its proximity to the Tidal Basin and its cherry trees, the Jefferson Memorial draws overwhelming crowds in late March and early April. Photo by Debbie K. Hardin.

the memorial every day. In 1941, artist Rudolph Evans was commissioned to create the 19-foot bronze statue of Jefferson that now resides inside the rotunda; the statue gazes directly toward the White House. Five quotations taken from Jefferson's writings are engraved on the walls of the memorial. Rangers present 30-minute programs throughout the day, but, if possible, visit at night when the exterior is flooded with light and the interior glows.

INSIDER TIP: *Although parking is always tight anywhere near the National Mall, one of the lesser known lots lies behind the Jefferson Memorial on Ohio Drive. If you come early or late in the day, you're more likely to find a spot here than anywhere else within easy walking distance of a memorial.*

Korean War Veterans Memorial (202-426-6841; www.nps.gov/kwvm; Independence Ave., southeast of the Reflecting Pool on the Mall; nearest Metro: Smithsonian, Blue and Orange lines). One of the most accessible memorials on the Mall, the Korean War Veterans Memorial commemorates the sacrifice and service of more than 1.5 million Americans who participated in the three-year Korean War. The memorial includes the serene "Pool of Remembrance" surrounded by a thick grove of trees and the "Field of Service," which depicts eerily lifelike statues patrolling with heavy packs and foul-weather gear. Nearby is a 164-foot granite wall with etched depictions of individuals who served in the war. There is also a listing of the 22 nations that contributed to the United Nation's campaign in Korea.

Lincoln Memorial (202-426-6841; www.nps.gov/linc; westernmost end of the Mall, between Constitution and Independence Aves.; nearest Metro: Smithsonian, Blue and Orange lines). One of the most beloved monuments in D.C. is the Lincoln Memorial, which honors America's 16th president. Architect Henry Bacon designed the memorial to the "Great Emancipator" to resemble a Greek temple, with 36 columns to reflect the 36 states of the Union at the time of Lincoln's death. Dominating the interior space is a commanding 19-foot white marble statue of a seated Lincoln designed by Daniel Chester French. The memorial, which was completed in 1922, also features murals by artist Jules Guerin, and the interior walls are engraved with moving passages from the Gettysburg Address and Lincoln's second Inaugural Address. To the east of the monument is the 2,000-foot-long Reflecting Pool that points to the new World War II Memorial and the Washington Monument (and Capitol) beyond. In August 1963, the Lincoln Memorial was the site of Martin Luther King Jr.'s "I Have a Dream" speech; an inscription on the 18th step down from the top of the memorial was added later to mark the exact spot where King delivered this historic address. Crowds are intense day and night at the Lincoln Memorial; if you have a hard time getting an unobstructed photo of the memorial, never fear: You probably have the image in your pocket (on the back of the penny).

Vietnam Veterans Memorial (202-426-6841; www.nps.gov/vive; northeast of Lincoln Memorial; nearest Metro: Blue and Orange lines). The Vietnam Veterans Memorial is a moving, simple statement of loss that honors the men and women who sacrificed and served during the Vietnam War. The centerpiece of the memorial (known as "the Wall") was completed in 1982, after college student Maya Lin's elegant design won a national contest. Because of the controversial nature of the war, Lin envisioned a memorial that makes no political statement. The stark, reflective black granite of the Wall is inscribed

Many urban myths are attached to the Lincoln Memorial, including one that insists this statue of Lincoln is sending a message using American Sign Language. (It is not.) Photo by Debbie K. Hardin.

with nearly 60,000 names of fallen soldiers, as well as those still considered missing in action, listed in chronological order of loss (starting on the west end of the Wall). The National Park Service occasionally adds names as individuals continue to die from injuries sustained during the war. Information books located at the western end of the Wall chronicle every name inscribed, along with the number of the panel on which it can be found; thin slips of paper and pencils are provided so that visitors can make rubbings of names. In 1984, a life-sized statue of three soldiers who seem to be staring at the Wall was created by Frederick Hart and installed nearby. And in 1993, the Vietnam Women's Memorial, designed by Glenna Goodacre, was erected on the grounds. This memorial shows three uniformed women nurses caring for a wounded soldier. Guests should exercise decorum when visiting the grounds of this memorial; it is an overwhelmingly emotional place for many who come to pay tribute to their loved ones, most of whom died much too young.

Washington Monument (202-426-6841; www.nps.gov/wamo; on the National Mall, midway between the Capitol and the Lincoln Memorial; nearest Metro: Smithsonian, Blue and Orange lines). Arguably the most recognizable architectural feature in Washington, D.C., the Washington Monument is an elegant, commanding memorial to the nation's

Guests to the Vietnam Veterans Memorial often leave flowers, flags, notes, and other small gifts at the base of the Wall; the National Park Service collects these each evening and stores them off-site. Photo by Debbie K. Hardin.

first president, George Washington. Despite its seeming simplicity—it is rendered in the style of a classic Egyptian obelisk—the monument is on a grand scale, topping out at a little more than 555 feet tall and weighing in at more than 80,000 tons. The structure is made with 36,491 blocks of white marble and is surrounded by 50 flags at the base, each symbolizing a state of the union. The monument was designed by architect Robert Mills, who originally conceived of a much more elaborate memorial: The current obelisk was to be surrounded by statues of Revolutionary War heroes along with a large statue of a toga-clad Washington driving a chariot. Money—and enthusiasm for the grand theme—ran short, however, and eventually the plans were scaled back. In 1848, the cornerstone of the obelisk was laid on the Fourth of July. But building progressed slowly because of financial constraints, and by 1854, funds dried up completely. The country entered into the bitter Civil War soon after, and the monument thus stood unfinished for more than 20 years. When the war was finally over and construction began again, the stones dug from the same quarries were a slightly different shade of white. If you look about a third of the way up the monument, you'll see the demarcation between the old building and the new.

Today the tiny observation floor at the top of the Washington Monument, accessed via an elevator that can reach the top in 70 seconds, offers one of the best views in the city. Although the tour of the monument is free, all visitors must have tickets (even small children). The ticket kiosk at the base of the monument on 15th Street opens at 8:30 AM (although lines often form as much as an hour and a half earlier). Free tickets are available on a first-come, first-served basis. One person may pick up a maximum of six tickets. Guests may reserve a ticket in advance either by visiting the National Park Service Web site at www.reservation.nps.gov or by calling 1-877-444-6777. There is a $1.50 fee per order to reserve tickets ahead of time. Pick up these tickets at the will-call window of the monument ticket kiosk the day of your tour. Open 9–5; closed July 4 and December 25.

World War II Memorial (202-426-6841; www.nps.gov/nwwm; east of the Lincoln Memorial; nearest Metro: Smithsonian, Blue and Orange lines). The World War II Memorial is an oval, 7?-acre park built in 2004 to honor the 16 million individuals who served during World War II, including the more than 400,000 people who gave their lives doing so. The memorial sits at the eastern base of the Lincoln Reflecting Pool, and critics complain that it breaks up the expansive view that used to run from the Lincoln Memorial to the Washington Monument. The neoclassical park features 56 granite pillars arranged in a semicircle; each 17-foot pillar is adorned with two bronze wreaths and is marked with the name of a state or U.S. territory. On either side of the pillars are massive archway pavilions symbolizing the wars in the Atlantic and the Pacific, and in the center of the central plaza is a large pool with explosive fountains. The "Freedom Wall" to the west contains more than 4,000 stars—one for every 100 soldiers who died during the war. Visitors will find a registry kiosk to look up the names of veterans. (Note that this is also available at www.wwiimemorial.com.)

WHERE THE NATION'S BUSINESS IS CONDUCTED

Library of Congress (202-707-8000; www.loc.gov; 10 First St., S.E., Washington; nearest Metro: Capitol South, Blue and Orange lines). Founded in 1800, the Library of Congress was conceived as a repository of books and papers for use by members of Congress. The Library was housed within the Capitol itself until 1814, when the collection of 3,000 vol-

The Washington Monument as seen from the base of the Reflecting Pool. Photo courtesy of Juliane Preimesberger. Used with permission.

umes was destroyed when British soldiers tried to burn down the city. A few months after the fire, Thomas Jefferson offered his extensive personal library for sale to replenish the collection. The U.S. government bought 6,487 volumes from Jefferson for $23,950. Sadly, another fire destroyed nearly two-thirds of these books in the mid-19th century. It didn't take long, however, for the Library to build back its collection—and then some.

Today the Library of Congress is the largest library in the world, with more than 130 million items in its permanent collection, including such priceless treasures as one of three surviving Gutenberg Bibles and what is said to be the smallest book in the world— *Old King Cole,* which measures $\frac{1}{25}$ of an inch square (you'll need a needle to turn its pages). There are more than 530 miles of bookshelves in the Library; in addition the Library collects maps, recordings, photographs, letters, and manuscripts, including presidential papers dating back to George Washington; the earliest daguerreotype of the U.S. Capitol; and the first surviving film registered for copyright (*Fred Ott's Sneeze,* 1894). Each day the Library adds another 10,000 or so new items to its collection; these vast resources remain available to members of Congress as well as to the American public.

The Library occupies three buildings on Capitol Hill: The magnificent Thomas Jefferson Building, which dates to 1897; the John Adams Building (1939); and the James Madison Memorial Building (1981). The Jefferson Building—where most visitors will want to spend their time—is an extraordinary example of Italian-Renaissance-style architecture; inside, guests will find miles of intricate marble floor mosaics, allegorical paintings on ceilings worthy of a Roman cathedral, more than 100 murals, a soaring staircase that seems too fine to be housed in a public building, and ornate plasterwork and embellishments reminiscent of a European castle. Visitors will also find numerous exhibits open to the public, including "American Treasures of the Library of Congress," which offers a rotating display of some of the rarest items in the Library's collection, including the Bible on which Abraham Lincoln took the oath of office, Thomas Jefferson's rough draft of the Declaration of Independence, and the Huexotzinco Codex, an eight-sheet document recording the testimony in a 1531 legal case against the colonial government in Mexico.

Beneath the massive dome in the Jefferson Building is the stunning Reading Room, which is accessible to visitors on 45-minute docent-led tours, offered regularly throughout the day. (Pick up a ticket at the information desk at the front entrance for same-day tours.) In addition, adults wishing to do research in the Reading Room may do so after first securing a reader identification card; cards are free and can be obtained in Room LM 140 on the first floor of the Madison Building, near the Independence Avenue entrance. Present a valid driver's license, passport, or a state-issued ID and complete a computerized self-registration process in person; the Library will verify the information, take an ID photo, and issue a photo card on the spot. Note that no one under 18 is admitted inside the Reading Room.

The World War II Memorial is punctuated by several bombastic fountains. Photo courtesy of Jon Preimesberger. Used with permission.

Inside the Jefferson Building, the most picturesque of the three structures that make up the Library of Congress. Photo by Debbie K. Hardin.

The Library's Coolidge Auditorium is the site of numerous arts performances throughout the year, including live music and dance. Tickets to these performances are free, but seats must be secured in advance through Ticketmaster (1-800-551-SEAT). The tiny Mary Pickford Theater, housed in the Madison Building, has frequent free screenings of early films and TV programs as well. Open 10–5; closed Sunday and all federal holidays.

INSIDER TIP: *For more in-depth tours of the Library of Congress, ask your House representative in advance for tickets to special congressional tours, which are held twice a day on weekdays.*

Supreme Court Building (202-479-3211; www.supremecourtus.gov; 1 First St., N.E., Washington; nearest Metro: Capitol South, Blue and Orange lines). Home of the highest judicial authority in the U.S., construction of this exceptionally beautiful, classic building, which resembles a Greek temple, began in 1932. Designed by Cass Gilbert, the building boasts an outcropping of splendidly ornate and perfectly symmetrical Corinthian columns over which is inscribed "Equal justice under law." There are also fine sculptural works in bas relief on the pediments and massive bronze doors. Court is in session here October through late June or early July; during this period, the court usually sits for two weeks each month and hears arguments from 10–noon and 1–3 on weekdays. Members of the public can view cases Monday through Wednesday, but be prepared to wait for hours; seats are limited (about 100 spots) and provided on a first-come, first-served basis. Call for specifics in advance, or check the argument calendar at www.supremecourtus.gov. When court is not in session, visitors can tour the building and catch a live lecture on the inner workings of the Court. These lectures, generally available on the hour, are subject to change and cancellation. Call ahead for specifics. Open 9–4:30 weekdays.

United States Capitol (202-225-6827; www.aoc.gov; First St., between Constitution and Independence Aves.; nearest Metro: Capitol South, Blue and Orange lines). The regal U.S. Capitol building has housed Congress since 1800; the west-facing steps are the site of modern presidential inaugurations, and inside is the location of the annual State of the Union address. President Abraham Lincoln's funeral was held within the halls of the ceremonial Rotunda (the room that lies beneath the enormous dome), and most presidents who have died in the modern era have lain in state here as well. The original design for the Capitol was by William Thornton, who won a countrywide architectural competition. Construction on this neoclassical beauty began in 1793, and George Washington laid the cornerstone. The Capitol was built on top of a hill so that it would tower over the rest of the city—and in fact, in 1901 Congress passed a law that ensured the Capitol dome would remain the tallest building in the city: It is 287 feet, 5.5 inches tall, and by law no building in D.C. may exceed this height. The emblematic statue of the *Goddess of Freedom*, rendered by artist Thomas Crawford, was added to the top of the dome in 1863.

Since 9/11, there have been numerous security updates to the building, and a new Visitor Center was built underground recently. The tragedy of 9/11 has also drastically changed the accessibility of this building (and every other federal building in the country), and guests are no longer allowed to visit without a prearranged tour. If you want to get a peek inside, secure tickets the same day in person at the Visitor Center. Tours begin at 9 AM and lines queue up as early as 7 to secure timed tickets. Be sure to arrive no

The Capitol has no back door; the building was designed with an East Front and a West Front (shown here), which faces the National Mall. Photo by Debbie K. Hardin.

later than 10, because the number of tickets are limited and are generally gone by late morning. Note that each member of your party must be present to obtain a timed ticket. Line up 10 minutes before the appointed time, and expect the total tour (including the security check) to take a little more than an hour. Visitors may not bring food or liquids into the Capitol, and no bags larger than 14 inches by 13 inches by 4 inches are allowed. In addition, other prohibited items include aerosol and nonaerosol bottles and cans; any sort of sharp object, including knitting needles; and, of course, all weapons (even toys) and ammunition. When Congress is in session, you may obtain tickets to visit the galleries that overlook the government in action. Secure these passes in advance from your House representative; most will be able to accommodate your request the day of your visit, but it's a good idea to call ahead to verify availability. Non-U.S. citizens may obtain gallery tickets at the security office once inside the building. Those requiring accessible tours should call 202-224-4048 in advance to arrange special accommodations.

These public tours can be brutally crowded during high tourist seasons, and given the waits involved to secure the tickets and pass through security, visitors are well advised to wear comfortable shoes and pack extra patience. Forty individuals are taken every five minutes per tour, beginning in the Rotunda. Your group will share the floor with at least a dozen others, and the sounds inside this big old stone structure are cacophonous. Add to this the frustrating requirement that you stay in one spot with your designated tour guide, which means you'll see most of the room from a distance. If you can stomach the crowds and noise, however, the place is magnificent. The Rotunda is tall enough to accommodate an upright Statue of Liberty (if she were standing in her bare feet). Four enormous paintings by John Trumbull hang inside, each of which depicts scenes from the early days of the republic. Most impressive, however, is the enormous painting on the inside of the dome, 180 feet above the Rotunda floor. Painted by Constantino Brumidi and titled *The Apotheosis of Washington*, the classical scene shows George Washington surrounded by symbols of Democratic progress. Brumidi also painted many of the corridors and other rooms throughout the Capitol, as well as a good portion of the frieze depicting scenes from American history that encircles the Rotunda.

Next on the tour is the Old Hall of the House of Representatives, which is now National Statuary Hall, so-named because of the dozens of state-owned statues that have been placed here. Visitors will wonder at the variety of people memorialized here, from Confederate General Robert E. Lee to King Kamehameha I of Hawaii; states may place (at their own expense) whatever statues they wish in the Hall, as long as the subject is deceased and the statue is made from marble or bronze. The ornate moldings throughout the Hall, its off-center dome, and plethora of statuary are interesting, but the real draw in this massive space is its irregular acoustics. Because of the architecture of the dome, it is possible to hear a whisper from across the room.

Tours terminate in the relatively uninteresting crypt, where you can continue on to a gift shop, find rest rooms, or exit. If you would like to get a little closer to the folks who decide how your tax dollars get spent, be sure to visit your representative or senator. To find your House representative, head to the Cannon, Longworth, and Rayburn Buildings on the south side of the Capitol. Offices of senators are on located in the Dirksen, Hart, and Russell Buildings on the north side of the Capitol, on Constitution Avenue.

INSIDER TIP: *You can tell when Congress is in session by looking for the flags that fly over the House and Senate on those days. At night, look for the light that shines from the Goddess of Freedom, the statue that sits on top of the Capitol dome.*

White House (202-456-1414; www.nps.gov/whho; 1600 Pennsylvania Ave., N.W., Washington; nearest Metro: Farragut West, Blue and Orange lines). City architect Pierre L'Enfant's original plan for the District called for the White House to be nearly 10 times its current size to keep it in proportion to the much larger Capitol building. But later planners scaled back the size of the president's house considerably, and today many visitors are surprised by how small the White House really is—especially considering the West Wing houses many employees of the Executive Office of the President and the East Wing houses largely ceremonial rooms. Although the building has been renovated many times over the years, the original concept came from James Hoban, who won a government-sponsored competition with his Georgian design. Thomas Jefferson also entered the design competition (under the pseudonym "A. Z.") and lost. John and Abigail Adams moved in in 1800; George Washington was the only president who never lived here.

As a result of increased security post-9/11, White House tours can only be arranged through your congressional representative, and only for groups of 10 or more. Note that these must be requested six months ahead of time. You will be notified of your specified day and time a month in advance; note, however, that the White House can and does cancel these tours at a moment's notice. Call the visitor's information desk, 202-456-7041, the day before your scheduled tour to confirm it. Also note that the White House has a long list of prohibited items: Visitors may not bring purses or bags of any type; cameras, video recorders, or audio recorders (this includes cell phones that can take

Even at night, sharpshooters patrol the grounds of the White House; security is even more intense when the president is in residence. Photo by Debbie K. Hardin.

and transmit photos); strollers; tobacco; and personal grooming products like lotions, lipsticks, brushes, and combs. Not surprisingly, sharp objects that can be used as weapons and any actual weapons or explosive devices are also not allowed. Guests *can* bring cell phones that do not take photographs, umbrellas, and car keys. In addition to the obvious security concerns the White House must address, at least one administration has taken steps to prevent fashion crimes as well: In the summer of 2007, the George W. Bush administration instituted a dress code for anyone visiting the White House. Guests may not wear shorts, jeans, miniskirts, T-shirts, tennis shoes, and—as noted in boldface print on signs posted prominently throughout the complex—absolutely no flip-flops.

Tours are scheduled 7:30–12:30 Tuesday through Saturday (excluding federal holidays), although this is subject to change at any time. There are 132 rooms on six floors in the White House, but if you are lucky enough to get a White House tour you will see only a limited section that includes ceremonial public rooms like the Red Room, the Blue Room, the Green Room, the East Room, the State Dining Room, and the China Room. Tours do not get anywhere near the Oval Office, nor will visitors be allowed to see the presidential residence.

If you cannot arrange a White House tour, don't despair: Visit the **White House Visitor Center** (at the southeast corner of 15th and E Sts., N.W.) to see an exhibit on the architecture of the White House, as well as displays on artifacts and furnishings. There is also a 30-minute video about the history of the structure and its famous occupants through the years. Open 7:30–4, weekdays.

Next door to the White House, on 17th Avenue, N.W., is the **Eisenhower Executive Office Building**, or EEOB (formerly the Old Executive Office Building, or OEOB). This building's extravagant French Empire-style architecture boasts more than 900 columns, two dozen chimneys, and houses the White House staff overflow. Nicknamed the "Wedding Cake," many architectural critics have derided its over-the-top exterior; wit Mark Twain called the EEOB the "ugliest building in America," and in the early 20th century there were plans to cover the building with a Greek-Revival façade. Thankfully for those of us who are fans of this fanciful structure, funding ran short and the remake never happened.

INSIDER TIP: *If you are able arrange a tour of the White House, call the day of your visit for current dress codes, or you risk being turned away from the presidential mansion.*

Columns from the U.S. Capitol were removed after a remodel and placed amid the trees at the United States National Arboretum. Photo by Debbie K. Hardin.

BEYOND THE MALL

Cultural Rewards of the Republic

As discussed in the previous chapter, many visitors to D.C. never get past the National Mall. Although the monuments and museums clustered in this small area of the city are iconic and certainly should not be missed, tourists who never venture beyond do themselves a great disservice. Washington, D.C., is a multicultural feast for the senses, from the eclectic, multiethnic neighborhood of Adams Morgan to the upscale shopping and dining of Georgetown to the energy and intensity of the historic, revitalized Penn Quarter. And beyond the city limits, across the Potomac River and into Virginia in the thriving and fast-growing city of Arlington, as well as the charming and historic Alexandria, more history, fine dining, and cultural opportunities await those willing to leave the National Mall long enough to find them.

GARDENS

Among the many joys of the D.C. area are the glorious gardens, and their expansiveness and ubiquity often surprise visitors. In addition to the formal, federal gardens (see pages 95–101), there are pocket parks throughout the city (and into Arlington and Alexandria, as well) that offer the garden lover a chance to appreciate the myriad flora found in the region; these include the well-known cherry blossoms in the spring, as well as delicately blooming dogwood trees, exuberant azaleas and rhododendrons, and carefully planned beds brimming with brilliantly colored tulips. In summer you'll find crepe myrtles in nearly every shade, as well as banks of brown-eyed Susans, roses—wild and cultivated—and miles of vibrant daylilies. Throughout the region you'll find lovingly tended home gardens in most neighborhoods, and even the tiniest patches of earth in front of town homes generally overflow with blossoms. In early spring you'll find tens of thousands of daffodils blooming along the sides of the highways, and in the summer wild poppies decorate the commute route.

Even though D.C. is nicknamed "the city of trees," many first-time visitors are surprised to see the number and maturity of trees scattered both along wide boulevards and clustered down residential streets; in summer (especially after adequate rainfall), the wild areas alongside roads are akin to jungles, with emerald green foliage on trees, tangled vines that wind themselves around any vertical structure, and waist-deep undergrowth.

We've outlined some of the most well-known gardens below, but if gardening is your passion, keep an eye out for the numerous small parks around the city where you'll be able

The whimsical, opulent gardens at Dumbarton Oaks in Georgetown offer plenty of space to get away from the crowds. Photo courtesy of Juliane Preimesberger. Used with permission.

to enjoy a quiet respite from city life; these are especially easy to find in tony neighborhoods like Georgetown and Dupont Circle and on the grounds of museums throughout the region.

Bishop's Garden at the National Cathedral (202-537-6200; www.nationalcathedral.org; 3101 Wisconsin Ave., N.W., Washington; nearest Metro: Tenleytown, Red line). Adjacent to Washington National Cathedral (see page 145) is the lovely 3-acre Bishop's Garden, tucked between charming stone walls fashioned to look medieval. Formal beds include two herb gardens, a rose collection, two perennial borders, and statuary and artifacts sprinkled throughout, including a seventh-century baptismal font, a Celtic cross dating to the early Christian pilgrimages, and a modern sculpture by Heinz Warneke called *The Prodigal Son*. Look for the Shadow House, a charming gazebo at the east end of the garden that was taken from President Grover Cleveland's summer home. Also on the Cathedral grounds, located just southeast of the church, is **Olmsted Woods**, 5 acres of old-growth forest that feature a series of walkways through mature oaks and beeches. Open dawn to dusk daily.

Dumbarton Oaks (202-339-6401; www.doaks.org; 1703 32nd St., N.W., Washington; no Metro access). Located in a quiet Georgetown neighborhood that is home to multimillion-dollar mansions, the lovely Dumbarton Oaks garden is a surprising and delightful green sanctuary. Noted landscape architect Beatrix Farrand designed the grounds of what was once the breathtaking mansion of Robert and Mildred Bliss in 1920. The original property included an astounding 53 acres, of which 10 remain. Guests today may tour several formal garden spaces, including the lovely Orangery, which is draped with enormous potted figs that date to the Civil War; the Rose Garden, which features almost 1,000 rosebushes; and the unusual Pebble Garden, which features an elaborate design set in stones and highlighted with a whimsical fountain. Throughout the property there are beautiful examples of wrought iron, statuary, and water features. Be sure to look for the spreading katsura tree that drapes its branches perpendicular to the perfectly manicured lawn near the entrance; this is one of the oldest trees on the property, said to be a remnant of a 19th-century planting. Although this glorious garden is worth a visit any time of the year, early spring is perhaps the most rewarding, with flowering cherry trees, spring bulbs, forsythia, wisteria, azaleas, lilacs, and enormous star magnolias. Note that throughout 2008 (and perhaps beyond), the Dumbarton Oaks Museum and Museum Shop are closed for extensive renovations. Enter the garden at R and 31 Streets. Open 2–5 Tuesday through Sunday (with later hours in the summer), but call ahead, as the garden is frequently closed without notice because of inclement weather or other vagaries. Adults $8, seniors and children $5.

Kenilworth Aquatic Gardens (202-426-6905; www.nps.gov/kepa; 1550 Anacostia Dr., N.E., Washington; no Metro access). Step into a real-life Monet painting at this enchanting aquatic garden, which is awash in water lilies. Twenty-eight ponds on the property feature forests of cattails, exotic lotus blossoms, and the ubiquitous water lilies in nearly every shade. Blossoms are best in midsummer, but late summer and early fall are the only times to see the enormous Victoria water lilies, which are large enough to sit on (although this is not allowed!). Located in northeast D.C., near the Maryland border and running along the Anacostia River, the gardens can be difficult to access. The Metro is not nearby, and ongoing road construction complicates driving. Nevertheless, this is one of the few parks in the country dedicated to water gardens, and it's well worth the effort to get here. Call ahead and the helpful curators will direct you via the most current convenient route. Open 7–4 daily.

INSIDER TIP: *Water lilies don't appreciate the D.C. summer heat and close up when temperatures exceed 90 degrees. In hot weather, be sure to visit Kenilworth Aquatic Gardens early in the morning, while it is still relatively cool, to see the most vivid displays of blooms.*

United States National Arboretum (202-245-2726; www.usna.usda.gov; 3501 New York Ave., N.E., Washington; no Metro access). This undervisited gem is a true urban oasis, with an astounding 446 acres of pristine, carefully cultivated grounds overflowing with myriad varieties of trees, shrubs, and herbs, all of which are interlaced with more than 9 miles of walking trails. The expansive park was established in 1927 as a research facility for the U.S. Department of Agriculture, and remains both an educational facility and venue for public outreach. Guests can stroll through the species-specific gardens, hike the woodland trails, and drive along the scenic roads that encircle the collections. Every season offers its own treats, but don't miss the spring explosion of color as the more than 15,000 azalea bushes bloom alongside native dogwoods, peonies, lilacs, and wild roses. In summer look for the near-perfect water lilies that decorate the Administration

Lilies bloom at the United States National Arboretum water gardens throughout July and August.
Photo by Debbie K. Hardin.

Building pool where children, especially, enjoy feeding the ravenous koi that also make their home here. First-timers are startled to find what look like ruins in the distance; in fact, there is a surprising stand of original columns taken from the U.S. Capitol Building in the late 1950s during a remodel and placed here among the trees. Also on site is the **National Bonsai and Penjing Museum**, open 10–3:30 daily. Note that this lovely park falls in an iffy neighborhood and is somewhat challenging to reach. By Metro, exit via the Stadium Armory station, transfer to Metrobus Line B2, and get off on R Street. From there walk two blocks to the entrance gate. There is an express bus (X6) from Union Station that runs directly to the Arboretum on weekends and holidays. If you're driving, look for gates along New York Avenue (accessed via an unmarked service street that runs parallel) and on R Street off Bladensburg Road. Open 10–5 daily.

INSIDER TIP: *Come early to feed the koi in the pool behind the Administration Building of the United States National Arboretum; the food dispenser is only filled once a day, and when all the food has been purchased, it is not refilled until the next day to avoid overstuffing the fish.*

HISTORIC SITES

Arlington National Cemetery (703-607-8000; www.arlingtoncemetery.org; Arlington;
nearest Metro: Arlington Cemetery, Blue line). More than 300,000 American soldiers
are buried on this hillside cemetery just across the river from Washington, D.C., and the
symmetrical rows of small, white marble tombstones seem to stretch endlessly over the
peaceful hills. The most famous grave is likely that of John F. Kennedy, whose final resting place is marked with an eternal flame. Just down a small hill lies his brother, Bobby,
whose grave is marked with a simple white cross. Also here is the Tomb of the Unknown
Soldier, patrolled 24/7 by a dress guard; every hour on the hour (and every half hour in
the sweltering summer months), witness the precise, theatrical changing of the guard.
Open 8–5:30; extended hours in the summer.

This is also home to the **Arlington House** (the **Robert E. Lee Memorial**), one-time
home of the famous general. Lee didn't actually own the house—it was the family home
of his wife, Mary Custis—but the family lived in this yellow Virginia sandstone home
overlooking the Potomac for many years, and Lee was said to have been extremely fond
of the property. When Lee left the home to fight for the South in the Civil War, the house
was surrounded by more than 1,000 acres of plantation. In his absence, Union forces
confiscated Arlington House for back taxes and then buried soldiers extremely close to
the house itself. Soon the federal government took over the property altogether for the

Symmetrical rows of grave markers at Arlington National Cemetery. Photo courtesy of Jon Preimesberger.
Used with permission.

The Basilica of the National Shrine of the Immaculate Conception is modeled after the grand cathedrals in Europe. Photo by Debbie K. Hardin.

national cemetery. Lee never returned to the home after the war, and judging by what he wrote in personal letters, he remained bitter about his loss until the day he died. Visitors can tour the interior of the home, which appears much as it did when Lee left it. Note that this is hilly terrain, and hiking up to the top of the cemetery can be strenuous, especially in the heat of summer. If mobility is a problem for anyone in your party, consider taking the Tourmobile (page 52), which is the only tour vehicle allowed to drive to the top of the cemetery. Just to the north of Arlington Cemetery is the **Marine Corps War Memorial** (www.nps.gov/archive/gwmp/usmc.htm), better known as the Iwo Jima statue, which commemorates Marines who have died in battle since 1775. The 100-ton sculpture is one of the largest bronze statues in the world; it re-creates the scene of five Marines and one Navy corpsman raising the U.S. flag on Iwo Jima, site of the World War II battle in which more than 6,000 Marines perished.

Basilica of the National Shrine of the Immaculate Conception (202-526-8300; www.nationalshrine.com; 400 Michigan Ave., N.E., Washington; no Metro access). This breathtaking Catholic church in northeast Washington, D.C., near Catholic University, is the largest church in the Western Hemisphere and among the 10 largest in the world. The Basilica is a marvel of neoclassical architecture that boasts stunning panoramic mosaics, colored marble floors and columns, and a large collection of statuary. The Basilica comprises dozens of small chapels on two levels, as well as the main church upstairs. Downstairs you'll find an expansive bookstore, as well as a separate gift shop selling innumerable religious items. There's even a cafeteria that serves up a nice breakfast at a reasonable price. Parking is plentiful, and although this monument to faith is a bit far flung, it is well worth a visit. Open 7–6; extended hours in the summer.

Carlyle House (703-549-2997; 121 N. Fairfax St., Alexandria; nearest Metro: King Street, Blue and Yellow lines). One-time home of wealthy Scottish merchant John Carlyle, this grand 18th-century manor house was used as British headquarters while General Edward Braddock held a council to discuss the funding of the French and Indian War. Guests can tour the re-created opulence on the half-hour. Open 10–4 Tuesday through Saturday, noon–4 Sunday. Adults $4, children $2.

Christ Church (703-549-1450; 118 N. Washington St., Alexandria; nearest Metro: King Street, Blue and Yellow lines). George Washington and dozens of other Founding Fathers worshiped in this historic church, which was built in 1767 and is still an operating parish. Guests can tour the building with a trained docent 2–4 Monday through Saturday.

Dumbarton House (202-337-2288; www.dumbartonhouse.org; 2715 Q St., N.W., Washington; no Metro access). Dating to 1799, this lovely Federal-style mansion in Georgetown hosted Dolley Madison when she fled the burning White House during the War of 1812, as well as many other leading citizens of the early republic. Visitors today can tour the property to see fine examples of period furnishings and art displayed throughout seven restored rooms in the home. Tours operate on the quarter hour from 10:15–1:15 Tuesday through Saturday. Adults $5.

Embassy Row (www.embassy.org; nearest Metro: Dupont Circle, Red line). Running along Massachusetts and New Hampshire Avenues north of Dupont Circle and stretching to the National Cathedral is an area known as Embassy Row, where you'll find more than 150 foreign embassies housed in a neighborhood of stately old mansions. Embassies are generally collections of buildings that serve as offices and residences for ambassadors and other embassy employees. Look for the buildings flying foreign flags. A particularly lovely example is the **Indonesian Embassy** (2020 Massachusetts Ave., N.W., Washington), which is housed in the historic Walsh-McLean House, the most expensive private home to be built in its time. (Mrs. McLean was a one-time owner of the Hope Diamond.) Most embassies are closed to the public, but in the **Canadian Embassy** (202-682-1740; 501 Pennsylvania Ave., N.W., Washington), guests can visit displays of Canadian arts and culture 9–5 weekdays. (Visitors must bring a government-issued I.D. to be admitted to the embassy.)

Frederick Douglass National Historic Site/Cedar Hill (202-426-5961; www.nps.gov/frdo; 1411 W St., S.E., Washington; nearest Metro: Anacostia, Green line). Abolitionist and orator Frederick Douglass was arguably the most influential African American in the 19th century. He was born into slavery but escaped to the North and to freedom as a young man. Thereafter he worked to free others and further equality among all people, regardless of race, ethnicity, or gender. This National Historic Site located in the former home of the "Sage of Anacostia," as he was known, is open after a three-year, $2.7 million preservation effort that updated the home's heating and ventilation systems and restored its 1893–1895 appearance. Guests can tour the cozy parlor, guest bedrooms, a small kitchen, and the private bedrooms of the Douglass family. Reservations are recommended (877-444-6777; there is a $1.50 fee for advance reservations). Open 9–4 daily.

Gadsby's Tavern Museum (703-838-4242; www.gadsbystavern.org; 134 N. Royal St., Alexandria; nearest Metro: King Street, Blue and Yellow lines). Founding luminaries such as George Washington, Thomas Jefferson, John Adams, and James Madison lifted their steins on this site just across the street from the Alexandria Court House. Today the tavern, which dates to 1785, and an adjacent hotel (circa 1792) are restored to the appearance of their heyday, when they served as an important gathering place for folks visiting the capital city, as well as the site of many important celebrations. (George Washington's annual "Birthnight Ball" was held here, and the president himself attended in 1798 and 1799.) Guided tours begin at a quarter past and quarter before the hour. Open April–October, 10–5 Tuesday through Saturday and 1–5 Sunday and Monday; November–March, 11–4 Wednesday through Saturday and 1–4 Sunday. Adults $4, children $2. June–August, the museum offers 30-minute lantern tours from 7–10 PM. Ages 5 and older $5.

Kreeger Museum (202-337-3050; www.kreegermuseum.org; 2401 Foxhall Rd., N.W., Washington; no Metro access). This residential museum was once the home of wealthy businessman David Kreeger and his wife Carmen, who were avid art collectors. The small gallery is now open to the public and includes works by Kandinsky, Monet, Picasso, and Rodin. There is also a collection of African masks and pre-Columbian artifacts on display. Reservations are required to visit Tuesday through Friday and can be made by

Gadsby's Tavern served as a hotel, restaurant, and pub as early as the 1700s. Photo courtesy of Jon Preimesberger. Used with permission.

telephone or via the Web site; drop-by guests are admitted 10–4 Saturday; the museum is closed throughout August. Adults $8, seniors and students $5.

Mary McLeod Bethune Council House National Historic Site (202-673-2402; www.nps.gov/mamc; 1318 Vermont Ave., N.W., Washington; nearest Metro: McPherson Square, Blue and Orange lines). The first headquarters of the National Council of Negro Women and influential political activist and presidential adviser Mary McLeod

Bethune's last home, this town house is now a national historic site open to visitors. National Park Service rangers lead guests through the house after an orientation film about Bethune's extraordinary life. Open 10–4 Monday through Saturday; extended hours in the summer.

Mount Vernon (703-780-2000; www.mountvernon.org; 3200 Mount Vernon Memorial Hwy., Mount Vernon; no Metro access). George Washington said of his Mount Vernon home, 20 miles downriver from Old Town Alexandria, "No estate in United America is more pleasantly situated than this." Visitors will soon agree that the 500 acres that remain of Washington's original 8,000 are indeed breathtaking, sited on a bucolic bend of the Potomac River and surrounded by old-growth trees, many of which have been on the property since the 18th century. Critics have complained about the "Disneyfication" of the old estate in recent years, thanks to a new orientation center that is admittedly a little slick for a historic property. Nevertheless, once you make your way through the jarring new architecture of the visitor's center (which shows an optional 15-minute orientation film) and take the short hike toward the mansion, it is still possible to glimpse the expansive Bowling Green lawn in front as a guest of George and Martha's might have. The arcade of huge trees that rims the perfectly maintained lawn dwarfs the whitewashed, red-roofed home, making it appear smaller than it really is.

Guests enter through the formal dining room, a study in bright color (decorated with a paint called verdigris, one of the most expensive hues available in the 18th century) and delicate plasterwork. A stunning centerpiece fireplace—a gift to GW from one of his many wealthy and influential friends—is crafted of three kinds of Italian marble, and it was believed to have been dismantled from an English manor and brought to Mount Vernon just for this room. The fireplace's intricately carved frieze shows a gentle farming scene with lambs and cattle, and indeed the whole room is decorated in a farm motif, proof that Washington believed his calling as a farmer was his highest occupation.

George Washington often wrote that he loved his home, Mount Vernon, more than any other place in the world. Photo by Debbie K. Hardin.

In the center of the room is a large banquet table set for a feast—including George's favorite, stuffed duckling.

A highlight of the tour downstairs is Washington's personal office, a manly wood-paneled library where he is said to have spent the earliest hours of the day catching up on his voluminous correspondence (he is known to have written more than 25,000 letters in his lifetime, and historians believe he probably wrote another 15,000 that are unaccounted for). On display is a letter press where George was able to make an early "Xerox" by pressing still-wet ink on his original document against onion-skin copy paper. Guests during the hot summertime months will marvel at his fan chair, a contraption that allowed him to sit back and read or work while peddling a foot treadle that drove a wooden fan blade suspended over the top of the chair. More remarkable, the desk chair Washington used as president, first in New York and then in Philadelphia, sits within steps of guests. The black leather chair seems small for his height (he was about 6-foot-2), but it offered the latest in technology: It swiveled.

Upstairs half of the 10 bedrooms in the house are on display, all featuring authentic 1799 decorations (although not all of the furnishings on display actually belonged to the Washingtons). Be sure to look for the baby crib in the "Nelly Custis" bedroom—a gift from Martha to her daughter. Guests can also peek into the room where the Marquis de Lafayette stayed when he visited—one of the grandest bedrooms in the home, festooned with rich carpets, more bright paint colors, and ornately patterned fabrics. George and Martha's bedroom, at the end of a private hallway, is much more subdued, with white walls, white bed linens, simple wooden desks and tables, and only a touch of color on the painted moldings. In fact, this was the only bedroom Martha decorated herself, so it isn't clear if this quieter design reflected her personal tastes or if the Washingtons chose to put their money into decorating the public rooms. Regardless, this serene space houses the bed where the couple slept and where George died in 1799. (Martha was so distraught after his death that she never used the room for herself again.)

Step outside the mansion and enjoy the Washingtons' phenomenal view of the back lawn and the river beyond. A row of wooden chairs on the rear-facing porch invites guests to rest a spell before moving on to the extensive gardens—the lower gardens grow vegetables, herbs, and fruit, and the upper gardens feature decorative flowers. A short hike leads to a larger fruit orchard and nursery, and at the far reaches of the property is a pioneer farmer exhibit that demonstrates Washington's innovation (he was one of the first farmers in the country to rotate crops). Also on the property are the poignant slave quarters, a slave memorial and burial ground, the kitchen, the clerk's quarters, the smokehouse, a wash house, a coach house, stables, various "necessaries"—what we now call outhouses—and Washington's tomb, set on a site he selected himself.

On the way out of the property, visitors will pass through the Donald W. Reynolds Museum and Education Center, another recent addition to the property. The small museum is worth a look (it houses original letters to and from Washington, an original key to the Bastille that Lafayette gave to GW, and artifacts that belonged to Washington, such as china and weaponry). The adjacent education center was designed to engage younger visitors in hopes that they leave Mount Vernon understanding Washington better. Here are life-sized wax creations of the general during various stages of his career, interactive exhibits about Washington's occupations, and several theaters that show films depicting the most important events in his public life—including a full-sensory experience with vibrating theater chairs and special effects like fog and "snow." Although this is no doubt appealing to many children, it is a cacophonous sensory overload for most adults. The good news is that it is easily bypassed on the way to the extensive gift shop and food court. The nicest choice for a meal on site is the **Mount Vernon Inn**, where guests can dine on Colonial-style food like peanut soup in a period setting *and* at a reasonable price (a cup of soup is only about $3).

Mount Vernon offers a number of seasonal activities, including holiday tours throughout December in which the mansion is decorated with natural greenery and the third floor (normally closed to the public) is available for touring; a Revolutionary War encampment in late September in which re-enactors act as soldiers, camp in authentic Colonial tents, and demonstrate military maneuvers; and a patriotic Fourth of July celebration that includes live music, "Happy Birthday, America" cake for guests, and a ceremony at Washington's tomb, where guests are invited to leave a flower. Weekends in April and September and daily May through August, guests can catch a 40-minute narrated cruise on the Potomac from the Mount Vernon dock (additional fees apply). It's also possible to catch a cruise from D.C. to Mount Vernon via Spirit Cruises (see page 244). Open daily; hours vary by season. Adults $13, seniors $12, children $6.

Old Post Office Pavilion (202-289-4224; www.oldpostofficedc.com; 1100 Pennsylvania Ave., N.W., Washington). Billed as D.C.'s "first skyscraper," this 19th-century building that once housed both the D.C. Post Office and the U.S. Post Office stands 12 stories high and affords one of the nicest views of the city from its tower (accessible by elevator for a fee). Today the magnificent old structure is stuffed full of souvenir shops and fast-food joints, and we find it a little depressing. The exterior structure is still grand, however, and you can't miss the tower from most vantage points on the National Mall. Stores open 10–7 Monday–Saturday, noon–7 Sunday.

The Old Stone House in Georgetown, as seen from the bucolic back garden. Photo by Debbie K. Hardin.

Old Stone House (202-895-6070; www.nps.gov/olst; 3051 M St., N.W., Washington; no Metro access). The Old Stone House in the heart of Georgetown is the only pre-Revolutionary building still standing in D.C. It was built in 1765 for Christopher and Rachael Layman and their two sons, who moved to Georgetown in 1764 to work in the growing port town. Legend had it that the home served as George Wash-

The towering Washington National Cathedral is visible throughout many parts of the District, as well as from Arlington, Virginia. Photo by Debbie K. Hardin.

ington's headquarters during the war; this was later disproved, but the mistaken notion probably saved the structure from the wrecking ball. It remains a nice example of a lower-middle-class home of the middle 18th century, with simple construction—3-foot-thick walls and packed dirt floors—and low ceilings to conserve heat. (Visitors will wonder if 18th-century folks were shorter than their 21st-century counterparts; check out yard-sticks in the main room that show how tall George and Martha Washington really were.) Although the Old Stone House was originally just a one-room home, later owners financed additions, including a rear kitchen in 1767 and a second floor sometime in the late 18th century, which now houses re-created sleeping quarters. The home was privately owned until 1953, when the federal government purchased it. Since then the National Park Service has administered it as part of Rock Creek Park. Visiting days and hours vary, but the pretty and peaceful garden in the back is open from dusk to dawn daily.

Pentagon (703-697-1776; pentagon.afis.osd.mil/tours.cfm; Army Navy Dr. and Fern St., Arlington; nearest Metro: Pentagon, Blue and Yellow lines). Headquarters for the Secretaries of Defense, Army, Navy, and Air Force, the Pentagon in Arlington, Virginia, is the third-largest building in the world: There are 17.5 miles of corridor inside the building, but because of the clever box-in-a-box design, it is said to take no more than 10 minutes to walk from any given point in the building to another (provided you know where you're going). The Pentagon was the site of the September 11, 2001, terrorist attack in the D.C. area: An airliner crashed into the side of the building, killing more than 100 people inside as well as all of those onboard the aircraft (see page 38). The damage to the building was repaired quickly, and as this book went to press a memorial was planned to commemorate those who perished. One-hour walking tours of the building are conducted by active-duty military personnel, and tickets must be requested from your state congressional representative at least two weeks in advance. Expect purses and handbags to be X-rayed and be sure to leave battery-operated devices, cameras, and backpacks at home. Children 12 and younger do not require ID to enter the Pentagon; children 13–17 must bring a photo ID and be accompanied by a parent or guardian; adults must bring two forms of ID, one of which must be a photo ID.

INSIDER TIP: *Even though the Pentagon's physical address is in Virginia, when mailing a letter to the Pentagon you must address it to "Washington, D.C." And note that each branch of the military is assigned its own Pentagon ZIP code.*

Washington National Cathedral (202-537-6200; www.cathedral.org; 3101 Wisconsin Ave., N.W., Washington; nearest Metro: Tenleytown, Red line). Carved from Indiana limestone, Washington National Cathedral is the second-largest cathedral in the United States and the sixth largest in the world. It took more than 83 years to complete: President Theodore Roosevelt laid the foundation stone in 1907 and President George H. W. Bush laid the final finial in 1990. Designed in the shape of a cross, with a nave onetenth of a mile long, this Gothic beauty is reminiscent of the magnificent cathedrals in Paris and Chartres, complete with flying buttresses and an army of gargoyles. The cathedral is nondenominational and regularly holds Episcopal, interfaith, and ecumenical services. It has been the site of important State funerals such as Ronald Reagan's in 2004. Look for the magnificent rose window (one of more than 200 stained glass windows) in the north transept depicting the Last Judgment; the high altar at the east end of the Cathedral that houses 110 sculptures of men and women who represent the ideals of Christianity; and the window on the nave level called "Scientists and Technicians," which depicts planets and stars and is embedded with an actual piece of moon rock in the center. After touring the interior of the Cathedral, be sure to visit the lovely grounds (see page 134). And don't miss tea and crumpets at 1:30 PM Tuesday and Wednesday, part of a special tour that must be reserved in advance.

Woodlawn Plantation (703-780-4000; www.woodlawn1805.org; 9000 Richmond Hwy., Alexandria; no Metro access). Woodlawn was a gift from George Washington to his beloved nephew, Major Lawrence Lewis, and his wife, Eleanor Custis (Martha's granddaughter). Washington gave the couple 2,000 acres from his vast estate, and prominent architect William Thornton was hired to design a lavish mansion on the property, which was begun in 1800. Guests can tour the expansive home and grounds with a docent. Open March through December, 10–5 Tuesday through Sunday. Adults $7.50, children $3. Also on site is the **Pope-Leighey House** (703-780-4000; www.woodlawn1805.org; 9000 Richmond Hwy., Alexandria), a 1940s suburban home designed by famous architect Frank Lloyd Wright that was moved to the grounds of Woodlawn in 1964, when construction of Highway 66 threatened its original site in nearby Falls Church, Virginia. Adults $7.50, children $3. Combined tickets can be purchased for Woodlawn and the Pope-Leighey House at a slight discount.

MORE MEMORIALS

African American Civil War Memorial (www.afroamcivilwar.org; 1240 U St., N.W., Washington; nearest Metro: U Street, Green line). A bronze statue memorializes African American troops who served during the Civil War, as well as liberated slaves. Plaques are inscribed with the names of more than 200,000 soldiers who fought as part of the Union forces.

Freedmen's Memorial (11th and E. Capitol St., N.E., Washington; no Metro access). Located in Lincoln Park, this memorial dedicated to Abraham Lincoln was funded by donations from freed slaves, many of whom served in the Union army. A sculpture shows Lincoln sawing off the chains of a slave, a metaphor for his Emancipation Proclamation. Also in Lincoln Park is a memorial to political activist and educator Mary McLeod Bethune, which marks the first statue of an African American woman to be erected on public ground in Washington, D.C.

George Washington Masonic Memorial (703-683-2007; www.gwmemorial.org; 101 Callahan Dr., Alexandria; nearest Metro: King Street, Blue and Yellow lines). This highly visible memorial to the first U.S. president stands on a hill in Alexandria and overlooks the capital city across the river. Financed entirely by Masons (a group to which Washington belonged), the 333-foot tower offers an observation deck that has panoramic views of Alexandria and D.C. Guests to the memorial can also tour the George Washington Museum, which features GW's family Bible and a leather field trunk he used throughout the Revolutionary War. Open 9–4 daily. Adults $4, children $2.

National Japanese American Memorial (www.njamf.com; D St. and New Jersey and Louisiana Aves., Washington; nearest Metro: Union Station, Red line). This graceful memorial near the Capitol honors the Japanese Americans who fought and died for this country during World War II and commemorates the sacrifice of the thousands of Japanese Americans who were relocated to internment camps during the war. The focal point of this memorial is a sculpted crane tangled in barbed wire; there is also a peaceful pond and a small area for quiet contemplation.

National Law Enforcement Officers Memorial (202-737-3213; www.nleomf.org; Visitors Center, 605 E St., N.W., Washington; nearest Metro: Judiciary Square, Red line). A national memorial dedicated to the U.S. law enforcement officers who have given their lives in the line of duty lists names on two low, curving walls that surround a small, serene park. At the head of the walls, massive bronze lions stand watch. To the right of the adjacent Metro exit is a locator book with pencils and slips of paper to allow guests to take away rubbings of the engraved names.

An oversized sculpture of Teddy Roosevelt welcomes visitors to Memorial Plaza with an outstretched hand on Theodore Roosevelt Island. Photo courtesy of Jon Preimesberger. Used with permission.

Theodore Roosevelt Island (across from the Kennedy Center; access via Arlington on a footbridge off George Washington Parkway; www.nps.gov/gwmp; no Metro access). This wooded nature preserve in the middle of the Potomac River is well known to hiking enthusiasts, and it is often the jumping-on point of the Mount Vernon bike and jogging trail (see page 255). Also here, within a quick walk from the footbridge that runs from its parking lot, is a memorial to the island's namesake, the 26th president, an ardent out-doorsman who would surely have appreciated the natural setting in which his larger-than-life statue was erected. The plaza housing the statue is surrounded by tranquil pools and fountains, and stone footbridges arch gracefully over canals to the several walking trails that crisscross the island. If you have the opportunity to visit in the early morning hours, you are likely to see several species of birds, small water mammals that live in the wetlands, and deer, which are surprisingly inured to the noise of jets headed for Reagan National Airport.

U.S. Air Force Memorial (www.airforcememorial.org; 1 Air Force Memorial Dr., Arlington; nearest Metro: Pentagon, Blue and Yellow lines). Honoring the men and women who have served in the U.S. Air Force, including the more than 54,000 who sacrificed their lives in the line of duty, the U.S. Air Force Memorial in Arlington, Virginia, looks over the Pentagon and is visible when crossing most of the bridges leading out of the city. The 270-foot-tall memorial, completed in 2006, comprises three curving stainless steel spires that are reminiscent of jets speeding through the sky.

MUSEUMS: BEYOND THE MALL

The National Mall offers one of the finest collections of museums in the world, and every visitor to D.C. should see as many of them as possible. But there are numerous—and often less crowded—cultural and educational opportunities beyond the Mall. These include private museums, community museums, and even farther flung branches of the Smithsonian.

Anacostia Community Museum (202-633-1000; www.anacostia.si.edu; 1901 Fort Pl., S.E., Washington; no Metro access). Founded in 1967 as the first federally funded neighborhood museum, this institution is dedicated to the historic Anacostia neighborhood in southeast D.C., one of the first suburbs in the city and one-time home to abolitionist Frederick Douglass. Changing exhibits focus on various aspects of the community as portrayed in visual arts, poetry, literature, and photography; in addition, there are more than 6,000 artifacts in the permanent collection dating to the early 1800s. By Metro, take the Green line to the Anacostia station (take the "local" exit) and then transfer to the W2 or W3 bus, which can be picked up on Howard Road to the left of the escalators. Open 10–5 daily.

Corcoran Museum of Art (202-639-1700; www.corcoran.org; 500 17th St., N.W., Washington; nearest Metro: Federal Triangle, Blue and Orange lines). This often-overlooked museum was actually the first public art collection in Washington, D.C., founded in 1859 by wealthy Georgetown banker and art collector William Wilson Corcoran, who originally kept the artwork in his home and opened his own galleries twice a week for the edification of visitors. The museum's new digs are in a beautiful Beaux-Arts building across the street from the White House. The permanent collection features 18th-through 20th-century American art and includes pieces by Albert Bierstadt, Mary Cassatt, Edward Hopper, and John Singer Sargent. A ground-floor café features a Southern-style Sunday brunch complete with grits and gospel singers, and guests are treated to live jazz at 12:30 on the first and third Wednesday of each month in the Frances and Armand Hammer Auditorium. Note that this is a working art school as well, with regular student exhibits. Closed Tuesday; every other day open at 10 AM, with closing times varying by season. Adults $14, children $10.

Decatur House Museum (202-842-0920; www.decaturhouse.org; 1610 H St., N.W., Washington; nearest Metro: Metro Center, Blue, Orange, and Red lines). Just around the corner from the White House, the Decatur House is one of the oldest surviving homes in the city and one of only three remaining residential buildings to be designed by noted architect Benjamin Henry Latrobe, who built the home in 1818 for naval officer Stephen Decatur. Today guests can tour the town house—which is undergoing restoration—every hour on the quarter hour. The large gift shop has a unique collection of china that reproduces presidential patterns, as well as a good bookstore. Open 10–5 Monday through Saturday, noon–4 Sunday. (Note that tours are not available on Monday.)

District of Columbia Arts Center (202-462-7833; www.dcartscenter.org; 2438 18th St., N.W., Washington; nearest Metro: Woodley Park, Red line). Other than live music venues and a few restaurants and pubs with local art adorning their walls, DCAC remains the only spot for the arts in the Adams Morgan neighborhood. More an experimental theater and gallery than a mainstream cultural venue, it boasts a 750-square-foot gallery and an intimate 50-seat black-box theater. Typical shows include audience-oriented improv comedy; music circles composed of locals; alternative small-cast plays; and a steady rotation of photography, painting, and multimedia exhibits. DCAC typically hosts events on weekend nights; due to limited capacity, presale tickets are a must.

INSIDER TIP: *Art fans should carve out some time to gallery crawl in Chinatown/Penn Quarter and Dupont Circle. In the former neighborhood, the galleries are clustered around Seventh Street between D and H Streets, and in Dupont, explore the streets surrounding the Phillips Collection (see page 156).*

Donald W. Reynolds Center: The Smithsonian American Art Museum and National Portrait Gallery (202-633-1000; www.npg.si.edu; Eighth and F Sts., N.W., Washington; nearest Metro: Gallery Place, Green, Red, and Yellow lines). The Smithsonian American Art Museum, the National Portrait Gallery, and the Lunder Conservation Center are all under the same roof, and it is sometimes difficult to know when you've wandered out of one space and into another. Nevertheless, the shared entrance makes admittance easier (there's only one bag check), and there are handy lockers just off the main entrance to store your stuff (especially helpful if you come straight from the International Spy Museum gift shop across the street, as many visitors do). The shared space is an awfully

The Corcoran Museum of Art offers popular workshops for adults and children throughout the year.
Photo by Nathan Borchelt.

nice one as well; the collections are housed in a lovely Greek Revival structure that dates to 1868. The building started out as the U.S. Patent Office and was the site of Lincoln's inaugural ball.

The National Portrait Gallery features portraits of important Americans from pre-Colonial days through the Revolutionary and Civil Wars, and also showcases 20th-century Americans, including pop icons like Marilyn Monroe, Babe Ruth, and Tallulah Bankhead. A second-floor gallery offers the only complete collection of presidential portraits outside the White House, including Gilbert Stuart's famous painting of George Washington. The American Art Museum section is an expansive space with ample seating to allow visitors to view the artwork in comfort. This is where you'll find the entertaining *Electronic Superhighway: Continental U.S., Alaska, Hawaii,* a mesmerizing video piece by Nam June Paik. If you stand in the right spot (in front of a video camera), you can see yourself in the section that marks D.C. Also look for Georgia O'Keeffe's *Manhattan* and Albert Pinkham Ryder's *Flying Dutchman.*

The Lunder Conservation Center houses conservation staff from both museums who often work behind glass walls to allow visitors to see the techniques they use to preserve and clean artwork. Note that this is one of the few Smithsonian museums that opens late; regular hours are 11:30–7 daily.

Ford's Theater and Lincoln Museum (202-347-4833; www.fordstheatre.org; 511 10th St., N.W., Washington; nearest Metro: Federal Triangle, Blue and Orange lines). This theater is infamous for being the place where President Abraham Lincoln was assassinated in 1865 by John Wilkes Booth, a popular actor who blamed all the nation's ills on the president. After Lincoln's death, the theater was closed for more than 100 years. As a tribute to Lincoln's love of the theater, however, the site was reopened in the late 1960s, and is now designated as a National Historic Site. The theater and museum are open after an extensive renovation completed in 2007, but note that hours will vary and the museum will close altogether at times because of the requirements of ongoing theatrical productions.

George Washington's Distillery and Grist Mill (703-780-2000; www.mountvernon.org; VA 235, Mount Vernon; no Metro access). Three miles down the road from Mount Vernon (see page 141), guests can tour a re-created gristmill on the site where Washington (his servants, anyhow) used to process his wheat and corn. The gristmill is powered by a 16-foot waterwheel, which moves huge wooden gears that in turn power the grinding stones. Also on site is a distillery that mimics one that Washington operated in his later years; on display are 18th-century distilling techniques using copper stills, enormous mash tubs, and an aromatic boiler. Although encroached on by nearby McMansions, the setting is relatively bucolic, and the stream running along the back of the property makes a nice picnic spot. Note that a commuter bus (Fairfax Connector Bus #152) runs from Mount Vernon 42 minutes past the hour to the Distillery and Grist Mill and back (#151) hourly 10–5. Open April through October, 10–5 daily. Tours begin every 20 minutes. Adults $4, children $2; discounts apply when tickets are purchased in conjunction with admission to Mount Vernon.

Hillwood Museum and Gardens (202-686-8500; www.hillwoodmuseum.org; 4155 Linnean Ave., N.W., Washington; no Metro access). Adjacent to Rock Creek Park, Hillwood Museum and Gardens is the former home of Marjorie Merriweather Post, a wealthy philanthropist and avid antique collector. The tastefully opulent, over-the-top compound that is now a museum includes decadent gardens, priceless antique pieces, overflowing

The Japanese gardens at Hillwood Museum have bridges to cross and waterfalls to behold.
Photo by Debbie K. Hardin.

greenhouses, and an art research facility (available by appointment only). Once inside the ornate gates of this expansive estate, visitors are surrounded by luxury, refinement, and the lovely excess that only the extraordinarily wealthy will ever enjoy. After passing through a visitor's center that once served as the gardener's home, guests are able to enter the red-brick mansion that houses Post's extensive collection of Russian imperial art and artifacts—which includes thousands of porcelains, liturgical artifacts, and priceless religious icons—as well as 18th-century French decorative art. Visitors will see bejeweled eggs fashioned by renowned Russian jeweler Carl Fabergé, including one created for Nicholas II, Russia's last czar; an enormous dining room table inlaid with more than a dozen colors of Italian marble that Mrs. Post specified in her will be transported from her Florida home to Hillwood Museum (sadly, the luminous table is often covered with a tablecloth); and an oversized chandelier made with rock crystals the size of softballs in the entry hall. Not to be missed are the 12 acres of gardens and 13 acres of surrounding woodlands, which include a formal French parterre garden, a rose garden (the final resting place of Post's ashes, which are stored beneath the base of a pink granite monument); and a lively Japanese-style garden with a plunging waterfall and numerous

Appropriately enough, one of the buildings that make up the International Spy Museum once housed the headquarters of the U.S. Communist Party. Photo by Debbie K. Hardin.

bridges traversing the running waters. Guests will also discover a traditional dacha, a country house that highlights rural Russian motifs; an Adirondack building that is meant to recall Mrs. Post's summer retreat in upstate New York (it was built a decade after her death); and a greenhouse with thousands of orchids. Because the estate is located in an upscale residential area, it is difficult to reach without a vehicle. If you come via Metro, prepare to hike in from the Van Ness/UDC station (exit on the east side of Connecticut); save a little shoe leather for the grounds and take the L1 or L2 bus at Connecticut Avenue and Tilden Street instead, then walk east toward Rock Creek Park and turn left onto Linnean Avenue. If you drive, parking is plentiful, but be sure to make reservations because the number of guests per day is limited (regardless of their mode of transportation). Although walk-in visitors are sometimes accommodated when the reserved numbers are low enough, it is likely that you'll be turned away without prior arrangements. Open 10–5 Tuesday through Saturday and on select evenings and Sundays. Closed throughout January and on national holidays. Adults $12, children $5.

International Spy Museum (202-393-7798; www.spymuseum.org; 800 F St., N.W., Washington; nearest Metro: Gallery Place, Green, Red, and Yellow lines). Housed in a complex of carefully restored historic buildings, the International Spy Museum is the only public museum in the world that celebrates the trade of espionage. Permanent exhibits include the largest collection of international spy-related artifacts on public display. Start your visit by assuming an identity, memorize your new name and background, and then check in at video screens along the way to make sure you've kept your cover. At each stop you'll receive additional details of your mission, which gets increasingly complicated. Throughout you'll watch archival films that include OSS and C-130 training films from World War II; interviews with former intelligence agents who explain their often complex motivations; cartoon shorts from WWII that encourage citizens to pay their "taxes to beat the Axis"; and a training video on how to pick a lock. Check out gadgets that would make Maxwell Smart drool, like a compass hidden in a button; a Bulgarian umbrella that can fire a poison-filled pellet; a KGB-issue shoe with a heel transmitter; a cigarette pistol; and eye glasses that conceal a cyanide pill. Kids will not want to miss the chance to crawl through overhead duct work to eavesdrop on conversations. In late 2007, the museum launched a new interactive tour called "Operation Spy," in which guests play the role of U.S. intelligence officers on a mission to locate a stolen nuclear device. Participants conduct video surveillance of a secret meeting, crack a safe to search for clues, and administer a polygraph test to a suspect.

Note that this museum is extremely popular, especially with children, and visitors are well advised to purchase tickets online in advance (they can be picked up the day of admittance at the will-call center at the Information Desk). During busy seasons, the line to purchase tickets can stretch outside the building, and the exhibits themselves become too congested to appreciate. Whenever you visit, come early to avoid the worst crowds that build in the early afternoon. If the wait to enter is just too long, check out the gift shop instead; it's almost as much fun. Choose from a large collection of books, videos, and novelty T-shirts and caps. For kids, look for disappearing ink, edible paper, and dozens of books filled with spy adventures. On site is the **Spy City Café,** a fast-food restaurant that continues the museum's ambiance with spy-inspired decor. Open 9–8 daily April through mid-August, 10–6 daily the rest of the year. Adults $16, seniors and active military and intelligence agents $15, children $13.

INSIDER TIP: *TSA agents at the local airports are not amused by many of the items from the International Spy Museum gift shop, especially those that disguise their functions (e.g., pens that look like lipstick; coin safes that look like peanut butter jars, etc.). If you pack them in carry-on luggage, they may get confiscated.*

Madame Tussaud's Wax Museum (202-942-7300 or 1-888-WAX-IN-DC; www.madame-tussauds.com; 1025 F St., N.W., Washington; nearest Metro: Federal Triangle, Blue and Orange lines). Opened in late 2007, Madame Tussaud's has brought its lifelike wax sculptures to D.C., featuring famous politicos from the past and present like Abraham Lincoln, Bill and Hillary Clinton, and Al Gore, as well as superstars from popular culture like Angelina Jolie and Jennifer Lopez. Guests can pose for photographs in a convincing recreation of the Oval Office, or give the president a big smooch. Open 10–6 daily. Adults $25, children $18.

Marian Koshland Science Museum (202-344-1201; www.koshland-science-museum.org; Sixth and E Sts., N.W., Washington; nearest Metro: Judiciary Square, Red line). This small museum offers compelling interactive experiences that focus on topics such as global climate change, the spread of infectious diseases, and the expanding universe. Hands-on exhibits use cutting-edge technology and sophisticated software designed for adults, although older children will appreciate the museum as well. Open 10–6 daily except Tuesday. Adults $5, children and students $3.

National Building Museum (202-272-2448; www.nbm.org; 401 F St., N.W., Washington; nearest Metro: Judiciary Square, Red line). This unusual and expansive museum explores architecture, engineering, and building through exhibits on both historical and cutting-edge practitioners in the field. The museum is housed in the magnificent 1887 U.S. Pension Building. The Great Hall atrium might well be the most impressive "lobby" you will ever see, with soaring Corinthian columns that rise up to the ceiling and lovely arched arcades that run the length of the hall. This impressive space is also used as the site of presidential inaugural balls, charity events, and special museum presentations. Smaller galleries on the first and second floors display historic—and stunningly artistic—building materials such as bricks, terra cotta pediments, steel adornments, and ornate hardware; a lovely copper dormer surround taken from the 1900s-era Carnegie mansion in New York; and walls full of architectural plans and drawings. There are hands-on opportunities for children and adults here, such as miniature bricks with which one can practice creating a Flemish bond (instructions provided!), sketching pads and drafters' tools to bring out the visitor's creativity, and listening stations and video displays to illuminate the work of a particular architect or the characteristics of a featured city. As enthralling as this innovative museum is, perhaps the greater draw is the outstanding museum gift shop, which has one of the finest collections of books on architecture in the country, including a vast selection on building (and living) in harmony with the environment; high-design house and kitchen wares; handcrafted art objects; imaginative toys you won't find on the shelves of the neighborhood mall; and specialty papers and stationery. Open 10–5 Monday through Saturday, 11–5 Sunday. Closed major holidays. Suggested donation $5.

National Geographic Museum at Explorers Hall (202-857-7588; www.nationalgeographic.com/museum; 1145 17th St., N.W., Washington; nearest Metro: Farragut North, Red line). Explore interactive exhibits that are part of the public outreach program of this famous magazine. Temporary and permanent exhibits on display in the main gallery space highlight travel, adventure, and educational experiences. An outside portico displays relief maps and artifacts, and a courtyard is filled with photography displays. Near the entrance you'll find the National Geographic Store, full of books, toys, videos, and magazines especially appealing to children. Open 9–5 Monday through Saturday, 10–5 Sunday.

National Museum of Health and Medicine (202-782-2200; www.nmhm.washingtondc.museum; 6900 Georgia Ave., N.W., Washington; nearest Metro: Takoma Park, Red line). This offbeat museum houses more than 5,000 skeletons and more than 10,000

The atrium of the inspiring National Building Museum is more than 300 feet long and 100 feet wide.
Photo by Debbie K. Hardin.

preserved bodies—including remains from Presidents Abraham Lincoln and James Garfield. Visitors can gaze at actual specimens to compare a healthy lung with a smoker's lung; see a hairball removed from the stomach of a 12-year-old girl; and view an exhibit that shows the development of early human embryos. A friend calls this the "gross-out museum," and she is right that it isn't for the faint of heart. Open 10–5:30 daily.

National Museum of Women in the Arts (202-783-5000; www.nmwa.org; 1205 New York Ave., N.W., Washington; nearest Metro: Metro Center, Blue, Orange, and Red lines). Located northeast of the White House, this is the only museum in the city that displays works exclusively by women. The permanent collection includes 16th- through 20th-century art, including pieces by Georgia O'Keeffe, Mary Cassatt, and Frida Kahlo. Open 10–5 Monday through Saturday, noon–5 Sunday. Adults $10, students and seniors $8.

National Postal Museum (202-633-1000; npm.si.edu; 2 Massachusetts Ave., N.E., Washington; nearest Metro: Union Station, Red line). Located in the old post office building on Capitol Hill, just west of Union Station, this museum is dedicated to everything pertaining to mail. Philatelists can browse the collection of stamps for hours; tens of thousands of international stamps are housed in vertical drawers that visitors can slide out themselves. There are also rotating exhibits of stamps that highlight the permanent collection; these change regularly, but expect to see some of the rarest stamps in the world. You'll also see displays of creative mailboxes, examples of antique postmarks, exhibits that explain the work of postal inspectors, and interactive stations where you can create and send personalized postcards. Don't miss Owney the dog, the scruffy, now-stuffed (and slightly creepy) mascot of the Railway Mail Service.

Newseum (1-888-639-7386; www.newseum.org; 555 Pennsylvania Ave., N.W., Washington; nearest Metro: Federal Triangle, Blue and Orange lines). This relatively new museum quickly outgrew its original Arlington, Virginia, space, and a new facility recently opened in downtown D.C. Poised adjacent to the National Mall between the White House and the Capitol, the new venue has spectacular views of some of the most important real estate in the District. Galleries on six levels highlight the history of news and media; visitors can also explore an interactive newsroom, visit a journalist's memorial dedicated to the more than 1,600 journalists who have lost their lives while reporting; and see a real "Checkpoint Charlie" tower and the largest segment of the Berlin Wall outside of Germany. Look for **The Source**, Hollywood darling Wolfgang Puck's first full-scale dining venture on the East Coast.

Phillips Collection (202-387-2151; www.phillipscollection.org; 1600 21st St., N.W., Washington; nearest Metro: Dupont Circle, Red line). Housed in a stately 1897 Georgian-revival mansion once owned by founder Duncan Phillips, a successful industrialist and avid art collector, the Phillips Collection was the first modern art museum in the U.S. It boasts more than 2,500 pieces in its permanent collection, ranging from Impressionism through the modern masters of America and Europe. Look for works by Miro, Rothko, Picasso, Van Gogh, and Georgia O'Keeffe, and don't miss the most famous piece in the collection, Pierre-August Renoir's luminous *Luncheon of the Boating Party.* Part of the charm of this small gallery is the old home in which it is housed; especially beautiful is the music room, which is clad in dark, intricately carved paneling. Be sure to catch the concert series that runs at 4 PM Sunday, October through May. Admission to the regular collection is free on weekdays; prices for special exhibits vary. Front-desk folks, who are sometimes pushy, request a $15 per person donation to visit the permanent collection, but you should understand that this rather pricey request is not required and often costs

The Phillips Collection remodeled and expanded into a modern space next door several years back, but many folks prefer the galleries that are still housed in the original mansion near Embassy Row. Photo by Debbie K. Hardin.

more than the mandatory ticket to view a special exhibit, which includes access to the permanent collection anyhow.

Renwick Gallery of the Smithsonian American Art Museum (202-633-1000; www .AmericanArt.si.edu; 1661 Pennsylvania Ave., N.W., Washington; nearest Metro: McPherson Square, Blue and Orange lines). Directly across the street from the Eisenhower Executive Office Building and the White House, Renwick Gallery is dedicated to American crafts from the 19th century onward, including pieces in glass, ceramic, wood, metal, textiles, and mixed media. The magnificent red stone building dates to 1859, when it was built as the District's first art museum, originally housing the Corcoran collection, which has since moved down the street (see page 148). The gallery was reopened in 1972 and named after James Renwick Jr., the building's architect—the same architect responsible for the Smithsonian Castle on the National Mall. The Grand Salon at the top of the dramatic staircase was designed to resemble a 19th-century collector's gallery, and today it features artist George Catlin's "Indian Gallery," a collection of more than 250 paintings—including many portraits, landscapes, and animal studies—the early

A hands-on room upstairs at The Textile Museum allows guests to try their skills at weaving, spinning, and creating original designs. Photo by Debbie K. Hardin.

19th-century artist created to document the lives of Native Americans. The vivid paintings are hung as Catlin himself displayed them, from floor to ceiling, and numbered frames correspond to an information panel that explains the subject of the piece. A museum store offers arts and crafts books as well as reasonably priced handcrafted jewelry, pottery, and hand-painted scarves. Open 10–5:30 daily.

Stabler-Leadbeater Apothecary Museum (703-838-3852; www.apothecarymuseum.org; 105–107 S. Fairfax St., Alexandria; nearest Metro: King Street, Blue and Yellow lines). This recreated 1792 apothecary shop offers a glimpse into the strange world of medicines in the 18th century, with examples of potions, elixirs, and medicinal teas. It also provides an overview of Colonial family businesses. Open daily April through October; closed Sunday through Tuesday the rest of the year. Hours vary seasonally. Adults $4, children $2.

The Textile Museum (202-667-0441; www.textilemuseum.org; 2320 S St., N.W., Washington; nearest Metro: Dupont Circle, Red line). This small museum tucked into Embassy Row is dedicated to handmade textile arts, including fabrics, weavings, needle art, quilts, and carpets. The permanent collection includes more than 7,000 pieces from Persia, India, China, Peru, and Egypt, among others, some dating back to 3000 B.C. Exhibits focus on extraordinary textiles of a given genre (or even a given color) that include items from the museum's own collection as well as pieces on loan. A small garden in the back offers a quiet spot to relax. An additional gallery is set to open in late 2008. Open 10–5 Monday through Saturday, 1–5 Sunday. Closed all federal holidays. Admission is free, but a donation of $5 is suggested.

Woodrow Wilson House (202-387-4062; www.woodrowwilsonhouse.org; 2340 S St., N.W., Washington; nearest Metro: Dupont Circle, Red line). This surprisingly large 1915 brick structure near Embassy Row was home to Woodrow Wilson and his second wife in the years immediately following his presidency. It is a delight to find the home much as the Wilsons left it: It still seems residential (one has to ring the doorbell to be admitted), and 95 percent of the contents are those that the Wilsons owned themselves, still in their original settings. Begin the tour with a somewhat dry 15-minute orientation film about the former president, and then you will be led among the 1920s-style furnished rooms, including Wilson's personal office (nicknamed "The Dugout" because of his love of baseball), a well-stocked library that also features a movie screen, and a fascinating kitchen and pantry stocked with foods typical of the era. While visiting you can sneak a peek into Mrs. Wilson's closet, and you might even have the chance to plunk out a tune on the Wilsons' grand piano. Guided tours begin on the hour. Open 10–4 every day except Monday. Adults $7.50, students $3.

INSIDER TIP: *The Woodrow Wilson House does not have central air conditioning, so in summer months visit first thing in the morning to avoid the stifling heat that builds up later.*

PERFORMING ARTS

Washingtonians love the arts, which means the diversity, number, and quality of performing arts in the city are exceptional. It also means there's a lot of competition for the best seats. A majority of seats at the most sought-after performances go to season ticket holders, especially for the opera and the major theater companies in town. In addition, a good chunk are reserved for VIPs—either by the arts companies themselves or by elite hotels, which offer them as perks for their deep-pocket guests. This is good news if you're staying at one of the finer lodging establishments in the city; check with your concierge, as she or he may be able to get tickets for you at the last minute.

If you are interested in catching a show while in town and don't qualify as a VIP (we don't, either), try to secure tickets as far in advance as possible. But if you decide at the last moment to see a show, all is not lost—and you might even be able to score seats at a considerable discount. Check out **TICKETplace** (202-842-5387; www.ticketplace.org; 407 Seventh St., N.W., Washington) for half-price, day-of-the-show discounts. They often have last-minute cancellations to pass along, and you're even more likely to get a seat if your party doesn't mind sitting separately. TICKETplace is open 11–6 Tuesday through Friday, 10–5 Saturday. Tickets for Sunday and Monday performances are sold on Saturdays. Tickets purchased online can be picked up at the performance theater's will-call window. (Be sure to bring the credit card you used to purchase the tickets, along with a photo ID.)

Capitol Steps: Irreverent Musical Satire

For a town as obsessed with politics as Washington, D.C., it's difficult to find something that amuses a local crowd more than the **Capitol Steps** (703-683-8330; www.capsteps.com), a comedy group that sets humorous lyrics about current political scandals to familiar show and pop tunes. This group of irreverent performers spares no one: They poke fun at both the Left and the Right, with Hollywood icons thrown in for good measure. The comedy troupe started out as congressional aides performing at a 1981 Senate Christmas party, and in the more than quarter century since, they've played on national TV programs and National Public Radio broadcasts, and for the past several years have offered live performances in a venue not far from Capitol Hill. Routines change regularly to stay in sync with the news events of the day, but performances could include a parody of the left-leaning Supreme Court justices singing about their longevity to the tune of the Bee Gees' "Stayin' Alive," or a parody of a song from *The Sound of Music* called "How Do You Solve a Problem Like Korea?" A highlight of every performance is a hilarious bit called "Lirty Dies" in which a fast-talking double speaker transposes the first letters of words and creates a soliloquy of popular topics in the news while uttering double entendres and intentionally silly gibberish. Backdrops, costumes, and lighting are minimal, to showcase the talent of the half dozen performers who display pitch-perfect comedic timing—and aren't half-bad singers, either. Performances are held at 7:30 every Friday and Saturday in the 600-seat amphitheater on the concourse level of the Ronald Reagan Building and International Trade Center (just off the Federal Triangle Metro station). Guests must bring a photo I.D. and have their bags X-rayed to be admitted to the federal building. For advance reservations, call 202-397-SEAT. Tickets $35.

Arena Stage (202-488-3300; www.arenastage.org; 1101 Sixth St., N.W., Washington; nearest Metro: Waterfront, Green line). The Arena Stage, the first regional theater in the country to receive a Tony Award, has received many other accolades in its 50-year history. The focus is on American theater; expect to see the classics as well as exciting new plays. This not-for-profit company attracts an annual audience of 250,000 and offers numerous educational opportunities for students throughout the region. True to its name, the company boasts an arena theater (also known as a theater in the round) as well as a more traditional proscenium-arch stage.

Carter Barron Amphitheatre (202-426-0486; 16th and Colorado Aves., N.W., Washington; no Metro access). This peaceful outdoor arena located in Rock Creek Park opened in 1950 as a venue for the celebration of D.C.'s sesquicentennial; it was envisioned by its founders as an outlet for accessible performing arts. The schedule includes plays, concerts, ballet, and performance art. Admission to many performances is free, and even when tickets are sold, they are generally a bargain. Don't miss the annual summer Free for All: two weeks of free Shakespeare plays performed in the open air. The National Symphony Orchestra also puts on amazing weekend concerts for free. Performance seasons are summer and fall.

Folger Shakespeare Library (202-544-4600; www.folger.edu; 201 E. Capitol St., S.E., Washington; nearest Metro: Capitol Hill South, Blue and Orange lines). Located just one block east of the Capitol, the Folger boasts the world's largest collection of Shakespeare's printed works, in addition to a fine selection of rare Renaissance manuscripts. The Library's magnificent Great Hall houses rotating exhibits that feature artwork, manuscripts, and theatrical memorabilia. A small re-created Elizabethan theater on the premises stages plays by Shakespeare and his contemporaries, as well as concerts, poetry readings, and other dramatic presentations. Reading rooms are reserved for scholars who come from around the globe to take advantage of the Folger's extensive collections. Don't miss the small garden next door, which features sculptures of Shakespeare's characters as well as plantings of herbs true to his time.

Ford's Theatre (202-347-4833; www.fordstheatre.com; 511 10th St., N.W., Washington; nearest Metro: Federal Triangle, Blue and Orange lines). This historic theater is best known as the site where President Lincoln was shot, and tours are available on site when the theater is not in use. But this is also a working theater specializing in 20th-century plays. The theater is actively involved in the community with workshops for inner-city children and through the popular Operation Discovery program, which subsidizes performances for thousands of low-income individuals. Note that because the theater maintains its historic design (complete with inconveniently placed columns), some seats are partially obstructed.

John F. Kennedy Center for the Performing Arts (202-467-4600; www.kennedy-center.org; 2700 F St., N.W., Washington; no Metro access). Although Dwight Eisenhower was the president to sign bipartisan legislation to fund and create this national cultural center back in 1958, the stunning theater complex—opened in 1971—was ultimately named after President John F. Kennedy to honor his lifelong commitment both to the arts and, during his presidency, to funding the center. The Kennedy Center is the pre-

The Folger Shakespeare Library features sculptures depicting characters from some of the Bard's most beloved plays. Photo by Debbie K. Hardin.

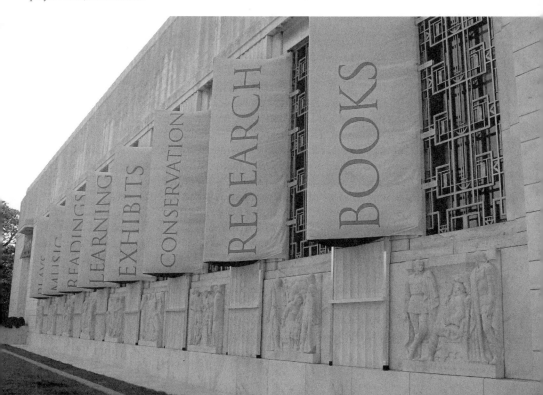

A large bust of John F. Kennedy sits on the main level of the Kennedy Center foyer, just behind the Opera House. Photo by Debbie K. Hardin.

mier performance venue in the city, and comprises several theaters under one roof, including the magnificent Concert Hall where the National Symphony Orchestra performs; the Opera House, home of the very popular Washington National Opera company as well as international ballet companies; the Eisenhower Theater, where dramatic productions are staged; the charming Terrace Theater, home of chamber music and smaller productions; and the Theater Lab, which offers new plays and experimental works. As part of an encompassing community outreach program, the Kennedy Center presents free one-hour concerts at 6 PM every evening, ranging from live jazz to string quartets. This is also a great place to expose children to the theater; look for special matinee performances of original plays aimed at youngsters. The casual **KC Cafeteria** and the more elegant **Roof Terrace Restaurant** on the top floor of the Kennedy Center offer panoramic views of the District, the Potomac River, and Georgetown—and are convenient spots to grab a light snack or a more substantial meal. Note that underground parking is extensive, but it'll cost you $15 (although there is free one-hour parking on Level B to allow guests to purchase tickets at the box office or to visit the gift shop; be sure to get your ticket validated at the time of purchase). If you are arriving by Metro, the Center runs a free shuttle bus every 15 minutes between 9:30 AM and midnight from the Foggy Bottom Metro station to the Kennedy Center. Free tours of the facility are given 10–5 weekdays and 10–1 Saturday and Sunday. Call ahead for schedules.

INSIDER TIP: *The Concert Hall and the Opera House at the Kennedy Center have presidential boxes in the center of the first balcony that are reserved for every performance, should the president choose to attend. These plush boxes have their own private sitting rooms with wet bars and bathrooms. You can tell when the president is in the house, because the Kennedy Center hangs a presidential seal in front of the box.*

Master Chorale of Washington (202-471-4050; www.masterchorale.org). This symphonic chorus is the only one of its kind in the D.C. area, and traditional performances are well worth the cost of admission. The chorus performs in the Kennedy Center's Concert Hall and in venues throughout the region.

National Symphony Orchestra (202-416-8100; www.kennedy-center.org/nso). This could very well be the hardest working orchestra in the country: These extraordinary musicians perform a 52-week season that includes approximately 175 concerts annually. The National Symphony provides the musical backdrop for presidential inaugurations, state occasions, and national holiday celebrations in the District. Many NSO performances are the centerpieces of free large-scale events such as the annual Memorial Day and Labor Day concerts at the Capitol and the Fourth of July celebrations on the National Mall. In addition to maintaining a full performance schedule at its home venue, the Kennedy Center, the orchestra stages special performances throughout spring and summer at the Carter Barron Amphitheatre in Rock Creek Park. In the summer, the NSO Pops also performs at **Wolf Trap National Park for the Performing Arts** (703-255-1868; www.wolf-trap.org; 1645 Trap Rd., Vienna), a lovely outdoor venue about 15 miles west of the District in Northern Virginia.

National Theatre (202-783-3372; www.nationaltheatre.org; 1321 Pennsylvania Ave., N.W. Washington; nearest Metro: Metro Center, Blue, Orange, and Red lines). Behind the unassuming façade of this theater just blocks from the White House, patrons will find the hottest touring Broadway shows in the city, and the most respected stage actors in the country have played here. Past luminaries include John Barrymore, Helen Hayes, and Laurence Olivier. In addition, Arlington, Virginia, natives Warren Beatty and his sister Shirley MacLaine worked here in their teens—as a stage doorman and usher, respectively. The theater offers a wildly popular free Saturday morning program for children at 9:30 and 11; complimentary tickets are distributed at the box office a half hour before the shows. There is also a well-attended summer cinema series that celebrates classic films.

Shakespeare Theater Company (202-547-1122; www.shakespearedc.org; 450 Seventh St., N.W., Washington; nearest Metro: Gallery Place, Green, Red, and Yellow lines). Washington, D.C., is crazy for the Bard, and the Shakespeare Theater Company is fan central. Located in the now-trendy Penn Quarter, the theater comprises two venues: the original Lansburgh Theatre at Seventh and E Streets, N.W., and the new Harman Hall at Sixth and F Streets, N.W. As noted, the company is dedicated to Shakespearean plays, but other classical dramatic productions are also staged. A limited number of discounted tickets are available to students and seniors.

The Studio Theater (202-332-3300; www.studiotheater.org; 1501 14th Street, N.W., Washington; nearest Metro: U Street, Green and Yellow lines). The Studio Theater is artist-

Cinema in the Capital City

Although many of D.C.'s independent movie houses have been swallowed by chains, there are a few stalwarts in the region that offer an alternative to traditional Hollywood fare. Leading the charge is **E Street Cinema** (202-452-7672; www.landmarktheatres.com; 555 11th St., N.W., Washington), an eight-screen underground theater near Metro Center that specializes in first-run art, indie, documentary, and foreign films, with concession stands that sell beer and veggie dogs alongside conventional movie snacks. The **Avalon Theater** (202-966-3464; www.theavalon.org; 5612 Connecticut Ave., N.W., Washington), D.C.'s oldest surviving movie house, was saved from demolition by a nonprofit organization in 2003. Today the theater screens first-run art and foreign films. Cinophiles also should make it a point to visit the **American Film Institute Silver Theatre and Cultural Center** (301-495-6720; www.afi.com/silver/new; 8633 Colesville Rd., Silver Spring) in the Maryland suburb of Silver Spring, which hosts first-run art, indie, foreign, and documentary films along with retrospectives focused on directors, actors, or trends—typically with special guests and lectures. The Silver Theatre also hosts **Silverdocs** (www.silverdocs.com), a documentary film festival held each June. Throughout the District you'll find a variety of other film festivals, including **Reel Affirmations** (www.reelaffirmations.org), an international gay and lesbian film festival; **FilmFest DC** (www.filmfestdc.org); and **Screen on the Green** (see page 298), a free outdoor event held on the National Mall Monday nights from late July to mid-August. Lovers of old-school cinema houses should also drop in on the single-screen Art Deco treasure known as the **Uptown Theater** (202-966-5400; 3426 Connecticut Ave., N.W., Washington). With the biggest screen in the city, this classic movie house relives the glory days of the classical theaters, complete with a parting red curtain as the opening credits start to roll. Finally, film buffs should check out museums like the Hirshhorn and the National Gallery of Art, which typically hold thematic film series.

founded and artist-driven, and the dramatic façade of the venue articulates its central focus: The use of close-up, black-and-white photos of the actors' faces, enlarged to fill the theater's wall-sized street-level windows, expresses a love for the dramatic and thoroughly contemporary, while strokes of neon red above the awning capture the Studio's flare for the whimsical. In operation for more than 30 years, the Studio boasts three 200-seat stages, including its famed 2ndstage. Work from playwrights like Neil LaBute and Tom Stoppard are staged here, along with edgier fare like *Reefer Madness: The Musical,* making it one of the more eclectic and consistently modern theater companies in the area.

Warner Theater (202-783-4000; www.warnertheater.com; 13th and E Sts., Washington; nearest Metro: Metro Center, Blue, Orange, and Red lines). This glamorous 1924 structure decked out with crystal chandeliers, gilded molding, and exclusive box seats is a mix of Louix XIV and late Empire design styles. The beautiful old theater started out life as a venue for vaudeville and silent films, and continued as a movie house through the 1960s, when it unfortunately fell into disrepair, for a time showing pornographic movies. In the late 1970s, however, the theater rebounded as a live venue, hosting world-class acts like the Rolling Stones and Frank Sinatra, and since then has undergone a dramatic renovation that has restored its nostalgic elegance. Today patrons can see concerts, comedic acts, dance performances, musicals, and plays here.

Washington Ballet (202-362-3606; www.washingtonballet.org). The premier ballet company in the District, the Washington Ballet performs both classical dance and new ballets. The company is heavily involved in community outreach programs, including innovations such as the acclaimed DanceDC, which combines creative movement with a language arts curriculum for students of D.C. public schools. Washington Ballet also has a dance school located in Anacostia—the only theater in this southeast neighborhood—that allows low-income children to widen their horizons through the performing arts. Performances are staged at the Kennedy Center for the Performing Arts.

Washington National Opera (202-295-2400; www.dc-opera.org). Under the general direction of the legendary Placido Domingo, the Washington National Opera is recognized as a world-class company, and performances at the Kennedy Center are almost always standing-room only. The company presents classical opera, but thrives on presenting lesser known works of great composers and staging new productions. The reputation of the company—as well as the incomparable Domingo—attracts the brightest opera stars in the world, and many performances are taped for later broadcast on PBS. The best seats in the house generally go to subscribers, but even a bad seat offers a superlative experience. Ticket prices are steep (as much as $300), but to expose a wider audience to the world of opera, the WNO offers special discounted rates to patrons aged 18–35 through its "Generation O" program. Don't worry if you aren't fluent in German or Italian; you'll still understand the plot at WNO productions, thanks to "supertitles" projected above the stage.

Woolly Mammoth Theatre Company (202-393-3939; www.woollymammoth.net; 641 D St., N.W., Washington; nearest Metro: Archives, Green and Yellow lines). On the cutting edge of the performing arts, the Woolly Mammoth Theatre is a daring, often irreverent outlet for new drama and exciting, up-and-coming actors. The group has received nearly 100 Helen Hayes Washington Theater award nominations, and is well known for its community outreach programs. The company used to share venues around town, but in 2005 opened the doors to its own 265-seat "courtyard-style" theater in downtown, the industrial-style architecture of which has won many accolades of its own. The company stages approximately a half dozen plays each season.

The well-endowed sign for Madam's Organ. Photo by Nathan Borchelt

6

RESTAURANTS AND NIGHTLIFE

Wine, Dine, and Dance

Washington, D.C., attracts people from around the world, and thus the region has always known how to accommodate demanding, international palates. In addition, local eateries have learned to handle deep-pocket lobbyists looking to impress. But over the past 10 years, the tried-and-true culinary traditions of Washington have been infiltrated by a host of new, inventive chefs who have pushed the envelope on fine dining in the city, and in the process proven themselves to be some of the world's best culinary artists. All-stars like Michel Richard and CityZen's young executive chef Eric Ziebold now work along such famed artisans as Jeff Tunks (DC Coast), José Andrés (Jaleo), Ashok Bajaj (Ardeo), and Arlington's own Cathal Armstrong (Restaurant Eve). In fact, many of these chefs have pioneered bona fide movements in the region, complete with mini-empires. As a result, portions of the following pages are dedicated to their innovative restaurants. Staple D.C. spots like Georgetown's 1789, however, continue to shine amid this new influx, and with world-renowned chefs like Charlie Palmer, Laurent Tourondel, and Wolfgang Puck now on the scene, the competition—and diners' options—are really heating up.

Whether you want to drop $10 or $100 for dinner, D.C. will accommodate. The region's diverse cultures result in a mélange of cuisines, from Malaysian to Mexican, from Thai to Ethiopian, from the famed half-smokes at Ben's Chili Bowl to entrées composed entirely of sustainable seafood at Georgetown's Hook.

Prices
Rather than provide exact menu prices that quickly become outdated, we've offered price range categories to help you gauge the costs. Prices are per person, and include appetizer, entrée, dessert, tax, and tip, but exclude drinks.

Inexpensive: Up to $15
Moderate: $15–30
Expensive: $30–75
Very Expensive: $75 and up

RESTAURANTS

AROUND THE MALL
BLT STEAK
Executive Chef: Laurent Tourondel
202-689-8999
www.bltsteak.com
1625 I St., N.W., Washington, D.C. 20006
Open: Daily
Price: Expensive
Cuisine: American
Serving: L, D
Credit Cards: AE, MC, V
Handicap Access: Yes
Reservations: Yes
Nearest Metro: Farragut West, Blue and
Orange lines

Veteran New York City chef Tourondel chose the locale for his first foray into D.C. wisely. This sizable, classically stylish restaurant lies only a few blocks west of Lafayette Park and the White House, but BLT Steak leaps beyond traditional steak house expectations. An open dining room with polished dark-wood furniture and hardwood floors, plush fabrics, and intimate lighting already take the experience one step beyond the darker chop houses in the city. You can still find aged porterhouse and shrimp cocktail, but those staples share space on the menu with rewarding Kobe beef (the real thing, organically raised and processed in Japan) and aquatic specialties like Dover sole. Start off with selections from the raw bar—just select from the large chalkboard of the latest, freshest offerings. Proximity to the White House and K Street ensure a few politico spottings, but it's best to turn your attention to the menu—particularly in the summer, when they unveil a special salad and sandwich menu. Choose from Kobe salad, the beef cooked to heavenly perfection, or the soft-shell crab BLT.

CENTRAL MICHEL RICHARD
Executive Chef: Cedric Maupillier
202-626-0015
www.centralmichelrichard.com
1001 Pennsylvania Ave., N.W., Washington, D.C. 20004
Open: Monday–Saturday
Price: Moderate
Cuisine: American/French
Serving: L, D
Credit Cards: AE, D, MC, V
Handicap Access: Yes
Reservations: Recommended
Nearest Metro: Federal Triangle, Blue and Orange lines

Famed chef Michel Richard, founder of the world-renowned Citronelle (see page 193), followed the recent D.C. trend of taking haute cuisine to a brasserie-style establishment in an effort to present culinary artistry on more affordable plates. But while Central

Michel Richard, the man behind Citronelle and Central. Photo by Len Depas. Used with permission.

may be less expensive, the food remains some of the best in the city. Witness the lobster burger, a patty of the delicate meat enriched by a scallop mousse and served on a bun with medallions of crisp potatoes, with frites cooked in a mixture of Canola oil and clarified butter. But we're getting ahead of ourselves; the starters really set the stage for this whimsical approach to American dishes touched with a hint of France. The "faux" foie gras is made with chicken liver (instead of duck liver) infused with butter, and other menu items like hamburgers and an inventive banana split drenched in house-made caramel firmly display affection for traditional U.S. cuisine. A heady selection of gourmet beers sits comfortably alongside blue-collar favorites, and a vast, affordable selection of wines complements the food. The finishers, one of Richard's staple successes, also match (and sometimes exceed) expectations, from an eclectic twist on the Kit Kat bar to a heavenly orange soufflé that seems to dance on the fork. The decor is suitably dressed down as well, with an open kitchen in the back and a casual dress code that welcomes jeans and dinner jackets alike. Half the dining room is dedicated to the long bar that stretches the length of the restaurant—which is your best bet for a seat should you drop in without a reservation.

CEIBA

Chef de Cuisine: Victor Albisu
202-393-3983
www.ceibarestaurant.com
701 14th St., N.W., Washington, D.C. 20005
Open: Monday–Saturday
Price: Expensive
Cuisine: South and Central American
Serving: L, D
Credit Cards: AE, D, DC, MC, V
Handicap Access: Yes
Reservations: Recommended
Nearest Metro: Metro Center, Blue, Orange, and Red lines

Ceiba takes its name from an umbrella-shaped tree indigenous to South and Central America that is rumored to contain mythical powers, and the same could be said for this whimsical spot. Like Executive Chef Jeff Tunks's other restaurants—Acadiana, DC Coast, and TenPenh—the emphasis is split between the decor and the cuisine. The former embraces an elegant mix of candles, terra-cotta, small window-side tables, and a banquet-hall-sized room with views of the kitchen. But the latter leaves the lasting impression. Each dish takes its influence from particular regions of Latin America with an artful, contemporary twist, from the Peruvian parihuela seafood stew, to whole crispy red snapper Vera Cruz, to fava bean plantain and mixed mushroom tamales. Start with one of four ceviches (or hedge your bets and order the sampler), and don't miss the "hot lava stone" queso fundido, a mixture of grilled skirt steak, poblano chilis, and Oaxacan cheese served in (you guessed it) a warm lava-stone bowl. If you can't decide, you can safely rely on staff recommendations. Better yet, ask your server to pair wines with each course. Ceiba's famed cocktails, like the pisco sour and the Brazilian pita cachaca (a mix of sugarcane rum, tamarind extract, passion fruit puree, and pineapple juice) pull a steady, loyal happy hour crowd. And at the end of each meal, every table receives caramelized popcorn wrapped in newsprint, proving once again that sometimes the best things are also the simplest.

INSIDER TIP: *Each cocktail at Ceiba and Ten-Penh (see page 185) comes with a whimsical blue plastic figurine: an ox and a monkey, respectively. They're great little souvenirs for the kids should parents break away to dine in one of these top establishments.*

CITYZEN

Executive Chef: Eric Ziebold
202-787-6006
1330 Maryland Ave., S.W., Washington, D.C. 20024
Open: Tuesday–Saturday
Price: Expensive
Cuisine: American
Serving: D
Credit Cards: AE, D, DC, MC, V
Handicap Access: Yes
Reservations: Highly recommended
Nearest Metro: Federal Center, Blue and Orange lines

A neighboring restaurant on the rapidly developing waterfront will find vying for attention with CityZen quite challenging. The signature restaurant at the chic Mandarin Oriental Hotel offers one of the best culinary experiences in the city. Everything hits the right note, from the gracious host and attentive service to the exhibition kitchen and the dining room's refined decor, a subdued mixture of polished wood, limestone, stainless steel, and textured fabrics. But once the food arrives, everything fades into the background as young Chef Ziebold demonstrates that he's one of the most inventive cooks working today. Diners can choose from one of three tasting menus: the meat-centered three- or six-course chef's menu or the six-course vegetarian menu. Timidity is not rewarded here, especially when the rotating menu could include dishes like sautéed Chesapeake Bay soft-shell crab with applewood-smoked bacon, a saffron-infused shrimp bouillon paella soup with squid and puffed rice, herb-roasted Elysian Fields Farm lamb with couscous and summer squash, or the CityZen falafel served with lemon cucumber and Greek yogurt. Up the ante by asking sommelier Andy Myers to pair each course with something from the restaurant's voluminous wine list. The dessert options rotate monthly as well, with summer confections like a honeydew and cavaillon melon salad or Ziebold's take on an old-fashioned chocolate malt with caramel macaroon and crystallized banana chips.

KAZ SUSHI

Owner and Chef: Kaz Okochi
202-530-5500
www.kazsushibistro.com
1915 I St., N.W., Washington, D.C. 20006
Open: Monday–Saturday
Price: Expensive
Cuisine: Japanese
Serving: L, D
Credit Cards: AE, D, DC, MC, V
Handicap Access: Yes
Reservations: Yes
Nearest Metro: Farragut West, Blue and Orange lines

Sushi fans have developed an unabashed admiration for Kaz Okochi, former chef at the Sushi-Ko (see page 201) and now the man behind this Foggy Bottom hot spot. But don't expect your typical sushi dishes. Dubbed "freestyle Japanese cuisine," the menu does offer some of the city's highest quality sushi, rolls, and nigiri, from tuna with roasted almonds, to yellowtail belly *buri toro,* to sweet shrimp *ama ebi* with Japanese rice. But the real emphasis lies in the menu's small-plate options, which couple non-Asian staples like Cornish game hen alongside Kobe beef miso soup. Foodies and the culinarily adventurous should opt for the "taste parade," an eight-course fixed-price meal drawn mostly from the night's specials. First-timers may be put off by the narrow dining room's decor—which includes laminated menus, lighting that seems a touch too bright, and a TV screen with rotating images of the entrées—but one taste of the smoked fatty mackerel on a bed of Japanese cucumbers and all attention turns to your enlivened taste buds. Lunch specials change daily, and a coveted seat at the sushi bar also presents additional options not on the menu. Plan accordingly.

OLD EBBITT GRILL

Owners: Stuart Davidson and John Laytham
202-347-4801
www.ebbitt.com
675 15th St., N.W., Washington, D.C. 20005
Open: Daily
Price: Moderate
Cuisine: American
Serving: B, L, D
Credit Cards: AE, D, DC, MC, V
Handicap Access: Yes
Reservations: Recommended
Nearest Metro: Metro Center, Blue, Orange, and Red lines

Just around the corner from the White House, the iconic Old Ebbitt Grill was founded more than 150 years ago (in 1856), when Franklin Pierce was president. The richly decorated main dining room is adorned with dark woods and features tweed-upholstered booths, manly leather chairs, and sporting paraphernalia as accent pieces. The testosterone-heady decor is enhanced with hunting trophies said to have been bagged by outdoorsman Teddy Roosevelt and with carved wooden bears once collected by Alexander Hamilton to spruce up his own personal bar. This institution is a tourist destination, but it gets its fair share of locals, too, thanks to the surprisingly satisfying fare. The Old Ebbitt is famous for its Oyster Bar, which is among the best raw bars in the city. Other tempting starters include the bubbling hot crab and artichoke dip served with a fresh baguette and the smoky New England clam chowder. Although entrée menus change daily, you can count on old favorites like the lightly crusted Virginia trout parmesan,

The well-known Old Ebbitt Grill is a perennial favorite. Photo by Ron Blunt Photography. Used with permission.

which is pan fried and topped with hollandaise sauce, and the delicate linguini with mussels. For dessert, don't miss the hot pineapple upside-down cake smothered in whipped cream. If you find yourself short on time, check out the new Ebbitt Express, which offers an abbreviated menu of to-go items.

INSIDER TIP: *The Old Ebbitt offers free valet parking after 6 PM—a welcome bonus, because otherwise parking this close to the White House is impossible.*

OCCIDENTAL

Executive Chef: Rodney Scruggs
202-783-1475
www.occidentaldc.com
1475 Pennsylvania Ave., N.W., Washington, D.C. 20004
Open: Monday–Saturday
Price: Expensive
Cuisine: American
Serving: L, D Monday–Friday; D only Saturday
Credit Cards: MC, V
Handicap Access: Yes
Reservations: Recommended
Nearest Metro: Federal Triangle, Blue and Orange lines

For more than 100 years, this D.C. fixture just down the road from the White House has been a watering hole and dining destination for some of the world's most powerful people. After a multimillion-dollar renovation in 2007, it continues to be a premier spot to see and be seen. The clubby interior with masculine dark woods; a gleaming, old-school bar; and nearly 2,000 autographed photos lining the walls in tribute to past loyal costumers like Richard Nixon, Winston Churchill, and Amelia Earhart has cache to spare. Thanks to Chef Rodney Scruggs's innovative approach to the surf and turf staples, the food is now as noteworthy as the patrons who pack the house. Start with the exquisite jumbo lump crab cakes served with tomato dill butter or the creamy English pea risotto with grilled shrimp. Notable entrées include roasted halibut served with champagne grapes and baby bok choy; guinea fowl with poached apricots and golden beets in a pink peppercorn sauce; and classic grilled filet mignon served in a Marsala tarragon reduction. Satisfy a sweet tooth with an eye-catching chocolate sampler plate ornamented with shards of pulled sugar candy or a collection of intense house-prepared sorbets. In temperate months, guests can also enjoy an expansive and festive outdoor dining patio.

ADAMS MORGAN
CASHION'S EAT PLACE

Chef: John Manolatos
202-797-1819
www.cashionseatplace.com
1819 Columbia Rd., N.W., Washington, D.C. 20009
Open: Tuesday–Sunday
Price: Expensive
Cuisine: American, European
Serving: D (brunch on Sunday)
Credit Cards: AE, MC, V
Handicap Access: Yes
Reservations: Recommended
Nearest Metro: Woodley Park, Red line

Chosen as one of *Gourmet* magazine's 10-best neighborhood restaurants, the French- and Mediterranean-inspired American cuisine seldom disappoints. Master chef Ann Cashion sold the restaurant in late 2007, and the new owner, John Manolatos, is transforming the menu, focusing—as always—on locally grown, organic ingredients. The scene itself is subdued—black-and-white photos, low lights, attentive staff, and legions of locals who routinely flock to this small neighborhood establishment—and the wine list has a variety of well-priced options. Cashion's is also a very popular weekend brunch spot, with diners typically spilling out onto the expansive front patio, blissfully dining in the spring sunshine.

THE GRILL FROM IPANEMA

202-986-0757
www.thegrillfromipanema.com
1858 Columbia Rd., N.W., Washington, D.C. 20009
Open: Daily
Price: Moderate
Cuisine: Brazilian
Serving: D (brunch on weekends)
Credit Cards: AE, D, DC, MC, V
Handicap Access: Yes
Reservations: Recommended
Nearest Metro: Woodley Park, Red line

Sip a few *caiparinhas*—a cocktail of soda, lime, and liquor distilled from sugarcane—while listening to the seductive whisper of bossa nova in this low-lit dining room and you may fool yourself into believing you've escaped to Rio. And the food at this Brazilian restaurant supports that illusion. Specialties like spicy conch soup, Bahia-style stews, and South American steak are highlights, while an eclectic mix of appetizers like *churrasquinhos* (Brazilian-style brochette with your choice of beef, chicken, or pork, served with ground yuca) round out the menu. The dress code is a grade up from some of the neighborhood's more mainstream restaurants, but that only adds to the experience. It's also a little removed from the chaos of the rest of Adams Morgan, which is a blessing on busy weekend nights. The three-course champagne brunch, which includes a house salad, a glass of libation, and your choice of an entrée and dessert, also draws a crowd most weekends.

LITTLE FOUNTAIN CAFÉ

202-462-8100
www.littlefountaincafe.com
2339 18th St., N.W., Washington, D.C. 20009
Open: Daily

Price: Moderate
Cuisine: American
Serving: D
Credit Cards: D, MC, V
Handicap Access: Yes
Reservations: Yes
Nearest Metro: Woodley Park, Red line

The intimate setting, low lights, and reliably imaginative food make this 38-seat basement-level restaurant something of a neighborhood anomaly. True to its name, a small fountain evokes a quiet, civilized atmosphere, but in most respects, it reflects a place found in New England, not Adams Morgan. A few highlights of the contemporary menu include appetizers like the grilled eggplant stack with feta cheese, sun-dried tomatoes, roasted red bell peppers, and a tomato-basil coulis; and fish and pasta entrées like Dijon-crusted baked red snapper with sautéed spinach and root vegetable gratin, or the spinach gnocchi with a pesto cream sauce. But the kitchen's strength lies in comfort food with a gourmet twist—their roast chicken will remind you of how it became a staple of American cuisine.

MESKEREM

202-462-4100
2434 18th St., N.W., Washington, D.C. 20009
Open: Daily
Price: Moderate
Cuisine: Ethiopian
Serving: D
Credit Cards: AE, DC, MC, V
Handicap Access: Yes
Reservations: Recommended
Nearest Metro: Woodley Park, Red line

Meskerem has some of the best Ethiopian food in Washington—which is saying something, considering the burgeoning Ethiopian population in the District. So, if you're a novice, this is one of the best places to get initiated. And if you've eaten eastern African before, it's a sure bet for high qual-

The line outside Perry's for Sunday morning's Drag Brunch. Photo by Nathan Borchelt.

ity and attentive service. The cuisine consists mostly of stews called *watts* made of lamb, beef, chicken, and vegetables, each offering varying degrees of spiciness (*alica watts* are the mildest). Diners eat communally by scooping the meal with soft, porous, pancake-like sourdough bread called *injera* (no silverware here). Favorites include *lega tibs,* a tender lamb dish with onion and spices, and veggies like pureed chick peas, mashed lentils, and potato salad. First-timers may want to simplify matters by ordering one of the menu samplers. The decor—three levels, skylights, a variety of traditional Ethiopian decorations, woven-basket tables, and upholstered leather poufs or carved wooden chairs for seats—completes the experience. A modest number of Ethiopian wines and beers keep you rooted in the African continent.

MIXTEC

202-332-1011
1792 Columbia Rd., N.W., Washington, D.C.
20009
Open: Daily
Price: Inexpensive
Cuisine: Mexican
Serving: L, D
Credit Cards: MC, V
Handicap Access: Yes
Reservations: No
Nearest Metro: Woodley Park, Red line

Don't expect a nacho platter the size of an Aztec volcano or sizzling shrimp fajitas here. Described by locals as the best Mexican food this side of the border, Mixtec specializes in the traditional cuisine of our neighbors to the south. Starters like the salsa are so fresh you understand why they charge for it. Traditional dishes like the pork-filled tamales and the chicken con-sommé perfectly balance competing flavors, and the *mole* (a traditional Mexican sauce made of chili, cinnamon, and chocolate) is everything it should be—spicy, rich, and delectable, particularly on the Fiesta Mexicana, a dish of grilled chicken with rice and beans. The overhead fluorescents and plastic tablecloths don't offer much ambience, but after a few sips of their stellar Cadillac margaritas, you'll likely be busier talking to your neighbor than squinting from the lighting. They also make tortas, a Mexican spin on the traditional sub sandwich, with pork, beef, or chicken mixed with chilies, salsa, and guacamole—great for a quick take-out.

PERRY'S

Owner: Saied Azali
202-234-6218
www.perrysadamsmorgan.com
1811 Columbia Rd., N.W., Washington, D.C. 20009
Open: Daily
Price: Moderate
Cuisine: Japanese, American
Serving: D (brunch on Sunday)
Credit Cards: AE, D, DC, MC, V
Handicap Access: No
Reservations: Recommended (none accepted during spring and summer)
Nearest Metro: Woodley Park, Red line

This second-story neighborhood staple—with accompanying roof deck during the warmer months—has long been a bastion for the celeb-conscious, but it deserves merit for reasons other than a Keanu sighting. After ascending a narrow flight of stairs, you enter the main dining room, a plush interior of dark wood and red curtains with a handsome bar; big, high-backed booths; and quasi-organic, Dali-esque fixtures. The menu specializes in sushi, and large helpings at that, but dishes like roast chicken or the roast snap-per should entice those not inspired by uncooked fish, and there's a variety of small plates for those just looking to nibble. On Sundays, the gay-friendly Perry's also puts on the city's craziest brunch buffet, drawing huge lines before doors open at 11. Known as the Drag Brunch, diners are interrupted every 15 minutes by diva-blessed drag queens who lip-sync a bass-pounding number while dancing through the main dining room.

THE REEF

Chef: Ken Kaiser
202-518-3800
www.thereefdc.com
2446 18th St., N.W., Washington, D.C. 20009
Open: Daily
Price: Moderate
Cuisine: American
Serving: D (brunch on weekends)
Credit Cards: AE, MC, V
Handicap Access: No
Reservations: No
Nearest Metro: Woodley Park, Red line

The first thing you notice about this place is the decor—an expansive second-story dining room with saltwater aquariums filled with tropical fish; floor-to-ceiling windows overlooking 18th Street; intimate two- and three-person tables; massive booth seating; and a huge central bar covered in copper scales. But the gastro-pub menu remains the chief attraction. The seasonal cuisine is created from all-local, all-organic ingredients, and includes a variety of starters and small gourmet pizzas, seafood and veggie entrées, the city's best bison (burger or sirloin), and a rotation of fresh desserts. By some standards the beer list isn't voluminous, but the 20 or so options on tap have been chosen *by* beer lovers *for* beer lovers (some nights they even feature special single-cask beer from the U.S. and overseas), and the kitchen retains a special pub menu

The Reef, crowned with a huge, tarp-covered roof deck. Photo by Nathan Borchelt.

long after the main kitchen closes. Downstairs, the street-level **Lush** bar—a narrow, dark room that looks like a fusion of the Amazon and *Apocalypse Now*—offers quiet respite if the scene upstairs gets hectic (as it can on weekend nights). The clientele ranges from tattooed hipsters to Capitol Hill scribes, and the unpretentious air from both staff and customers is a welcome change from some other Adams Morgan locales. The Reef also boasts one of the best roof decks in the neighborhood, recently supplemented with a series of massive tarps to shield its customers from the elements—and keep it open year-round.

CAPITOL HILL
AMERICA
General Manager: Matt Mitchell
202-682-9555
www.arkrestaurants.com
50 Massachusetts Ave., N.E., Washington, D.C. 20002
Open: Daily
Price: Moderate
Cuisine: American
Serving: B, L, D (brunch on Sunday)
Credit Cards: AE, D, DC, MC, V
Handicap Access: Yes
Reservations: No
Nearest Metro: Union Station, Red line

This sprawling restaurant inside Union Station seats up to 1,000—but it can still be hard to get a table here at lunch. That's because locals on Capitol Hill know this is one of the best places to find hearty comfort food, served in large portions and with a dash of patriotism courtesy of decor that pays homage to the 50 states. Patrons can dine in the cozy bar downstairs, in "patio" seating that spills out onto the wide expanse of Union Station, in an exclusive wine vault room tucked away from view, or in an appealing upstairs loft that allows diners to look over the bustling crowds as well as appreciate the ornate rococo details of this amazing train station. The menu is exhaustingly long, and includes pasta, soups, salads, a huge variety of sandwiches, and familiar entrées like an oversized chicken pot pie and meat loaf doused in mushroom gravy. For something *slightly* lighter, try the crab cake sandwich, served plain on a toasted bun, or the Navajo fry bread sandwich stuffed with grilled chicken, caramelized onions, and guacamole. A specialty you aren't likely to find elsewhere are the patriotic red, white, and blue enchiladas made with tricolor tortillas, black beans, and stir-fried veggies. Desserts include favorites from around the country, like key lime pie from Florida, pecan pie from Atlanta, and cheesecake from New York.

BISTRO BIS

Owner and Executive Chef: Jeffrey Buben
202-661-2700
www.bistrobis.com
15 E St., N.W., Washington, D.C. 20001
Open: Daily
Price: Expensive
Cuisine: French
Serving: B, L, D
Credit Cards: AE, D, DC, MC, V
Handicap Access: Yes
Reservations: Recommended for dinner
Nearest Metro: Union Station, Red line

The elegant interior of this Capitol Hill gem is a clean-lined, modern interpretation of a classic French bistro. An inviting zinc bar at the entry shimmers with backlighting and polished glassware; the gleaming open kitchen is visible behind a wall of glass; and honey-toned woods and earthy fabrics contrast with colorful antique French posters. Although housed inside the Hotel George (see page 72), which is run by the Kimpton hotel group, this restaurant is independently owned and operated by D.C. food maverick Jeffrey Buben, whose vision and dedication to excellence is evident in each carefully chosen menu item. Starters include the luscious crab salad, a molded wonder created from enormous chunks of jumbo lump crab, creamy avocado, mango, and the slightest hint of pink grapefruit; and, when in season, the delicate fried squash blossoms stuffed with lobster, goat cheese, and prosciutto. For the main course, try Chef Buben's interpretation of the traditional beef bourguignon, made with spoon-tended braised short ribs served in a red wine sauce with mushrooms, root vegetables, and bacon. The more adventurous will want to try the truffle-scented sweetbreads *à l'ancienne,* which are pan roasted with asparagus and pearl onions and served alongside an artichoke puree. Whatever your entrée, don't miss a side order of the light, crisp *pommes frites,* which come to the table in a towering paper cone. The dessert menu changes with the seasons, but expect to find the roselike apple bistro tart served with crème fraîche ice cream and the chocolate gateau with layers of ganache, chocolate panna cotta, mocha butter cream, and espresso gelée. You'll also find a nice selection of artisinal cheeses. To round off one of the finest meals you'll find in the city, there is an extensive selection of wines by the glass and a voluminous list available by the bottle, including a nice variety of sparkling wines.

CHARLIE PALMER STEAK

Executive Chef: Bryan Voltaggio
202-547-8100
www.charliepalmer.com/steak_DC
101 Constitution Ave., N.W., Washington,
D.C. 20001
Open: Monday–Saturday
Price: Expensive
Cuisine: American
Serving: L, D Monday–Friday; D Saturday–
Sunday only

Credit Cards: AE, DC, MC, V
Handicap Access: Yes
Reservations: Recommended
Nearest Metro: Archives, Green and Yellow
lines

This recent addition to the District steak
house scene isn't your grandfather's chop
house. Rather than the expected dim lights
and wood paneling, this place evokes an
L.A. vibe: The white interior houses a large

The Charlie Palmer Steak "wine cube" houses 3,500 bottles from the 10,000-bottle cellar. Photo by Hoachlander Davis
Photography, LLC. Used with permission.

main dining room and a central bar that is grounded by an expansive all-glass wine "cube." But one glance out the window at the Capitol and there's no question where you are. D.C. local Bryan Voltaggio lives up to his boss's marquee name, offering steaks like filet mignon that's been aged 21 days or the "cowboy cut" rib eye, along with more contemporary French dishes like the roasted foie gras with crisp duck confit, blood orange, and candied ginger—one of the most flavor-infused and generously proportioned foie gras dishes in the city. Starters include a heady number of seafood options, as well as lighter fare like red endive salad with caramelized honey-poached pears, medjool dates, and goat cheese. In addition to the USDA-certified beef, entrées include Sonoma County duck with balsamic lacquer and a puree of maroon carrots, and the Pacific halibut with roasted artichokes and fennel confit. Side dishes like the creamed spinach, baby bok choy, and pancetta-tossed brussels sprouts will make you love to eat your vegetables. The wine list specializes in U.S. vintages that deliver surprising flavors at half the cost of their Euro counterparts.

INSIDER TIP: *Political groupies may want to hit Charlie Palmer Steak for lunch; a fixed-price menu and close proximity to the Hill keeps this spot on the radar regardless of party affiliation.*

LOCANDA

Executive Chef: Brian Barszcz
202-547-0002
www.locandadc.com
633 Pennsylvania Ave., S.E., Washington, D.C. 20003
Open: Tuesday–Sunday
Price: Moderate
Cuisine: Italian
Serving: L, D
Credit Cards: AE, MC, V
Handicap Access: Yes

Reservations: Yes
Nearest Metro: Eastern Market, Blue and Orange lines

When owner Aykan Demiroglu opened this Northern Italian restaurant in July 2007, he gave the neighborhood what it had been longing for: a local spot high on quality and easy on the wallet. A simple, subdued decor of white walls, bright orange modern chairs, old maps of Italy adorning the walls, and an intimate bar in the back successfully present an overall sense of inviting sophistication. Yet that apparent simplicity disguises Demiroglu's dedication to wholly eco-friendly practices, which include everything from wind-powered energy, recycled paper menus, and sustainable textiles on the wood banquettes. Chef Barszcz also embraces this "green" approach, perusing the veggie, cheese, and meat stalls of nearby Eastern Market each day to ensure that the menu's offerings use only the freshest, locally grown ingredients. The menu features small-plate appetizers like zucchini fritters, followed by an antipasta course featuring house-made pastas married with fresh veggies like eggplant, or the veal crudo with capers and parsley. These are followed by entrées like a juicy hanger steak or the pork chop Milanese, with meat that's been brined for three days. The vast array of selections will lead to sumptuous overeating, but carve out enough room for one of Locanda's traditional Italian desserts, from house-made sorbets to the Meyer lemon panna cotta. The wine list reflects both the restaurant's home country and Locanda's desire to give you everything you need without draining your wallet.

CHINATOWN/PENN QUARTER

ACADIANA

Executive Chef: Jeff Tunks
202-408-8848
www.acadianarestaurant.com
901 New York Ave., N.W., Washington, D.C. 20001

The summer crayfish and shrimp boil at Acadiana.
Photo by Nathan Borchelt.

Open: Daily
Price: Expensive
Cuisine: Cajun
Serving: L, D
Credit Cards: AE, D, DC, MC, V
Handicap Access: Yes
Reservations: Recommended
Nearest Metro: Gallery Place/Chinatown,
Green, Red, and Yellow lines

Forget counting calories. This rich, decadent, delicious Southern-cuisine restaurant is tailor-made for shameful culinary indulgence. Executive Chef Tunks, who spent four years cooking down South, describes Acadiana as "a contemporary interpretation of a Louisiana fish house," and the latest in his D.C. restaurant empire lives up to his marquee reputation. Roux, rémoulades, bisques, étoufées, even New Orleans-style beignets—it's all here, presented with an artful flair in a triangular, all-glass dining room wedged between K Street and New

York Avenue. The fried green tomatoes and trio of deviled eggs with crab, shrimp, and Louisiana choupique caviar are the stuff of legend. Regardless of the appetizers you order, anticipate an *amuse bouche* from the kitchen to awaken the palate and senses. Entrées are drawn heavily from the sea, including a grilled gulf fish with seafood jambalaya risotto that's good enough to eat solo and the New Orleans-style barbecue shrimp with yaya eggplant fries. Landlubbers can choose from a pan-crisped roasted duck or a beef tenderloin filet with buttermilk mashed potatoes. Sides like the collard greens, jalapeño grits, and the aforementioned potatoes offer a contemporary twist on traditional Southern staples, while the sinful array of desserts tantalizes even the most overfed with doses of sugary perfection. During the summer, the back patio overlooking K Street opens at 4:30 for a deliciously messy crayfish and shrimp boil. Armed with a bucket of chilled Abita Light beer (a New Orleans original, naturally) and a few pounds of both shellfish, killing the humidity of a July evening in D.C. has never been so enjoyable.

INSIDER TIP: *With the Woolly Mammoth Theater and the Shakespeare Theater both situated in the southern region of Chinatown/Penn Quarter, most restaurants in this area offer pre-theater fixed-priced menus, perfect if you're pressed for time.*

CAFÉ ATLANTICO
Executive Chef: Katsuya Fukushima
202-393-0812
www.cafeatlantico.com
405 Eighth St., N.W., Washington, D.C.
20004
Open: Daily
Price: Expensive
Cuisine: South American and Caribbean
Serving: L, D
Credit Cards: AE, D, DC, MC, V
Handicap Access: Yes

Reservations: Yes (especially for Minibar)
Nearest Metro: Archives, Green and Yellow lines

This four-level restaurant just north of the Navy Memorial echoes more than a touch of *Alice in Wonderland* whimsy. The ground floor gives way to a narrow dining room alongside a long bar, while stairs wind around the large rectangular space, first passing the tile-lined, second-floor open kitchen; up to a third floor with seats overlooking the kitchen or Eighth Street; then upward to the top floor, a more intimate, low-lit collection of tables. Like its architecture, the menu offers an eclectic array of Mexican, Spanish, and South American dishes. To heighten the fairy tale vibe, try one of their signature cocktails. Their *caipirinhas* are mixed with a burst of crushed pineapple, and the *pulparindo* combines lemon vodka and fresh tamarind with *piloncillo* syrup. Be sure to sample a few appetizers, particularly the tuna-coconut ceviche with avocado and jicama; and the arugula salad with Cabrales cheese, corn, and raspberry, both of which deliver explosive forkfuls of texture and flavor combinations. Entrées continue the contemporary theme, from the Cornish hen with *mole* and watermelon to a deconstructed *feijao tropeiro*, a Brazilian classic of beans, pork, rice, oranges, and collard greens. Better still, opt for a tasting menu and let Chef Fukushima take you on a culinary tour of his inspirations. The wine list is exhaustive, and the dessert list will convince you that maybe you do have enough room for the house-made seasonal sorbet. The third-floor **Minibar**, meanwhile, remains one of Café Atlantico's chief draws. With just eight seats arranged in front of a narrow bar, this is part theater, part dining experience. Two chefs (or more) serve the willing patrons about 30 small-plate concoctions like "tumbleweeds" of fried, stringed beets; conch fritters with caviar; and a caramelized "liquid" olive that explodes on your tongue. The brainchild of José Andrés, rising Food Network celeb and the executive chef behind D.C.'s Jaleo (see page 182), Minibar is *the* must-dine spot for adventurous gourmands in D.C. If you are intrigued, plan well in advance. Prix-fixe seats have a one-month waiting list.

DC COAST

Executive Chef: Jeff Tunks
202-216-5988
www.dccoast.com
1401 K St., N.W., Washington, D.C. 20005
Open: Monday–Saturday
Price: Expensive
Cuisine: American
Serving: L, D
Credit Cards: AE, D, DC, MC, V
Handicap Access: Yes
Reservations: Recommended
Nearest Metro: McPherson Square, Blue and Orange lines

The first thing you see when entering Executive Chef Tunks's flagship restaurant is the oversized mermaid. It makes for an apt first impression; DC Coast is of the sea, and the portions are bountiful. Hometown hero Chef de Cuisine Travis Timberlake imbues everything on the menu with a playful, contemporary twist, from appetizers like Buffalo-style crispy fried oysters to cast-iron-steamed Blue Hill mussels with Lemoncello thyme cream. The entrées continue the oceanic love affair: grilled yellowfin tuna Nicoise with roasted fingerling potatoes, and the pistachio-crusted Atlantic salmon on a bed of saffron couscous are two particular successes. But nonseafood lovers also benefit from Timberlake's skills. The seared pork chop with sweet potatoes, green beans, and fruit chutney alone is worth the reservation. At first glance, the Art Deco interior can seem a bit too bustling, but when you find your table in the sizable dining room, the angled mirrors

DC Coast's graceful mermaid statue at the entrance to Jeff Tunks's flagship restaurant. Photo by Fredde Lieberman. Used with permission.

afford panoramic views of the action and the setting becomes surprisingly intimate. This is in part thanks to the servers, who offer enough attention to make you feel like a visiting dignitary without becoming overbearing. Small touches like a gratis *amuse bouche* help to dilute the cushy-yet-corporate vibe, and desserts like the crispy chocolate Gianduja bar with salted-caramel ice cream and poached kumquats or warm and gooey beignets ensure that you'll leave sated.

JALEO

Executive Chef: José Andrés
202-628-7949
www.jaleo.com
480 Seventh St., N.W., Washington, D.C. 20002
Open: Daily
Price: Moderate
Cuisine: Spanish
Serving: L, D
Credit Cards: AE, D, DC, MC, V
Handicap Access: Yes

Reservations: Recommended
Nearest Metro: Gallery Place/Chinatown,
Green, Red, and Yellow lines

One of the *tapas* (small-plate) pioneers in
the District, this large restaurant at Seventh
and E Streets has kept things fresh and
exciting since it opened in April 1993—a
commendable feat given the now-ubiqui-
tous presence of small plates in the area.
Much of this continued success rests on
Executive Chef Andrés. The menu boasts
more than 50 tapas divided into cold, hot,
and seasonal. Mainstays like grilled house-
made chorizo on a bed of mashed potatoes
sit next to marinated-fried shark, sweet
peppers stuffed with goat cheese and mushrooms, and a crisp green apple and
Manchego cheese salad. Andrés also offers a
variety of proper Spanish entrées, including
seared salmon with sautéed spinach, pine
nuts, raisins, and apples; and four types of
paella. Beverages include the delicious
(read: dangerous) sangria and a robust wine
list, with a vast variety of whites without
oak. And if you go the tapas route, best hold

Jaleo's José Andrés, one of D.C.'s pioneer chefs. Photo by
Lourdes Delgado. Used with permission.

on to a menu—you'll likely go back to peruse
the options for one more dish... or three,
and give over to the Spanish translation of
this restaurant's name: uproar, revelry, and
merrymaking. Also located in Arlington,
Virginia (703-413-8181) and Bethesda,
Maryland (301-913-0003).

INSIDER TIP: *Jaleo is perfect for parties of three
or more. The dishes arrive when they're ready,
and the shared-dining experience lends to a
convivial atmosphere.*

MATCHBOX

Chef: Jonathan McArthur
202-289-4441
www.matchboxdc.com
713 H St., N.W., Washington, D.C. 20001
Open: Daily
Price: Moderate
Cuisine: Italian
Serving: L, D
Credit Cards: AE, MC, V
Handicap Access: Yes
Reservations: Recommended
Nearest Metro: Gallery Place/Chinatown,
Green, Red, and Yellow lines

Forget NYC-style pies; this narrow, multi-
leveled establishment, which describes
itself as a "vintage pizza bistro," serves
some of the city's best wood-oven gourmet
pizza, along with a heady list of pasta. But its
fame rests equally on one appetizer: the
mini-hamburgers, tiny, handcrafted patties
of Angus beef on toasted brioche with a
slice of pickle served in orders of three, six,
and nine alongside lightly battered onion
rings. Most gravitate toward house specialties like the pizza called Fire and Smoke,
which comes with fire-roasted red peppers,
sweet onions, chipotle pepper, tomato
sauce, smoked gouda, and fresh basil. Vegetarians, meanwhile, can sate themselves
with the fresh portobello pie with marinated artichoke, fresh garlic puree, olive
oil, and mozzarella; or the veggie with

Oyamel's decor features a festive use of traditional Day of the Dead imagery. Photo by Pablo Deloy. Used with permission.

sautéed cremini mushrooms, sweet onion, roasted red peppers, and a healthy dose of stringy mozzarella. The exposed-brick walls, framed matchbooks on the walls, and a 150-seat outdoor patio (a Chinatown first) reinforce the bistro vibe, while an impressive variety of beer and wine pulls a steady group of loyalists.

OYAMEL COCINA MEXICANA

Chef: Joe Raffa
202-628-1005
www.oyamel.com
401 Seventh St., N.W., Washington, D.C. 20004
Open: Daily
Price: Moderate
Cuisine: Mexican, South American
Serving: L, D
Credit Cards: AE, D, DC, MC, V
Handicap Access: Yes
Reservations: Recommended
Nearest Metro: Gallery Place/Chinatown, Green, Red, and Yellow lines

Oyamel takes Mexican street food to the next level. And, lest you forget their point of inspiration, there's a live Web-cam feed of an actual street in Mexico City projected on one wall. In keeping with the theme of bite-sized dishes, most of the menu is composed of *antojitos,* or small plates, divided into salads, seafood, meats, and veggie dishes. Try the baby cactus salad with tomatoes in a lime dressing alongside seared salmon with a green *mole* sauce, or fried potatoes in a *mole poblano* sauce of almonds, chilies, and a touch of chocolate. But some of the kitchen's most inventive touches await in Oyamel's famed handmade tortilla tacos. Options vary from the contemporary (grilled marinated chicken breast with guacamole) to the inventive (sautéed seasonal wild mushrooms with garlic and shallots) to the traditional (braised oxtail with tomatoes, braised beef tongue with radishes, and a confit of baby pig with green tomatillo sauce) to the legendary (the Oaxacan specialty of sautéed grasshoppers with shallots, garlic, and tequila). A terra-cotta ceviche bar serves up five versions of this cold seafood appetizer, and a variety of soups and entrées round out the menu along with bottled Coke imported from Mexico and *aguas frescas*—some of the best fruit juices going.

RASIKA

Chef: Vikram Sunderam
202-637-1222
www.rasikarestaurant.com
633 D St., N.W., Washington, D.C. 20004
Open: Monday–Friday
Price: Moderate
Cuisine: Indian
Serving: L, D
Credit Cards: AE, D, DC, MC, V
Handicap Access: Yes
Reservations: Recommended
Nearest Metro: Archives, Green and Yellow lines

Rasika (the word means "flavors" in Sanskrit) takes traditional Indian cuisine in new directions. The restaurant's chic interior instantly separates it from typical curry-and-samosas expectations. Low lights, electro-lounge music, saffron-colored walls, brushed wood floors, red curtains, strings of dangling jewels, and an all-tile kitchen evoke the Mumbai of today, not tradition. And the menu complements the setting. The flash-fried baby spinach should be a requisite order for every table; cooked for a heartbeat, it literally melts in your mouth and primes you for what's to come. Some of the entrées that depart South Asia are a bit hit-and-miss, but when D.C.-by-way-of-London Chef Sunderam gets it right, the food is a revelation. Goan halibut curry, barbecued mango shrimp, a perfectly spiced wild boar vindaloo: The menu's a complex dance of sweet and spice. It comes as no surprise that vegetarians have their pick of delicacies, from a street-food-inspired *chaat* of avocado, mango, and

papaya to the *tawa baingan*—grilled eggplant with spiced potato and olive oil in peanut sauce. Pairing a wine with such a revolutionary mix of flavors proves challenging, but a sizable wine list—and a refreshingly informed staff—level the playing field while leaving room for surprises.

TENPENH

Executive Chef: Jeff Tunks
202-393-4500
www.tenpenh.com
1001 Pennsylvania Ave., Washington, D.C. 20004
Open: Daily
Price: Expensive
Cuisine: Asian
Serving: L, D
Credit Cards: AE, D, DC, MC, V
Handicap Access: Yes
Reservations: Recommended
Nearest Metro: Federal Triangle, Blue and Orange lines

Nestled on the ground floor of an unassuming office building and close to both the theater district and the National Mall (at Tenth and Pennsylvania—hence the name), this stylish gem personifies the best in contemporary Asian cuisine. Subdued lights,

TenPenh's whole fish is sumptuously graceful on the plate. Photo by Fredde Lieberman. Used with permission.

stretches of colorful silk, teak furniture, and a collage of Japanese hanging lanterns hovering over the elevated main dining room set an elegant mood. The menu takes you on a culinary tour of Thailand, China, and Vietnam, with detours provided by Chef Cliff Wharton's modern touch. Don't miss the Kobe beef tartare, a brisk, heavenly mixture of flavors crowned with a fried quail egg, or the wok-seared calamari, which adds a punch of heat amid a salad of tatsoi greens, lime, and toasted cashews. Signature fish entrées like the red Thai curry shrimp, artfully served with golden pineapple and steamed jasmine rice, live up to the expectations bred by the tasteful decor. But be sure to consider one of several nightly specials like the 1.5-pound lobster dish served on a bed of fried spinach. Desserts like the made-to-order cinnamon donuts or the warm ginger lemongrass pound cake ensure a decadent end to the evening. To best experience TenPenh, fortify your constitution by selecting the proper evolution of beverages: Start with a signature cocktail like the Asian pear mojito, pair the food with a bottle from the vast and worldly wine list, and finish up with a chilled Vietnamese coffee—a mix of espresso and condensed cream that'll give you the energy you need to walk away from such a decadent feast.

ZAYTINYA

Owner: José Andrés
202-638-0800
www.zaytinya.com
701 Ninth St., N.W., Washington, D.C. 20001
Open: Daily
Price: Moderate
Cuisine: Middle Eastern, Mediterranean
Serving: L, D
Credit Cards: AE, D, DC, MC, V
Handicap Access: Yes
Reservations: Recommended
Nearest Metro: Gallery Place/Chinatown, Green, Red, and Yellow lines

Ignore the gaudy statue in front of this expansive restaurant and go straight inside. The moment the scene hits you—the scent of fresh bread, the clatter of cocktail shakers, the sound of sizzling lamb, the soothing candlelight glow—you're transformed. And that's even before you see the belly dancer. The menu consists of *mezze,* the term for small plates in the Mediterranean and Middle East, inviting a communal dining experience. Steaming cones of airy bread come to the table almost instantly, ready to be torn into and dipped in a mixture of olive oil and . . . wait, is that pomegranate? The mezze themselves are divided among veggies, seafood, meats, and seasonal dishes, and despite their diminutive size, each is a treasure, from homemade Mahanek sausages of lamb and beef to the chicken with orzo in a tomato sauce and the sautéed shrimp with dill and shallots. The menu boasts more than 70 mezze, and the indecisive are well advised to ask for recommendations. A sweeping dining room; a tiered, second-floor balcony; and a wide, long bar complete a chic scene more at home in Manhattan, and the cocktails and wine list match that expectation. To avoid geographic displacement (and to enjoy the fresh air when D.C.'s weather permits), target a seat outside, within shouting distance of the National Museum of American Art.

INSIDER TIP: *Adventurous eaters should absolutely visit the Chinatown/Penn Quarter neighborhood, which features Oyamel's Tacos de Chapulines (sautéed grasshoppers), or up the ante with Full Kee's traditional Chinese dishes like sea cucumber, sautéed frog, cold jellyfish, and pig skin with duck blood.*

ZOLA

Chef: Franco Morales
202-654-0999
www.zoladc.com
800 F St., N.W., Washington, D.C. 20004
Open: Daily

Price: Moderate
Cuisine: American
Serving: L Monday–Friday; D daily
Credit Cards: AE, D, DC, MC, V
Handicap Access: Yes
Reservations: Recommended
Nearest Metro: Gallery Place/Chinatown, Green, Red, and Yellow lines

Taking its aesthetic cue from the neighboring Spy Museum, Zola evokes a playful '60s vibe that's more chic than kitsch. Details like spy holes that look into the kitchen, declassified intelligence documents pressed between Plexiglas on the walls, and a back stairway that leads to the Spy Museum reinforce the playful theme. But the quality of food elevates Zola beyond mere gimmick. Chef Morales's dishes perfectly merge traditional with gourmet, resulting in such wholesome fare as the lunch-fave lobster mac and cheese, and dinner entrées like the sweet garlic-glazed chicken with eggplant, zucchini, tomato, and onions; or prosciutto-seared skate wing with blue crab, cured Virginia ham, and pasta pearls. A sleek hallway leads to a mirrored wall that swings open like a secret door from *Get Smart,* revealing the bathrooms. Expect large crowds during happy hour (and sometimes into the wee hours); the drinks, while pricey, are expertly poured, and appetizers like the famed tuna tartare or the "no fuss" mussels with ham, tomatoes, arugula, lemon, and garlic keep Zola's regulars coming back.

DUPONT CIRCLE AND FOGGY BOTTOM
BISTRO DU COIN
Owners: Yannis Felix and Michel Verdon
202-234-6969
www.bistrotducoin.com
1738 Connecticut Ave., N.W., Washington, D.C. 20009
Open: Daily except Labor Day
Price: Moderate
Cuisine: French
Serving: L Monday–Friday; D daily

Credit Cards: AE, MC, V
Handicap Access: Yes
Reservations: Recommended
Nearest Metro: Dupont Circle, Red line

Although this bistro sits just north of Dupont Circle, if you squint your eyes you'd swear you were on the Left Bank. Sepia lighting that evokes the stain of nicotine sans the smell, tall ceilings cluttered with Parisabilia, free-flowing wine, a zinc-covered bar, and a main dining room packed with parchment-covered tables and giddy diners reinforce the blissful state of geographic displacement. The encyclopedic menu offers loads of options, but we suggest you start with a salad of grilled asparagus and artichoke hearts, or the warm goat cheese salad with walnuts, then graduate to the restaurant's true draw: one—or several—of the 10 steamed mussel dishes. Traditional (white wine, garlic, and fennel) or less conventional (pesto with French ham and prosciutto), large order or small, each dish comes steaming and drenched in broth tasty enough to drink, along with bread for dipping and an order of *frites.* The menu also boasts a large array of entrées like the hanger steak with béarnaise sauce; appetizers that include a variety of house-made pâtés; and rich desserts. And although service is occasionally abrupt—perhaps intentionally evoking one of France's less commendable traits—the buzzing, convivial atmosphere makes Bistro du Coin one of D.C.'s most successful, evenly priced restaurants.

MALAYSIA KOPITIAM
Owners: Leslie and Penny Phoon
202-833-6232
www.malaysiakopitiam.com
1827 M St., N.W., Washington, D.C. 20036
Open: Monday–Saturday
Price: Inexpensive
Cuisine: Malay
Serving: L, D

Credit Cards: MC, V
Handicap Access: No
Reservations: No
Nearest Metro: Farragut North, Red line

Malaysia's geography has resulted in one of the world's most intoxicating cuisines: a flavorful mixture of Indian and Chinese with traditional Malay influences. The decor of this basement-level restaurant transports you from the bustle of M Street into an otherworldly realm of leaf-covered roofs and servers adorned in brightly colored dresses. Start with a traditional Malay appetizer of *rota canai*, a thin, Indian-style bread served with a creamy curry chicken dipping sauce, or several of the *satay* skewers, perfectly grilled chunks of chicken, pork, or beef on bamboo shoots, served alongside a tangy, peppery peanut sauce with cucumbers, and fresh onion. You could make a full meal from this section of the menu alone (as most vegetarian patrons tend to do), but then you'd miss spicy entrées like tamarind squid with pineapples, okra, and red onion, or the beef rending, curried meat simmered in a thick sauce of coconut milk and spices. The noodle dishes and soups are also treasures—the sweet-and-spicy *assam laksa* soup in particular raises the concept of a spicy broth with tuna and noodles to new culinary heights. To end, order the sticky rice with fresh mango in sweet coconut milk, or try one of their famed shaved-ice desserts like the ice *kachang*, a dizzying mixture of kidney beans, creamed corn, gelatin, evaporated milk, and palm sugar served on a crisp bed of ice. Trust us: The list of ingredients doesn't do justice to the spectacular tastes.

OBELISK
Owner: Peter Pastan
202-872-1180
2029 P St., N.W., Washington, D.C. 20036
Open: Tuesday–Saturday
Price: Expensive

Cuisine: Italian
Serving: D
Credit Cards: DC, MC, V
Handicap Access: Yes
Reservations: Yes
Nearest Metro: Dupont Circle, Red line

The five-course, fixed-price menu at this restaurant is derived solely from the freshest, locally grown ingredients, which has translated into some of the city's best Italian countryside cooking for more than 20 years. Chef Jerry Corso typically starts with an antipasta course like a zesty octopus salad, slices of house-cured meats, or heirloom tomatoes with aged mozzarella drizzled with Tuscan olive oil. This sets the tone for the dishes to come, like bluefin tuna on roasted peppers, or lamb chops alongside fresh pasta. Guests choose between two or three dishes per course, and each dish comes mostly unadorned to let the natural flavors shine through. After the third course, you've got a cheese plate to consume, followed by a sinfully simple dessert like panna cotta with fresh fruit or one of the house-baked pastries. Despite the apparent formality of the meal, the dining experience itself is thoroughly casual.

PESCE
Owner: Regine Palladin
202-466-FISH
www.pescebistro.com
2016 P St., N.W., Washington, D.C. 20036
Open: Daily
Price: Moderate
Cuisine: Seafood
Serving: L, D Monday–Friday; D Saturday–Sunday
Credit Cards: AE, D, DC, MC, V
Handicap Access: Yes
Reservations: For lunch; for dinner only for parties of six or more
Nearest Metro: Dupont Circle, Red line

Although *pesce* is the Italian word for fish, this tiny seafood bistro has French flair,

Come to Pesce's at lunchtime and expect to see fresh fish being delivered by the crateload. Photo by Debbie K. Hardin.

thanks to gracious owner Regine Palladin, who knows many of her customers by name. The small town house storefront is decorated with brightly colored wooden fish art and strung with twinkling lights. A cozy bar tucked into the back offers an eclectic wine menu, and tiny tables packed tightly into the space are sunny with the colors of Provence. The large menu changes daily and comes to the table printed on a poster-sized blackboard; thankfully, the friendly servers give guests ample time to decide. Although there are a few vegetarian options—like seasonal melon soup with mint and fresh greens—seafood predominates. Light and flavorful starters include the well-seasoned tuna tartare served with black olive tapenade and, when available, crispy soft-shell crabs plated with a lemony chopped avocado—

among the best soft shells we've tasted in the city. Entrées vary with the catch of the day, but when you can find it, don't miss the rockfish in a carrot-ginger sauce served with potatoes and baby veggies. Also worth noting are the whole-fish options, especially when roasted in a salt crust. Desserts are presented artistically and include freshly made ice creams and sorbets and an assortment of delectable tarts. Valet parking is available starting at 6 PM.

RESTAURANT NORA

Chef: Nora Pouillon
202-462-5143
www.noras.com
2132 Florida Ave., N.W., Washington, D.C. 20008
Open: Monday–Saturday
Price: Expensive
Cuisine: American
Serving: D
Credit Cards: AE, MC, V
Handicap Access: Yes
Reservations: Yes
Nearest Metro: Dupont Circle, Red line

As America's first certified-organic restaurant, D.C.'s Nora qualifies as a true culinary pioneer. And this flagship restaurant has not lost its touch. The main dining room was once a 19th-century grocery store, but the entire property—from the red exterior bricks to the museum decor in the several small rooms branching off the main dining area—echoes the charm of D.C.'s row houses. The menu, however, is thoroughly contemporary. Since 95 percent of the menu *must* come from all-organic sources for the restaurant to qualify as "all-organic," the dishes rotate daily. Best, then, to go for the four-course tasting menu (veggie or meat) and let the artistry unfold. À la carte, consider an antipasta or salad to start. The ridiculously fresh flavors will encourage you to pace yourself for what's to follow, from meat dishes like grass-fed rib eye, to the

Tokyo hot pot of shichimi-crusted tofu, udon noodles, and crispy yams, while the desserts offer universally fresh confections of fruit pies, tarts, and cakes.

VIDALIA
Chef: Jeffrey Buben
202-659-1990
www.vidaliadc.com
1990 M St., N.W., Washington, D.C. 20036
Open: Daily
Price: Expensive
Cuisine: American, Southern
Serving: L, D Monday–Friday; D Saturday–Sunday only
Credit Cards: AE, D, MC, V
Handicap Access: Yes
Reservations: Recommended
Nearest Metro: Farragut North, Red line

This sophisticated Southern gem is hidden below ground in a noisy business corridor of downtown, and from the moment guests step inside the calm, friendly space, it's clear that this is meant to be a calming sanctuary. Visitors can slow down and enjoy the whimsical artwork and brightly glazed pottery that decorate the space, which is saturated with the browns, greens, and golden yellow shades of Vidalia onions. The dining room is a modern, formal space, broken into intimate sections to allow for private conversations. Menus change regularly, but whatever the offerings, Chef Buben's refined Southern comfort food provides a fusion of hominess and glamour; a friend notes that "this is the food your Southern Grandma would serve—if she took cooking lessons in New York City." Start with home-style corn bread and popovers served with a sweet-savory onion jam. When available, do not miss the remarkable chicken noodle soup, served with house-made linguini and a poached egg; the fortifying broth is added theatrically at the table. Other specialties of the house include the creamy shrimp and grits and the "What's

Up, Doc," a rabbit loin and sweetbread sausage served with a carrot-ginger puree. As when eating at any good Southerner's place, be sure to save room for dessert. Pastry Chef Caitlin Kelly's lemon chess pie is not to be missed—rich and sweet but not cloying, and served with a tiny vanilla meringue and huckleberry gelée. A recent renovation to the restaurant added an extensive wine bar up front, where guests can order more than 30 vintages by the glass and partake of an extensive bar menu as well.

Georgetown
1789 RESTAURANT
Chef: Nathan Beauchamp
202-965-1789
www.1789restaurant.com
1226 36th St., N.W., Washington, D.C. 20007
Open: Daily
Price: Expensive
Cuisine: American
Serving: D
Credit Cards: AE, D, DC, MC, V
Handicap Access: Yes
Reservations: Recommended
No Metro access

A Georgetown establishment since it opened in 1960, this converted town house echoes the city's storied past, when men wouldn't think of dining without a dinner jacket (and yes, that dress code is still politely enforced). Each of the six dining rooms in this narrow building retains a distinctive, historical flair, from Civil War-era prints in the Manassas Room to the Currier and Ives prints, paintings of nearby Georgetown University, and framed maps of D.C. in its infancy on the walls of the John Carroll Room. The staff is attentive and formal, yet comfortable enough to read the temper of its customers and act accordingly, whether they're visiting dignitaries, a couple celebrating their 30th wedding anniversary, or two college kids learning the art of

1789's John Carroll Room. Photo by Ron Blunt. Used with permission.

credit card debt before a formal dance. Chef Beauchamp, rated by *Gourmet* magazine as one of the country's rising stars, manages to infuse a touch of contemporary flair in the largely classical American seasonal cuisine. The surprisingly subtle mix of flavors in first- and second-course options—like the steak tartare with quail egg or the veal short rib with grilled corn—reinvents the dishes without divorcing them from their time-honored legacy. Lamb comes cooked to perfection, crusted in pancetta on a bed of goat cheese potato mousseline.

BISTRO FRANÇAIS
Owner: Gerard Cabrol
202-338-3830

www.bistrofrancaisdc.com
3128 M St., N.W., Washington, D.C. 20007
Open: Daily
Price: Moderate
Cuisine: French
Serving: L, D
Credit Cards: AE, MC, V
Handicap Access: Yes
Reservations: No
No Metro access

Tiny tables are pushed so close together that it's hard to avoid eavesdropping on one's fellow diners; dark wood paneling and gold-painted metal tiles line the ceilings and walls; and overly loud French music is piped in: Is it a bistro in Montmartre? One

A graceful crudo at Hook. Photo by Chris Eiehler. Used with permission.

might believe so, especially after perusing the menu, which features standard French café fare like rustic French onion soup, garlicky *moules Nicoise* (mussels baked with tomatoes, butter, and black olives), and *coq au vin de Bourgogne* (juicy chunks of chicken cooked in red wine). Dessert choices include old favorites like crème brûlée with a paper-thin topping of burnt sugar, swirls of velvety chocolate mousse, and shimmering fruit tarts. Most dishes are quite respectable, although the kitchen has trouble delivering meats to the requested doneness (skirt steaks, especially, tend to be overcooked). Any remaining similarity to a bistro in Paris truly ends with the service, however, which is courteous and fast, and also with the prices, which are completely reasonable. Order an "early-bird special" (5–7 on weekdays) for only \$20, which includes a glass of house wine, soup of the day, an entrée, and a dessert.

CLYDE'S

Owner: Stuart Davidson and John Laytham
202-333-9180
www.clydes.com
3236 M St., N.W., Washington, D.C. 20007

Open: Daily
Price: Moderate
Cuisine: American
Serving: L, D (brunch on Sunday)
Credit Cards: AE, D, DC, MC, V
Handicap Access: Yes
Reservations: Recommended for dinner
No Metro access

Clyde's in Georgetown opened its doors in the early '60s as a saloon catering to college students and businessmen, and at that point its food was little more than an afterthought. The beloved "Railroad Bar"—a 1917 wooden beauty salvaged from an old hotel in Baltimore—continues to dominate the narrow, cacophonous main dining room of Clyde's, where guests will also find gleaming wood booths and wood-paneled walls thick with sporting-themed art and collectibles. Although Clyde's is still a popular bar, these days the food's the thing. The restaurant serves to a capacity crowd every night, attracting tourists and locals alike to enjoy its famous spicy chili and generous portions of crab cakes. Clyde's also offers steaks, burgers, and oversized salads. Be sure to notice the hardworking waitstaff, who are specially trained by Clyde's to maneuver with as many as six dishes of steaming food stacked from their shoulders to their wrists, a signature style of service developed because the restaurant is too narrow to carry large trays. This successful local chain also has outlets in Chinatown, as well as the suburbs of Maryland (Chevy Chase and Columbia), and Virginia (Alexandria, Reston, Tysons Corner, and Vienna).

HOOK
Executive Chef: Barton Seaver
202-625-4488
www.hookdc.com
3241 M St., N.W., Washington, D.C. 20007
Open: Daily
Price: Expensive
Cuisine: Seafood
Serving: B, L, D
Credit Cards: AE, MC, V
Handicap Access: Yes
Reservations: Recommended
No Metro access

Simplicity can be tricky. Minimal decor, food served with subdued flair without the bells and whistles of nouveau garnish, and a modest selection of entrées rather than an encyclopedic list may leave diners feeling like they're missing out. But Hook hits all marks, marrying complex cooking with refreshingly flavorful, simple results. Young Executive Chef Seaver founded the restaurant in April 2007 on one central philosophy: Serve only seafood species not threatened by overfishing. As a result, expect dishes you've never encountered, like weakfish, Arctic char, and bluefish. Lest you get lost in a sea of unfamiliarity, your server offers a curt explanation of the texture, taste, and appearance of the fish on offer, making the meal part feast, part education on sustainable fishing practices. Start with a flight of three crudo, an Italian spin on sushi, like salmon with a slice of

Fuji apple, before moving on to appetizers like the house-made ham plate or the grilled calamari salad. Entrées are decidedly focused on seafood (on a recent visit only the grass-fed sirloin and a saffron risotto originated from terra firma), but the fish is amazingly fresh; Seaver is said to get text messages from Tobago fishermen, telling him what they've caught so he can start to plan that night's menu. If the culinary menu is minimal, the wine and champagne lists are voluminous. But whatever you order, save space for dessert. Finishers like the brown butter almond cake or the pineapple carpaccio with basil ice cream demand more than one demure forkful. In keeping with the clean and simple approach, the entire kitchen sits in plain view (typically, Seaver himself will deliver the entrées to your table).

MICHEL RICHARD CITRONELLE
Executive Chef: Michel Richard
202-625-2150
www.citronelledc.com
3000 M St., N.W., Washington, D.C. 20007
Open: Daily, except closed Sunday in July and August
Price: Very expensive
Cuisine: French
Serving: D
Credit Cards: AE, D, DC, MC, V
Handicap Access: Yes
Reservations: Required well in advance
No Metro access

Tucked into the basement of the unassuming Latham Hotel in the heart of Georgetown, Michel Richard Citronelle is considered to be among the finest restaurants in the world—and hands-down the pinnacle of fine dining in D.C. Chef Richard has accumulated dozens of prestigious accolades over the years, including a spot on *Gourmet* magazine's "Top Twenty Restaurants in the Country" and inclusion in the prestigious *Les Grandes Tables du Monde,* an honor given to little more than a dozen restaurants in the United States. Not surprisingly, it is exceedingly difficult to get a table here, and reservations are recommended *at least* two weeks in advance. But once inside, guests will find Citronelle a surprisingly comfortable, accessible place. Except for an intriguing wall of light that slowly cycles through the colors of the rainbow, the understated interior offers a neutral palette. This elegant restraint puts the focus where it belongs: on the gleaming open kitchen, bustling with an astonishing number of skilled chefs, choreographed by the masterful Chef Richard. Nothing short of a culinary genius, Richard—a delightful teddy bear of a man—is quick to visit and joke with his guests, be they star-struck tourists or some of the most powerful people in D.C. Maitre d' extraordinaire Jean Jacques Retourne oversees the formal yet friendly service, and world-renown sommelier Mark Slater is available to guide patrons through the exhaustive wine list.

The power of the space and its inhabitants is palpable, but all else pales when the food arrives. Presentation is impeccable and artful, and the dishes are sublime, prepared with ingenuity, passionate attention to detail, and a sensuality not often seen in this otherwise button-down city. Menu offerings change daily, which gives Richard's creativity full reign and allows the freshest ingredients to shine. Cuisine is a fusion of French and new Californian, with nods to myriad global influences. Pricey dining options include a three-course meal, which starts with a playful *amuse bouche* (a little taste of something special from the chef); an appetizer that might include a heavenly salad made from lobster and tiny pearls of squid ink pasta presented whimsically in a caviar tin, or a chestnut soup swirling around a delicate island of duck *confit*; an entrée that could include perfectly moist *sous vide* Alaskan halibut served with a tantalizing lemon-tomato relish, or Maine lobster with a colorful Creole-inspired sauce and miniature vegetable gnocchi; and finally fanciful desserts like a chocolate sampler of sorbet, pastries, and truffles or a cloudlike citrus soufflé accompanied by house-made ice cream and paper-thin almond cookies. For an extra charge, foodies will get a kick out of eating at the chef's table, which is *inside* the revered kitchen—but be sure to reserve *far* in advance for this indulgence.

MIE N YU

Chef: Tim Elliott
202-333-6122
www.mienyu.com
3125 M St., N.W., Washington, D.C. 20007
Open: Daily, except closed Sunday in July and August
Price: Moderate
Cuisine: Asian
Serving: L Wednesday–Friday; D daily (brunch on weekends)
Credit Cards: AE, D, DC, MC, V
Handicap Access: Yes
Reservations: Recommended
No Metro access

Like its punny name, Mie N Yu comes close to being *too* clever for its own good; in lesser hands, the Silk Road decor could become some kind of Asian-infused Epcot Center. But somehow the low lights, driftwood chairs, red velvet walls, crystal chandeliers, golden statues of Hindu gods, a belly dancer whirling through the dining rooms, hanging lanterns, silk-draped tables, a huge wooden goddess sculpture, a Tibetan lounge, tables resting in giant bird cages tucked next to a revolving staircase—even the bathrooms, a series of unisex rooms centered around communal sinks, the water trickling through bamboo pipes into barrels lined with smooth river stones—all work. The end result? This is the place you'll be telling your friends about. Like the decor, the seasonal menu derives

Even the unisex bathroom at Mie N Yu impresses. Photo by Michael Moran. Used with permission.

its influences from Asia, North Africa, and sprinkles of America and the Mediterranean. A variety of chef's tastings let you try Chef Elliott's more inventive recipes, like watermelon gazpacho, grilled beef tataki, or the tuna tartare, a leaning tower of fiery habañero and cool, raw ahi. Entrées (or proteins, as they're labeled on the menu) follow the restaurant's world bent in rewarding dishes like red curry scallops with tomatoes and okra, and the blueberry encrusted lamb loin with truffled wild-mushroom flan. The 350-plus-bottle wine list is presented in magazine format, transforming the task of locating that perfect bottle into equal measures education and discovery. Expect to see large crowds, especially on weekends, when the chill, low-lit lounge pulls a steady stream of well-dressed scenesters and college kids sipping ginger-infused cocktails.

INSIDER TIP: *For a romantic tête-à-tête with all the chic underpinnings, make a reservation for one of Mie N Yu's secluded tables that are wonderfully removed from the rest of the circus-like restaurant. Or just tuck yourselves away at the lounge and order from the chef's tasting menu.*

Look for the unfurled flags in the heart of Georgetown, and you've found Old Glory.
Photo by Debbie K. Hardin.

OLD GLORY

Owner: Capitol Restaurant Concepts
202-337-3406
www.oldglorybbq.com
3139 M St., N.W., Washington, D.C. 20007
Open: Daily
Price: Moderate
Cuisine: Barbecue
Serving: L, D (brunch on Sunday)
Credit Cards: AE, D, DC, MC, V
Handicap Access: Yes
Reservations: No
No Metro access

In a city that knows its barbecue, Old Glory stands out from the tie-stained crowd. This rambunctious two-story joint on the main drag of Georgetown boasts butcher paper on the tables, a wooden bar that runs nearly the full length of the place, and Elvis memorabilia to spare. Start with a bowl of piping hot hush puppies and a bottomless glass of sweet tea. Then dig into succulent pulled pork, generous portions of ribs, fork-tender beef brisket, whole chickens, and even slow-cooked lamb—all served "dry"; a half-dozen varieties of house-made sauces based on recipes from around the country stand at the ready so that guests can slather up their orders as they like them. Portions are large, but those with heroic appetites will want to try the down-home banana pudding with vanilla wafers or the spoon-licking-good peach cobbler. Don't worry about getting messy in *this* place: There's a sink smack in the middle of the dining room for guests to tidy up.

ZED'S

Owner: Zed Wondemu
202-333-4710
www.zeds.net
1201 28th St., N.W., Washington, D.C. 20007
Open: Daily
Price: Moderate
Cuisine: Ethiopian
Serving: L, D
Credit Cards: AE, MC, V
Handicap Access: No
Reservations: Yes
No Metro access

Ethiopian eateries are not on every street corner in the U.S.A., but D.C. is blessed with several superb Ethiopian restaurants, including this quaint one on the east end of Georgetown. Zed's is housed in a small converted town house and has dining space upstairs and down. Look out onto overflowing window boxes and the bustle of Georgetown beyond, and look in on an understated interior accented with African art and musical instruments. Be sure to visit Zed's with friends, because dining here is more fun as a communal experience. No utensils are provided; entrées are served on a large, shared platter, and guests tear off small bits of *injera*—a pliable, spongy bread that resembles a delicate pancake—and scoop up the offerings with their fingers. Try the spicy chicken *doro watt,* prepared with red pepper sauce and served with a boiled egg, or the cubed beef *alica* in a buttery herb sauce. Vegetarians will find plenty of choices here as well, including the hearty harvest vegetable specialty with cauliflower, green beans, and carrots, and the chopped collard greens with garlic and onion. Service can be a little distracted, but the waitstaff is friendly and will happily initiate guests who've never enjoyed Ethiopian food before.

U STREET AND THE 14TH STREET CORRIDOR
CAFÉ SAINT EX
Chef: William Klein
202-265-7839
www.saint-ex.com
1847 14th St. N.W., Washington, D.C. 20009
Open: Tuesday—Sunday
Price: Moderate
Cuisine: American

Serving: L Tuesday—Friday, D (brunch on weekends)
Credit Cards: AE, MC, V
Handicap Access: Yes
Reservations: No
Nearest Metro: U Street, Green and Yellow lines

Equal measures restaurant and hip night spot, Café Saint Ex stands out from like-minded establishments populating this stretch of 14th Street. This classic bistro draws its aesthetic inspiration from author-pilot Antoine de Saint-Exupéry, with black-and-white photos of pilots and airplanes, clocks on the wall set to the times of cities around the world, period postcards and posters, and a massive wooden prop. The menu features locally produced, all-organic ingredients, and it shifts with the seasons, but a few of the traditional all-star options include the roasted chicken and the grilled hamburger, made with Virginia grass-fed beef and served alongside a handful of sweet potato fries. Lighter fare includes dishes like duck eillette with grilled rustico

The façade at Saint Ex displays its affection for the aviation aesthetic. Photo by Nathan Borchelt.

and baby arugula, or the fried green tomato BLT with applewood smoked bacon, tomato mayonnaise, and mixed greens. A robust list of beers and wines and a heavy-handed pour on most cocktails serve as the collective foundation for Saint Ex's post-dinner scene—along with **Gate 54**, a friendly downstairs lounge that hosts DJ events and serves as a cool, dark shelter from the summer swelter. Both locals and suburbanites crowd the place, especially on the weekends; if you come for the nightlife and find a line stretching out the door, migrate a few blocks south to **Bar Pilar** (see page 233), Saint Ex's sister pub. A three-course fixed-price theater meal is also available, and open patio seating is offered when the weather cooperates.

COPPI'S

Chef: Elizabeth Bryant
202-319-7773
www.coppisorganic.com
1414 U St., N.W., Washington, D.C. 20009
Open: Daily
Price: Moderate
Cuisine: Italian
Serving: D
Credit Cards: AE, D, DC, MC, V
Handicap Access: Yes
Reservations: Recommended
Nearest Metro: U Street, Green and Yellow lines

Since it opened in 1993, Coppi's has generated some of the city's best, most affordable Northern Italian food. Its success is largely derived from its governing philosophy: Work with local organic farmers and food co-ops, cook what's in season, and always have wine on hand. The brick-oven, Neapolitan-style pizzas are revelations, the crust simultaneously crisp and soft, and each pie is covered with fresh ingredients proportioned so that they complement each other. Antipastas and main courses rotate almost daily and include such stars as sweet parsnip roots oven-fried in olive oil with garlic and parsley, or pasta with smoked wild salmon in a sun-dried tomato, asparagus, and red onion cream sauce. Even better, most of the entrées can also be ordered as an appetizer for half the entrée price. The decor echoes the glory days of the Italian bicycling team and sports Bianchi bike frames, cycling jerseys, and black-and-white photos of Fausto Coppi, the charismatic Italian cycling star who died in 1960 and is the source of the restaurant's name. Low light gives the small dining room an intimate vibe, and there's a tiny bar overlooking the brick oven and pizza-dressing station if you're forced to wait for a table.

TABAQ BISTRO

Owners: Omer and Melih Buyukbayrak
202-483-7669
www.tabaqdc.com
1418 U St., N.W., Washington, D.C. 20009
Open: Tuesday—Sunday
Price: Moderate
Cuisine: Middle Eastern
Serving: D (brunch on weekends)
Credit Cards: AE, MC, V
Handicap Access: No
Reservations: Recommended
Nearest Metro: U Street, Green and Yellow lines

Prepare yourself for a workout. This multilevel Mediterranean restaurant and lounge is crowned by one of the best roof decks in the city, an expansive dining area and full bar encased in glass that can completely retract when the weather cooperates. If you can handle the cardio workout to ascend the four stories to the top, you're rewarded with panoramic views of the Washington Monument and the Capitol dome. The menu comprises more than 40 mezze, or small plates, like seared scallop on a braised tomato, vegetarian specialties like stuffed grape leaves, and the requisite—and routinely successful—lamb and beef dishes. A small smattering of entrées reinforce Tabaq's Middle Eastern roots, like the chicken tangine or the vegetarian trio of tomatoes stuffed with polenta cheese and tomato-basil sauce. And if you've got the time and the appetite, take the waiter's advice and try one of the dessert soufflés. They take 20 minutes to prepare, but the results are sinfully rewarding. Downstairs the interior decor is an even mix of elegant dining and mod-influenced lounge, and the basement-level bar pulls in a well-dressed crowd most weekends. Late-night diners take note: Sometimes the bar and dancing scene can overtake the roof deck.

UPPER NORTHWEST
2 AMYS
Owner: Peter Pastan
202-885-5700
www.2amyspizza.com
3715 Macomb St., N.W., Washington, D.C. 20016
Open: Daily
Price: Moderate
Cuisine: Italian
Serving: L Tuesday–Sunday; D daily
Credit Cards: MC, V
Handicap Access: Yes
Reservations: Recommended
No Metro access

Expect to wait for a table at this neighborhood joint in Tenleytown, because the secret is out: 2 Amys serves some of the best pizza in town, in large part because of their near-religious devotion to creating the perfect Neapolitan pizza, which was formally recognized by the Italian government in 1998 as "a traditional food worthy of preservation." The wafer-thin, crispy pie was thus awarded D.O.C. (*Denominazione di Origine Controllata*) status, meaning that only certain ingredients and methods of preparation are allowed. Only soft-grain flour, fresh yeast, water, and sea salt can be used for the crust, and only Italian plum tomatoes, *mozzarella di bufala*, extra-virgin

olive oil, and fresh basil or dried oregano can be used for the toppings—and all pizzas must be cooked in wood-burning ovens. In addition to the near-perfect D.O.C. pizzas, 2 Amys' menu also boasts a variety of more contemporary pies, stuffed pizza, myriad salads, and a simple array of small plate "little things," like oven-roasted olives, potato-and-prosciutto croquettes, and grilled sardines. And if you get one of the cannolis, homemade ice creams, or sorbets, you'll understand why the tables take a while to turn over. The place is typically noisy, families make ritualized visits each week, the decor is simple and unadorned, and the food is an Italianized slice of heaven.

ARDEO
Chef: Trent Conry
202-244-6750
www.ardeorestaurant.com
3311 Connecticut Ave., N.W., Washington, D.C. 20008
Open: Daily
Price: Moderate
Cuisine: American
Serving: D (brunch on Sunday)
Credit Cards: AE, D, DC, MC, V
Handicap Access: Yes
Reservations: Recommended
Nearest Metro: Cleveland Park, Red line

Elegant and refined, this hip New American bistro in Cleveland Park serves food as confident and effective as its sleek interior. The contemporary menu boasts inventive dishes that align the perfect measure of ingredients. The asparagus and goat cheese appetizer comes wrapped in brick paper with grilled endive, pistachio, and honey-garlic balsamic, while the foie gras is paired with riesling apricots and chipotle syrup. Entrées like the herb-coated salmon with fennel confit, curried apples, and kaffir-almond froth, or the grilled Tasmanian ocean trout with avocado relish and bal-

The vertical wine rack at Ardeo. Photo by Michael Colella. Used with permission.

Price: Moderate
Cuisine: Indian
Serving: L, D
Credit Cards: AE, MC, V
Handicap Access: No
Reservations: Recommended
No Metro access

The latest hybrid Indian fusion cuisine notwithstanding, sometimes you crave a good, earnest curry. Should you be so inclined, look no further than Heritage India. While there are less expensive Indian restaurants around, this formal establishment in upper Georgetown prepares food worth the extra price. The two-story restaurant is a touch bright, and the service is a touch schizophrenic (either disappearing entirely or rushing you from entrée to bill), but one taste and all is forgiven. The samosa appetizers may convince you to forgo your entrée and just re-order another one. Don't, lest you miss the curries, the smoked grouper, the fiery lamb vindaloo, or the tandoor-cooked naan bread, perfect for sopping up the buttery broth of the chicken tikki masala. There's also a Heritage India in Dupont Circle (202-331-1414; www.heritageindiadupont.com; 1337 Connecticut Ave., N.W., Washington), billed as a lounge rather than a full-service restaurant. This second location serves street-food-inspired small plates like *chaat*—a salad of chick peas mixed with spices, tomato, and lime—along with a killer happy hour from 5–7 weekdays, when all dishes are half price.

INSIDER TIP: *Although there's no direct Metro access to the upper northwestern stretches of Wisconsin Avenue restaurants like Heritage India and Sushi-Ko, you can sometimes hop on an American University bus at the Tenleytown Metro stop (Red line) and get to the Glover Park neighborhood.*

samic onions in a citrus-cumin reduction reinforce Ardeo's affection for the ocean, but the consistency of the kitchen ensures that almost anything will be top quality. Not surprisingly, Ardeo has generated a steady following among both visiting politicians and locals who appreciate gourmet food at reasonable prices. During the warmer months, guests can dine on the roof deck. Blue jeans or a coat and tie—both are welcomed by an amiable staff.

HERITAGE INDIA

202-333-3120
www.heritageindiaofgeorgetown.com
2400 Wisconsin Ave., N.W., Washington, D.C. 20007
Open: Daily

LEBANESE TAVERNA

202-265-8681
www.lebanesetaverna.com
2641 Connecticut Ave., N.W., Washington,
D.C. 20008
Open: Daily
Price: Moderate
Cuisine: Lebanese
Serving: L, D
Credit Cards: AE, D, DC, MC, V
Handicap Access: Yes
Reservations: Recommended
Nearest Metro: Woodley Park, Red line

This huge restaurant serves traditional Lebanese meat dishes alongside inventive veggie *mezze* (Lebanese small plates) that keep non-meat-eaters enthusiastic for this local chain. An amiable staff can guide the uninitiated through the encyclopedic menu of salads, dips, breads, small plates, and entrées. The baba ghannouj, an eggplant puree with tahini, lemon juice, and garlic, may qualify as simple culinary heaven spread on a pita, while other traditional small plates like the chick pea falafel or the goat cheese blended with hot paprika served with olives demonstrates why this cuisine has become a global staple. It's best to order several, then decide from a huge selection of main dishes, like the rotisserie-cooked boneless chicken shawarma served with garlic puree and potatoes; the kafta kabob, a mixture of lamb and beef with onions and herbs grilled on a skewer; or the fresh veggie of the day, stuffed with rice, tomato, and pine nuts. Also located in Arlington, Alexandria, and McLean, Virginia; and Annapolis and Baltimore, Maryland.

SUSHI-KO

Chef: Koji Terano
202-333-4187
www.sushiko.us

2309 Wisconsin Ave., N.W., Washington,
D.C. 20007
Open: Daily
Price: Moderate
Cuisine: Japanese
Serving: L, D
Credit Cards: AE, MC, V
Handicap Access: Yes
Reservations: Recommended
No Metro access

Positioned next to a strip club in the unassuming, upper-Georgetown neighborhood of Glover Park, Sushi-Ko has long been regarded as the benchmark for top-notch sushi in the District. And well it should—after all, it's D.C.'s oldest Japanese restaurant. Its menu, however, rests firmly in both the traditional and the thoroughly modern. The miso soup comes with smoked mussels and eggplant; a modest selection of small plates like aged tofu or a rockfish-and-asparagus tempura edge toward the more adventurous side; and a delicate, fresh selection of sashimi, nigiri, charishi, and maki and temaki rolls prove Chef Terano's knife skills are beyond compare. To break from the menu, swap a table at the two-room bilevel dining floor for one of 16 seats at the sushi bar and let Terano's inspiration and the freshest ingredients dictate what appears on your plate. Miss scoring a coveted seat? Then order one of several moriawase, chef-selected dishes from the day's freshest fish. The beverage menu rests heavily on an impressive array of Burgundies and (not surprisingly) sake, along with a small, inventive selection of sake-infused cocktails.

INSIDER TIP: *Be sure to visit the Waterfront region while in D.C. With the new Nationals baseball stadium just opening, this rapidly developing neighborhood will soon attract some of the city's latest and greatest restaurants.*

ARLINGTON, VIRGINIA
CAFÉ PARISIEN EXPRESS
Owners: Yannis and Lydie Stefanopoulos
703-525-3340
4520 Lee Hwy., Arlington, VA 22207
Open: Daily
Price: Inexpensive
Cuisine: French
Serving: B, L, D
Credit Cards: Cash only
Handicap Access: Yes
Reservations: No
No Metro access

This tiny bistro in the Cherrydale neighborhood of Arlington (less than a mile from the Ballston Metro station) offers more authentically European fare than one would expect in the suburbs, thanks to the enthusiasm of French owner Lydie Stefanopoulos and her Greek husband Yannis. The walls are plastered with faded posters of Paris, and the same Édith Piaf CD has been playing for a decade, but the aromas of garlic, butter, and freshly baked pastries wafting from the kitchen are tantalizing. The casual French dishes, served on paper plates to keep down costs, almost never disappoint. Specialties include a rich onion soup; classic quiche served with bacon, spinach, or asparagus; and steak frites, a juicy sirloin with a side of thin fries. As with most French establishments, the desserts here are luscious; look for the decadently rich chocolate mousse and the homemade Madeleines sold by the dozen. The outside patio is a lovely alternative when the weather permits. Service is a bit slow, but always cheerful.

GUAJILLO
703-807-0840
www.waheeyo.com
1727 Wilson Blvd., Arlington, VA 22201
Open: Daily
Price: Inexpensive
Cuisine: Mexican
Serving: L, D
Credit Cards: D, MC, V
Handicap Access: Yes
Reservations: No
Nearest Metro: Courthouse, Orange line

Bright orange walls, a ceiling reminiscent of a crisp spring day, and swaths of cowhide identify this family-owned Arlington restaurant as distinctly south of the border. But rather than rely on sombreros ringed with stale corn chips, Guajillo—named after a chili pepper—has composed a small, confident menu of some of the best Mexican food in the area. Broken into groups like small plates, platters, and Mexican favorites, some of the dishes will ring familiar. But unlike your last burrito or chimichanga, the right touch of ingredients—like chorizo and green salsa—make these entrées hearty, flavorful, and honest. Fajita lovers can choose from beef, chicken, or shrimp, and the sauce on the *mole poblano* is wonderfully complex, a must-have chocolate-and-nut Mexican standard. But perhaps the most successful dishes are the house specials, where the freshest ingredients join forces in unexpected ways, like the duck breast in almond *mole* sauce, an enchilada composed of shrimp and goat cheese, or chunks of grilled chicken and chorizo served in a hollowed-out passilla pepper. You'll never look at Taco Bell the same way again.

LIBERTY TAVERN
Chef: Liam LaCivita
703-465-9363
www.thelibertytavern.com
3195 Wilson Blvd., Arlington, VA 22201
Open: Daily
Price: Moderate
Cuisine: Italian
Serving: D
Credit Cards: AE, D, DC, MC, V
Handicap Access: Yes
Reservations: Necessary
Nearest Metro: Clarendon, Orange line

Liberty Tavern bucked the trend in Clarendon, and instead of knocking down and rebuilding, the owners restored this old brick beauty. Photo courtesy of Liberty Tavern. Used with permission.

This elegant property in the revitalized Arlington neighborhood of Clarendon has a split personality: Downstairs it is a noisy, popular bar where 30-somethings hang out after work. Upstairs it is a noisy, popular restaurant where 30-somethings feast on light, inventive interpretations of Italian classics. Menus change seasonally, but expect bright flavors in unexpected pairings, like a cooling, colorful watermelon salad with fresh tarragon and Smithfield ham, or a hanger steak grilled in a wood-burning oven and served with a black-eyed pea succotash. Inventive pasta dishes can be ordered in half portions and include treats like gnocchi tossed with fava beans and sage and served in a brown butter sauce, or ziti prepared with chard, chilies, and sheep's milk feta. Also worth note are the thin, crispy pizzas with diverse toppings like granny smith apples, Vermont white cheddar, and prosciutto; or grilled chicken and

Getting Crabby in the Capital City

Philadelphia has cheesesteaks; Chicago has deep-dish; San Diego has fish tacos. Washington, D.C., is lucky enough to have it *all*: eclectic ethnic restaurants from around the world as well as American eateries representing the best of just about everyone's hometown. But if you want to get an authentic taste of the mid-Atlantic region, look no farther than Chesapeake Bay blue crabs. During the summer months, you'll find this sweet shellfish in abundance in crab shacks from Baltimore to D.C. Buy them by the half dozen or dozen, depending on size. They'll come to the table steamed a bright red, usually covered with spicy Old Bay seasoning. Don't expect niceties like silverware or even plates at most local crab shacks. Servers bring out the bodacious crustaceans in buckets or barrels and then dump them directly onto tables covered with butcher paper. You'll generally be given a mallet to pound out the stubborn bits, as well as a selection of knives, crackers, and picks. A pitcher of ice cold beer to accompany your bounty is *de rigueur*.

Start by snapping off the legs. There isn't much meat in the skinniest of the appendages, but many folks like to suck out the juices. The pincer claws offer the greatest rewards for the least effort; whack them gently with your mallet to crack the shell (but not so hard that you smash the delicate meat inside), then peel it away to leave a luscious lump of snow-white meat. Once the legs are dispensed with, move on to the body. Turn the crab onto its back, and on the belly you'll see a white apron with a slot in the middle that looks like either the Washington Monument (the males, or "jimmies"—preferred by many connoisseurs because they tend to be meatier) or the U.S. Capitol (the females, or "sooks" or "sallys"). Slip the tip of your knife under these tabs and pry them up like a pop-top. This will lift off the bottom of the crab to reveal a thickish golden substance called "mustard" and spongy white tubes that are the gills (sometimes called "dead man's fingers"). Use a knife to get rid of these. Now you're left to the good stuff: Cut the cartilage down the middle and have at it. You can cut around the shell in an effort to peel off the inedible hard pieces and leave only the lumps of crab, or you can use your knife and picks to pry loose the meat.

It can take hours to pick enough crabs to get a full meal—but it's a messy, festive, communal activity that is well worth the effort. Some of the best crab houses in the region include **The Dancing Crab** (202-244-1882; 4615 Wisconsin Ave., N.W., Washington), **Ernie's Original Crab House** (703-765-1000; 6319 Richmond Hwy., Alexandria), **Phillips Flagship** (202-488-8515; 900 Water St., S.W., Washington), and **The Quarterdeck** (703-528-2722; 1200 N. Fort Meyer Dr., Arlington). If you find yourself loving crab but not loving crab picking, never fear: In season, crab is available prepicked in delicious crab cakes, crab soups, and crab salads, and you'll find it on just about every menu in town.

arugula. Desserts are creative takes on familiar favorites, like a red velvet cake layered with fruit and cream and covered in Italian meringue, or a crème brûlée laced with a touch of fennel. Servers are friendly and accommodating, albeit a little slow. It cannot be stressed enough that this is *not* the place to come for quiet conversation; the din from the bar below as well as from fellow diners in the poorly insulated upstairs dining room can be overwhelming, even as it is a tribute to the popularity of this relatively new business.

RAY'S THE STEAKS

Owner: Michael Landrum
703-841-7297
1725 Wilson Blvd., Arlington, VA 22209
Open: Daily
Price: Inexpensive
Cuisine: American
Serving: L, D

Credit Cards: AE, MC, V
Handicap Access: Yes
Reservations: Recommended
Nearest Metro: Courthouse, Orange line

Consider this a steak house revolution. Not just because the menu or the decor—unadorned walls, no linens—are far cries from the region's more traditional chop houses, but because the price is considerably less than its competitors. The service and quality of the dishes, however, don't reflect the lower price tags. Anticipate lines outside the restaurant's nondescript storefront; they're locals in the know, craving the bone-in rib eye, the filet mignon, or any of the other meats hand-selected, butchered, and aged by owner Michael Landrum. The wait can be long, but the ultra-efficient kitchen gets the dishes out quickly, all entrées come with complimentary sides like creamed spinach, and each bill is accompanied by a chunk of sinfully delicious fudge.

THAI SQUARE

703-685-7040
www.thaisquarerestaurant.com
3217 Columbia Pike, Arlington, VA 22204
Open: Daily
Price: Inexpensive
Cuisine: Thai
Serving: L, D
Credit Cards: AE, MC, V
Handicap Access: Yes
Reservations: No
No Metro access

Consistently described by Southeast Asian ex-pats as *the* best Thai food in the area, this little box-shaped restaurant is a low-cost, high-return treasure. Admittedly, its decor—bright lights that reflect off the glass-surface tables clustered into one small dining room—doesn't inspire confidence. But all is forgiven when your order arrives. Just about everything on the menu delivers, so order a lot—especially traditional dishes like the green papaya salad,

one of several curries, the fried and crispy squid, some sticky rice to numb the spiciness, and either the coconut or lemongrass soup with chicken, which comes in a donut-shaped communal bowl complete with an open flame to keep things warm. As in Bangkok, the food arrives whenever it's ready, and it's best to sample and share—and to ask about the daily specials. The kitchen can adjust the spiciness to accommodate Western palates or amp it to eye-watering levels without sacrificing flavor. The Thai coffee is sure to keep you up long after you depart the restaurant, which is a godsend considering that the sheer amount of food consumed at this inexpensive gem practically guarantees a food coma.

ALEXANDRIA, VIRGINIA
A LA LUCIA

Owner: Michael Nayeri
703-836-5123
www.alalucia.com
315 Madison St., Alexandria, VA 22314
Open: Daily
Price: Moderate
Cuisine: Italian
Serving: L, D
Credit Cards: AE, MC, V
Handicap Access: Yes
Reservations: Recommended
Nearest Metro: Braddock Road, Blue and Yellow lines

In a restaurant landscape that's quickly becoming high on flash, A La Lucia is an understated revelation. Nestled alongside a row of shops on a quiet street in Old Town Alexandria, this small restaurant and wine bar operates with only the freshest ingredients for its traditional southern Italian cuisine. One taste of antipastas like fresh mozzarella and sliced tomatoes with basil, or the roasted pepper with olive oil, capers, and anchovies, and you'll understand why. The menu also boasts a variety of soups and salads, and entrées split between pasta like linguini with shrimp, calamari, and mus-

The interior of Gadsby's Tavern Restaurant shows off its 18th-century splendor. Photo by Debbie K. Hardin.

sels in a spicy white sauce, and fish and seafood dishes, from grilled sea scallops with fresh zucchini to veal scallopini with mushrooms and a Marsala cream sauce. But consider one of a dozen daily specials, which take their lead from the freshest ingredients available that day. The wine list is expansive. The decor and clientele is quite casual, more boisterous than romantic, but silence reigns whenever the desserts arrive. Try either the cannoli, tiramisu, panna cotta, or *moscato zabaglione* with fresh berries. The one thing you're left wanting is an espresso to help muster the energy you need for that eventual, unfortunate departure.

BASTILLE

Chefs: Christophe Poteaux and Michelle Garbee
703-519-3776
www.bastillerestaurant.com

1201 N. Royal St., Alexandria, VA 22314
Open: Wednesday–Sunday
Price: Moderate
Cuisine: French
Serving: L, D (brunch on Sunday)
Credit Cards: AE, MC, V
Handicap Access: Yes
Reservations: Recommended
No Metro access

This contemporary spin on the traditional French bistro takes expected dishes in new, exciting directions—without the accompanying price tag. Small plates are a great place to start, from fresh organic goat cheesecake with a fig compote to the foie-gras crème caramel. Entrées also ring familiar, but most have taken a tour through the Mediterranean thanks to judicious use of spices like fennel and cardamom. The paella is everything that dish should be: a richly textured, flavorful mélange of Spanish chorizo, grilled lobster, mussels, and market fish. The roasted lamb chop, meanwhile, is accompanied by merguez lamb sausage, summer vegetable ragout flavored with harissa, cumin, and star anise, all served over steamed couscous with raisins. Even the requisite Parisian bistro steak comes with a spicy Indonesian long pepper sauce. The decor, however, is more rooted in French tradition: open, dimly lit, and friendly, with a secluded Zen garden-like back terrace during the temperate months. The wine selection—more than 60 bottles, including a refreshing number available by the glass or half glass—also remains true to form. Before ordering dessert, try a choice of three or five of Bastille's artisinal cheeses, and then move on to finishers like warm peach tatin or the key lime cheesecake with lime-vanilla marmalade. Sundays, they feature a three-course fixed-price brunch, while pretheater and chef's tasting menu options are offered nightly.

EVENING STAR CAFÉ

Chef: William Artley

703-549-5051

www.eveningstarcafe.net

2000 Mt. Vernon Ave., Alexandria, VA 22301

Open: Daily

Price: Inexpensive

Cuisine: American

Serving: L Tuesday–Saturday, D daily (brunch on Sunday)

Credit Cards: AE, D, DC, MC, V

Handicap Access: Yes

Reservations: Not necessary

No Metro access

This hip little café and bar resides in the equally hip Alexandria neighborhood of Del Ray, serving consistently reliable fare in a relaxed, friendly environment. The menu takes its lead from Louisiana, with dinner entrées like bone-in chicken breast with

root veggies and white thyme gravy or mushroom ravioli. But start with almond-crusted Brie, a bowl of chicken-and-Andouille-sausage gumbo, or one of six other appetizers. The café also benefits from its relationship with two other 'hood establishments under the same general management: **Planet Wine,** which offers its entire inventory in case the 20 on-tap beers or 19 wines offered by the glass don't grab you, and **Buzz Bakery,** which supplies desserts. The main dining room successfully executes a 1950s-meets-the-mod-scene décor, with brightly-colored walls, muted red vinyl booths, and dim lighting. Follow the narrow hallway past the bathrooms, and you enter the **Majestic Lounge,** a casual local hang-out. Climb the stairs instead of hitting the lounge, and you'll find **No. 9,** a casual spot with overstuffed couches and live music on Mondays, Wednesdays, and Thursdays.

GADSBY'S TAVERN RESTAURANT

Manager: Andrew Creemer

703-548-1288

www.gadsbystavernrestaurant.com

138 N. Royal St., Alexandria, VA 22314

Open: Daily

Price: Moderate

Cuisine: American

Serving: L, D

Credit Cards: AE, D, MC, V

Handicap Access: Yes

Reservations: Recommended for dinner

Nearest Metro: King Street, Blue and Yellow lines

This delightful colonial tavern dates to 1785 and can boast with certainty that George Washington ate here—as did John Adams, Thomas Jefferson, James Madison, and James Monroe. Next door to the Gadsby's Tavern Museum (see page 140), this meticulously restored brick structure is lovingly decorated in traditional Federal style, with painted trim work, wide-plank floors that creak loudly with every step, and softly glowing brass candle chandeliers. Servers dress in period costumes, and recipes are based on traditional 18th-century fare, adapted to 21st-century tastes. Modern-day diners will enjoy freshly baked Sally Lunn bread (so sweet it tastes closer to pound cake) and to start partake of traditional favorites like peanut soup or Smithfield ham biscuits served with cranberry relish. For the main course, don't miss "George Washington's Favorite," a cider-glazed duck served with smoked bacon spoon bread; also worth note are the jumbo lump crab cakes (but only when in season) and the compelling "carpetbagger," a filet of beef stuffed with fried oysters and creamed spinach. Finish off with one of the tavern's extensive dessert wines—Madeira was GW's favorite—or the tipsy English trifle, a sponge cake drenched in sherry and served with fresh whipped cream and berries. On weekend evenings, you might enjoy live period music or meet up with "Benjamin Franklin," who will regale you with entertaining, sometimes saucy tales.

THE GRILLE

Chef: Dennis Marron
703-838-8000
www.morrisonhouse.com/mrr-dining
116 S. Alfred St., Alexandria, VA 22314
Open: Daily
Price: Expensive
Cuisine: Continental, American
Serving: B, D (brunch on Sunday)
Credit Cards: AE, DC, MC, V
Handicap Access: Yes
Reservations: Recommended
Nearest Metro: King Street, Blue and Yellow lines

Hotel restaurants can be a gamble, but thanks to the bold, fearless style of wunderkind Chef Marron, The Grille—housed inside the Morrison House hotel (see page 91)—is a sure bet. Marron has a passion for the freshest in-season ingredients, and he pairs them in surprising combinations—such as foie gras and fresh pineapple in his award-winning appetizer, a bit of oxtail in a delicate potato hash, or classic (and flawless) Maryland crab cakes served over a bed of fresh Silver Queen corn. Dishes are elegant and the flavors are clean and inventive. Menus change with the season, but when available, don't miss the Berkshire pork served with a black currant pinot noir reduction, or the wild game fish, prepared simply and accompanied by a vegetable the chef probably picked out himself at the Alexandria Farmer's Market that morning. For dessert, seasonal grilled peaches presented with ginger ice cream are light and astonishingly delicious. If it's chocolate you crave, Marron and his pastry chef have your back: Marron admits to being obsessed with the confection, so look for his trio of chocolate desserts—or better yet, come for breakfast and indulge in cloud-light pancakes studded with Valrhona chocolate chips. Service is exceptionally friendly and professional, and the subdued, neo-Colonial interior is quiet and sophisticated—that is, until the piano karaoke starts up at the adjacent bar. Thursday through Saturday, a pianist plays tunes popular from the 1920s to the 1940s, and dedicated regulars (including some professionals from the local opera company) show up around 9:30 to accompany her. Although the show can be overly exuberant, it is generally entertaining—and this is one of the few places in town that offers live karaoke. A full bar keeps the crowd well lubricated, so singalongs can go on for hours.

INDIGO LANDING

Chef: Bryan Moscatello
703-548-0001
www.indigolanding.com
1 Marina Dr., Alexandria, VA 22314
Open: Daily; closes in winter
Price: Moderate

Chef Dennis Marron of The Grille at the Morrison House hotel showcases the freshest ingredients in inventive and surprising dishes. Photo by Debbie K. Hardin.

Cuisine: Southern
Serving: L, D (brunch on Sunday)
Credit Cards: AE, D, DC, MC, V
Handicap Access: Yes
Reservations: Recommended
No Metro access

The real estate mantra "location, location, location" summarizes one of the chief attractions of Indigo Landing. Positioned on Virginia's Daingerfield Island just off George Washington Parkway, this Southern low-country restaurant sits right on the Potomac, sporting panoramic views of the city, including the Capitol dome and the Washington Monument. Watch sailboats ply the waters and airplanes swooping in and out of the sky from Reagan National Airport while reclining in the large, window-lined dining room or on the waterfront porch. A fair portion of the menu draws from the sea, including oysters on the half shell, sweet corn-glazed rockfish, and roasted halibut with applewood smoked bacon. But

mainlanders will also find plenty to choose from, especially if you like the "frogmore" approach (read: a love for bacon) made popular in South Carolina. Chef Moscatello's adoration for that state's cuisine, specifically the recipes of Charleston, also brings "buckets" of Southern dishes like cornmeal-crusted okra and grilled and chilled mussels to the menu. The food is routinely rich and the portions are sizable, from the tower of thick-battered fried green tomatoes with shrimp rémoulade to the jumbo crab cake. But if you manage to save space, the house-made ice creams and sorbets are delicate and full of flavor, as is the chilled sweet potato chiffon cake with pecan brittle and praline sauce. The decor continues the nautical theme, with fishing nets, maps, and tanks, but the restaurant's central aesthetic focus remains the slow-flowing Potomac River and city skyline, from lunch to dinner to the all-you-can-eat gourmet Sunday brunch buffet.

THE MAJESTIC

Chef: Cathal Armstrong
703-837-9117
www.majesticcafe.com
911 King St., Alexandria, VA 22314
Open: Daily
Price: Moderate
Cuisine: American
Serving: L, D
Credit Cards: AE, D, DC, MC, V
Handicap Access: Yes
Reservations: Recommended
Nearest Metro: King Street, Blue and Yellow lines

An Alexandria landmark for more than 75 years, this Art Deco treasure was facing closure until restaurateurs Cathal and Meschelle Armstrong, the duo behind the wildly successful Restaurant Eve (see below), teamed up to return this eatery to its former glory. The renovations sync with the restaurant's period identity, and the '50s-era cocktail list proves the previous generation had it right (try the Tom Collins ... trust us). The menu, meanwhile, takes its lead from Virginia's countryside and seaboards, with deceptively simple-sounding entrées like rack of lamb and roasted chicken. Although the offerings may *sound* pedestrian, every bite reveals a subtle sophistication, especially when coupled with sides like peas mixed with mint and lemon zest. The narrow dining room is lined with booths on one side, a row of catty-cornered tables down the center, and a long bench on the opposite side (perfect for larger parties), all within clear view of the open kitchen. A terraced ceiling infused with muted light creates a friendly, festive atmosphere that invites you to linger, which should provide the time you need to digest dinner and then sample one of the seasonal desserts. And for those longing to feel at home (no matter how far away from it they may be), make a reservation for Nana's Sunday Dinner, where a massive feast of the

The unassuming façade of Alexandria's famed Restaurant Eve. Photo by Nathan Borchelt.

best of Italian food is served, family style, to a perpetual crowd of eager diners.

RESTAURANT EVE

Chef: Cathal Armstrong
703-706-0450
www.restauranteve.com
110 S. Pitt St., Alexandria, VA 22314
Open: Tuesday–Saturday
Price: Expensive
Cuisine: American
Serving: D (except Saturday)
Credit Cards: AE, MC, V
Handicap Access: Yes
Reservations: Highly recommended
Nearest Metro: King Street, Blue and Yellow lines

Before you call for that sought-after reservation at Restaurant Eve (and trust us, you should), first you must decide what type of dining experience you're longing for. If you lean toward the slightly more casual, this pillar of culinary perfection provides a 100-seat bistro. The bright decor complements the inventive menu, a playful take on modern American interwoven with classical French influences, with all dishes derived from locally grown ingredients. Here the lunch-only Irish BLT comes with pork tenderloin instead of bacon alongside house-made potato chips, while dinner entrées like the Muscovy duck breast married with veggies and bing cherries, and the soft-shell crabs with sungold tomatoes and avocado emulsion create a bright, delightful array of options. After deciding, go for the cheese plate . . . and *then* move on to one of pastry chef Rebecca Willis's many confections. Fans of fine wine may face a challenge here, however. Although sommelier Todd

Thrasher knows his vintages, his cocktail-inventing skills rank him as one of the region's best mixologists. Best to hedge your bets and start with one of his inspired concoctions before moving on to that bottle (he's also the mad scientist behind Old Town's **PX** bar—see page 238). Those who are celebrating a special occasion or who want to turn the night into something special should opt for the Chef's Tasting Room, a 34-seat dining room adjacent to the bistro. Whether you go for the five- or nine-course menu, you'll be wowed by Chef Armstrong's culinary showcase. Each course is modeled after the seasons, organized into a palate-cleansing "Creation," followed by "Ocean" (seafood), "Earth and Sky" (meats and game), "Age" (cheese), and "Eden" (desserts). Because these entrées are created with the freshest ingredients and only sustainable proteins, the menu shifts daily—which just may provide the excuse you'll want to schedule a repeat visit.

QUICK EATS

AROUND THE MALL

Breadline (202-822-8900; thebreadlinedc.blogspot.com; 751 Pennsylvania Ave., N.W., Washington; nearest Metro: Archives, Green and Yellow lines). Close proximity to the White House and K Street create a frantic pace in this eclectically disorganized sandwich and breakfast spot on Pennsylvania Avenue. The seasonal menu changes constantly, but daily regulars have their pick of favorites, from custom salads with up to three toppings, to crisp empanadas, to sandwiches like prosciutto on walnut bread with mascarpone, gorgonzola, and fig jam. The emphasis is on the proper measure of ingredients, not Herculean servings, so that the quality shines through. As the name implies, all the bread is house-made, and they sell some of the best baguettes this side of Paris.

Five Guys (202-393-2135; www.fiveguys.com; 1331 Pennsylvania Ave., N.W., Washington; nearest Metro: Metro Center, Blue, Orange, and Red lines). Nothing tastes better than a burger done right, and this local chain has everything dialed in: handmade patties made to order that can include a laundry list of add-ons, hand-cut fries carved from Idaho potatoes (served boardwalk style or with Cajun spices), and peanuts to munch on while you wait. On the second floor of the food court at the Press Center, close to the White House, this restaurant pulls ranks of loyal construction workers and white-collar office-goers in hearty doses, especially at lunch. (Other locations include Old Town Alexandria, Georgetown, Chinatown/Penn Quarter, and the Courthouse neighborhood of Arlington.)

INSIDER TIP: *Forgo the hot dogs and half-smokes when you're on the National Mall and head a few blocks north to the food court at the National Press Center at 13th and F Streets, or Penn Quarter spots like Teaism (see page 214) and the Footnotes Café at Olsson's bookstore (see page 273) for healthier, more varied fare.*

ADAMS MORGAN

Amsterdam Falafel Shop (202-234-1969; www.falafelshop.com; 2425 18th St., N.W., Washington; nearest Metro: Woodley Park, Red line). Heralded as a godsend by locals tired of pizza as their only late-night Adams Morgan option, Amsterdam Falafel is a narrow, no-frills spot typical of the kind of place you'd find throughout Europe. Falafels (patties of fried chick peas) come in small (three) and regular (five) orders, wrapped in a warmed wheat or white pita with enough space to load up at the self-serve bar of toppings. Baba ghannouj, hummus, pickled beets, chili peppers, cucumber and tomato salad—it's all there. Amsterdam also serves Belgian *frites* with curry, mayo, and ketchup for dipping.

The Astor International Cuisine (202-745-7495; 1829 Columbia Rd., N.W., Washington). Located just west of the main strip in Adams Morgan, this no-frills eatery specializes in home-style entrées, sandwiches, and salads—that is, if your home is the Mediterranean.

Adams Morgan's institution and 24-hour refuge, The Diner. Photo by Nathan Borchelt.

The lamb slips off the bone; the gyro and kufta sandwich (a kabob of both lamb and beef) are hearty and served with tomato and lettuce; and the variety of vegetarian options, from stuffed grape leaves and falafels to roasted mixed veggies and tomato-cucumber salad, do not disappoint.

The Diner (202-232-8800; www.trystdc.com/diner; 2453 18th St., N.W., Washington; nearest Metro: Woodley Park, Red line). Simple is as simple does? Witness Adams Morgan's The Diner. This 24/7 spot serves all the traditional diner fare, including breakfast all day, to an eclectic cast of characters: students, locals, families, and tourists. Seating can be cozy whether you're at the bar, the booths, or the row of narrow tables, and if you come during peak times (brunch or lunch on the weekends), you can expect a wait. But if you're craving pancakes, a burger, a BLT, or just a place to grab a pint, this is your spot. It also becomes a haven for soccer-obsessed residents, who flock here all hours of the night during the World Cup to catch their team on the projection-screen TV.

Tryst (202-232-5500; www.trystdc.com; 2459 18th St., N.W., Washington; nearest Metro: Woodley Park, Red line). Like The Diner a few doors down, Tryst has become an Adams Morgan institution (not surprisingly, they have the same owners). Where The Diner excels at efficiency, Tryst has perfected the art of lingering. Customers can settle into a couch or a plush armchair, or snag a table and wile away the hours. Lighting remains moody without giving over to shadows, and if the weather's nice, the front doors swing open to let in a gentle breeze. Art by locals (sometimes for sale) adorns the walls, and amenities like wireless Internet, inexpensive coffee, specialty drinks, alcohol, and a sinful array of desserts make Tryst a staple for students and young professionals. The menu offers a variety of veggie and nonveggie sandwiches, salads, and snacks. The staff can sometimes take on a cooler-than-thou vibe, but for relaxing, writing, reading, or the time-honored pastime of people watching, Tryst can't be beat. To-go coffee and food orders are also available at the bar.

CAPITOL HILL

Market Lunch (202-547-8444; 225 Seventh St., S.E., Washington; nearest Metro: Eastern Market, Blue and Orange lines). A massive fire gutted the Eastern Market in 2007, transforming one of the most unique elements of D.C. into a boarded-up shell of its former self. But plans for reconstruction started before the smoke faded, and Eastern Market once again offers great, inexpensive fast seafood in the midst of a riot of food sellers with some of the freshest produce, meats, and cheeses available in the city. Try one of the best crab cakes in town, along with eggs and grits, burgers, and loads of other down-home cooking. This is a great place to stop for a bite while exploring the expansive flea market that surrounds the building every weekend. The main "South Hall" room is slated to reopen in 2009.

Marvelous Market (202-544-7172; www.marvelousmarket.com; 303 Seventh St., S.E., Washington; nearest Metro: Eastern Market, Blue and Orange lines). Don't let the name fool you. In addition to selling an eclectic array of gourmet groceries, organic produce, fresh bread, and pasta, this local chain also sells fantastic sandwiches, coffee, and pastries. Try the curry chicken wrap or the *jambon beurre*—imported French ham thinly sliced and served with sweet butter and cornichons on a crusty Parisian baguette. And don't miss the brownies—among the city's best—a moist, rich, artful collision of chocolate, chocolate, and...um...more chocolate. Other locations include Dupont Circle, Georgetown, Upper Northwest, and K Street.

CHINATOWN/PENN QUARTER

Capital Q (202-347-8396; www.capitalqbbq.com; 707 H St., N.W., Washington; nearest Metro: Gallery Place/Chinatown, Green, Red, and Yellow lines). This Texas BBQ joint might seem out of place given its Chinatown address, but put one foot inside and you'll swear you're in the Lone Star State. The signature beef brisket—slow-cooked for 12 hours—does Texas's barbecue legacy proud, as does the spicy sausage. But other items like the pulled chicken, the half-chicken, and the pulled pork (added by popular demand) are equally rewarding, whether you go for the mild or the spicy sauce. An array of side dishes, all steaming in the counter right before your eyes, are universally successful, but most diners tend to gravitate to the collared greens with near-religious loyalty. The servings are massive; the decor is a hearty hodgepodge of Texanalia, with signed 8-by-10s of damn near every Texan politician, George W. included; and the beer on the menu keeps this tiny spot hopping during both the lunch and dinner rushes.

Full Kee (202-371-2233; www.fullkeedc.com; 509 H St., N.W., Washington; nearest Metro: Gallery Place/Chinatown, Green, Red, and Yellow lines). Marked with a yellow awning and a large window overlooking H Street, Full Kee is arguably the best, most authentic of D.C.'s Chinatown restaurants. The decor is unapologetically minimal, only cash is accepted, they have no liquor license, and the service is blunt, but the food here is the draw—as evidenced by the large lunch crowds and the many chefs who drop in late at night after their shifts end. The menu ranges from traditional Chinese American fare to an array of delicacies like deep-fried spicy frog. One of the best items on the menu remains the Honk Kong-style noodle soup with baby shrimp wrapped in dumplings and bathed in a delectable broth.

The endless options at Teaism. Photo by Nathan Borchelt.

Teaism (202-638-2010; www.teaism.com; 400 Eighth St., N.W., Washington; nearest Metro: Archives, Green and Yellow lines). This graceful spot a few blocks south of the National Museum of American Art serves a variety of Asian-inspired meals for breakfast, lunch, and dinner. The bento boxes, a play on traditional Japanese cold meals, may be the best pick on the menu; options include salmon, chicken, and grilled veggies, each with sides like edamame, rice, or cucumber-ginger salad. But small dishes like the miso soup, a long list of organic sandwiches, and more traditional entrées like Thai chicken curry with sticky rice are equally successful. As its name implies, a wide variety of teas are also offered, from cold sweet green to a variety of oolong, black, green, and white. Teaism also offers two afternoon teas, traditional and Asian, from 2:30–5 daily. Next door, the Tea Shop offers a variety of tea sets along with bulk dried teas. Other locations include 800 Connecticut Ave., N.W., and 2009 R St., N.W.

INSIDER TIP: *Teaism's salty oak cookie with raisins has created an almost orgiastic response among those in the know. Pair it with the sweet green tea or a warm chai in the winter.*

DUPONT CIRCLE AND WEST END

Jack's Restaurant and Bar (202-332-6767; 1527 17th St., N.W., Washington; nearest Metro: Dupont Circle, Red line). The fact that well-regarded Swiss chef Herbert Kerschbaumer named his latest endeavor in the D.C. dining scene after his dog reflects his intentions: high-quality food in a friendly, neighborhood atmosphere at reasonable prices. Specials like half-priced hamburgers or half-priced bottles of wine and a weekly fondue night pull a loyal, local crowd, and although the service is somewhat topsy-turvy, what comes out of the reliable kitchen—from lamb shanks to mushroom risotto to burgers to the lightly breaded calamari—will not disappoint.

INSIDER TIP: *A crop of gourmet grocery stores new to the city, including Trader Joe's and Whole Foods, also offer a low-cost alternative for a quick, picnic-friendly meal. Or just check out a few of our picks of the best in deli and specialty stores (see page 221).*

Luna Grill and Diner (202-835-2280; www.lunagrillanddiner.com; 1301 Connecticut Ave., N.W., Washington; nearest Metro: Dupont Circle, Red line). True to its diner name, breakfast is available anytime and diners are welcome to mix and match pastas and sauces. Homegrown art adorns the walls and the confined space is crowded with locals, who take to the back patio when the weather cooperates. The menu consists of nouveau American comfort food: appetizers, pasta, sandwiches, and entrées like back-fin crab cakes, grilled salmon, and roasted turkey with stuffing. Try the sweet potato French fries and homemade lemonade, and always ask what's on special. Mondays and Tuesdays offer half-priced pasta, an early-bird special is available daily from 4:30–6:30, and Luna (which has been family-owned and -operated since 1970) hosts a special wine tasting dinner each month. Also located in the Shirlington neighborhood of Arlington (703-379-7173, 4024 28th St. S., Arlington).

Pizza Paradiso (202-223-1245; www.eatyourpizza.com; 2029 P St., N.W., Washington; nearest Metro: Dupont Circle, Red line). Housed in a tiny town house in Dupont Circle with no more than a dozen tables, the bohemian Pizza Paradiso cranks out extraordinary fire-baked, thin-crust pizzas topped simply with tomato, mozzarella, and a hint of fresh basil, or with more unusual ingredients like *bottarga* (a salty fish roe), egg, or potato and pesto. A second, larger shop serves the Georgetown neighborhood, where you'll also find **Birreria Paradiso**, a small beer joint downstairs that specializes in microbrews and hard-to-find Belgian beers; the bar offers 16 brews on tap and more than 80 bottled varieties (202-337-1245; 3282 M St., N.W., Washington).

INSIDER TIP: *Don't miss the intensely flavored homemade gelatos at Pizza Paradiso; if you drop by after 2 PM, you have a good chance of scoring a table at which to enjoy your treat.*

The Giant Slice

Pizza certainly wasn't invented in D.C., but pie shops in the Adams Morgan neighborhood may have "perfected" its most extreme variant. Just take a profusion of bars; legions of hungry, mostly drunk bar-goers; and *voilà!* Introducing the D.C. giant slice: a massive triangle of pizza roughly the size of an elephant's ear, dripping with cheese and grease, wrapped in aluminum foil, served on three paper plates, and eaten on the street. A years-long arms race exists among the three proprietors of the giant slice, each claiming to be the original, each trying to offer the largest piece, and each fostering near-religious loyalty among locals. While some may claim that the giant slice is manna from the bar gods, it's probably not the best slice you'll ever eat—but it does a great job of soaking up the alcohol after that 2:30 last call.

Pizza Mart (202-234-9700; 2445 18th St., N.W., Washington)
Pizza Boli's (202-244-2800; 5029 Connecticut Ave., N.W., Washington)
Pizza Movers (202-483-8787; 2471 18th St., N.W., Washington)

Georgetown

Amma Vegetarian Kitchen (202-625-6625; 3291-A M St., N.W., Washington; no Metro access). Follow a narrow flight of stairs to this second-floor, shoe-box-sized restaurant and you'll discover one of the neighborhood's best-kept secrets. Look past the blasé decor and focus on the food—the server's graciousness and the hip, multicultural crowd let you know you've found something special. Amma offers mostly south Indian delicacies like airy-light, sizable *dhosas,* which look like a thin burrito by way of Mumbai, made from lentils and rice, pan-fried and then filled with a variety of vegetables. Try it with a few sides like the mango chutney, and don't miss the sweet, tangy yogurt lassi, a refreshing drink. This is one of the best bargain meals in the city.

Moby Dick House of Kabob (202-333-4400; www.mobysonline.com; 1070 31st St., N.W., Washington; no Metro access). This hole-in-the-wall Georgetown institution offers some of the city's best Iranian food. The traditional pita bread is made by hand, and the kabobs are evenly spiced varieties of lamb, chicken, and beef. A variety of Middle Eastern salads and sides like the mix of cucumbers, tomato, and fresh herbs or garlic buds marinated in vinegar elevate this place far beyond the ordinary kabob shop.

INSIDER TIP: *Moby Dick's interior is small and blindingly bright. Escape those fluorescents by getting your order to go, and then enjoy them on a bench alongside the nearby C&O Canal (see page 243).*

U Street and the 14th Street Corridor

Ben's Chili Bowl (202-667-0909; www.benschilibowl.com; 1213 U St., N.W., Washington; nearest Metro: U Street, Green and Yellow lines). If you're longing for quintessential D.C. grub, look no further. This joint has slung breakfast, lunch, and dinner for a wide array of hungry locals since 1958—and it's a fave for celebs in the know (check out the pictures on the wall). Try the signature D.C. half-smoke (be sure they slice it down the middle and cook it on the grill) covered with beef chili, onions, and cheese. The chili-cheese fries are gooey, unhealthy poetry (especially when enjoyed late-night), and non-meat-eaters rave about the veggie chili. The scene, especially at night, is a buzz of activity, with cabbies, students, and damn near everyone else jockeying for room at the booth seats or the Formica bar.

Bus Boys and Poets (202-387-7638; www.busboysandpoets.com; 2021 14th St., N.W., Washington; nearest Metro: U Street, Green and Yellow lines). Equal measures restaurant, bookstore, and performance space, this little bastion of hipness takes its name from poet Langston Hughes. The book inventory swings liberal/political; the menu consists of inexpensive items like burgers and pizza along with a few soul-food and Mediterranean dishes; the service is a bit too cool for its own good; and the performances range from film screenings to open-mic poetry readings, local musician jams, and writers' tributes. Late-night crowds vary from bookworms fueled on coffee and intellectuals sipping libations, to DJs spinning dub and electro with hungry customers ordering from the kitchen, which stays open late.

Love Café (202-265-9800; lovecafe.cakelove.com; 1501 U St., N.W., Washington; nearest Metro: U Street, Green and Yellow lines). This small café and coffee shop provides a sane alternative to the Starbucks dominating every other city street corner. Food Net-

The real D.C. monument: Ben's Chili Bowl. Photo by Nathan Borchelt.

The neon glow may seem glam, but Nam Viet's pho is culinary poetry in a bowl. Photo by Nathan Borchelt.

work star Warren Brown (owner of the Cake Love bakery across the street) opened this narrow, sunlit, brightly colored spot to cater to locals eager for good coffee and sweets culled from his signature and sinfully delicious style. His recent addition, a make-your-own-cupcake, is a resounding success as well, and from 5–7:30 weeknights Love Café offers its version of happy hour: pieces of Brown's "lava cake" for only a few bucks.

UPPER NORTHWEST

Nam-Viet and Pho-79 (202-237-1015; www.namviet1.com; 3419 Connecticut Ave., N.W., Washington; nearest Metro: Cleveland Park, Red line). Anyone who knows of the curative effects of a bowl of *pho*, a traditional Vietnamese beef soup, should target this narrow, brightly lit, Cleveland Park establishment. Aesthetics aside, it consistently produces some of the city's best *pho* in a wide variety, as well as an encyclopedic list of Vietnamese salads, appetizers, entrées, and desserts. Service is routinely professional and the kitchen's fast. Also located in Alexandria (703-548-0440; 3819 Mount Vernon Ave.) and Arlington (703-522-7110; 1127 N. Hudson St.).

Rocklands BBQ and Grilling Company (202-333-2558; www.rocklands.com; 2418 Wisconsin Ave., N.W., Washington; no Metro access). Peanut shells litter the floor and seating is limited to a central communal table and a small stretch of bar stools lining the window, but this barbecue institution consistently generates the city's best vinegar-infused BBQ meals, bar none. The buzzing kitchen offers pulled pork, beef, and chicken, along with top-notch ribs. Side dishes like coleslaw and collard greens leave something to be desired, so concentrate on the meat—and be sure to ask for extra sauce. Also located in Alexandria (703-778-9663; 25 S. Quaker Ln., Alexandria).

THE WATERFRONT

Pruitt Seafood Market (202-554-2669; 1100 Maine Ave., S.W., Washington; nearest Metro: Smithsonian, Blue and Orange lines). One of D.C.'s most original and seldom-seen spots, the D.C. Maine Avenue Seafood Market attracts an eclectic crowd of seafood lovers yearning for the freshest fish available and fishmongers shouting out the daily deals—as has been the scene for more than 200 years. Pruitt has been here since 1933, serving daily catch fish alongside steamed crabs and other picnic-ready items. But half the fun is lingering and soaking in the carnival-esque scene only a few blocks from the Tidal Basin and a world away from most of D.C.

ARLINGTON, VIRGINIA

Delhi Dhaba Indian Café (703-524-0008; 2424 Wilson Blvd., Arlington; nearest Metro: Courthouse, Orange line). The inexpensive, café-style Indian fare seldom disappoints, and the Bollywood films on perpetual loop on the TVs evoke the right measure of Delhi-by-way-of-Virginia vibe. Try the tandoori chicken, and be sure to accompany whatever you order with naan, a traditional hot Indian bread.

Hard Times Café (703-528-2233; www.hardtimes.com; 3028 Wilson Blvd., Arlington; nearest Metro: Clarendon, Orange line). Hard Times Café lives up to its low-end name by offering no-frills food at rock-bottom prices. Although this rough-around-the-edges joint also offers salads, burgers, and grilled chicken, its claim to fame is its chili,

Vapiano's vibrant chalk board menu captures the chain's festive atmosphere. Photo by Fredde Lieberman. Used by permission.

served in big bowls without beans, ladled over spaghetti in enormous portions of chili-mac, or as the main ingredient in old-fashioned Frito "pies" (chili poured over corn chips and topped with shredded cheddar cheese and sour cream). Hard Times offers four varieties of chili, including a Cincinnati version flavored with cinnamon that tastes vaguely Middle Eastern, and a fantastic vegetarian chili made with soy and loaded with mushrooms, green peppers, and peanuts. A huge stack of beer-battered onion rings goes well either before or with the chili, and Hard Times' own vanilla-heady root beer washes it all down nicely—or if you prefer, there is a full bar with a happy hour from 3–7 weekdays.

Vapiano (703-528-3113; www.vapiano.com; 4401 Wilson Blvd., Arlington; nearest Metro: Ballston, Orange line). The all-Italian menu at this German-owned chain is made to order—literally. You pay for the dishes here by the ingredient, whether you opt for the spicy crayfish pasta, a salad, or a thin-crust pizza of plum tomatoes and mozzarella. All the pastas are house-made; the communal tables are lined with growing herbs that you're encouraged to tear into to season your dish; and true to its origins, the portions are more Euro than supersized American. The full-service bar offers a variety of libations and a buzzing, hip vibe. Locations also in Dupont Circle and Penn Quarter/Chinatown.

ALEXANDRIA, VIRGINIA

Buzz (703-600-2899; buzzonslaters.com; 901 Slaters Ln., Alexandria; nearest Metro: Braddock Road, Blue and Yellow lines). Those easily lured by sweet temptations like cupcakes, cookies, and Belgian waffles may never leave this personable coffee shop, open 6–midnight. Breakfast lovers take note: They serve some of the best egg sandwiches around. Or head here later at night just for dessert (choose from the aforementioned sweets or a cheese plate) and a few glasses of wine or an after-dinner drink in a calm, low-lit atmosphere. The free Wi-Fi doesn't hurt, either.

Eamonn's a Dublin Chipper (703-299-8384; www.eamonnsdublinchipper.com; 728 King St., Alexandria; nearest Metro: King Street, Blue and Yellow lines). The slogan on the door reads "Thanks be to cod," and no truer words have been penned for the owners of Eamonn's, the same folks behind The Majestic and Restaurant Eve (see page 210). At this small and simple eatery, the mostly fish-and-chip menu is scribbled on a chalkboard behind the low-slung counter. You place your order, decide which sauce to try (go for the hot chili—trust us), and wait. The fish is routinely fresh, the chips crisp and dense, and everything arrives unceremoniously in a paper bag. Get it to go or grab a seat at one of the few communal tables. Feeling adventurous? Chase your meal with a fried Milky Way and wash it down with one of several beers offered by Eamonn's.

FOOD PURVEYORS

Ice Cream

Dickey's Frozen Custard (703-418-0700; 2451 Crystal Dr., Arlington; nearest Metro: Reagan National Airport, Blue and Yellow lines). This generations-old local chain serves soft-serve custard in sugar cones in both Arlington and downtown (202-861-0669; 1710 I St., N.W., Washington).

Pop's Old Fashioned Ice Cream parlor, complete with 1940s-era whitewashed wrought-iron furniture.
Photo by Debbie K. Hardin.

Dolcezza (202-333-4646; www.dolcezzagelato.com; 1560 Wisconsin Ave., N.W., Washington; no Metro access). This chic Argentine ice creamery in Georgetown serves freshly made sorbets and thick, creamy ice cream closer to gelato than your traditional scoop.

Maggie Moo's Ice Cream Treatery (202-232-0676; 2324 18th St., N.W.; Washington; nearest Metro: Woodley Park, Red line). This national chain is part dessert paradise, part exhibition center. Ice creams are mixed on a cold slab of marble right before your eyes. In addition to the store in Adams Morgan, there are outlets downtown, on U Street, and in Alexandria and Arlington.

Max's Best Ice Cream (202-333-3111; 2416 Wisconsin Ave., N.W., Washington; no Metro access). Homemade and down-home, this family-owned ice cream parlor in Upper Northwest keeps things simple and delicious enough to justify visits through the years from several presidents.

Pop's Old Fashioned Ice Cream (703-518-5374; 109 King St., Alexandria; nearest Metro: King Street, Blue and Yellow lines). In the heart of Old Town Alexandria, Pop's makes its ice cream on the premises from recipes passed down from the owner's father, who claims to have made these same frozen treats for Eleanor Roosevelt to serve in the White House.

Deli and Specialty Foods

CakeLove (202-588-7100; www.cakelove.com; 1506 U St., N.W., Washington; nearest Metro: U Street, Green and Yellow lines). Lawyer-turned-baker and star of the Food Network's *Sugar Rush*, Warren Brown shows there's life beyond the courtroom by pro-

Old Italy meets Cleveland Park at Vace. Photo by Nathan Borchelt.

ducing the city's most sinfully delicious cakes, cupcakes, and "crunch feet"—miniature versions of his popular bundt cakes. Another CakeLove is located in the Village at Shirlington (703-933-0099; 4150 Campbell Ave., Suite 105, Arlington).

Cowgirl Creamery (202-393-6880; www.cowgirlcreamery.com; 919 F St., N.W., Washington; nearest Metro: Gallery Place/Chinatown, Green, Red, and Yellow lines). Cheese lovers unite! This California-based gourmet *fromage* shop serves some of the most flavorful, dynamic, all-organic cheeses to be found in the city in a sample-friendly environment.

The Italian Store (703-528-6266; www.italianstore.com; 3123 Lee Hwy., Arlington; nearest Metro: Clarendon, Orange line). Part gourmet Italian market, part deli, this little gem in Arlington serves some of the best to-go subs in the city, along with copious Italian wines, lobster ravioli, NYC-style pizza, and a good selection of fresh meat.

So's Your Mom (202-462-3666; 1831 Columbia Rd., N.W., Washington; nearest Metro: Woodley Park, Red line). Along with its kitschy name, this place offers an amazing deli with some of the city's best bagels and made-to-order sandwiches, along with a long line of oddball prepackaged items and homemade desserts and coffee.

Vace Italian Delicatessen (202-363-1999; 3315 Connecticut Ave., N.W., Washington; nearest Metro: Cleveland Park, Red line). Homemade pastas and sauce, a wide variety of fresh Italian meats and cheeses, and the best NYC-style pizza (by the slice or whole pie) make this narrow Upper Northwest store a true find.

Yes! Organic Market (202-462-5150; www.livingnaturally.com; 1825 Columbia Rd., N.W., Washington; nearest Metro: Woodley Park, Red line). This local chain enthusiastically celebrates its all-organic inventory of fruits, veggies, breads, and other grocery items—perfect for a picnic. In addition to the Adams Morgan location, there are stores in Upper Northwest, Capitol Hill, and Northeast.

FARMERS MARKETS

Proximity to the farmlands of Virginia, Maryland, and Delaware makes D.C. one of the country's better cities for freshly grown, all-organic produce; handmade pasta; and cheese. Some markets have been around for decades—or, like the Alexandria Farmers Market, for centuries. Others have cropped up as real estate becomes available. Following is a list of some of the more noteworthy throughout the region. Markets are open year-round unless otherwise noted.

Alexandria Farmers Market (301 King St., Market Square, Alexandria; nearest Metro: King Street, Blue and Yellow lines). Open 5:30–10:30 AM Saturday.

Adams Morgan Farmers Market (18th St. and Columbia Rd., N.W., Washington; nearest Metro: Woodley Park, Red line). Open May through December, 8–2 Saturday.

D.C. Farmers Market (1309 Fifth St., N.E., Washington; nearest Metro: New York Avenue, Red line). Open 7–5:30 Tuesday, 7–6 Saturday, 7–2 Sunday.

Dupont Circle Freshfarm Market (www.freshfarmmarket.org; 1500 20th St., N.W., Washington; nearest Metro: Dupont Circle, Red line). Open 9–1 Sunday (January through March, opens at 10 AM).

Eastern Market Outdoor Farmers Market (Seventh St. between C St. and North Carolina Ave., S.E., Washington; nearest Metro: Eastern Market, Blue and Orange lines). Open 7–4 Saturday and Sunday.

Georgetown Freshfarm Market (www.freshfarmmarket.org; 3219 Q St., N.W., Washington; no Metro access). Open June through October, 9–1 Saturday.

USDA Farmers Market (www.ams.usda.gov/farmersmarkets; 12th St. and Independence Ave., S.W., Washington; nearest Metro: Smithsonian, Blue and Orange lines). Open June through October, 10–2 Friday.

WINE

D.C.'s wine scene has grown exponentially with the region's increasingly diversified food landscape. Below is a short list of some of the best, from the veterans to the newer kids on the block. All offer periodic wine tastings and expert recommendations.

Best Cellars (202-387-3146; www.bestcellars.com; 1643 Connecticut Ave., N.W., Washington; nearest Metro: Dupont Circle, Red line). Also located in Arlington (703-741-0404; 2855 Clarendon Blvd., Arlington).

The Curious Grape (703-671-1549; www.curiousgrape.com; 4056 28th St., Arlington; no Metro access).

De Vinos (202-986-5002; www.de-vinos.com; 2001 18th St., N.W., Washington; nearest Metro: Dupont Circle, Red line).

Grape Legs Fun (202-387-9463; 2001 18th St., N.W., Washington; nearest Metro: Dupont Circle, Red line).

Planet Wine (703-549-3444; www.planetwineshop.com; 2004 Mount Vernon Ave., Alexandria; no Metro access).

Schneider's of Capitol Hill (202-543-9300; www.cellar.com; 300 Massachusetts Ave., N.E., Washington; nearest Metro: Union Station, Red line).

The Wine Specialist (202-833-0707; winespecialist.com; 2115 M St., N.W., Washington; nearest Metro: Foggy Bottom, Blue and Orange lines).

NIGHTLIFE

Although perhaps not as varied as the food scene, nightlife in D.C. holds its own, thanks in large part to its diverse musical history and ample live music venues. Choice neighborhoods will define your experience: Catch live jazz on U Street or Georgetown's famed Blues Alley (see page 232), crawl from bar to bar—or elbow up on an expansive rooftop—in Adams Morgan, rub shoulders with politicians and their countless hardworking minions in Capitol Hill, or dance the night away to the multicultural rhythms and crowds of Dupont Circle, which also lays claim to the largest gay community in the country after San Francisco. But what's possible in regional nightlife has also been conspicuously raised by the alchemy found in Old Town Alexandria's PX, a 21st-century speakeasy that specializes in drinks that will forever change the way you taste cocktails.

"Marilyn's" heavenly gaze, overlooking Woodley Park/ Adams Morgan at the Duke Ellington Bridge. Photo by Nathan Borchelt.

Although bars and lounges are plentiful, the city's clubs are admittedly sparse. Miami and New York City may dominate that scene, but D.C. boasts live-music icons like the international grooves of 18th Street Lounge and Nightclub 9:30, consistently ranked among the country's best spots for catching up-and-comers and established acts. On the Virginia side of the Potomac, Arlington's Iota and Alexandria's Birchmere provide an environment more intimate than your living room. Truth be told, it's difficult to gauge exactly what's happening when in a city as diverse as D.C. To aid your efforts, consult the free weeklies like the gay-friendly *Blade* (www.washblade.com) and the indie-oriented *Washington City Paper* (www.washingtoncitypaper.com); the free daily *Washington Post Express* (www.readexpress.com); and online resources like Daily Candy (www.dailycandy.com) and dcist.com to keep informed on the latest shows, DJ events, concerts, and pub crazes.

AROUND THE MALL

Elephant and Castle (202-347-7707; www.elephantandcastle.com; 1207 Pennsylvania Ave., N.W., Washington; nearest Metro: Federal Triangle, Blue and Orange lines). An impressive UK-centric beer list, including the hand-pulled Fuller's Porter, and high-quality pub food define this chain establishment, but this D.C. outpost is most noteworthy for its massive outdoor patio overlooking Pennsylvania Avenue. It's one of very few places in the neighborhood to grab a pint and a bite and people-watch during D.C.'s mild spring temps—and it's also one of the central routes for the president's motorcade as it zips from the Capitol to the White House. As you'd expect with its Euro origins, soccer and rugby games are televised live, sometimes on a huge screen on the patio.

Round Robin Bar (202-637-7348; 1401 Pennsylvania Ave., N.W., Washington; nearest Metro: Federal Triangle, Blue and Orange lines). Henry Clay introduced the first mint julep here in the 1800s, and today you can find that classic cocktail alongside others like a gin rickey or a negroni, each poured with military precision in this popular bar in the Willard Hotel (see page 70). A mixture of politicians and lobbyists exchange hushed words while leaning against the dark green walls; office workers collect en masse for happy hour; and you're liable to fall into hours-long conversations while sitting at the circular mahogany bar that dominates the room.

Sky Terrace Restaurant (202-638-5900; 515 15th St., N.W., Washington; nearest Metro: Metro Center, Blue, Orange, and Red lines). It's the view—not the food or the atmosphere—that serves as the chief draw to this rooftop spot at the Hotel Washington (see page 66). But what a view! Crowning the top floor of the hotel, the terrace overlooks the western side of the White House. Snag one of the tables for a late-morning Bloody Mary or come for the early happy hour, a prime time to catch a seat before sunset. Note that the bar is only open from April to October, and it will close for 12 to 18 months starting in 2008, as the Hotel Washington undergoes extensive renovations.

The Atlas District

As the line of gentrification continually shifts eastward, so does D.C.'s nightlife. Consider the Atlas District, a small stretch of bars, clubs, and restaurants that sprung up on an unlikely stretch of H Street, N.E., between 12th and 14th Streets. What was once a neighborhood populated by boarded-up row houses now carries an indie-hip cred. While surrounding blocks can be a bit sketchy, once you reach the Atlas, just about anything is available, from sword-swallowing bartenders to haircuts that come with a shot, the latter sheered by professional stylists at a fraction of their typical rates. A few highlights include **The Red and the Black** (202-399-3201; www.redandblackbar.com; 1212 H St., N.E., Washington), a narrow, two-level space with a New Orleans theme dedicated to live music; **The Rock and Roll Hotel** (202-388-7625; www.rockandrollhoteldc.com; 1353 H St., N.E., Washington), pulling some of the best indie, punk, and electro shows along with an endless stream of DJs; and **The Palace of Wonders** (202-398-7469; www.palaceofwonders.com; 1210 H. St., N.E., Washington), easily the weirdest bar in D.C., with sideshow oddities like a taxidermied body of the "last living unicorn," 9-foot-tall mummies, and weekend performances like the aforementioned sword swallowers and '50s-style burlesque dancers. The scene is going strong, and more venues will certainly join the fray. Only catch? The closest metro—Union Station—is about 1.5 miles away. Expect to take a cab there, but area businesses have teamed up to provide free shuttles from H Street to Union Station from 10–2:30 nightly. Just ask for the number, call the cab, and they'll show up within 10 to 15 minutes.

ADAMS MORGAN

Bedrock Billiards (202-667-7665; www.bedrock-billiards.com; 1841 Columbia Rd., N.W., Washington; nearest Metro: Woodley Park, Red line). Descend into this pub and discover an Adam's Morgan anomaly: a local hangout. Here you'll find pool tables, shuffleboard tables, dart boards, jovial bartenders, a good variety of drinks—and drink specials—and a jukebox with indie and classic rock. Decor is thrift store kitsch: '50s furniture, a central bar, and local artists' work adorning the walls. It can get tight on weekends after 9, but early weekend evenings and weekday nights are relaxed and friendly. Pool is charged by the hour, while darts and a variety of games like chess and Connect Four are free.

Bourbon (202-332-0800; www.bourbondc.com; 2321 18th St., N.W., Washington; nearest Metro, Woodley Park, Red line). The initial draw? Not surprisingly, the bourbon menu—more than 50 varieties along with a few Tennessee specials. But this three-story establishment also offers 12 wines by the glass, an assortment of on-tap

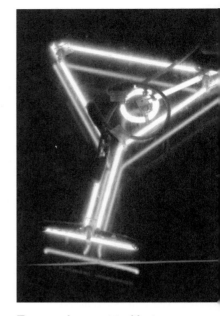

The warm glow promising libations at Toledo Lounge. Photo by Nathan Borchelt.

micro- and macro-brews, and other spirits in a friendly, no-frills environment. A series of first-come tables and booths and a bar line the ground floor, with a small outdoor patio open during the temperate months. Upstairs there are special monthly events that rally interesting artists into a casual Q&A forum, melded with lounge and hip-hop DJs. The rest of the time, expect indie music; decent-sized, unpretentious crowds; and an amiable staff. This Bourbon is an extension of the first Bourbon, located in the Upper Northwest neighborhood of Glover Park (202-625-7770; 2348 Wisconsin Ave., N.W., Washington).

Ghana Café (202-387-3845; www.ghanacafe.com; 2465 18th St., N.W., Washington; nearest Metro: Woodley Park, Red line). This West African establishment is one of several spots to sample the culture and cuisine of the Dark Continent, but Ghana truly steps into its own every Friday and Saturday night, as the second floor turns into one of the best Afrodance parties going thanks to well-versed DJs and an accommodating crowd. Downstairs is a quiet dining room offering affordable West African cuisine, with windows that look out onto the churning chaos of 18th Street, but upstairs roils until well past midnight—and often past last call—with an amiable, loud dance-groove scene.

INSIDER TIP: *Most of the restaurants in Adams Morgan and Dupont Circle, including The Reef and Bourbon, turn into nightlife hot spots as the night evolves. If you find a place you like, stake your claim to the prime real estate early and watch the weekend mayhem ensue.*

Madam's Organ (202-667-5370; www.madamsorgan.com; 2461 18th St., N.W., Washington; nearest Metro: Woodley Park, Red line). The exact location of this Adams Morgan institution has shifted up and down 18th Street since it first opened back in the early

1980s, but it's been one of the only places in the neighborhood that has consistently offered nightly live music, and it's also the only place in Adams Morgan to get singled out by *Playboy* as one of the country's best bars. The mural—the controversially well-endowed Madam herself—has also been a constant, marking the building's façade. Musical genres shift each night, but house bands include bluegrass, country, blues-inspired rock, and Latin, and the ground floor is typically swallowed by gyrating party-goers. Upstairs, find red-felt pool tables, a decor that echoes the Delta South, a scattering of tables, and a small seasonal outdoor deck.

Toledo Lounge (202-986-5416; 2435 18th St., N.W., Washington; nearest Metro: Woodley Park, Red line). Less a lounge and more a divey throwback to an aesthetic best described as '50s automotive—as evidenced by the street signs and eclectic paraphernalia on the walls—this honest, no-frills bar can be an oasis in the typical chaos of an Adams Morgan weekend night. Pub food is simple and inexpensive, the beer list is short, drinks are strong, the jukebox is varied, the mostly local crowds are friendly, and so is the staff.

CAPITOL HILL

Bullfeathers (202-543-5005; www.bullfeatherscapitolhill.com; 410 First St., S.E., Washington; nearest Metro: Capitol South, Blue and Orange lines). Named after one of Teddy Roosevelt's expletives (rather than "bull——"), this Capitol Hill institution has been the watering hole and refuge for the House of Representatives since 1980. The crowd is more staffers than interns, the pub aesthetic is decidedly 1900s (save for the profusion of flat-screen TVs), and the food and beer offerings are inexpensive and don't aspire to much, with nightly specials aimed at helping you narrow the small list of options. For cheap beer, lively conversation, and the occasional politician sighting, Bullfeathers reigns supreme.

Capitol Lounge (202-547-2098; www.capitolloungedc.com; 231 Pennsylvania Ave., S.E., Washington; nearest Metro: Capitol South, Blue and Orange lines). A devastating fire leveled this local favorite back in 2005, but the Capitol Lounge reopened the following January and it's as if this Hill-staffer-and-sports-fan favorite never missed a step, though the remodeling did brighten the place up a bit. Two big rooms are adorned with political memorabilia, and there's an old school lounge downstairs equipped with its own bar and plush leather seats. Expect a wait at the billiards room—and lots of laminated security cards dangling from the necks and belts of patrons, especially at happy hour. As evidenced by the growing collection of foreign soccer scarves, this pub also pulls huge fans of "the greatest sport in the world" (MLS, European clubs—you name it), which makes for an occasionally rowdy multicultural scene at odd and unpredictable times of the day.

Hawk 'n' Dove Bar (202-543-3300; www.hawkanddoveonline.com; 329 Pennsylvania Ave., S.E., Washington; nearest Metro: Eastern Market, Blue and Orange lines). Six rooms, including one with a roaring fireplace and another with pool tables; food served well past midnight; and a laid-back, convivial atmosphere define this pub popular with Hill staffers and locals eager to blow off steam. Nightly food specials, free food during happy hour, and a raucous upstairs dance party every Friday and Saturday night keep various interests coming back, regardless of which side of the aisle they sit on during daylight hours.

Kelly's Irish Times (202-543-5433; 14 F St., N.W., Washington; nearest Metro: Union Station, Red line). There's something admirable about an Irish Bar without pretense, a place that knows how to pour a pint of Guinness and serves cocktails in a pint glass. The

Hawk 'n' Dove's modest façade. Photo by Nathan Borchelt.

decor—booths and tables strewn across the narrow space—keeps things simple, and the bar food is satisfying. But the true pleasure can be found by elbowing up to the long wooden bar, checking out the collage of police patches, political memorabilia, and photos of Nixon and Elvis on display while chatting up the local barflies, who range from politicians to businessmen to broadcast journalists. At night a downstairs dance floor caters to an always-chaotic college crowd, and the place gets packed on weekend nights. But those in need of respite from the summer sun and some friendly company while wandering near Union Station should look no further.

Pour House (202-546-1001; www.pourhouse-dc.com; 319 Pennsylvania Ave., S.E., Washington; nearest Metro: Eastern Market, Blue and Orange lines). This cavernous Capitol Hill hot spot has something for all takers on three floors that are ideal for laid-back debauchery. Popular with Hill staffers and work softball teams, the somewhat divey, lived-in vibe is matched by an amiable staff, fantastic drink specials, and special quiz nights.

Tune Inn (202-543-2725; 331? Pennsylvania Ave., S.E., Washington; nearest Metro: Eastern Market, Blue and Orange lines). Described by one loyal patron as an "ultradive," this small pub offers a much-needed antidote to the sometimes stuffy Capitol Hill scene—so needed, in fact, that Tune Inn has been around since 1955. Stuffed deer heads are mounted on the wall; cheap beer is sold by the pitcher; and good, honest, greasy food (breakfast entrées included) is served late into the night. And if you carve through the crowds orbiting the bar, you may be lucky enough to snag one of the back booths.

The Ugly Mug (202-547-8459; www.uglymugdc.com; 723 Eighth St., S.E., Washington; nearest Metro: Eastern Market, Blue and Orange lines). Twenty-four beers on tap, nightly specials Monday through Saturday, a flat-screen TV always within view, and a reliable kitchen serving pizza, mini-burgers, and other classic American fare has earned this sports-oriented pub a steady following among laid-back city residents.

Union Pub (202-546-7200; www.unionpubdc.com; 201 Massachusetts Ave., N.E., Washington; nearest Metro: Union Station, Red line). The spacious, 80-seat patio at the Union Pub elevates this bar and restaurant above its Capitol Hill competition. The emphasis here rests solely on relaxation, with copious, ever-evolving nightly drink specials; potent pitchers of the house margarita; and traditional American food served by an impeccably professional staff. Not surprisingly, the pub is popular with unpaid interns eager to stretch their dollar and with groups of fanatic sports fans who cluster to watch the game on the indoor big-screen TVs.

CHINATOWN/PENN QUARTER

IndeBleu (202-333-2538; www.indebleu.net; 707 G St., N.W., Washington; nearest Metro: Gallery Place/Chinatown, Green, Red, and Yellow lines). Although the products coming from the kitchen at this full-service restaurant can be a bit spotty, the same can't be said for the cocktails at the bar, aptly dubbed the Tantric Lounge. More than 50 specialty drinks are spread out on a creative menu inspired by—and modeled after—the D.C. subway map, with South Asian—influenced concoctions like lichi-flavored martinis and the Holy Basil, a mixture of champagne and herb-infused simple sugar. The decor is decidedly modern, including flat-screen TVs that stand in for mirrors in the bathrooms. A roster of well-known DJs lay down worldly electro-lounge music, and the bar staff keeps things friendly and casual—even if you try to pocket one of those cool Metro menus.

Lucky Strike Lanes (202-347-1021; www.bowlluckystrike.com; 701 Seventh St., N.W., Washington; nearest Metro: Gallery Place/Chinatown, Green, Red, and Yellow lines). This national chain is responsible for bringing bowling back to D.C.—but don't expect your grandfather's lanes. This hip spot—which enforces a dress code that bars work boots and back-facing baseball caps—brings the lounge scene to the American pastime, with DJs, signature cocktails, pool tables, 14 shimmering blue lanes, and an over-21 policy after 9. True to the boutique experience, the prices are also a notch up from what you might expect. Anticipate long waits and rates that vary by the hour or the game on weekend nights. Located on the second floor of Chinatown's movie theater complex adjacent to the Verizon Center.

R.F.D Washington (202-289-2030; www.lovethebeer.com/rfd.html; 810 Seventh St. N.W., Washington; nearest Metro: Gallery Place/Chinatown, Green, Red, and Yellow lines). The owners of the Brickskeller (see page 230) opened this massive Chinatown pub to further express their love for beer. But unlike its sister pub in Dupont Circle, R.F.D. (short for Regional Food and Drink) boasts 30 beers on tap, which rotate seasonally, as well as close to 300 bottles from around the world encased in massive, glass-door coolers. Famous quotes about the glories of beer are painted onto the walls, flat screens crown the wraparound bar, and there is an expansive dining room and back patio. The affection for hops also results in some inventive food from the kitchen: Try the ale-marinated brew burger alongside a pilsner you've never heard of.

INSIDER TIP: *Chinatown/Penn Quarter can get overrun with concert-goers or sports fans any night the Verizon Center is holding an event. On such nights, visit during the scheduled event and take off before the crowds let out and the neighborhood devolves into bar-crawling craziness.*

Rocket Bar (202-628-7665; 714 Seventh St., N.W., Washington; nearest Metro: Gallery Place/Chinatown, Green, Red, and Yellow lines). Unlike most of Penn Quarter's watering holes, Rocket Bar—almost lost in the Times Square-esque chaos of Chinatown—offers a casual neighborhood atmosphere. Enter through the small doorway, walk down the lime-green stairs, and you'll discover a basement pub stocked with four pool tables, long shuffleboard tables, dart boards, and the occasional video game. Walls are adorned with a kitschy, *Jetsons*-style sci-fi theme. The beer on tap comprises familiars and the unusual, and you'll also find ciders, made-to-order cocktails, bottled beer, and a small selection of wine by the glass. Nooks and crannies decorated with '70s-era furniture offer a chance to tuck away and play one of the board games on loan from the bar, and you're invited to eat take-out from any of the neighboring establishments. Owned by the folks behind Bedrock Billiards (see page 226).

Dupont Circle and West End

18th Street Lounge (202-466-3922; www.eslmusic.com; 1212 18th St., N.W., Washington; nearest Metro: Dupont Circle, Red line). An unmarked door next to Mattress Discounters leads into this hipster haven, a narrow, multilevel lounge and dance club that also serves as the headquarters of the Eighteenth Street Lounge Music label and D.C.'s own Thievery Corporation. Although the door policy is arbitrary, it's one of the best places in town to hear new lounge music, international DJs, and occasional live bands in a warm environment with plush couches, expertly mixed cocktails, and many of the city's beautiful people. Roaring fireplaces in the winter are cozy and intimate; during the summer, 18th Street Lounge opens a massive roof deck, playing some of the world's best electro-lounge underneath a ceiling of stars.

INSIDER TIP: *To avoid high cover charges at the 18th Street Lounge, dress nicely and appear confident—and by* nicely *we don't mean you should wear a suit or an evening gown. Go for a casual, hip look, and you may slip in without paying as much as others who appear less trendy.*

The Brickskeller (202-293-1885; www.lovethebeer.com/brickskeller.html; 523 22nd St., N.W., Washington; nearest Metro: Dupont Circle, Red line). This D.C. establishment has long been on beer-lovers' maps for its expansive menu of more than 1,000 foreign bottles. And although the place is also somewhat notorious for being out of stock of the one bottle you simply *have* to try, the staff is knowledgeable enough to steer you in the direction of an equally good choice. The low ceiling and exposed brick of the basement-level series of rooms evokes a cavernous atmosphere, while upstairs is a more traditional place to dine on standard pub fare. They also host special beer tastings.

Café Citron (202-530-8844; 1342 Connecticut Ave., N.W., Washington; nearest Metro: Dupont Circle, Red line). One of the neighborhood's most popular happy hour spots, this salsa-infused lounge and restaurant offers some of the best mojitos in the city, as well as one of the most accessible dance scenes. Get there early on the weekends to avoid the lines, and dress to impress. The place gets crowded fast, and scoring a drink requires the patience of a saint, but the tone remains refreshingly unpretentious. Special events like flamenco dancing and live Brazilian music keep things perpetually fresh.

Five (202-331-7123; www.fivedc.com; 1241-B 19th St., N.W., Washington; nearest Metro: Dupont Circle, Red line). Ever since the banner club Nation closed and its real estate was swallowed by the new baseball stadium, Five has been one of the central focal points for D.C.'s floundering nightclub scene. International DJs spinning electronica, hip-hop, and reggae, and an attitude one step beyond the moneyed vibe of the downtown warehouse scene dominate this three-level, medium-sized club, which includes a Caribbean-themed rooftop when the weather cooperates. Hours that stretch to dawn make it a perennial night-owl hall-of-famer.

INSIDER TIP: *Weekend nights can get chaotic in Adams Morgan, Dupont Circle, and U Street, so consider hitting the town on weeknights for a more subdued scene. Summer weekends are also less hectic because the area's college students are on break.*

The Fox and Hounds (202-232-6307; 1537 17th St., N.W., Washington; nearest Metro: Dupont Circle, Red line). Teetotalers steer clear! This refreshing dive on bustling 17th Street serves its drinks with unabashed honesty: Order a vodka and tonic, and you get a glass of vodka and a bottle of tonic. Whether you take advantage of the large open-air patio or stick to the crowded bar area—stool, booth, or vinyl-covered small table—the people-watching is almost as good as the jukebox.

The Improv (202-296-7008; www.dcimprov.com; 1140 Connecticut Ave., N.W., Washington; nearest Metro: Dupont Circle, Red line). Those with a hearty appetite may find themselves in an uncomfortable position—the menu here brims with filling options, but eat too much and you risk exhaustion from laughing hysterically on a full stomach. This spot just south of the circle wrangles some of the country's best up-and-coming and established comedy acts. If you've seen *Seinfeld* (the namesake star has played here several times), you know the score: exposed brick backdrop, a bar, a bunch of tables, and an MC taking the stage between acts. Ticket prices vary by performer, and the Improv has a two-item limit (food or drink).

Ozio (202-822-6000; www.oziodc.com; 1813 M St., N.W., Washington; nearest Metro: Farragut North, Red line). This high-end cigar and martini bar was already popular before the 2007 smoking ban, but now it's a godsend for the nicotine-craving, well-dressed cocktail set (its status as a "cigar bar" saved it from the Districtwide smoking ban). Despite nominal sitting space and a weekend cover fee, it still pulls a crowd of the see-and-be-seen set, though Ozio also invites the opportunity to hang with the ones you're with. Fireplaces, a dance floor, Georgia O'Keeffe reproductions, and even a running waterwheel are scattered throughout this contemporary Art Deco, four-story property. Ozio also boasts a smoke-free dining room serving Mediterranean and South and Central American cuisine.

Russia House (202-234-9433; 1800 Connecticut Ave., N.W., Washington; nearest Metro: Dupont Circle, Red line). Housed in what was once a private supper club, this small, ultra-chic lounge is one of D.C.'s best. Dim lights, red silk damask-covered walls, polished wood, marble banisters, portraits of Russian czars, and a motley collection of plush couches and tables evoke an Old World feel popular with East European expats and hipsters who appreciate eclectic vodka, unique cocktails, and Russian caviar. Try to snag a place in the upstairs lounge or at the small bar and pick from more than 90 types of vodka on the menu (try one of their herb-infused varieties), or ask for a table in the maze-like, basement-level dining rooms.

For the Record: Part of D.C.'s Musical Legacy

When compared to other major metropolises like New York City or New Orleans, D.C.'s musical legacy flies under the radar. But listen closely, and you'll discover that the nation's capital served as the bedrock for two of the country's most vital musical genres: jazz and punk rock. Jazz reigns as U Street's perpetual soundtrack, with the mural of D.C. native Duke Ellington looking down with sage-like wisdom. Clubs on this strip hosted the likes of Dizzy Gillespie, Billie Holiday, Charlie Parker, Miles Davis, Lester Young, and other hometown legends like pianist Billy Taylor and sax player Frank Wess. The 1968 riots that followed the assassination of Martin Luther King Jr. destroyed much of the venerable jazz clubs, but the scene was rebuilt in the late 1990s, and now clubs like **Twins Jazz** (see page 235), **Jojo's** (202-319-9350; 518 U St., N.W., Washington; nearest Metro: U Street, Green and Yellow lines), **HR-57** (202-667-3700; www.hr57.org; 1610 14th St., N.W., Washington; nearest Metro: U Street, Green and Yellow lines), **U-topia** (202-483-7669; www.utopiaindc.com; 1418 U St., N.W., Washington), the venerable **Bohemian Caverns** (see page 233), and Georgetown's marquee **Blues Alley** (below) have rekindled the live jazz scene in the city.

D.C. also served as one of the central havens for the U.S. hard-core punk scene of the 1980s. Dubbed hard core, bands like Bad Brains, Minor Threat, Teen Idles, Rites of Spring, Dag Nasty, and Youth Brigade engaged in a fast and furious, blitzkrieg musical attack that rebelled against the Reagan-era mainstream. The scene gave birth to straight edge—a drug- and alcohol-free lifestyle—and spawned some of the genre's most influential albums, many issued by Dischord Records (www.dischord.com), cofounded by Ian McKay, lead singer of Minor Threat and member of Fugazi, one of D.C.'s seminal bands. The scene is still alive and kicking. Clubs like the **Black Cat** (see page 233), **Nightclub 9:30** (see page 235), and the venues in the Atlas District (see page 225) still host punk and hard-core bands, and the summer concert series in Upper Northwest's **Fort Reno Park** (www.fortreno.com; 3950 Chesapeake St., N.W., Washington; no Metro access) showcases other up-and-coming local talent.

GEORGETOWN

Blue Gin (202-965-4005; www.bluegindc.com; 1206 Wisconsin Ave., N.W., Washington; no Metro access). Georgetown's typical nightlife, made up of sports bars and unimaginative dance clubs, received a much-needed boost when this two-story, 4,500-square-foot club and lounge first opened in 2004. Boasting three bars, a sizable dance floor, a collage of film and abstract patterns on flat-screen TVs, a state-of-the-art sound system, a lounge room, and more than 12 types of martinis (including a signature mix of Tanqueray No. 10 gin, lime, elderflower syrup, and blue Curacao with a slice of sweet star fruit), Blue Gin attracts a slightly older crowd than most Georgetown venues, drawn in by good music and well-prepared cocktails. Expect a cover charge and a dress code barring sneakers and shorts on weekends. Best to arrive early.

Blues Alley (202-337-4141; www.bluesalley.com; 1073 Wisconsin Ave., N.W., Washington; no Metro access). This venerable D.C. jazz institution has been a local landmark since 1965, and its low stage has been graced by all the big names, from Stan Getz to Sarah Vaughan to Dizzy Gillespie. The intimate environs are colored by dim lights with scattered small tables and not a single bad seat in the house—this is the jazz club of your dreams. Attendance has its price, including a ticketed admittance fee and a modest commitment to spend $10–15 once you're inside, but the Creole cuisine is universally delicious, and it's a small price to pay for an experience of a lifetime.

Martin's Tavern (202-333-7370; www.martins-tavern.com; 1264 Wisconsin Ave., N.W., Washington; no Metro access). A bar as aged as the cobblestone streets of Georgetown itself, Billy Martin's Tavern was once a Civil War prison and a Corcoran family art gallery—and it's served every president since Harry Truman. Regardless of its storied history, Georgetown's oldest bar remains a quintessential corner pub. The decor stretches back to its 1933 origins: Tiffany lamps, nicotine-stained walls, wooden chairs and tables covered in linen, and framed hunting posters that create a homey atmosphere reinforced by the menu of reliable comfort food.

Sequoia (202-944-4200; 3000 K St., N.W., Washington; no Metro access). This classy establishment on the Georgetown waterfront almost feels more Miami than D.C., with its multilevel patio on the Potomac and glass-walled, high-ceiling dining room specializing in seafood. Consider it a pricey but relaxed way to chill in the sun and intermingle with the boat-bum crowd after a day of shopping in Georgetown, especially on warm days when the open-air patio pulls daylong crowds.

U STREET AND THE 14TH STREET CORRIDOR

Bar Pilar (202-265-1751; barpilar.com; 1833 14th St., N.W., Washington; nearest Metro: U Street, Green and Yellow lines). Just a few blocks south of its sister establishment, Saint Ex (see page 197), this down-to-earth pub offers refuge to legions of D.C. natives eager for a pint or cocktail and lazy, absurd conversation. The long bar dominates the right side of this narrow establishment as you walk in; the other side is flanked with a row of high tables. Farther back, a tight hallway leads past an old working photo booth and into a room with a series of coveted group tables. A nightly selection of tapas and entrées made from local, farm-fresh ingredients crafted by Executive Chef Justin Bittnery elevate pub fare beyond your standard expectations—and the price point is also grounded in reality. Be forewarned: The crowds can get out of hand on the weekends.

Black Cat (202-667-4490; www.blackcatdc.com; 1811 14th St., N.W., Washington; nearest Metro: U Street, Green and Yellow lines). *The* holy ground in Washington for emerging local, national, and international music acts, the Black Cat filled a noticeable void when the shoe-box-sized Nightclub 9:30 upgraded to its new digs. Co-owned by Foo Fighter Dave Grohl, the second-story main stage at this music venue provides room for 1,000 gyrating fans, while downstairs the no-cover Red Bar attracts a local crowd sporting torn jeans, tattoos, and a welcome lack of pretension. The small, hot, sweaty back room hosts DJ events on weekend nights and the occasional secret show of big-name artists like Beck. The Food for Thought kitchen serves a variety of vegetarian- and vegan-friendly dishes, and there's an all-ages policy for all shows. On New Year's Eve, the Black Cat hosts Peaches O'Dell and Her Orchestra, a festive, big-band alternative to a more expensive night out.

Bohemian Caverns (202-299-0801; www .bohemiancaverns.com; 2001 U St., N.W., Washington; nearest Metro: U Street, Green and Yellow lines). You'll either find the

The detailed wood carvings at the door to the Bohemian Caverns. Photo by Nathan Borchelt.

The Duke Ellington mural on U Street. Photo by Nathan Borchelt.

basement-level subterranean decor—complete with faux stalactites—atmospheric or over the top, but either way, one look at the roster of musicians who've graced this stage (Ellington, Armstrong, Holiday, Fitzgerald, Monk, Basie) and you know you're in a club that jazz built. At the street level, Bohemian Caverns serves slightly overpriced meals and holds special DJ hip-hop events that have generated quite a following. But downstairs is where the magic happens, even if the furniture and bar made of petrified wood evoke an unfortunate Disney vibe. When the lights dim and the musician takes the stage, everything but the music fades into a comfortable blur.

Chi-Cha Lounge (202-234-8400; 1624 U St., N.W., Washington; nearest Metro: U Street, Green and Yellow lines). Low-lit and ultra-chill, this Latin-influenced lounge is chock-full of plush velvet couches, live South American acoustic music, and plumes of exotic tobacco smoked from hookahs. The expansive main room consists of nests of couches and chairs, and a smaller back room is typically reserved for private parties dining on Peruvian tapas. A narrow side room offers more discrete seating. The clientele is heavily multicultural and well dressed, and a nominal dress code (no branded T-shirts) keeps the frat boys at bay.

Halo (202-265-2828; 1435 P St., N.W., Washington; nearest Metro: Dupont Circle, Red line). A frosted-glass façade marked by an embossed titular circle graphic may hide the mob scene inside. But even during happy hour (which can get really packed), this two-story, gay-friendly Logan Circle bar is casual and friendly. Much of the attitude derives from a sleek decor of leather couches and subdued lighting—or perhaps it's the two-for-one drink special from 5–9.

Local 16 (202-265-2828; 1604 U St., N.W., Washington; nearest Metro: U Street, Green and Yellow lines). The owners of the 18th Street Lounge (see page 230) are behind this wildly successful corner bar and restaurant, which boasts one of the city's largest roof decks. Although the name is taken from a Maryland ironworkers union, prices are matched to the urban hipster rather than to the blue collar, but deep-red walls, a central bar, and hardwood floors make for an honest, refined atmosphere. There is also a second-floor dining room and a third-floor roof deck, open year-round with the help of a huge collection of space heaters. The food menu offers upscale American dishes made from mostly local ingredients.

Nightclub 9:30 (202-393-0930; www.930.com; 815 V St., N.W., Washington; nearest Metro: U Street, Green and Yellow lines). Ladies and gentleman, Washington, D.C.'s finest live-music venue. What first started as a narrow dive of a club at 930 F Street has since graduated into a state-of-the-art experience. The stage rests on rollers to accommodate various-sized crowds; a wraparound second-floor balcony offers a birds-eye view (as does a third-level bar); and two long bars on the main floor keep the libations flowing. The downstairs bar, meanwhile, offers respite should the impeccable speaker system get too intense. The club books local, national, and international bands on the cusp of graduating to the stadium scene, along with a who's who of eminent indie, folk, rock, hip-hip, electronic, lounge, and hard-core artists—from Sonic Youth to Bob Dylan.

Twins Jazz (202-234-0072; www.twinsjazz.com; 1344 U St., N.W., Washington; nearest Metro: U Street, Green and Yellow lines). Climb the stairs to this small, second-level spot and you'll find a laid-back, knowledgeable crowd vibing in an intimate setting to the workmanlike musicianship of its performers, both local stars and national heroes on 365-day tours. Ethiopian and Caribbean food that complements the music nicely, and an inexpensive entry fee are bonuses, but the service can get spotty. That's a small trade-off to catch some of the best jazz in the city.

UPPER NORTHWEST

Aroma (202-244-7995; 3417 Connecticut Ave., N.W., Washington; nearest Metro: Cleveland Park, Red line). Under the same management as neighboring basement-level Comet Billiards, this narrow street-level lounge serves some of the city's most creative, reliable cocktails in a friendly atmosphere. Equal measures intimate and social, the decor embraces a retro-mod vibe with lounging couches in the back, high-table seating and a long tiled bar flanking the main room, and local art displayed for sale. Catch lounge, electronica, hip-hop, and world DJs on the weekends.

Nanny O'Briens Irish Pub (202-686-9189; www.nannyobriens.com; 3319 Connecticut Ave., N.W., Washington; nearest Metro: Cleveland Park, Red line). This Irish pub gets it right: dimly lit rows of whiskey lined up behind a scratched wooden bar that stretches the length of the narrow room, cracked green booths, and good beer on tap with staff who know how to pour it. A small stage near the back hosts the expected Irish tunes, and their Monday night Celtic jam sessions are legendary.

Aroma, Cleveland Park's understated drinking hole for the cocktail set. Photo by Nathan Borchelt.

ARLINGTON, VIRGINIA

Clarendon Grill (703-524-7455; www.cgrill.com; 1101 N. Highland St., Arlington; nearest Metro: Clarendon, Orange line). Live musicians whose talent sometimes doesn't measure up to their ambitions, '80s DJ nights, packed crowds, and a friendly and social (if chaotic) atmosphere personify this young-professionals happy-hour spot. If the noise becomes too much, retreat to the 75-seat back patio.

The Continental (703-465-7675; www.modernpoollounge.com; 1911 N. Fort Myer Dr., Arlington; nearest Metro: Rosslyn, Blue and Orange lines). Located in the Rosslyn neighborhood, this très modern, tiki-style lounge houses two bars, two dart boards, room for a live band, and nine pool tables covered in purple felt. But this place is about more than pool. Taking its aesthetic direction from nightclubs from the '50s–'70s (think *Barbarella,* not *Austin Powers*), the main property is divided into theme rooms like the Jet-Set Dining Room, Space-Age Bar, and the Exotica Bar and Lounges, where artfully crafted cocktails keep the well-dressed crowds drunk on libations as much as the opulent decor.

Galaxy Hut (703-525-8646; www.galaxyhut.com; 2711 Wilson Blvd., Arlington; nearest Metro: Clarendon, Orange line). There's always something going on at this friendly dive, from free movie night to karaoke to Wednesday "hump night" events where anyone can be the DJ. Saturday through Monday catch live indie shows from local and about-to-break national bands. The decor is unapologetically no-frills, with old-school arcade games and outsider art for sale on the walls. The prices match the utter lack of pretension.

Iota (703-522-8340; www.iotaclubandcafe.com; 2832 Wilson Blvd., Arlington; nearest Metro: Clarendon, Orange line). Part café, part club, this little gem on Wilson Boulevard caters to both vegetarians looking for good, cheap eats and music lovers eager to catch the next big thing in a space as intimate as a living room. Acts lean toward the country/folk variety, although the venue carries a hefty and well-deserved reputation among most accomplished touring musicians, whether they're rockers or soul singers. Iota also hosts poetry nights, open-mic nights for musicians, and afternoon all-ages shows.

Ireland's Four Courts (703-525-3600; www.irelandsfourcourts.com; 2051 Wilson Blvd., Arlington; nearest Metro: Clarendon, Orange line). Sure, it's got framed pictures of Dublin and an overreliance on forest green, but when the bartenders know how to pour a good pint of Guinness, stereotypical Emerald Isle trappings are tolerable—especially when the pub is as easygoing as Ireland's Four Courts. A roaring fireplace, dark wood, live acoustic music, and a clientele composed of friendly locals and young professionals from the surrounding business parks make this spot a no-frills treasure.

ALEXANDRIA, VIRGINIA

Birchmere Music Hall (703-549-7500; www.birchmere.com; 3701 Mount Vernon Ave., Alexandria; no Metro access). If you like to see your favorite musician rather than the back of a shaggy-haired head, and you prefer to hear the music rather than someone screaming for another drink, then the Birchmere is your place. In music circles the venue and its impeccable sound system are legendary: The artist takes center stage (literally), patrons sit at rows of tables and are asked to stay quiet and stay seated (unless a dance floor has been cleared), and a variety of surprisingly decent food is served. True to its relaxed atmosphere, mellower acts dominate the calendar, from The Decemberists to Emmylou Harris to k.d. lang, and they typically rise to the reverent setting to create an experience that you *share* with the performer. Beyond the main room, Birchmere also boasts a few recent additions, including a German-style beer garden and a billiards room.

O'Connell's in Old Town Alexandria offers ample bar space and a rowdy, friendly crowd. Photo by Nathan Borchelt.

O'Connell's Restaurant & Bar (703-739-1124; www.danieloconnells.com; 112 King St., Alexandria; nearest Metro: King Street, Blue and Yellow lines). The stats of this sprawling Old Town bar speak volumes: 8,200 square feet spread across two floors, with four bars (constructed from old woodwork salvaged from Dublin watering holes) offering 11 beers on tap in a convivial, jolly atmosphere. Because it's marketed as a "modern" Irish bar, you probably won't find beer-splattered floors or drunkards crooning along with the Pogues—but if you do and you want to escape, keep wandering through the property and you'll find a room exactly your speed. The kid-friendly establishment also has a small second-floor balcony.

PX's luminous, old-fashioned interior, leather-covered walls and all. Photo by Meshelle Armstrong. Used with permission.

Pat Troy's (703-549-4535; www.pattroysirishpub.com; 111 N. Pitt St., Alexandria; nearest Metro: King Street, Blue and Yellow lines). Almost disguised by its nondescript storefront a few blocks off King Street, this old-school pub envelops you with the sense of familiarity Irish pubs have somehow monopolized. The dining room dominates this bilevel establishment, but the 14-stool bar remains the room's main emphasis (at least until the live music starts each night). The dark-wood bar is crowned by a row of military uniforms encased in glass, with police patches lining the wall alongside a citadel of liquor bottles.

PX (703-299-8384; www.eamonnsdublinchipper.com; 728 King St., Alexandria; nearest Metro: King Street, Blue and Yellow lines). Modeled after Prohibition-era speakeasies, PX has no sign, just a wooden door around the corner from its sister establishment, Eammon's (see page 220). Look for a pirate flag and the glow of a subtle blue bulb, ring the bell, wait for the panel to slide open, and if you're wearing a jacket and you've timed it right, you'll enter one of the region's most spectacular drinking spots. The emphasis here is on artful, one-of-a-kind libations, from tobacco-infused cocktails to a life-changing twist on the traditional Manhattan. The brainchild of mixologist Todd

Thrasher, the sommelier at Restaurant Eve (see page 210), every ingredient has been made in-house, from the bitters to the soda water. The result? Cocktails that look almost too good to drink and evolve in complexity with every sip. Space is limited to two lounges and a few stools at the bar—and PX keeps the customer count capped at around 35, which adds to the refined, old-school successes of this labor of love. It's best to call Eammon's well in advance to reserve space at PX.

Union Street Public House (703-548-1785; www.usphalexandria.com; 121 S. Union St., Alexandria; nearest Metro: King Street, Blue and Yellow lines). First impressions are a bit deceiving at this first-rate Old Town pub and restaurant. You may pass right through the revolving door and settle into a booth or onto a bar stool at the cozy front bar—all dark wood, brass, and exposed brick—order a pint, and not explore. But then you'd miss the small back room with one of the city's best raw seafood bars, a second room cluttered with tables, and an entire second-floor dining room. The beer selection isn't the most expansive in the city, but the lively, friendly crowd, a mix of locals and out-of-towners, and inexpensive food easily make up for that shortcoming.

The towering forest of Rock Creek National Park. Photo by Nathan Borchelt.

7

RECREATION

The Great Outdoors

Known as the City of Trees since 1872, when D.C. Governor Alexander Shepherd called for 60,000 arboreal specimens to be planted throughout the District, Washington boasts thousands of acres of green space, a 185-mile-long hike-and-bike trail alongside a tranquil and historic canal, a 2,000-acre national park, and more than 3,700 cherry trees that explode in constellations of white and pink flowers each spring. Add to that the waterfront stretches of D.C., Alexandria, and Arlington; a host of municipal, county, and state parks; the 146-acre National Mall; and D.C.'s low horizon line and wide streets, and the region easily exceeds the expectations of any outdoor enthusiast.

BICYCLING

D.C. seems to have been designed with cyclists in mind. The terrain is mostly flat, save a few modest-grade hills in Upper Northwest and Capitol Hill, and the city is rapidly increasing the number of dedicated bike lanes on city streets, which makes exploring the city on two wheels a breeze—whether solo or in an organized tour. But don't limit your biking to the city streets; a wide variety of dedicated bike trails within the District and on the other side of the Potomac unveil the region's vast, verdant persona in ways a motorized vehicle could never allow. Please note: Wearing helmets is required by law, and biking on sidewalks is strongly discouraged. In addition to bike shops, rentals are available at several of the region's boat houses (see pages 244–245). Bicycles are allowed on the Metro, but not during rush hour, and the bikes must be transported by elevator and taken on only through the doors at the ends of the train cars (not the center doors).

Beach Drive (202-895-6070; www.nps.gov/rocr; no Metro access). This is paved paradise for the active set. Sections of this two-lane road, the main thoroughfare in Rock Creek National Park, close to motorized traffic from 7 AM to 7 PM on weekends and federal holidays year-round. Flocks of loyal locals—bikers, hikers, inline skaters, joggers, even families pushing baby strollers—cruise the road as it winds over the titular creek, past picnic grounds and hiking trailheads, and through old-growth forests. The terrain is moderately hilly, and side paths at the northern section of the park link up to well-marked, easy to navigate trail systems that run throughout the Maryland suburbs. The road is closed from Broad Branch Road to Military Road, from Picnic Grove 10 to Wise Road, and from West Branch Drive to the D.C. border. To access the southernmost point, park at Peirce Mill, located at Tilden Street/Park Road and Beach Drive. Please note: Biking on the hiking trails is strictly prohibited, and if caught, your bike will be confiscated. But beyond Beach Drive lie a few single-track routes in regional parks. Just look for the purple blaze painted on the trees, which marks the path.

Big Wheel Bikes (202-337-0254; www.bigwheelbikes.com; 1034 33rd St., N.W., Washington; no Metro access). A cycling institution in D.C. since 1971, Big Wheel Bikes is one of the best places in the city for rentals, in part because its flagship store is located within a few pedal strokes from the Chesapeake and Ohio Canal Towpath. Bikes of all description—from simple kids' models to full-suspension mountain bikes, tandems, and triathlon bikes—are available by the hour (three-hour minimum) or the day, and come with helmets, but not locks. In addition to the Georgetown location (just look for the big yellow building with a bike on it), Big Wheel Bikes has branches in Arlington (703-522-1110; 3119 Lee Hwy.) and Alexandria (703-739-2300; 2 Prince St.). Open 11–7 Wednesday through Friday; 10–6 on weekends. Closed Monday and Tuesday.

Capital Crescent Trail (www.cctrail.org; no Metro access). This 11-mile multiuse trail travels from Georgetown to the suburbs in Bethesda, Maryland, and is constructed on the abandoned rail bed of the Georgetown branch of the B&O Railroad. The first 7 miles are paved, cutting out of the western edge of K Street alongside the Potomac River before turning inland. At Bethesda, the trail shifts into crushed gravel after passing through a

D.C.'s bike-friendly landscape extends from bike-only lanes on many of its streets to paved paths through national parkland. Photo by Nathan Borchelt.

The Real D.C.: Neighborhood Heritage Trails

Tourists understandably flock to the National Mall as if it sits at the center of a gravitational force. But if you're also interested in tapping into D.C.'s varied urban history, consider traversing one—or several—of the recently established Neighborhood Heritage Trails. Organized by **Cultural Tourism D.C.** (202-661-7581; www.culturaltourismdc.org), these self-guided walks zoom in on the history of particular neighborhoods, with easy-to-find, illustrated signs that outline the route and offer historical and cultural background on the thriving locales within the District. Trace the influence of jazz down the famed U Street Corridor, learn the history of immigrants in the colorful neighborhood now known as Adams Morgan, explore the U Street/Shaw neighborhood (which predated Harlem as a mecca for African Americans), or wander the tree-lined "village-within-a-city" that is Mount Pleasant. The options are as varied as the city's history, and each offers an ideal way to step beyond D.C.'s well-trotted tourist track. Cultural Tourism provides printer-friendly PDF brochures, with maps and explicit directions, on its Web site, along with extensive information on a variety of guided tours throughout the District.

tunnel. You can cycle this trail as an out-and-back, or link up with Rock Creek National Park and loop back into Northwest D.C. by heading south down Beach Drive. Expect heavy crowds on weekends, especially during the warmer months; on weekdays a small army of dedicated cycling commuters ride the trail.

Chesapeake and Ohio Canal Towpath (202-653-5190; www.nps.gov/choh; 1057 Thomas Jefferson St., N.W., Washington; no Metro access). Part of the National Park System, the C&O Canal Path, as it's known locally, meanders alongside the Potomac River for 184.5 miles, from Georgetown to Harper's Ferry, West Virginia, and also links D.C. to the Maryland stretch of Great Falls National Park (see page 252). Once a lifeline for the communities and business that sprouted up along it, today the canal attracts cyclists and hikers out on daytrips or longer overnight hauls (campsites are available throughout the park on a first-come, first-served basis). Dirt hiking trails wind off the main canal, but don't get tempted—cycling is permitted solely on the crushed-gravel towpath. The park's Visitor Center in Georgetown also offers numerous kids' programs that illustrate the canal's historical importance.

Mount Vernon Trail (703-289-2500; www.nps.gov/gwmp; nearest Metro: Arlington Cemetery, Blue line). Located on the Virginia side of the Potomac River since 1973 and maintained by the National Park System, this 17-mile trail connects the District to George Washington's estate at Mount Vernon (see page 141). Entirely paved, it follows George Washington Memorial Parkway along a long stretch of the Potomac River, looping past Gravelly Point (where you can watch airplanes soar into the sky or come in for a roaring landing at Reagan National Airport) and cutting through Old Town Alexandria before a gradual 1-mile climb through a grove of trees to Mount Vernon. Pick up the trail by crossing the Memorial Bridge and turning left. Note: Bikes are not allowed on the grounds of Mount Vernon, so bring a lock if you plan to explore GW's estate.

The Washington and Old Dominion Trail (703-729-0596; trail office: 21293 Smiths Switch Rd., Ashburn, VA; no Metro access). The W&OD Trail, built on the former rail bed of its namesake railroad, is so frequently traveled that a yellow line divides its 9-foot-wide center for every one of its 45 paved miles. It starts just north of Arlington's

National Cemetery, in the neighborhood of Shirlington, and runs all the way to Purcel-lville in rural Virginia. For the ambitious, two-day trips are made simpler with easy access to an impressive array of trailside hotels and B&Bs, and a parallel horse trail offers a touch of variety for off-road cyclists. Expect crowds, especially on weekends in the closer suburbs, though things thin out as you get farther from the metro area. The W&OD also links up with the Mount Vernon Trail at Theodore Roosevelt Island (see page 147).

INSIDER TIP: *Road cyclists should consider pedaling to East Potomac Park (see page 251). The street that lines this peninsula doesn't get much car or pedestrian traffic—even during spring, when canopies of cherry blossoms shade the one-way road.*

BOATING

D.C.'s Potomac and Anacostia Rivers make it easy to break free of terra firma and explore the region by boat, whether heading to Roosevelt Island by rental kayak or taking a daylong cruise to Mount Vernon.

The Boat House at Fletcher's Cove (202-244-0461; www.fletcherscove.com; 4940 Canal Rd., N.W., Washington; no Metro access). This National Park Service-run boat house is located just northwest of Georgetown, ideally positioned between the C&O Canal and the Potomac River since the 1850s. You can rent rowboats, canoes, and kayaks by the hour or the day; enroll in beginner canoe and kayaking lessons; or purchase a D.C. fish-ing license and cast right off the property into the Potomac for the white perch, which start to migrate in early March. Fletcher's also rents bikes for cycling up and down the crushed-gravel towpath. Open 7–7 daily, early March through fall.

Jack's Boathouse (202-337-9642; www.jacksboathouse.com; 3500 K St., N.W., Washing-ton; no Metro access). Despite the fact that this family-owned boat house has been in operation at the same spot since 1945, Jack's remains one of D.C.'s best-kept secrets. Rowboats, canoes, and kayaks (both single and tandem) are available for rent by the day or the hour, and special tours can be arranged that delve into the city's history. Jack's location in Georgetown at the end of K Street, right on the Potomac River, puts Washing-ton Harbor, Roosevelt Island, and water-level views of the National Mall within (rela-tively) close paddling distance. Open 10–sunset Monday through Friday, 8–sunset on weekends.

INSIDER TIP: *Planning to stay in D.C. on the Fourth of July? Reserve a kayak or canoe with Jack's Boathouse and watch the fireworks from the Potomac River.*

Spirit Cruises (202-554-8000 or 1-866-302-2469; www.spiritofwashington.com; Pier 4, Sixth and Water Sts., S.W., Washington; nearest Metro: Shaw, Green and Yellow lines). You can arrange to take a day cruise to Mount Vernon or ply the waters of the Potomac for a few hours at this D.C. tourist institution, which offers all varieties of boat trips on the Potomac and Anacostia Rivers. The shorter cruises are organized around lunch, early and late dinner, and moonlit outings, along with live music and spectacular views of the monuments and Old Town Alexandria. Longer cruises include the aforementioned trip to Mount Vernon, one-time home to George Washington (see page 141), and a variety of private yacht charters. The food isn't spectacular and the required business-casual dress seems a touch forced, but the city shines when viewed from the river, especially as evening grows into night.

Thompson Boat Center (202-333-9543; www.thompsonboatcenter.com; 2900 Virginia Ave., N.W., Washington; no Metro access). Located at the intersection of Virginia Avenue and Rock Creek Park, Thompson's serves as the racing hub for many of the university rowing teams. In addition to renting canoes and kayaks (day-long or hourly), Sunfish sailboats and racing shells are available for those with certification, and Thompson offers instructional and racing programs. They also rent mountain and cruise bikes by the hour or the day. Open 8–6 daily.

Washington Sailing Marina (703-548-9027; www.washingtonsailingmarina.com; 1 Marina Dr. at Daingerfield Island, Alexandria; no Metro access). This sizable marina 1.5 miles south of Reagan National Airport off George Washington Parkway offers sailing and windsurfing lessons for all ages and hosts one-design and small sailboat racing. Hourly rental options include 19-foot Flying Scots and Aqua Fin sailboats, as well as mountain and cruise bicycles. Open 9–6 daily.

Period costumes and slow cruising on the C&O Canal offer a playful window into the ways of Georgetown's past. Photo by Nathan Borchelt.

The National Mall Carousel can offer restless children some much-needed play time between museums.
Photo by Nathan Borchelt.

FAMILY FUN

The nation's capital and children go together like summertime and ice cream. In addition to the exhaustive list of Smithsonian museums that continually capture the imagination, D.C. has a top-notch zoo, a carousel on the National Mall, paddleboats in the Tidal Basin, and an array of eclectic museums and kid-specific events that'll ignite their imagination and educate (without making it too obvious). In addition, most Smithsonian museums offer special kids' programs as part of their monthly schedules. Visit www.si.edu/visit for more information. And be sure to call 202-633-1000 for a recorded list of "Ten Tips for Visiting the Smithsonian Museums with Children."

Bureau of Engraving and Printing (1-866-874-2330; www.bep.treas.gov; 14th and C Sts., S.W., Washington; nearest Metro: Smithsonian, Blue and Orange lines). As much as $541 million is produced—daily—at this federal office, and a 45-minute tour lets you fol-low how money is made, from observing the large, blank sheets of paper to peering down on the actual printing floor as the bills come flurrying out in massive reams of currency. Tours are free, but same-day tickets are required during the prime tourist season from March to August (available at the ticket booth on Raoul Wallenberg Place). Also, Homeland Security measures often close the building to the public, so be sure to call in advance. Open 9:30–10:45 am and 12:30–2 pm, Monday through Friday.

Chesapeake and Ohio Canal National Historic Park (202-653-5190; www.nps.gov/choh; 1057 Thomas Jefferson St., N.W., Washington; no Metro access). Peer into the storied past of the once-vital Georgetown C&O Canal as period-dressed park rangers take you and your brood on an hour-long, mule-drawn boat ride. As you traverse through the canal's historic lift locks, the guides explain what life was like back in the 1800s. If you're lucky, you'll be treated to period tunes performed by a musically inclined ranger. Don't forget to bring along some fruit or veggies to feed the mules! Special historical walks can also be arranged out of the C&O Visitor Center during the summer, delving into the neighborhood's architecture and Civil War history. Open during daylight hours, with guided walks held during the summer months.

Miniature Golf at East Potomac Park Golf Course (202-554-7660; www.golfdc.com/gc/ep /mini.htm; 972 Ohio Dr., S.W., Washington; nearest Metro: Smithsonian, Blue and Orange lines). Come expecting challenging putts and quirky angles, not dinosaurs and imitation Eiffel Towers, and you'll love this 18-hole miniature golf course. This quiet spot just beyond the Tidal Basin offers perfect refuge from the typical tourist hot spots. The park also has a playground, swimming pool, tennis courts, and picnic facilities. Open 11–7 weekends only, April through October.

National Mall Carousel (202-357-2700; 1000 Jefferson Dr., S.W., Washington; nearest Metro: Smithsonian, Blue and Orange lines). Perfectly positioned for between-museum distractions on the south side of the Mall near the Smithsonian Arts and Industry building adjacent to the Smithsonian Castle, this 50-year-old carousel is outfitted with horses, dragons, and sleighs. You'll find smaller crowds on weekday mornings, but longer lines sometimes crop up during the prime tourist season, from March through August. Tickets required. Open 10–5:30 daily.

National Zoo (202-633-4800; nationalzoo.si.edu; 3001 Connecticut Ave., N.W., Washington; nearest Metro: Woodley Park, Red line). Although it resides far north of the Mall, in Upper Northwest between Cleveland Park and Adams Morgan, the zoo successfully draws legions of visitors—and with good reason. Orangutans swing overhead on an open cable system; lions and tigers and bears prowl in their simulated environments; and indoor exhibits like the Reptile and Amphibian House, the Invertebrate House, and the Bat Center offer shelter from any impending storm. The multistory Amazonia building reflects the diverse climate of that South American ecological treasure, complete with a walk-through rainforest and profiles of its resident animals. But arguably the zoo's biggest draw is Tai Shan, the lovable baby giant panda on display with his mother, Mei Xiang (acquire free tickets to gain entry into the Panda House, should the weather keep them inside, from the zoo's Web site). Special events are scheduled annually. Free admittance. Open 6–8 daily, April through October; 6–6 November through March.

Rock Creek Horse Center (202-362-0117; www.rockcreekhorsecenter.com; 5100 Glover Rd., N.W., Washington; no Metro access). The only active full-service horse center and provider of riding lessons in the District, Rock Creek Horse Center offers trail and pony rides, lessons, and summer day camps for children 8 and older. The trail rides penetrate scenic Rock Creek National Park and are open to children 12 and older, while by-appointment-only weekend pony rides accommodate children at least 2? years old and 30 inches tall. Open noon–6 Tuesday through Friday, 9–5 Saturday and Sunday.

Smithsonian's Discovery Theater (202-633-8700; www.discoverytheater.org; The S. Dillon Ripley Center, Third Sublevel, 1100 Jefferson Dr., S.W., Washington; nearest Metro: Smithsonian, Blue and Orange lines). For more than 25 years, the Discovery Theater has staged approximately 300 entertaining, educational live performances annually— each one geared toward kids. Music, theater, mime, puppetry, storytelling, all-ages shows, and events targeting specific age groups—it's all represented. Show themes vary annually, but they're typically staged at 10:15 and 11:30 AM Tuesday through Friday, and occasionally at noon on Saturday. Theater summer camps are held in consort with the larger Smithsonian Association's day camp program. Reservations are highly recommended.

Tidal Basin Boathouse (202-479-2426; www.tidalbasinpeddleboats.com; 1501 Maine Ave., S.W., Washington; nearest Metro: Smithsonian, Blue and Orange lines). Rent a two- or four-seater paddleboat for a few hours and ply the calm waters of the Tidal Basin, and take in staggering views of the Jefferson Memorial and the National Mall. It's a downright ethereal experience during the Cherry Blossom Festival, but expect to spend a fair amount of time navigating around the other boats that choke the water during prime tourist season. There's no age limit, though at least one person in the boat has to be 16 or older. Advance reservations (either online or by phone) are highly recommended. Open 10–6 daily from March 15 through Labor Day, Wednesday through Sunday after Labor Day until Columbus Day Weekend.

Upton Hill Regional Park (703-534-3437; www.nvrpa.org/parks/uptonhill; 6060 Wilson Blvd., Arlington; no Metro access). Everything from hiking trails to batting cages and a water park can be found at this densely wooded Arlington regional park a few miles from Washington, but the prime family draw remains the deluxe mini-golf course. The scenic course carves through a beautiful stretch of the parkland and boasts one of the world's longest mini-golf holes. Hours vary by season.

Washington Doll's House and Toy Museum (202-244-0024 or 202-363-6400; 5236 44th St., N.W., Washington; nearest Metro: Friendship Heights, Red line). The biggest challenge at this small Upper Northwest museum? Not touching anything, because although this impressive collection of Victorian-era dolls, dollhouses, and toys may beg to be used, it's strictly hands-off. But even without the tactile experience, the museum won't disappoint. Sip on refreshments in the Edwardian tea room, peer into miniature windows of the dollhouses to marvel at the tiny place settings, and peruse the two gift shops. And don't let the name fool you—the museum also has toy soldiers, wooden horses, and building blocks on display. Open 10–5 Tuesday through Saturday, noon–5 Sunday. Nominal entry fees apply.

GOLFING

The wealth of private courses in the D.C. metro area keep resident golfers well sated throughout the season, but the District and the surrounding 'burbs also benefit from some of the country's most scenic, high-quality, and challenging public courses perfect for visiting aficionados eager to swing the clubs. All the courses listed below also offer lessons. All greens fees listed are for 18 holes; carts are extra.

The Tidal Basin paddleboats provide leg-powered fun in an exceptionally beautiful environment. Photo courtesy of Jon Preimesberger. Used with permission.

East Potomac Park Golf Course (202-554-7660; www.golfdc.com; 972 Ohio Dr., S.W., Washington; nearest Metro: Smithsonian, Blue and Orange lines). This municipal golf center close to the National Mall resides on the scenic peninsula that stretches between the Potomac River and the Washington Channel, sporting views of the D.C. skyline. As such, it can get crowded, and the mostly flat course does not drain well after a rainstorm. Options include two nine-hole courses—the White Course (2,505 yards, par 34) and the Red Course (1,311 yards, par 27); an "executive course" featuring par 4s and 3s; the 18-hole, 6,599-yard, par-72 Blue Course; a two-deck, 100-stall driving range; and a snack bar with a patio that serves grilled food and on-tap beer. Greens fees around $25.

Greendale Golf Course (703-971-3788; www.fairfaxcounty.gov/parks/golf/greendale; 6700 Telegraph Rd., Alexandria; no Metro access). A mixture of modest challenges over 18 holes, this par-70 course typifies the type of public-access golf courses you'll find in the D.C. suburbs. Tight Bermuda fairways and water hazards are strewn along 148 acres of rolling terrain, with views of the entire course and surrounding region on the 17th hole. Facilities include a putting green, clubhouse with food service, pro shop, and warm-up net. Greens fees around $25.

Hilltop Golf Club (703-719-6504; www.hilltopgolfclub.com; 7900 Telegraph Rd., Alexandria; no Metro access). Unless someone told you, you'd never guess that this meandering nine-hole course sits atop what was once a landfill—a fact that makes Hilltop all the more a revelation. In light of the absence of deep soil, architect Lindsay Bruce Ervin turned to the treeless courses of Scotland for inspiration, and designed a grassy 2,300-yard par-31 course along with a lighted driving range with 68 stalls. Greens fees $25–50.

Langston Golf Course and Driving Range (202-397-8638; www.golfdc.com; 2600 Benning Rd., N.E., Washington; no Metro access). Rated by the *Washington Post* as the city's best public course, this 6,600-yard-long, relatively flat 18-hole course has mounded fairways on the front nine to keep things interesting, and a brutal back nine, including a stretch of marshy wetlands and a 538-yard, par-5 hole that starts with a drive across Kingman Lake. Forty driving-range stalls (five covered), a short-game practice green near the 18th hole, a pro shop, and a snack bar round out the long list of amenities. Greens fees under $25.

Pinecrest Golf Course (703-941-1061; www.fairfaxcounty.gov/parks/golf/pinecrest; 6600 Little River Turnpike, Alexandria; no Metro access). A familial vibe dominates at this 2,462-yard public course, with nine holes stretched across a narrow, out-and-back par-35 playing field scattered with ponds and paved pathways. An indoor practice area, 10

A scenic stone bridge crossing over the eponymous creek in Rock Creek National Park. Photo by Nathan Borchelt.

driving cages, a putting green, and a full-service clubhouse, pro shop, and snack bar are also on-site. Greens fees $25–50.

Rock Creek Golf Course (202-882-7332; www.golfdc.com; 1600 Rittenhouse St., N.W., Washington; no Metro access). Don't let the diminutive stats of this Upper Northwest golf course fool you. Although its 18 holes are only par 3s and par 4s, the hilly terrain, postage-stamp-sized greens, and the dense woodland that borders practically every inch of the back nine makes this one of the region's toughest. One local golfer's advice? "If you're playing Rock Creek, be sure to bring along a box of balls." Additional facilities include a putting green, pro shop, and snack bar, along with an outdoor grill offering hamburgers and chicken. Greens fees around $25.

PARKS

More than 19 percent of Washington, D.C., is devoted to public parks and open spaces—one of the highest ratios of any U.S. urban center. From a modest, blocks-wide patch of green in the middle of downtown, to the sprawling, 2.75-square-mile Rock Creek National Park, to the National Mall itself, which is part of the National Park System, dodging the city for a flirtatious afternoon with Mother Nature is a simple matter of deciding where you want to go. This list includes some of D.C.'s more remarkable parks and public lands, but it's far from definitive. Explore downtown on foot or by bus and you'll discover other stretches of urban parkland. In addition to exploring Rock Creek National Park, ardent hikers should consider day trips out to **Great Falls** and **Shenandoah National Parks** (see page 252). Birders tend to flock to the **U.S. National Arboretum** (see page 135), where hawks, sparrows, and owls congregate in the winter, while summer typically sees high numbers of northern bobwhites.

Battery Kemble Park (bounded by Chain Bridge Rd., MacArthur Blvd., 49th St., and Nebraska Ave., N.W., Washington; no Metro access). During the Civil War, this park served as a battery with two 100-pound Parrot rifles that covered the Chain Bridge and the Virginia shores of the Potomac River. Today, this stretch of public parkland rests within the larger Rock Creek National Park, tucked into an affluent neighborhood near American University. The 57-acre park is ideal for picnics, bird-watching, hiking, and trail-running, with paths that link up with Glover-Archbold Park and points beyond. Dog-lovers (and dog-haters) take note: Battery Kemble recently became a leash-free dog park.

East Potomac Park (Ohio Dr., S.W., Washington; nearest Metro: Smithsonian, Blue and Orange lines). One of D.C.'s most scenic and seldom visited locales (at least by tourists), 328-acre East Potomac Park rests on a narrow peninsula that juts out from the Tidal Basin, between the Washington Channel and the Potomac River. Spring brings an explosion of pink and white flowers as the cherry blossoms create a floral canopy over the 3.2-mile, one-way road that encircles the park, sheltering the legions of joggers and road cyclists. During the summer and fall, locals wile away the day picnicking or fishing in the river. Hains Point, the park's southernmost tip, marks the geographical spot where the Potomac and Anacostia Rivers converge, affording views of Reagan National Airport, the Bolling Air Force Base, Fort Lesley McNair, and the National War College. This is also the former home to *The Awakening*, a stunning bronze sculpture of a massive man clawing his way out of the earth. Unfortunately, this statue was sold in 2007 for $750,000 and moved to the National Harbor in Prince George's County, Maryland. The park also hosts a golf course and driving range, miniature golf, a swimming pool, a tennis center, and copious picnic tables.

Glover-Archbold Park (enter via Reservoir Rd., off Foxhall Rd., N.W., Washington; no Metro access). This narrow, 183-acre park is shaped like an elongated finger pointing out from Rock Creek National Park for about 2.6 miles, running from the Chesapeake and Ohio Canal north up to Van Ness Street, bordering the Upper Northwest neighborhood of Glover Park. The wild, wooden landscape, which boasts public gardens and a maze of dirt hiking and running trails, was donated to the city in 1924 as a bird sanctuary. Today you can still spy Kentucky warblers, winter wrens, white-throated sparrows, and thrushes.

National Parks Near and (Somewhat) Far

Great Falls National Park (703-285-2965; www.nps.gov/grfa) might only measure in at a modest 800 acres, but its geological wealth elevates the park to downright gargantuan proportions. The national park straddles two states and is bisected by the Potomac River. The Virginia side is noticeably wilder, with access to hikes that hug the rocky shoreline, serpentine lines of narrow single-track open to mountain biking, and plenty of picnic spots nestled in the woods. The Maryland side is a bit more established, home to a wooden deck overlooking the sizable falls from which the park derives its name, and one of the better hiking trails in the D.C. area, the rugged and rock-strewn Billy Goat Trail. And best of all, Great Falls is only a stone's throw from the Beltway, easily accessible by walking or cycling to the park's Maryland side via the C&O Canal Towpath. Open 7 AM to dark daily.

The rugged terrain of the Billy Goat Trail on the Maryland side of Great Falls National Park. Photo by Nathan Borchelt.

Shenandoah National Park (540-999-3500; www.nps.gov/shen), on the other hand, lies 75 miles east and a world away from Washington, D.C. Envision 197,411 acres of pristine wilderness stretched across the verdant Blue Ridge Mountains brimming with plant and animal life. During spring, the landscape is covered in wildflowers and emerald ferns. During summer, the park offers higher-elevation respite from D.C.'s sweltering humidity, while fall brings bursts of foliage, brilliant displays of orange, vermillion, purple, and red. Armchair nature-lovers should rent a convertible and tour Skyline Drive as it carves through the park, past staggering overlooks and public picnic spots. The more actively ambitious, meanwhile, can disappear for weeks, exploring more than 500 miles of hiking trails (including 101 miles of the famed Appalachian Trail), camping either in the backcountry (permit required) or one of the park's many established campsites. Special ranger-guided tours and children's activities, like the Junior Ranger Program, are available. Serious hikers in particular should not miss the hike up Old Rag Mountain, easily the best day-hike in the region.

A bird's-eye view of Rock Creek as it feeds into Woodley Park and Adams Morgan. Photo by Nathan Borchelt.

Lady Bird Johnson Park and Lyndon B. Johnson Memorial Grove (703-289-2500; www.nps.gov/gwmp; between 14th Street and Memorial Bridges, Arlington; no Metro access). D.C.'s iconic monuments serve as the backdrop for this 15-acre Virginia park, located on Columbia Island just off George Washington Memorial Parkway. The pink granite monument to Lyndon Johnson sits within a grove of white pine and dogwood trees, but the real lure here lies beyond the monument, where the hiking trails wind through the forestland alongside the Potomac. In spring, more than 1 million daffodils and 11,000 red tulips bloom in the park's formal flower beds. It's also a great spot to watch the Fourth of July fireworks without getting choked in the postcelebration traffic.

Meridian Hill National Park (202-895-6000; www.nps.gov/mehi; bounded by 15th, 16th, Euclid and W Sts., Washington; nearest Metro: U Street, Green and Yellow lines). Something of a D.C. secret hideaway, Meridian Hill Park (also known locally as Malcolm X Park) opened in 1914, but fell into disrepair during the city's troubled times in the 1980s and '90s. Today the 12-acre site offers four city blocks of open fields; views of the Washington Monument peeking out over apartment complexes; and an expansive terraced garden with statues, waterfalls, and fountains. It's a fantastic spot to escape the urban bustle of nearby Adams Morgan and U Street. On the evenings and weekends, locals play soccer or toss the Frisbee while students from nearby Howard University study on outstretched blankets under the sun. And on Sunday afternoons during the warmer months, a massive conflagration of drummers flocks to the stone benches near the overlook, pounding out tribal beats—African mixed with Latino—with flair and orchestral-like efficiency. That said, the park is best avoided at night, as the dark corners and lack of police patrols bring back the city's criminal elements.

Montrose Park (202-426-6827; 30th and R Sts., N.W., Washington; no Metro access). In the 19th century, rope-making baron and Georgetown resident Robert Parrot donated this land for local meetings and picnics. Today, it boasts 16 acres that include tennis courts, picnic tables, hiking trails, a boxwood maze for kids, new playground equipment, and access to the trails of Rock Creek National Park and the gardens of Dumbarton Oaks (see page 134).

Pershing Park (202-737-6938; 14th St. and Pennsylvania Ave., N.W., Washington; nearest Metro: Federal Triangle, Blue and Orange lines). This little downtown oasis within blocks of the White House could be accused of having seasonal-affective disorder. During the warmer months, the park's pond is occupied by a community of ducks, and the café hosts art events and sells ice cream, snacks, and souvenirs Wednesday through Sunday. Come winter, the park gives way to armies of ice-skaters in a family-friendly environment, complete with skate rentals and hot chocolate (see page 259).

Rock Creek National Park (202-895-6070; www.nps.gov/rocr; 5200 Glover Rd., N.W., Washington; nearest Metro: Woodley Park, Red line). Urban oasis personified, this narrow stretch of verdant parkland covers more than 2,000 acres (more than twice the size of New York's Central Park) in northwest D.C., stretching from the Maryland border all the way down to the National Mall. This patchwork of hiking and horseback riding trails, paved cycling routes, tennis courts, and copious historic monuments was the first urban natural area set aside by Congress as "a pleasuring place for the enjoyment of the people of the United States." Today, locals regard the park as their own back yard, with easy access from Adams Morgan, Georgetown, and Upper Northwest. The park also contains a number of car-accessible picnic areas like the historic Peirce Mill, a gristmill that dates back to the 1820s, along with public-use tennis and horse centers and the **Carter**

The National Mall commonly stands in as a makeshift baseball diamond for legions of office softball teams.
Photo by Nathan Borchelt.

The boardwalk trail through Theodore Roosevelt Island is popular with hikers. Photo by Debbie K. Hardin.

Barron Amphitheater (202-426-0486; 16th St. and Colorado Ave., N.W.), home to a free Shakespeare event each spring (see page 297). On weekends and holidays, sections of Beach Drive, the central road through Rock Creek, are closed to traffic, opening the smooth asphalt to cyclists, inline skaters, and families hunting for that perfect picnic spot or a trailhead leading into the park's Brothers Grimm-esque old-growth forests (see page 254). Open dawn to dusk daily.

Theodore Roosevelt Island (703-289-2500; www.nps.gov/this; accessible via a footbridge on the Virginia side of the Potomac River, off George Washington Parkway just north of the Roosevelt Bridge; also accessible via the Mount Vernon Trail; no Metro access). Within minutes you can travel from the chaos of Georgetown or the tourist hordes of the Mall and reach 91 pastoral acres of pristine, all-natural serenity. A 17-foot-tall statue of the island's namesake sits at the center of this teardrop-shaped island in the Potomac River (see page 147), but the real lure is the 2.5 miles of clearly marked dirt trails and a boardwalk that snake through the forest, marshlands, and riverfront terrain. Open dawn to dusk daily.

The Triumphant Return of the Washington Nationals

Baseball returned to the nation's capital in the spring of 2005, when the Washington Nationals (202-675-NATS; www.washington.nationals.mlb.com) played their first game at RFK Stadium. D.C.'s previous team, the Senators, actually had two incarnations in the city, both within the American League. The first Senators team played from 1901 to 1960 before moving to Minneapolis-St. Paul, becoming the Twins. The second team played from 1961 to 1972, when the franchise moved outside of Dallas and were renamed the Texas Rangers. At that point, most local fans turned to the Baltimore Orioles rather than harboring loyalty for displaced (and renamed) teams.

Then, in a twist of poetic justice, the first franchise relocation since the Senators left for Dallas brought the Montreal Expos to the District, who became the Washington Nationals. And although getting the National League team to D.C. proved to be a huge struggle—which included negotiating a deal between Major League Baseball and Orioles ownership to protect the Baltimore team from financial harm if its fan base dwindled—the Nats have been resoundingly embraced by D.C.'s long-neglected baseball supporters.

In May 2006, ground was broken for a new Nationals Stadium at the revitalized Anacostia Waterfront at South Capitol and N Streets in southeast D.C. near the Navy Yard metro stop. The state-of-the-art, 41,000-seat, open-air stadium is anchored by the city skyline south of the National Mall, including views of the Washington Monument and the dome of the Capitol from the upper level. The stadium was open for business as of the 2008 season.

PICKUP SPORTS

D.C.'s plentiful open spaces and parkland lend themselves to something of an urban anomaly: A profusion of terrain tailor-made for pickup sports. Witness the National Mall, where games of soccer and Frisbee football are played almost daily alongside office softball teams and registered kickball leagues. To tap the vein of some of the quasi-organized events, refer to **Craig's List D.C.** (washingtondc.craigslist.org), where pickup games are commonly posted. Or just grab your cleats and wander the Mall until you find a game.

Baseball and Football

These two American pastimes can be had pretty much anywhere there's open ground—particularly the National Mall, where office baseball and softball team league games are held. The fields just south of the Reflecting Pool also serve as prime staging ground. For full-on baseball diamonds, however, head to the Tidal Basin and West Potomac Park, where chain-link backstops and dirt diamonds reside just past the Roosevelt Memorial.

Frisbee

The National Mall and the Ellipse are the typical staging grounds for weekend morning matches of Frisbee football. A friendly smile and a basic understanding of the rules will typically gain access to the game. These expansive stretches of urban green land are also perfect for tossing the disc. For Frisbee golf, head to Arlington's **Bluemont Park** (703-228-4747; 601 N. Manchester St., Arlington; no Metro access; open dawn to dusk), which sports a 70-acre county park with a nine-hole course.

Soccer

As one of America's premier international cities, the world's most popular game certainly has its place in the District. Pickup matches can be found at practically any park—or concrete course—big enough to accommodate a handful of players and two goals, but games can be found on weekends on the National Mall just south of the Reflecting Pool or west of the Capitol, and most warm evenings—and all throughout the weekend—in Meridian Park just north of U Street (see page 253). To hook up with a more organized group, contact **Federal Triangles Soccer Club** (www.federaltriangles.org), a group of gay and lesbian soccer players with organized pickup games twice weekly.

Volleyball

Near the back of the Lincoln Memorial, in a narrow stretch of parkland at the base of the Memorial Bridge, sit the **Sand Courts of Washington** (3265 S St., N.W., Washington; no

---

Sports: A Washington Obsession

Baseball: The Nationals

Until 2008, the Nationals played in RFK Stadium (202-675-NATS; washington.nationals.mlb.com), but they now play at the 41,000-seat baseball stadium on the Anacostia Waterfront.

Basketball: The Wizards

Formerly known as The Bullets—a name that was changed around the same time D.C.'s murder rate skyrocketed—the Wizards now play in the recently built Verizon Center in the northwest neighborhood of Chinatown (202-661-5050; www.nba.com/wizards; 601 F St., N.W., Washington).

Basketball: The Mystics

Founded in 1998, a year after the start of the WNBA, the Washington Mystics quickly tapped into D.C.'s loyal fan base, recognized for the highest home-game attendance for five nonconsecutive years. So far, the team's success has been less noteworthy. They also play in Chinatown's Verizon Center (202-266-2200; www.wnba.com/mystics; 601 F St., N.W., Washington).

Football: The Redskins

Winners of five NFL Championships and three Super Bowls, the Washington Redskins (301-276-6050; www.redskins.com) are dearly loved by arguably the most loyal fans in the league. They practice in Ashburn, Virginia, and play their games at FedEx Field in Landover, Maryland. As you'd expect from such rabid followers, tickets are nearly impossible to get unless you can find friends with a season pass—and can convince them to let you join 'em.

Hockey: The Capitals

Although they've had a topsy-turvy few seasons, the Caps still pull a loyal following at the Verizon Center arena (202-266-2350; capitals.nhl.com; 601 F St., N.W., Washington).

Soccer: D.C. United

Victor of the first two Major League Soccer Cups in the mid 1990s, D.C. United continues to draw a loyal—if somewhat small—following to their spirited games at RFK Stadium (202-587-5466; dcunited.mlsnet.com; 2400 E. Capitol St., S.E., Washington), although there are plans for a 27,000-seat, soccer-specific stadium in the works for the same locale as the newly constructed baseball stadium on the Anacostia River. RFK also hosts exhibition games with clubs from Europe and South America.

Metro access), a fleet of 11 courts that typically see four and doubles pickup games in a friendly, convivial atmosphere with a healthy mix of international players.

RUNNING

D.C.'s relatively flat landscape, wide sidewalks, and ample public spaces make it ideal for jogging enthusiasts. The National Mall may offer the most iconically scenic route, but you can also trail run in Rock Creek National Park (see page 254) and on the gravel path of the C&O Canal (see page 243). Late-evening runners should consider running through the National Zoo (see page 247); thin crowds and a steady uphill grade from the back entrance, ending at Connecticut Avenue, offer a great workout. To better plan your routes, visit walkjogrun.net, a fantastic countrywide Web site that lets you map out potential routes (with mileage counts) and access routes created and saved by other people. **D.C. Run** (212-209-3370; www.dcrunningtour.com), meanwhile, offers guided jogging tours of the city in routes that range from 3 to 10 miles, along with routes customized to your particular interest and running proficiency. Also check out **Fleet Feet** (202-387-3888; www.fleetfeetdc .com; 1841 Columbia Ave., N.W., Washington; nearest Metro: Woodley Park, Red line), an independently owned running store in Adams Morgan that holds weekly club runs.

Runners stretching mid-workout at the benches that ring the Washington Monument. Photo by Nathan Borchelt.

INSIDER TIP: *Long-distance runners should consider a loop around the National Mall. Start at the Lincoln Memorial, jog around the Capitol, and then back to the steps of the Lincoln and you've clocked about 5 miles.*

SKATING

Ice Skating

D.C. has several indoor and outdoor ice-skating rinks, and although none match the larger scale urban skating spots like New York City's Rockefeller Center, D.C. does allow you to practice your double Lutz next to sculptures by renowned artists like Joan Miró and Alexander Calder.

Pentagon Row (703-481-6666; www.pentagonrowskating.com; 1201 S. Joyce St., Arlington; nearest Metro: Pentagon City, Blue and Yellow lines). This Arlington shopping mall offers outdoor ice skating daily from November through March—including holidays—amid an arena of outdoor cafés. Open noon–10 Monday through Friday, 10–11 Saturday, 10–7 Sunday.

Pershing Park (202-737-6938; www.pershingparkicerink.com; 14th St. and Pennsylvania Ave., N.W., Washington; nearest Metro: Federal Triangle, Blue and Orange lines). This small downtown outdoor ice rink just two blocks from the White House provides an intimate, family-friendly atmosphere for more inexperienced skaters, as well as lessons and learn-to-skate events. Open 11–9 Monday through Thursday, 11–11 Friday, 10–11 Saturday, 10–7 Sunday, November through mid-March.

Skating in circles on the ice rink at the National Gallery of Art's Sculpture Garden. Photo courtesy of Guest Services, Inc. Used with permission.

Sculpture Garden Ice Rink (202-289-3360; www.nga.gov; Seventh St. and Constitution Ave., N.W., Washington; nearest Metro: Archives, Green and Yellow lines). From November though March, the fountain at the center of this recently constructed sculpture garden just west of the National Gallery of Art transforms into a small rink, offering ice-level views of the surrounding artwork, including Roy Lichtenstein's whimsical house—a kid favorite. The Pavilion Café sells hot chocolate and food, and also offers respite from the cold (or from aching feet). Open 10–11 Monday through Saturday, 11–9 Sunday, November through mid-March.

Inline Skating

Inline skating is allowed on the city streets, but those not comfortable with skating in traffic may find themselves in over their heads in D.C. Although there are bike lanes, these are typically occupied by the numerous urban cyclists, and the city streets become a mad collage of commuters, pedestrians, and city buses—especially during rush hour. And don't even think about taking to the sidewalks unless you enjoy weaving around tour groups, Segway tours, office workers, and students.

That said, the two one-way streets that border the National Mall (Jefferson Drive, which runs west to east, and Madison Drive, which runs east to west) see less traffic (just watch out for tour buses). Alternatively, all of the paved trails around D.C. are open to Rollerbladers, including the Capitol Crescent Trail, Mount Vernon Trail, Chesapeake and Ohio Trail, and the paved trails in Rock Creek National Park, including Beach Drive (see pages 241–244).

TENNIS

Tennis is alive and well in the Washington, D.C., region. There are countless public-access courts throughout the city, from Capitol Hill to Adams Morgan to the scenic grounds behind the National Cathedral. There are also only-in-D.C.-type organizations like the **Capitol Hill Tennis Club** (703-927-5791; www.capitolhilltennis.org), composed of current and former members and staff of the U.S. Congress (public access is available, space permitting). In late July, D.C. also hosts the annual U.S. Open Series **Legg Mason Tennis Classic** (202-721-9500; www.leggmasontennisclassic.com), which features the world's top players competing for upwards of $1 million in Rock Creek National Park's William H.G. FitzGerald Tennis Center. Below we profile a few of the more established public-access courts, but by no means is it a complete list. Check out local community centers, Virginia county parks, and local schools and universities for other public-access courts.

INSIDER TIP: *To catch some of the world's best tennis athletes playing more for enjoyment than competition, get tickets to the prequalifying matches of the Legg Mason Tennis Classic, where the big names take to the court to warm up before this highly competitive portion of the U.S. Open Series starts.*

Bluemont Park (703-228-4747; 601 N. Manchester St., Arlington; no Metro access). This sprawling Virginia county park boasts nine lit tennis courts and a practice wall amid 70 acres of paved trails, baseball diamonds, fountains, volleyball courts, and picnic shelters.

East Potomac Tennis Center (202-554-5962; www.eastpotomactennis.com; 1090 Ohio Dr., S.W., Washington; nearest Metro: Smithsonian, Blue and Orange lines). One of the largest public facilities in the area, this tennis center sits on the shaded peninsula of East Potomac Park near Hains Point. Seasonal membership, walk-in, and by-appointment courts are available by the hour for their 10 clay and 14 hard-surface courts, including five indoor courts set to a comfortable 70 degrees year-round. EPTC also offers practice walls, ball machines, lessons, and full pro-shop services. Open 7–10 daily; clay courts open May through November.

Montrose Park (202-426-6827; 30th and R Sts., N.W., Washington; no Metro access). The opulent outdoor parkland surrounding these two lit tennis courts in Georgetown demands that we single them out from the other public-access hard surfaces in the city. And if the courts happen to be occupied, the park's proximity to Rock Creek National Park (see page 254) and the gardens of Dumbarton Oaks (see page 134) offers hours of distraction as you wait your turn.

Rock Creek Tennis Center (202-722-5949; www.rockcreektennis.com; 16th and Kennedy Sts., N.W., Washington; no Metro access). Host of the Legg Mason Tennis Classic, the only stop on the U.S. Open Series in the region, this public-access tennis facility in Upper Northwest sports 25 outdoor tennis courts (10 hard courts and 15 clay courts) and five heated indoor courts for year-round use. Lessons, clinics, ball machine and racquet rentals, and pro-shop services are also available. Its Web site also posts lists of players looking for partners. Open 7–11 Monday through Thursday, 7–8 Friday through Sunday, May through mid-September; 7–11 daily from mid-September through April.

Iconic D.C. shopping—for better or worse. Photo by Nathan Borchelt.

8

Shopping

What You Need and What You Want

For decades, the engine of politics that runs Washington, D.C., and its Virginia suburbs has resulted in a predominately conservative approach to that elusive element of life best described as "style." Even for liberal politicians, adventurous attire is typically limited to a three-button suit or judicious use of bold colors. And while classical variations on this theme stand the test of time, in the District there aren't many variations on the D.C. professional's uniform: pleated khaki pants and a blue button-down shirt for men, a pencil skirt and an unimaginatively tailored blouse for women—both typically accessorized with laminated work badges.

However, within the past 10 or so years a crop of new stores has sprung up across the region, geared to those eager to elevate Beltway fashion into the 21st century. Appropriately enough, most of the owners of the new boutique clothing stores come from the corporate world, having swapped their 9-to-5 lifestyle for projects that spark their true life's passions. As a result, consumers can reach beyond standby shopping neighborhoods like Georgetown and Old Town Alexandria and find a fresh approach to fashion, from vintage and consignment stores in Capitol Hill to boutique fashions along 14th Street, N.W. This new shopping sensibility has also translated into a cache of edgy, fashionable home-furnishing stores, copious locales that sell playful gifts with an eclectic D.C. spin, and a fantastic array of health and beauty facilities.

This sudden explosion of trendiness notwithstanding, D.C. is still proud of its storied legacy as the power-brokering capital of the country. This focused concentration on government and governing has naturally trickled down through the decades to influence new and used book and record stores and wonderfully eclectic shops that specialize in political memorabilia, antiques, art, and collectibles. The city's multicultural population has also resulted in truly unique artifacts from across the globe, from low-cost, high-quality ceramics in Chinatown or African artifacts in Adams Morgan, to Capitol Hill's purveyors of intricately woven rugs.

Our emphasis in this chapter is less on the chain stores and more on unique, independent, and regional outfits. But shopping enthusiasts will be happy to note that all of the nation's most popular stores, from Abercrombie & Fitch to Zara, are represented in the region as well. To tap those more familiar veins, explore Georgetown, Old Town Alexandria, and the newly established shopping district around Metro Center. To help you find more unique shopping and one-of-a-kind items, be sure to check out the **Daily Candy** e-mail

Artifactory is part museum, part global treasure trove. Photo by Nathan Borchelt.

newsletter (www.dailycandy.com), as well as **DC Scout** (www.washingtonpost.com/wp-srv/dcscout), the new shopping-specific e-mail product from the *Washington Post*.

ANTIQUES

Artifactory (202-393-2727; 641 Indiana Ave., N.W., Washington; nearest Metro: Navy Memorial, Green and Yellow lines). Open since 1972, this store offering an extensive collection of African and Southeast Asian artifacts—masks, strands of glass, textiles, sculptures of Hindi gods, Balinese puppets, South Asian batiks, the list is endless—offers a cornucopia of handcrafted artisanship. Prices range from affordable sale items to exorbitant collector's pieces. But if you simply have to have that life-sized Buddhist statue, this is the place (and yes, they can arrange shipping).

Brass Knob Architectural Antiques (202-332-3370; www.thebrassknob.com; 2311 18th St., N.W., Washington; nearest Metro: Woodley Park, Red line). As its name implies, Brass Knob specializes in home-decor accents and other architectural pieces that have been salvaged from residential and commercial properties. Doorknobs of all imaginable shapes, sizes, and materials sit beside gilded gas lamps, stained-glass windows, ornate tiles, chandeliers, and other elements that you might find—and envy—while touring someone's row house. The owners also have a huge downtown warehouse that sells bathtubs, doors, and other items too big to fit into their Adams Morgan showroom (202-265-0587; 57 N St., N.W., Washington).

Cherub Antique Gallery (202-337-2224; 2918 M St., N.W., Washington; nearest Metro: Rosslyn, Blue and Orange lines). This Georgetown antique store seems to have cornered the D.C. market for Art Nouveau and Art Deco treasures. In operation since 1974, the store has an ever-rotating inventory that includes unique sculptures, candleholders, chandeliers, glassware, cocktail shakers, and artwork—and for those longing for something older than the 19th century, Cherub shares the same address as Michael Getz Antiques (see below).

Frank Milwee Antiques (202-333-4811; 2912 M St., N.W., Washington; no Metro access). Oenophiles, this may be your version of antique heaven. This Georgetown shop carries a wide variety of wine corkscrews and vintage wine accessories amassed by owner Frank Milwee, a wine and corkscrew expert nonpareil.

Michael Getz Antiques (202-338-3811; 2918 M St., N.W., Washington; no Metro access). While coresident Cherub Antique Gallery (see above) specializes in Art Deco and Art Nouveau antiques, Michael Getz concentrates mostly on silver and decorative arts from the United States and England, as well as period fireplace tools and other eclectic items from the 18th to 20th centuries.

Millennium Decorative Arts (202-483-1218; www.millenniumdecorativearts.com; 1528 U St., N.W., Washington; nearest Metro: U Street, Green and Yellow lines). If you believe mid- to late-20th-century relics qualify as "antiques," this two-story converted U Street row house is your kind of place. Objects range from eclectic Art Deco lighting to '70s furniture to cocktail shakers from the '40s. You'll also find a veritable cornucopia of smaller items and one-of-a-kind knickknacks, along with vintage clothing, records, books, and rare pieces from famed designers like Charles and Ray Eames and Paul McCobb.

ART AND COLLECTIBLES

Allen Custom Framing & Biscarr Fine Art (202-628-1389; www.biscarr.com; 4620C Wisconsin Ave., N.W., Washington; nearest Metro: Tenleytown, Red line). Recently relocated from Georgetown, this unassuming frame and fine art store in the Tenleytown neighborhood in upper Northwest D.C. offers custom framing at highly competitive prices. But the real lure for out-of-towners? The store's impressive, perpetually rotating inventory of original and limited-edition prints from 20th-century artists like Picasso and Alexander Calder.

Après Peau (202-783-0022; www.aprespeau.com; 1430 K St., N.W., Washington; nearest Metro: McPherson Square, Blue and Orange lines). One of the most original and playful spots in the city for D.C.-centric gifts and collectibles, Après Peau (French for "after skin") was founded by Tina Alster, director of the Washington Institute of Dermatologic Laser Surgery and a clinical professor of dermatology at Georgetown University. Perfume and Lancôme products sit alongside D.C.-themed chocolates with names like Capitol Coconut and Smithsonian Salty Pretzel; stationery adorned with quotes culled from love letters written by U.S. presidents and their wives; and stunning ceramic artisan bowls designed by Louise Mathieson.

Art & Soul (202-548-0105; 225 Pennsylvania Ave., S.E., Washington; nearest Metro: Capitol South, Blue and Orange lines). This Capitol Hill spot boasts eclectic, nonconservative "wearable art" in the form of bracelets, rings, earrings, and necklaces. Run by a kind-

Get Kitschy in Tacoma Park

Longing for a lazy afternoon in a small-town community filled with eclectic, inexpensive shopping? Takoma Park has you covered. Founded in 1883, this 20,000-strong community straddles the borders of the District and Maryland, and was established as the first commuter suburb in the metro area. Young professionals still dominate this comfortable, colorful neighborhood, and their presence has generated a crop of quirky shops along Carroll Avenue, the neighborhood's unofficial main street. Fans of consignment stores and flea market finds will score treasures galore; the stores sell everything from vintage dresses and guayabera shirts to musical instruments, old magazines, furnishings, housewares, and collectible sports memorabilia—they've even got a gourmet store catering to dog-lovers and their canine companions. **Now and Then** (301-270-2210; 6927 Laurel Ave., Takoma Park) was one of the first stores on the scene, and it still sells some of the best "fine frivolities" in the area, while **Sangha** (301-891-3214; www.sangha.ws; 7014 Westmoreland Ave., Takoma Park) deals solely in fair-trade products from around the world, including Cambodia, Nepal, South Africa, and Guatemala. The neighborhood also boasts a variety of ethnic and American restaurants, and with easy access from the Red line's Takoma Metro stop, it's a fanciful, affordable place to wile away an afternoon far beyond the chaos of downtown.

hearted woman passionate about her inventory, Art & Soul also sells handmade scarves and shawls; beautiful, flowing clothes; and artisan ties for the menfolk.

Beadazzled (202-265-2323; www.beadazzled.net; 1507 Connecticut Ave., N.W., Washington; nearest Metro: Dupont Circle, Red line). Feeling crafty? As its name implies, Beadazzled is your one-stop shop for all things beaded—loose beads; glass beads from the Czech Republic and India; Chinese porcelain beads; beads made of bone, horn, shell, copper, and silver; bead strands; colorful seed beads; pearls, gemstones, and handcrafted glass beads—they even hold craft classes so you can learn what to do with your newfound treasures. This local chain (with stores in Baltimore and Tysons Corner, Virginia, as well) also sells glassworks, art supplies, textiles, woodcrafts, and jewelry.

Da Hsin Trading Company (202-789-4020; 811 Seventh St., N.W., Washington; nearest Metro: Gallery Place/Chinatown, Green, Red, and Yellow lines). One of the few spots in Chinatown that's still rooted in the neighborhood's Asian origins, Da Hsin sells all things Chinese: exotic packaged foodstuffs and dried herbs, embroidered house slippers, specialized cookware, and Buddha sculptures. But the real treasures are the competitively priced Asian ceramics—including tea and sake sets—and a large selection of home furnishings, statues, and Chinese paper lanterns.

Indian Craft Shop (202-208-4056; www.indiancraftshop.com; 1849 C St., N.W., Washington; nearest Metro: Farragut West, Blue and Orange lines). Housed inside the Department of Interior building is one of D.C.'s true treasures for collectors of Native American arts and crafts. In operation since 1938, this is one of the primary outlets for contemporary art by the Native American artists themselves. Tapestries and paintings; sculpture; beadwork; baskets; pottery; ivory and whale-bone carvings from Alaska; and extensive selections of jewelry and sand paintings—it's all here, attended by a knowledgeable, friendly staff whose contagious enthusiasm will likely encourage you to buy more than you had initially planned.

Keith Lipert Gallery (202-965-9736; www.keithlipertgallery.com; 2922 M St., N.W., Washington; no Metro access). Although the Washington branch opened in 1994, Keith Lipert has been in the business of selling fine glasswork, collectibles, and gifts for more than 20 years—first in London and then Manhattan—before establishing this Georgetown gallery. The majority of the inventory echoes the political origins of the city—its treasures have long stood as the go-to option for visiting dignitaries. But the store also sells fine jewelry, silver candle holders, and decorative art and accent pieces like ornate ceramic vases.

Movie Madness (202-337-7064; 1083 Thomas Jefferson St., N.W., Washington; no Metro access). The entrance to this basement-level Georgetown treasure trove of movie memorabilia is typically marked by a large movie poster propped near the door. Inside you'll fine reams of large-format movie posters from all eras (Hitchcock to Kubrick to Tarantino), along with a small collection of music posters.

Old Print Gallery (202-965-1818; www.oldprintgallery.com; 1220 31st St., N.W., Washington; no Metro access). Housed in an unassuming Georgetown row house since 1971, this is the country's largest retailer of U.S. and European prints and maps. Museums, restaurants, offices, and private collectors have benefited from an inventory that covers most genres, including nautical scenes, sporting events, city portraits and maps, natural history, war scenes, and genre pictures from such famed artists as Winslow Homer and George Caleb Bingham. Prices range from $40 to $10,000.

Oya's Mini Bazaar (202-667-9853; 2420 18th St., N.W., Washington; nearest Metro: Woodley Park, Red line). These narrow shops in Adams Morgan reflect the Ethiopian roots of the neighborhood, selling clothes, crafts, and collectibles from East Africa and the rest

Da Hsin's ceramic treasures line the back shelves of this Chinatown store. Photo by Nathan Borchelt.

Cards for all types—from the eclectic to the traditional—on display at Pulp. Photo by Nathan Borchelt.

of the continent. Almost the entire stock is imported, and prices range from 50-cent beads to $500 wooden giraffes. Some prices are a bit steep—but remember, you're in D.C., not Addis Ababa, and typically there are treasure troves of discount items. Weekend nights can get crowded as bar-goers wander the narrow aisles in search of an indulgent purchase.

The Paper Source (202-298-5545; www.paper-source.com; 3019 M St., N.W., Washington; no Metro access). Paper lovers and arts-and-crafts fanatics will lose themselves in this expansive Georgetown store, which specializes in handcrafted paper, cards, stationery, posters, and loads of do-it-yourself material. This shop, part of a small national chain, also boasts eclectic vases, paperweights, picture frames, notebooks, photo albums, pens, and kitschy publications. Also located in Alexandria (703-299-9950; 118 King St., Alexandria).

Pulp (202-462-7857; 1805? 14th St., N.W., Washington; nearest Metro: U Street, Green and Yellow lines). A hodgepodge of paper products, political gifts, eclectic stationery, and comical cards, this spot—one of several on the recently revitalized 14th Street—is ideal for those longing for unique, humorous, or downright embarrassing gifts. The inventory in this two-story store also includes tasteful home-decor accents, clothing, gift wrap, work by local artists, and a selection of progressive music. Also located in Capitol Hill (202-543-1294; 303 Pennsylvania Ave., S.E., Washington).

Tiny Jewel Box (202-393-2747; www.tinyjewelbox.com; 1147 Connecticut Ave., N.W., Washington; nearest Metro: Farragut North, Red line). Don't let the name fool you; there's nothing tiny about this gem of a store a few blocks south of Dupont Circle. It specializes in vintage estate and new jewelry and watches from some of the industry's top designers. Although a touch expensive, the quality and unique character of most pieces is beyond reproach. The six-floor property also carries high-end items like handbags, crystal, and home accessories and accents.

Torpedo Factory Art Center (703-838-4565; www.torpedofactory.org; 105 N. Union St., Alexandria; nearest Metro: King Street, Blue and Yellow lines). Part working art studio, part gallery, this 72,000-square-foot building reigns as one of the best places in the D.C. metro area to score original artwork at reasonable prices—and to meet the artist in the process. Nestled in Old Town, this warehouse venue serves as both work studio and gallery space. The myriad shops housed under one roof carry a wide variety of media: collage, painting, glasswork, jewelry, photography, printmaking, sculpture, enamel, and mixed media. The building used to be a munitions factory that produced MK-14 torpedoes in the 1920s. Today it's an art-lover's mecca, as well as a great place to take kids interested in the arts, because the artists themselves—about 160 at last count—often can be seen working on their latest creations. You'll also find art classes on site, as well as commissioned work and special gallery exhibits.

INSIDER TIP: *Collectors of original art should consider bar- and restaurant-crawling in the Adams Morgan, U Street, Capitol Hill, and 14th Street neighborhoods, where local art, typically marked with reasonable price tags, adorns the walls.*

Wake Up Little Suzie (202-244-0700; 3409 Connecticut Ave., N.W., Washington; nearest Metro: Cleveland Park, Red line). It's amazing that such a small, uncluttered store can collect so many playful, quality products. The emphasis is on the political, with products that skewer famed politicians from both sides of the aisles: T-shirts, paperweights, bumper stickers, antique campaign buttons, and a cornucopia of fun gift items as well as arty clocks, china, and a selection of tasteful jewelry.

Even the sign for Wake Up Little Suzie evokes the store's playful inventory. Photo by Nathan Borchelt.

The Written Word (202-223-1400; www.writtenword.invitations.com; 1427 P St., N.W., Washington; nearest Metro: Dupont Circle, Red line). This stationery store east of Dupont Circle specializes in all things associated with the time-honored act of writing. Graceful pens, antique letterpress printing, and spectacular handcrafted, custom-made invitations form the bulk of the store's inventory. You can also find reams of Japanese pattern paper, stationery, and inventive gift cards.

Beauty, Spa, and Health

18th and Yoga (202-462-1800; www.inspiredyoga.com; 1115 U St., N.W., Suite 202, Washington; nearest Metro: U Street, Green and Yellow lines). Don't let the name misdirect you to 18th Street for this studio on 12th Street. (Once you find the place, buzz 0203 to be let in.) This Vinyasa-based flow yoga studio offers walk-in appointments and a wide array of different classes organized by theme. The space is open and comfortable, and the staff affable and informed. They also sell a small variety of yoga-inspired clothing and supplies, organize retreats, and offer workshops and discount beginner-yoga classes.

Bluemercury (202-965-1300; www.bluemercury.com; 3059 M St., N.W., Washington; no Metro access). This internationally renowned local apothecary and spa has made a name for itself by selling only the highest quality, wonderfully indulgent, truly innovative products from the most coveted brands. In addition to hard-to-find imported salves and intoxicating aromas arranged in the aesthetically stunning wooden showroom, Bluemercury offers a full array of spa treatments, including skin care, aesthetic appointments, and body-care treatments like hot-stone massage. Also located in Dupont Circle (202-462-1300; 1619 Connecticut Ave., N.W., Washington).

Celadon Spa (202-347-3333; www.celadonspa.com; 1180 F St., N.W., Washington; nearest Metro: Metro Center, Blue, Orange, and Red lines). Tailor-made to ease the stresses of pounding the D.C. pavement or dissolve the strain of days-long business meetings, this downtown oasis offers a full array of spa and wellness treatments. Sign up for a 30- to 90-minute therapeutic massage or a variety of sensual options like body rubs with coconut and chocolate sugar or margarita salt, or a nourishing seaweed body wrap. This full-service health center also offers antiaging treatments; skin, hair, nail, and makeup appointments; and a heady variety of men's and women's health and beauty products and gift baskets.

Georgetown Yoga (202-342-7779; www.georgetownyoga.com; 1053 31st St., N.W., Second Floor, Washington; no Metro access). All classes are drop-in, save enrolled sessions and special workshops (refer to the Web site for scheduling info). The studio, in operation since 2002, holds classes organized by styles and skill levels, and also offers Thai yoga massage, private instruction, and prenatal yoga classes.

Grooming Lounge (202-466-8900; www.groominglounge.com; 1745 L St., N.W., Washington; nearest Metro: Farragut North, Red line). Think of this as the traditional barbershop elevated to metrosexual perfection (and to any guys who may be skeptical about this supposed fad: one visit and you're a convert). Sip on a beer or sparkling water while you wait your turn for a seat in one of the old-school barber chairs, then surrender to their signature hot lather shave, complete with hot towels and a soothing face massage. Other treatments—like a hot-stone massage, men's facials, haircut, waxing treatments, and a special golfer's massage—keep the crowds of professionals and politicians in constant monthly rotation. They also sell a variety of high-quality men's grooming products.

Lush (202-333-6950; www.lush.com; 3066 M St., N.W., Washington; no Metro access). The moment you walk into this Georgetown "beauty bar," the aromas inspire unabashed loyalty to this international chain specializing in fresh, handmade cosmetics. You'll find bath soaps, massage bars, and hair-care products, all dubbed with playful names like "Honey I Washed the Kids" soap and "Mask of Magnaminty" facial cleanser. Don't miss their "bath bombs," little balls of organic goodness that explode into aromatic froth in your tub.

Mint (202-328-6468; www.mintfitness.com; 1724 California St., N.W., Washington; nearest Metro: Woodley Park, Red line). Equal parts gym and spa treatment facility, this Adams Morgan health club will appeal to both the athlete and hedonist in you. Indulge with treatments like Swedish or aromatherapy massage in one of four private rooms tucked in the back of the facility, sign up for spin or yoga classes, or work out on state-of-the-art exercise equipment. The scene is subdued, and there is a welcome ban on cell phones. A new juice bar with Wi-Fi is also becoming a neighborhood hot spot.

Serenity Day Spa (202-362-2560; www.serenitygift.com; 4000 Wisconsin Ave., N.W., Washington; nearest Metro: Tenleytown, Red line). The name of this spa facility in Upper Northwest was a perfect choice; after giving in to one (or several) of their many wellness treatments, you will indeed be blissfully serene. Choose from a voluminous list of options that includes facials, a "serenity massage" that blends multiple techniques, or a 30-minute tension-relief massage. Other beauty treatments, including hair removal, nail care, and hair design, round out a laundry list of options, and they also offer daylong packages, couples massages, and customized "spa parties." Also located in Alexandria (703-549-9212; 209 Madison St., Alexandria).

Books and Music

ADC Map and Travel Center (202-628-2608; 1636 I St., N.W., Washington; nearest Metro: Farragut West, Blue and Orange lines). If you love to tour the world without leaving a single room, this little gem of a store is for you. And by *little,* we mean tiny. Its inventory of maps, globes, atlases, and guidebooks, however, remains ridiculously expansive: aeronautical and nautical charts, maps of city-street quadrants from around the world, topographical maps from the U.S. Geological Survey, and an ever-growing list of special-order products put the entire world at your fingertips.

Aladdin's Lamp Children's Books (703-241-8281; 2499 N. Harrison St., Suite 10, Arlington; no Metro access). Nestled in the lower level of Arlington's Lee Harrison Shopping Center, this store is heaven for budding bookworms. In addition to a huge inventory of hand-selected books for children struggling with their first sentence up to young-adult reading level, Aladdin's hosts special storytimes, author visits, workshops, and regularly scheduled story hours at 11 AM Friday.

American Institute of Architects Bookstore (202-626-7475; 1735 New York Ave., N.W., Washington; nearest Metro: Farragut West, Blue and Orange lines). It's not surprising that this bookstore, located within the American Institute of Architects building a few blocks west of the White House, has an inventory that centers on theoretical and practical resources for architects. But they also carry a nice selection of coffee-table-sized architectural photography books, note cards, watches, and other trinkets geared toward the structurally obsessed.

Barnes and Noble (202-965-9880; www.barnesandnoble.com; 3040 M St., N.W., Washington; no Metro access). An oasis of calm on M Street—and one of the choice spots for Georgetown students who want to escape campus to study—this three-story branch of the national chain carries a wide array of national magazines, travel books, literature, and music. Unlike other coffeehouses in the neighborhood, the ubiquitous Starbucks coffee shop on the second floor is massive, providing much-needed respite from the shopping hordes. Branches are also located in Arlington, Alexandria, Downtown, and Capitol Hill.

INSIDER TIP: *Public bathrooms in most neighborhoods are hard to come by—and most restaurants keep theirs reserved for customers. Instead, consider dropping in on one of the national bookstore chains, whose bathrooms are open to all (just leave that coffee-table book on the shelf, George Costanza).*

Beyond Comics 2 (202-333-8651; 3060 M St., N.W., Washington; no Metro Access). Fan boys—and fan girls—risk losing hours of their life in this Georgetown comic shop, which specializes in hard-to-find comics, a vast selection of the latest titles from around the globe (including Japanese manga), and all varieties of pop-culture mania. From action figures to posters, signed editions to the occasional piece of original comic art, this place is tailor-made for the comic enthusiast.

Borders (202-737-1385; www.bordersstores.com; 600 14th St., N.W., #100, Washington; nearest Metro: Metro Center, Blue, Orange, and Red lines). Just two blocks from the White House, this downtown store boasts an impressive collection of European magazines in addition to the expected cadre of books and gifts. The lower-level music section is one of the largest in the city, though the inventory tends to get picked over quickly. Also located in Dupont Circle, Upper Northwest, Alexandria, and Arlington.

Bridge Street Books (202-965-5200; www.bridgestreetbooks.com; 2814 Pennsylvania Ave., N.W., Washington; no Metro access). Expect to find a vast collection of paperbacks in a slightly vertiginous arrangement—a wide spy hole lets you peer up at the stocked shelves on the second floor and then at the Washington sky through a ceiling skylight. The emphasis here is mostly on film, poetry, and vast collections on the humanities. The no-frills Web site displays the store's recent acquisitions. Located next to Georgetown's Four Seasons Hotel.

Chapters, A Literary Bookstore (202-737-5553; www.chaptersliterary.com; Note: Store moving to new location at presstime. Please call or visit web site for new address.) In business for more than 20 years, this downtown bookstore displays a discerning interest in what they carry. Exploring their hand-selected collection of poetry, fiction, travel writing, cookbooks, and books on natural history and spirituality feels like thumbing through the library of a *very* well-read relative. Chapters also hosts readings almost every week, from the established fiction and political all-stars to up-and-comers who will become the next big thing (with or without Oprah's endorsement). The store also offers free tea and cookies Friday afternoons to encourage you to explore and discover what will likely become your next favorite book.

Crooked Beat Records (202-483-BEAT; www.crookedbeat.com; 2318 18th St., N.W., Washington; nearest Metro: Woodley Park, Red line). You probably won't find the latest *Bill-*

board #1 at this basement-level, independently owned record store, but if you're a music aficionado, expect to dedicate hours to this store's many crates of records and CDs. Because Crooked Beat specializes in hard-to-find new and used music, including loads of world and obscure labels, the stacks are typically populated by local DJs in search of otherwise-unattainable vinyl. The knowledgeable staff will point you in the right direction or help track down that elusive 45 that has long been on your must-have list. It's also a good place to get the lowdown on the better music events throughout the city.

DJ Hut (202-659-2010; www.djhut.com; 2010 P St., N.W., Floor 2, Washington; nearest Metro: Dupont Circle, Red line). Professional DJs, music lovers, and aspiring record-hounds alike will find themselves at home at this second-story Dupont Circle spot. New and vintage vinyl dominates the store's inventory, with special emphasis on electronica, big beat, jungle, and hip-hop. DJ Hut also sells DJ equipment and CDs from all genres. It's also one of the best places to dial into the week's best DJ gigs. You may even run into a few local record spinners.

Fairy Godmother (202-547-5474; 319 Seventh St., S.E., Washington; nearest Metro: Eastern Market, Blue and Orange lines). Occupying a tiny row house in Capitol Hill, this bookstore carries an impressive variety of classic children's literature (in French and Spanish as well as English), along with toys, CDs, puppets, and arts-and-craft supplies and kits.

Idle Time Books (202-232-4774; 2467 18th St., N.W., Washington; nearest Metro: Woodley Park, Red line). This neighborhood used bookstore, in Adams Morgan since 1981, carries a steady, revolving collection of used fiction, cookbooks, children's books, CDs, greeting cards, newspapers, and records. The three-floor establishment boasts an estimated 50,000 titles, including rare and out-of-print editions. The insanely knowledgeable staff can also help you track down that one title you've been hunting for (and yes, they will ship titles to you when they arrive).

Kramerbooks and Afterwords Café (202-387-1400; 1517 Connecticut Ave., N.W., Washington; nearest Metro: Dupont Circle, Red line). Combining the leisurely activity of book browsing and the impeccable allure of café society, this Dupont hot spot can swallow your entire afternoon. The carefully chosen inventory lends itself to fiction lovers, travelers, and politicos, while the sunny café, gracefully tucked into the rear of the store, carries a casual—if somewhat compressed—restaurant vibe, complete with table service. The best part? It's open late on weekdays and all night on weekends.

Lambda Rising (202-462-6969; www.lambdarising.com; 1625 Connecticut Ave., N.W., Washington; nearest Metro: Dupont Circle, Red line). A pioneer in D.C., this Dupont Circle landmark specializes in books and periodicals that focus on the gay community. In operation since 1974, it's become the cultural hotbed for GLBT issues, and also services the local population by supporting artists, authors, and other special events.

Melody Record Shop (202-232-4002; www.melodyrecords.com; 1623 Connecticut Ave., N.W., Washington; nearest Metro: Dupont Circle, Red line). Melody is a music-lover's retreat. The modest storefront reveals a deep collection of all musical genres—contemporary, world, electronica, pop, jazz, blues, the list goes on and on—on both CD and vinyl. They also have a huge bin of sale CDs in the front, will happily special-order any CDs they don't happen to stock, and are armed with some of the most musically informed staff in the city.

Olssons (202-638-7610; www.olssons.com; 418 Seventh St., N.W., Washington; nearest Metro: Archives, Green and Yellow lines). One of Washington's remaining independent bookstore chains, this spot is firmly rooted in the ever-expanding Penn Quarter restaurant-and-theater district. The store's inventory is split among books, music, and DVDs, and includes a variety of signed editions, discount copies, and one of the best selections of indie-film DVDs and music in the city. Monthly readings and occasional in-store performances keep the vibe local, and the adjoining **Footnotes Café** makes for a perfect low-key lunch spot. Also located in Alexandria, Arlington, and Dupont Circle.

Politics and Prose (202-364-1919; www.politics-prose.com; 5015 Connecticut Ave., N.W., Washington; nearest Metro: Van Ness, Red line). Although this bookstore is located a bit beyond the tourist-centric part of town, serious lovers of the written word are well served to search out this D.C. literary institution. Open since 1984, the store has an inventory of about 100,000 books that divides its interests among politics, fiction, and the humanities, and the adjoining café invites shoppers to stick around. But its enduring identity lives beyond the books on the shelves. Politics and Prose routinely holds readings, discussions, and other events with literary luminaries, from contemporary politicians to up-and-coming fiction writers.

Second Story Books (202-659-8884; www.secondstorybooks.com; 2000 P St., N.W., Washington; nearest Metro: Dupont Circle, Red line). This used bookstore just west of Dupont Circle is a treasure trove for the book-obsessed. The tightly packed rows brim with all types of publications, including an expansive line of art books, fiction, and history that ranges from first-edition treasures to well-thumbed paperbacks. Second Story

The overflowing shelves at Dupont Circle's Second Story used bookstore. Photo by Nathan Borchelt.

is D.C.'s largest antiquarian bookseller, and also specializes in hard-to-find period magazines, albums, and movie and music posters—along with the expected collection of secondhand CDs.

Smash Records (202-38-SMASH; www.smashrecords.com; 2314 18th St., N.W., Washington; nearest Metro: Woodley Park, Red line). Once the unofficial headquarters of punk in Georgetown, this recently relocated D.C. establishment now resides in the lower end of Adams Morgan. The emphasis is still on punk and D.C. hardcore (see page 232), but the used vinyl section covers all genres. Smash also serves as D.C.'s reliable outpost for temporary hair dye; Doc Martin shoes and boots; punk T-shirts, posters, and CDs; and loads of edgy accessories and secondhand clothes.

Som Records (202-328-3345; www.somrecordsdc.com; 1843 14th St., N.W., Washington; nearest Metro: U Street, Green and Yellow lines). Rock, funk, soul, disco, salsa, folk, blues, samba, jazz, punk, electronica, D.C.'s own go-go—all that and more can be found at this crate-diggers paradise of used and new vinyl.

Trover Shop (202-547-BOOK; www.trover.com; 221 Pennsylvania Ave., S.E., Washington; nearest Metro: Capitol South, Blue and Orange lines). Its close proximity to the Capitol, Library of Congress, and the Supreme Court hints at the topic of this family-owned Capitol Hill bookstore. Volumes on politics, books about and by politicians, newspapers and articles from across the country, and guides to such D.C. institutions as lobbying, fund raising, and the upcoming elections share shelf space with travel guides, fiction, and history spread across two floors. This decades-old store also has another location in Penn Quarter (202-347-6460; 1270 F St., N.W., Washington).

Yoshitoshi (202-338-3474; www.yoshop.com; 3207A M St., N.W., Suite A, Washington; no Metro access). Equal measures music store and lifestyle spot, this techno HQ was cofounded by the members of house music icons (and D.C. locals) Deep Dish. Named after their record label, this small Georgetown store specializes in hard-to-find, cutting-edge dance music and clothes, and is a must-stop for club-goers looking for the next big night in the city.

CLOTHING

Alex Boutique (202-296-2610; www.alexboutiquedc.com; 1919 Pennsylvania Ave., N.W., Washington; nearest Metro: Farragut West, Blue and Orange lines). Purveyor of fashion-forward and vintage attire for both men and women, this downtown boutique hot spot carries the latest European and U.S. fashions. Contemporary designers include Covet, Dubuc, Apartment, and Beth Lauren, while their vintage couture apparel and accessory labels read like a roster of fashion icons: Chanel, St. John, Dior, and Chloé, among others. They also specialize in locating unique vintage pieces from the '20s to the '70s and host special trunk sales and fashion shows for local designers.

All About Jane (703-243-4424; 2839 Clarendon Blvd., Arlington; nearest Metro: Clarendon, Orange line). One of the D.C.-area boutique pioneers, this Arlington gem deals in hip, fun, and fashionable women's attire from such indie labels as Shoshanna, Nanette Lepore, Rebecca Taylor, Belabumbum, Cammie Hill, Custo, and Easel. The friendly staff is knowledgeable without being pushy—but expect to spend more than you'd anticipated, because they also carry Lauren Merkin bags and jewelry from Lulet, Queen Bee, and Marie Chavez.

Adams Morgan, professing its affection for fancy shoes and the jumbo slice. Photo by Nathan Borchelt.

Annie Creamcheese (202-298-5555; anniecreamcheese.com; 3279 M St., N.W., Washington; no Metro access). The name of this Georgetown vintage clothing and accessories store evokes blissful overindulgence, and one step inside and you'll see why. A far cry from a typical vintage scavenger hunt, the clothes here are always of the highest quality, from sundresses of the 1970s to cocktail dresses from the 1920s to full-length ball gowns from the 1940s. Expect to pay more than you'd initially planned for all that behind-the-scenes vetting. Or play it safe and just peruse the wide variety of lesser priced vintage accessories, handbags, and jewelry.

Carbon (202-986-2679; www.carbondc.com; 2643 Connecticut Ave., N.W., Washington; nearest Metro: Woodley Park, Red line). Relocated from its former digs on U Street, this trendy spot has one desire: to shift D.C. from "federal" to "funky." Their exclusive selection of hip men's and women's footwear exceeds that of any other spot in the city, and they also carry women's accessories like handbags, cuff links, belt buckles, and jewelry, as well as a small variety of men's and women's clothing.

Commonwealth (202-265-1830; www.cmonwealth.com; 1781 Florida Ave., N.W., Washington; nearest Metro: Woodley Park, Red line). This urban-inspired Adams Morgan spot shies away from the expected patinas of black and gray for more vibrant explosions of color in their men's and women's apparel. Bold designer sneakers from Nike and Reebok, bright hoodies and baseball caps, and city-centric labels like Stüssy, Absurd, Haze, Heliz Beliz, Original Fake, and Staple Design dominate the inventory.

Current Boutique (703-528-3079; www.currentboutique.com; 2629 Wilson Blvd, Arlington; nearest Metro: Courthouse, Orange line). Billed as a "modern consignment shop," this Arlington store is the place to find contemporary, in-season, barely worn designer wears in primo condition. You may have to sift through the expected recycled apparel and accessories from Banana Republic, H&M, and Urban Outfitters, but prizes like Betsy Johnson, Marc Jacobs, and Kate Spade reward the diligent.

Denim Bar (703-414-8202; www.denimbaronline.com; 1101 S. Joyce St., Arlington; nearest Metro: Pentagon City, Blue and Yellow lines). For fashionistas obsessed with the latest trends and labels in the ever-evolving world of fashion jeans and denim wear, this is the spot for you. Owner Mauro Farinelli and his informed staff share your enthusiasm and will help point you to the best pair of jeans, from familiar designers like Seven and Diesel to elite brands like Blue Blood, Prps, and Rock and Republic. They also sell men's and women's T-shirts, sweaters, jackets, hoodies, and shorts.

H&M (202-637-0037; www.hm.com; 1025 F St., N.W., Washington; nearest Metro: Metro Center, Blue, Orange, and Red lines). This downtown branch of the Swedish chain—the city's largest—boasts two floors with an ever-shifting inventory of inexpensive, Euro-styled clothes and accessories for men, women, and children. Also located in Georgetown (202-298-6792; 3222 M St., N.W., Washington).

INSIDER TIP: *If the weather catches you by surprise, street-side vendors usually sell inexpensive sweatshirts. But to avoid looking like a poster child for ill-prepared tourists, consider low-cost, more fashionable stores like H&M or downtown's Filene's Basement (202-638-4110; 529 14th St., N.W., Washington).*

Maggie and Lola Boutique (202-234-2850; www.maggieandlola.com; 1013 E St., S.E., Washington; nearest Metro: Eastern Market, Blue and Orange lines). Calypso Kids, 317, Hanky Panky, Sweetess, and Chan Luu are just a few examples of the ever-expanding

---

Beware of Knockoff Handbags and Glad Rags

Purses used to be for hauling stuff—a wallet, keys, some cosmetics, maybe a book to read on the Metro. These days, handbags are a way to display style savvy, fashion correctness, and wealth. From divine evening clutches to oversized hobos, handbags are a prime status symbol—and as such, the most coveted designer versions can cost hundreds and even thousands of dollars. But in D.C., some of the hottest bags with the most mouth-watering labels *seem* to be on sale for a fraction of retail. Where? On street corners throughout the city you'll find small kiosks overflowing with purses boasting labels like Gucci, Prada, Chanel, Coach, Dior, Fendi, Kooba, Hermes, and Birkin—all with price tags of $20–30. Year-round, street-side vendors selling these apparent bargain bags—as well as sunglasses and designer scarves—pop up near subway exits, in busy downtown corridors, and amid pricey shopping meccas like Georgetown. Of course, the outrageously discounted products are knockoffs—and the folks making and selling these fakes are violating a handful of trademark infringement laws. In addition, although these curbside couture accessories resemble the originals, they aren't likely to fool anyone who's seen the real deal. And if you end up buying something from a knockoff vendor, note that they tend to move around frequently, so don't expect to come back the next day to make an exchange.

roster of top Los Angeles and NYC designers on offer at this Capitol Hill locale, which specializes in hip women's and children's apparel. But it all started with hand-embellished T-shirts by owner Katharine Ordway, still one of the biggest draws.

Nana (202-667-6955; store.nanadc.com; 1534 U St., N.W., Washington; nearest Metro: U Street, Green and Yellow lines). This charming boutique is tailor-suited for those with a discernible, playful fashion eye. Well-known, chic labels like LA Made, Mary Green, Soda Blue, Kasil Jeans, and Hobo International share real estate with the one-of-a-kind vintage pieces tucked into the back room. A variety of unique accessories round out the eclectic inventory, with prices that range from $20 shirts to $300 couture skirts.

women's and men's clothing and accessorie

Pop (202-332-3312; www.shoppop.com; 1803A 14th St., N.W., Washington; nearest Metro: U Street, Green and Yellow lines). A pioneer on now-flourishing 14th Street, this second-floor boutique makes up for its modest size with an impressive array of hip labels for both men and women, including Ben Sherman, Penguin, Speiwak, Dollhouse, and Free People. Like its sister store in Brooklyn, Pop also sells quirky handbags, T-shirts, hats, and home decor trinkets.

Proper Topper (202-842-3055; www.propertopper .com; 1350 Connecticut Ave., N.W., Washington; nearest Metro: Dupont Circle, Red line). Although its name refers to this Dupont store's main emphasis, Proper Topper carries more than men's and women's hats. Offering ready-to-wear apparel from some of the biggest labels in the business (including exclusive arrangements with Tracey Reese and Ted Baker), it's a one-stop shop for adult and children's clothes, accessories like jewelry and scarves, home decor,

Pop's vibrant sidewalk sign on the revitalized 14th Street corridor.
Photo by Nathan Borchelt.

and gift items like note cards, books, and writing paper. And their hat selection is consistently ranked the best in the city. Also located in Georgetown (202-333-6200; 3213 P St., N.W., Washington).

Redeem (202-332-7447; www.redeemus.com; 1734 14th St., N.W., Washington; nearest Metro: U Street, Green and Yellow lines). Luxury casual wear from labels like Orthodox, Bodybag, Alex & Chloe, and Earnest Swen personify this urban-hip retailer in the ever-expanding 14th Street clothing hub. The style is a touch gothic hipster, including screen-printed T-shirts, with a particular affection for blacks, browns, army greens, and just the right splash of color.

The Remix Vintage Fashion Shop (202-547-0211; www.remixvintage.com; 645 Pennsylvania Ave., S.E., Washington; nearest Metro: Eastern Market, Orange and Blue lines). Established by an experienced merchandiser and former window designer, Remix is a brightly colored confection for fashionistas. The store's vintage dresses, hats, jewelry, and handbags are whimsical and meld the styles of the old (think the 1950s and '60s) with a contemporary eye for the new.

Sassanova (202-471-4400; www.sassanova.com; 1641 Wisconsin Ave., N.W., Washington; no Metro access). Shoes, handbags, and jewelry that could pass as bona fide pieces of art have made this Georgetown store one of the must-hit hot spots in a shopper's tour of D.C. The use of cheetah prints and pinks inside the store sets the tone for its innovative lines, including boutique labels like Bettye Muller, Delman, Dolce Vita, Moschino, and Paul Smith.

Secondi Consignment Clothing (202-667-1122; www.secondi.com; 1702 Connecticut Ave., N.W., Second Floor, Washington; nearest Metro: Dupont Circle, Red line). Secondi dispels the notion that consignment implies secondhand. With equal focus on men's and women's apparel, the store prides itself on hand-selecting the very best clothes from the best labels with prices that may seem high, until you realize how much these clothes cost the first time around.

Shake Your Booty (202-518-8205; shakeyourbootyshoes.com; 2439 18th St., N.W., Washington; nearest Metro: Woodley Park, Red line). Welcome to one of the D.C. meccas for très hip, reasonably priced shoes. Pavement-stomping sneakers, knee-high stilettos, brightly colored rain slickers, they're all here, including brands like Me Too, NYLA, Berne Mev, Henry Ferrera, and Sugar. Sure, they might not be the names that make Carrie Bradshaw swoon, but the styles would—and at prices a *real* writer could afford. They also sell funky jewelry and handbags.

Shoefly (703-243-6490; www.shoefly.com; 2618 Wilson Blvd., Arlington; nearest Metro: Clarendon, Orange line). Searching for hip footwear that's a far cry from the typical department store? Shoefly has you covered, including styles for men and women from the likes of Camper, M.O.D., and more than 50 other brands. But what really sets this Arlington spot apart from its competitors: the price, which makes finding the funky shoes an affordable reality, not a haute dream. They also sell equally stylish clothing for men, women, and children, as well as handbags and watches.

South Moon Under (703-807-4083; www.southmoonunder.com; 2700 Clarendon Blvd., Suite R440, Arlington; nearest Metro: Clarendon, Orange line). What started as a surf shop in Ocean City, Maryland, in the 1960s has since graduated to one of the area's best stores for fashionable attire. South Moon Under concentrates on a hand-picked inventory of clothing and swimwear for both men and women (with labels like Penguin, Juicy

---

Outlet Stores

D.C.'s surrounding suburbs boast a wide array of low-cost, high-quality outlet shopping. You'll need to arrange your own transportation, as they lie beyond the city-centric public transportation, but for shopaholics, the effort will be rewarding.

Arundel Mills (410-540-5110; www.arundelmills.com; 7000 Arundel Mills Circle, Hanover, Maryland). Near Baltimore-Washington International Thurgood Marshall Airport, this is another of the area's largest outlet centers, with more than 200 stores like Kenneth Cole, Off 5th, and Old Navy.

Leesburg Corner Premium Outlets (703-737-3071; www.premiumoutlets.com; 241 Fort Evans Rd., N.E., Leesburg, Virginia). This self-contained outdoor shopping mall carries more than 100 upscale brands like Nike, Reebok, Calvin Klein, Jones New York, Crate & Barrel, and Pottery Barn. About a 15-minute drive from Washington Dulles International Airport.

Potomac Mills (703-496-9301; www.potomacmills.com; 2700 Potomac Mills Circle, Prince William, Virginia). This is one of the country's largest outlet centers, with more than 220 discount stores spread across both sides of I-95, about 30 minutes south of D.C. Includes Nordstrom, Polo, Mikasa, Banana Republic, as well as movie theaters and restaurants.

The global bazaar that is Go Mama Go! Photo by Nathan Borchelt.

Couture, Ben Sherman, and Citizens of Humanity) along with jewelry, home accents like candles and frames, and designer shoes.

Urban Chic (202-338-5398; www.urbanchic-dc.com; 1626 Wisconsin Ave., Washington; no Metro access). As its name implies, this women's apparel retailer in upper George-town blends up-and-coming and established labels and designers in a largely successful effort to shift D.C. from its conservative-dress routines. Explore a wide variety of jeans, T-shirts, dresses, and accessories in a comfortable environment of bleached-blond wood and artfully arranged displays.

Wink (202-338-9465; 3109 M St., N.W., Washington; no Metro access). One level below the perpetual bustle of Georgetown's M Street awaits a 16,000-foot space filled with some of the best designer women's clothing in the city. Jeans, dresses, T-shirt, pants, suits, skirts, and coats—the inventory targets the hip and young, with prices that range from $30 to $800.

HOME FURNISHINGS

Apartment Zero (202-628-4067; www.apartmentzero.com; 406 Seventh St., N.W., Wash-ington; nearest Metro: Archives, Green and Yellow lines). The contemporary home fur-nishings on display at this Penn Quarter establishment—part showroom, part art gallery—are for truly modern interiors. A showroom of bleached white floors, with walls of white and red, reinforces the contemporary perspective and displays a variety of couches, ottomans, lamps, clocks, and end tables, most with prices that reflect each piece's unique qualities.

Go Mama Go! (202-299-0850; www.gomamago.com; 1809 14th St., N.W., Washington; nearest Metro: U Street, Green and Yellow lines). The enthusiastically named store, which occupies one of 14th Street's largest display rooms, carries an artful, vast array of Asian home decor, trinkets, and dishware, along with gift cards, statues, brightly colored fabrics, and other items from around the globe. The place feels more like a world bazaar than a bona fide showroom, with a staff that proves helpful without being pushy.

Kosmos Designs and Ideas (703-837-0107; www.kosmosdi.net; 805 N. Royal St., Alexandria; nearest Metro: King Street, Blue and Yellow lines).This importer specializes in furniture and home furnishings from around the world. Tables made of recycled teak from Indonesian bridges and other furniture crafted from reclaimed wood from South Asia anchor the inventory, but they also sell artful accent pieces like lamps, pillows, mirrors, candle holders, and tableware. Prices carry the expected markup, but recycling these rare woods reinforces that each piece is a sound, holistic investment. Also located in Old Town (703-837-1955; 1010 King St., Alexandria).

Le Village Marché (703-379-4444; www.levillagemarche.com; 4050 S. 28th St., Arlington; no Metro access). This Paris-by-way-of-Virginia store housed in the Village at Shirlington shopping center specializes in French-influenced reproduction furniture, antiques, garden accessories, patterned glass, and recycled frames. They also carry a variety of charming trinkets, including glass jewelry and vintage scales, postcards from the 1930s, old seltzer bottles, glassware, handcrafted candles, and olive-oil-based soaps.

INSIDER TIP: *To find some of the city's best bargains in art, collectibles, and home decor, be sure to visit museum gift shops throughout the District, especially the National Gallery of Art (see page 106), the National Building Museum (see page 154), and the Freer and Sackler Galleries (see page 101), which offer high-quality products at surprisingly reasonable prices.*

Miss Pixie's (202-232-8171; www.misspixies.com; 2473 18th St., N.W., Washington; nearest Metro: Woodley Park, Red line). This secondhand furniture and trinket shop is a diamond in the rough for people looking for unique sofas, armchairs, silver-gilded mirrors, old-school poker chip sets—basically anything from the late 1800s through the current era. Its stock rotates often, thanks to an influx of goods from area estate auctions each Wednesday (read: if you see something you like, don't hesitate), and the prices are universally reasonable. Out-of-city shipping can be arranged, but Miss Pixie's also has a slew of take-it-home items, from tapestries and Tibetan prayer flags to antique silverware and crystal goblets.

Muleh (202-667-3440; www.muleh.com; 1831 14th St., N.W., Washington; nearest Metro: U Street, Green and Yellow lines). Owner Christopher Reiter describes the style of home furnishings in this U Street Corridor store as "tropical modern." Derived mostly from Bali-based designers, the furniture here blends organic materials with a distinctly modern style. Although the showroom is dominated by chairs, tables, couches, and other furnishings made of reclaimed wood and handwoven abaca fiber, Muleh also sells spectacular, high-end clothing and accessories from design houses based in Manhattan, Paris, and Milan.

Muleh's artful showroom. Photo by Nathan Borchelt.

Skynear and Company (202-797-7160; www.skynearonline.com; 2122 18th St., N.W., Washington; nearest Metro: Woodley Park, Red line). An Adams Morgan fixture for more than 15 years, this three-story showroom of contemporary furniture from around the globe has attracted a steady clientele, from recent grads eager for an Ikea alternative to diplomats looking for a touch of Polynesian exotica. The main floor displays the store's most contemporary, colorful, and playful items, while the second floor leans toward more traditional global imports from Asia, Europe, and Mexico. The inventory on the top floor, meanwhile, reflects a pragmatic appeal for urban living—after all, the furniture has to get up that narrow flight of stairs.

Vastu (202-234-8344; www.vastudc.com; 1829 14th St., N.W., Washington; nearest Metro: U Street, Green and Yellow lines). Named after the ancient Sanskrit philosophy that's the Indian equivalent of feng shui, this high-end furniture retailer deals exclusively in pieces that put design at the forefront. Custom-size your choice of sofa and chair designs, or peruse other pieces—crafted from fabrics like ultra-suede, bamboo, brushed nickel, and leather—including some of the sharpest looking outdoor furniture ever to grace a patio. They also sell an inventive selection of accessories, including lamps, cocktail paraphernalia, mirrors, trays, vases, and rugs.

West Elm (202-347-8929; www.westelm.com; 1020 G St., N.W., Washington; nearest Metro: Metro Center, Blue, Orange, and Red lines). The new D.C. branch of this national chain specializes in affordable, stylish home furnishings that meld contemporary designs with low-cost functionality. Everything from bed frames and kitchen tables to inventive picture frames and free-floating wall shelves is on display at this massive downtown showroom.

Woven History (202-543-1705; www.wovenhistory.com; 311–315 Seventh St., S.E., Washington; nearest Metro; Eastern Market, Blue and Orange lines). As close as you'll ever get to a Moroccan rug dealer in D.C., this Capitol Hill store gets some of the best handcrafted rugs and tapestries imported three times each year from big-league players in the craft: Turkey, Nepal, Iran, Pakistan, Afghanistan, Moldova, Egypt, Bosnia, and Macedonia, among others. The goods are of the highest quality, and the prices are as reasonable as you're liable to find this side of the Atlantic. Silk Road, its neighboring sister store, continues the global experience, with items like Nepali masks and musical instruments, Iranian trays, Turkish overcoats, silk dresses from China, and Afghan jewelry.

Souvenirs and Political Memorabilia

America's Spirit (202-842-0540; www.americastore.com; Union Station West Hall, 50 Massachusetts Ave., N.E., Washington; nearest Metro: Union Station, Red line). Politicos on either end of the party aisle will flip over this kitschy store jam-packed with only-in-D.C. memorabilia. Browse the White House collection, which includes items like toothbrushes, pens, and toilet paper stamped with the White House logo; nightgowns emblazoned with the slogan "Borrowed from the Lincoln Bedroom"; and mugs decorated with the presidential seal. Also available are current campaign buttons and bumper stickers; hats and T-shirts with FBI and CIA logos; DVDs of presidential "bloopers"; and a slightly disturbing collection of talking dolls in the images of Bill and Hillary Clinton, Dick Cheney, Condoleezza Rice, and Donald Rumsfeld. The store also has an outlet in Dulles International Airport.

Capitol Coin and Stamp Co. (202-296-0400; www.capitolcoin.com; 1001 Connecticut Ave., N.W., Suite 745, Washington; nearest Metro: Farragut North, Red line). Dubbed "the best little political shop" in the city, this collector's haven has been in operation in the same spot near the White House for more than 20 years. They specialize in all types of political items, from presidential memorabilia to electoral keepsakes like lapel pins, posters, matches, and autographs from the nation's beginning to the latest high-profile senate race. They also house an impressive collection of rare coins and stamps.

Chocolate Moose (202-463-0992; www.chocolatemoosedc.com; 1800 M St., N.W., Washington; nearest Metro: Farragut North, Red line). This gift store champions the quirky, oddball, and thoroughly memorable. Broken into different departments—hip housewares, tacky toys, artful accessories, jazzy jewelry, and so forth—the products here aren't really D.C.- or political-centric, but their eclectic variety means you'll find something for everyone on your list, from a small rubber Elvis head mounted on a spring to cake servers that double as dachshund sculptures.

Joe's Souvenir Headquarters (202-247-0875; F and 10th St., N.W., Washington; nearest Metro: Archives, Green and Yellow lines). If you're longing for a D.C. baseball cap, a snow globe with the Capitol or the Lincoln Memorial, or a sweater proclaiming that you're not enrolled in the FBI Witness Protection Program, you've found the mother lode. Packed to the ceiling with postcards, posters, coffee mugs, magnets, and various other tourist trinkets—all sold at ridiculously low prices—you may have to sift through stacks of pink T-shirts to find one that's just kitschy enough to qualify as ironic.

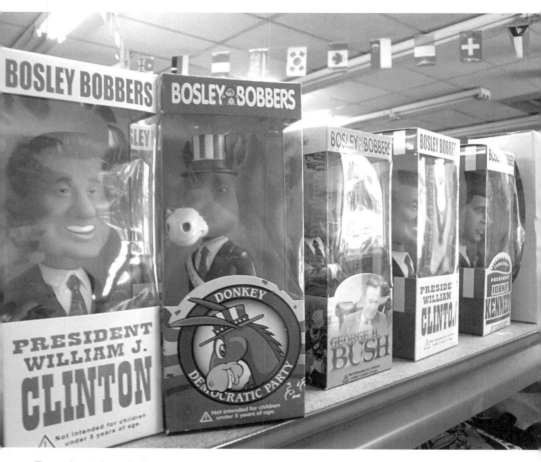

The wacky sit alongside the requisite postcards, key chains, and T-shirts at Joe's. Photo by Nathan Borchelt

Political Americana (1-800-333-4555; politicalamericana.com; 1331 Pennsylvania Ave., N.W., Washington; nearest Metro: Federal Triangle, Blue and Orange lines). A profusion of standard-fare D.C. souvenirs may be the first thing you notice, but Political Americana is also one of the few places in the country where you can find political collectibles like a lapel pin from Reagan's last campaign for governor of California, an inaugural letter of appreciation penned by JFK, a wide variety of historical photographs, and oddball items like an FBI baseball.

The Virginia Shop (703-836-3160 or 1-888-297-8288; www.thevirginiashop.com; 104 S. Union St., Alexandria; no Metro access). Most visitors to D.C. are sure to bring back souvenirs from the capital city, but this charming country shop in Old Town Alexandria encourages guests to bring back a little of Virginia as well. Virginia foods, wines, and trinkets are housed in a historic building that dates to 1765. Especially popular are the salty Smithfield hams and a large variety of flavored peanuts—many of which are laid out for sampling each day. Also look for crab seasoning and a delicious variety of bread and biscuit mixes; the Sally Lunn bread is a traditional Virginia favorite.

White House Visitor Center Gift Shop (202-737-8292; 1450 Pennsylvania Ave., N.W., Washington; nearest Metro: Federal Triangle, Blue and Orange lines). Even if you don't have an interest in touring the White House, the exhibits on display at the visitor center portray the fascinating history of the presidential residence. The adjoining gift shop proffers souvenirs and collectibles embossed with the White House insignia, from china and mugs to T-shirts, postcards, and books.

The National Mall lights up with brilliant color as fireworks explode near the Washington Monument. Photo courtesy of the Washington, D.C., Convention and Tourism Corporation. Used with permission.

9

Handy Facts

Know Before You Go

Surprises can be the most memorable parts of a vacation. But it never hurts to be prepared, in case one of these unexpected adventures turns unpleasant. What follows is a brief guide that may help you resolve problems or answer questions once you arrive in town. We've also included a short bibliography on Washington, D.C., and Northern Virginia, so that if you're interested, you can do a little research ahead of your visit. Use this page as a quick reference to find what you need:

AMBULANCE, FIRE, AND POLICE

Like everywhere else in the United States, dial 911 for medical and police emergencies as well as fires. For police matters that are not emergencies, call:

Washington, D.C.   311
Alexandria, VA   703-838-4444
Arlington, VA   703-558-2222

AREA CODES, TOWN GOVERNMENTS, AND ZIP CODES

Area Codes

When calling from the District to Virginia or vice versa, you must dial the area code first; you must also dial the area code to make a local call *within* Virginia, even if it's to the same area code. However, you need not dial "1" before the area code. There are no long-distance or additional toll charges for calling between Washington, D.C., Arlington, and Alexandria.

Washington, D.C.?202   Alexandria, VA?703   Arlington, VA?703

Town Governments

Washington, D.C., City Hall
202-333-5640
2218 Wisconsin Ave., N.W.
Washington, D.C., 20016

Alexandria City Hall
703-838-4000
301 King St.
Alexandria, VA 22314

Arlington County Board
703-228-3130
2100 Clarendon Blvd., Suite 300
Arlington, VA 22201

ZIP Codes

Washington, D.C.   20001–20599
Alexandria, VA   22201–22209
Arlington, VA   22301–22322

BIBLIOGRAPHY

Architecture and Art

Art in the United States Capitol. Washington, D.C.: U.S. Government Printing Office, 1978.

Goode, James M. *Best Addresses.* Washington, D.C.: Smithsonian Institution, 1988.

——. *The Outdoor Sculpture of Washington, D.C.: A Comprehensive Historical Guide.* Washington, D.C.: Smithsonian Institution, 1974.

Gutheim, Frederick. *Worthy of a Nation: The History of Planning for the National Capital.* Washington, D.C.: National Capital Planning Commission and Smithsonian Institution Press, 1977.

Lee, Antoinette J., and Pamela Scott. *Buildings of the District of Columbia.* New York: Oxford University Press, 1994.

Smith, Kathryn Schneider, ed. *Washington at Home.* Washington, D.C.: Columbia Historical Society, 1988.

Fiction

Blatty, William Peter. *The Exorcist.* New York: Harper and Row, 1971.

Brown, Rita Mae. *Dolley: A Novel of Dolley Madison in Love and War.* New York: Bantam, 1994.

Condon, Richard. *The Manchurian Candidate.* New York: McGraw-Hill, 1959.

Dos Passos, John. *The Grand Design.* Boston: Houghton Mifflin, 1949.

Roosevelt, Elliott. *Murder in the Red Room.* New York: St. Martin's Press, 1992.

Smith, Margaret Bayard. *A Winter in Washington; or Memoirs of the Seymour Family.* New York: E. Bliss and E. White, 1824.

Truman, Margaret. *Murder on Capitol Hill: A Novel.* New York: Arbor House, 1981.

——. *Murder at the FBI.* New York: Arbor House, 1985.

——. *Murder in the White House: A Novel.* New York: Arbor House, 1980.

Noteworthy architecture can be found throughout the District. Especially lovely are the many old federal structures, like the USDA Building just off the National Mall. Photo by Debbie K. Hardin.

Twain, Mark. *The Gilded Age.* Hartford, CT: American Publishing, 1883.
Vidal, Gore. *Empire: A Novel.* New York: Random House, 1987.
———. *Washington, D.C.: A Novel.* Boston: Little, Brown, 1967.

Films

Absolute Power (1996)	*The Manchurian Candidate* (2004; 1962)
All the President's Men (1976)	*National Treasure* (2004)
Bob Roberts (1992)	*National Treasure II* (2007)
Breach (2007)	*No Way Out* (1987)
Broadcast News (1987)	*The Sentinel* (2006)
Dave (1993)	*St. Elmo's Fire* (1985)
Dick (1999)	*Syriana* (2005)
The Exorcist (1973)	*X-Men* (2000)
A Few Good Men (1992)	*Wedding Crashers* (2005)

History and Politics

Abbott, Carl. *Political Terrain: Washington, D.C., From Tidewater Town to Global Metropolis.* Chapel Hill: University of North Carolina Press, 1999.
Apidta, Tingba. *The Hidden History of Washington, DC.* Washington, D.C.: The Reclamation Project, 1995.

The scandal at the Watergate complex helped make Carl Bernstein and Bob Woodward household names.
Photo by Debbie K. Hardin.

Bangura, Abdul Karim. *DC Vote: Fighting against Taxation without Representation.* Washington, D.C.: Writers Club Press, 2001.

Bernstein, Carl, and Bob Woodward. *All the President's Men.* New York: Simon & Schuster, 1974.

Carrier, Thomas J. *Images of America: Washington, D.C.: A Historical Walking Tour.* Charleston, SC: Arcadia, 1999.

Moore, John L. *Speaking of Washington.* Washington, D.C.: CQ Press, 1993.

O'Brien, Cormac. *Secret Lives of the U.S. Presidents.* Philadelphia: Quirk Books, 2004.

Williams, Paul K. *Images of America: Dupont Circle.* Charleston, SC: Arcadia, 2000.

CLIMATE, WEATHER, AND WHAT TO WEAR

Weather

Weather in D.C. is notoriously unpredictable, and transitional seasons (early spring and late fall) can fluctuate between steamy and icy in a matter of days. Precipitation is heavy throughout the year, so be sure to pack a good umbrella (although, frankly, in the heaviest rains, it won't do much good). It is also often quite windy, especially in the open expanses of the National Mall.

Winter: Count on winters being damp and cold (often bitterly so when wind-chill factors are taken into account). Although the area has received fewer snowstorms recently than in past decades, most winters see at least a few dustings of snow and one or two "accumulation events." The real threat in winter are the ice storms, which coat the tree branches in a delicate, glittery glaze—and make the streets and sidewalks downright treacherous. However, despite the likelihood of frigid weather at this time of year, there are often days of balmy relief.

Spring: Spring comes later here than winter-weary residents would like; the busiest tourist season—late March and into mid-April, when the cherry blossoms bloom and daffodils and tulips decorate the federal gardens—is often very chilly. Late spring is a wonderland of beauty in the District and Northern Virginia, with delicate pink and white dogwoods vying for attention with bombastic, brightly hued azaleas and rhododendrons. Note that this can be a particularly vicious time for allergy sufferers—many of whom don't even realize they *have* allergies until they visit D.C. in the spring.

Summer: Summer is generally the most consistent and predictable season: It is next to impossible to get away from the hot and very humid weather, which often culminates in dramatic lightning and thunderstorms and drenching rains in the late afternoons. However, despite the oppressive heat and stickiness, the trees are almost tropical in their displays of luxuriant deep greens, and sunsets are among the prettiest at this time of the year.

Fall: Fall is another lovely season, and a favorite with many locals because congestion drops off considerably as children go back to school. Expect generally mild temperatures day and night—although early fall can still feel like summer and late fall can be cold enough for snow and ice. Deciduous trees begin a spectacular color show as early as mid-October, generally peaking at the end of the month.

	Jan.	Feb.	Mar.	Apr.	May	June	July	Aug.	Sept.	Oct.	Nov.	Dec.
Avg. Temp. (°F)	43	47	55	66	76	84	89	87	80	69	58	48
Avg. Precip. (in.)	4	3	4	3	4	4	4	4	4	3	3	3

The North Lawn of the White House blanketed by a rare snowstorm. Photo courtesy of the Washington, D.C., Convention and Tourism Corporation. Used with permission.

What to Wear

Washington, D.C., is a formal city, and serious people in serious jobs dress to impress. Business wear is generally somber and conservative, with dark colors and little flash. Evening wear varies with the venue, of course; expect tuxedoes and evening gowns for the opera, suits and cocktail dresses for fine dining. Many finer restaurants insist on ties and jackets for gentlemen, while jeans and T-shirts are fine for just about every event on the National Mall.

Make sure you pack for a variety of weather conditions. In winter, bring a heavy water-proof coat, gloves, and hat; the February wind can be bone-chilling. But also pack a few lighter garments, because there are sometimes unseasonably warm spells throughout the winter, just as there are unseasonably hot spells during the spring. Throughout spring and fall, you'll want a sweater and light coat. As noted, summertime offers the least variable weather: It's going to be hot and it's going to be humid. Pack light-colored clothing that breathes, and although it's tempting to wear shorts and flip-flops in the 90-degree humidity, this attire isn't really appropriate outside of Smithsonian museums and recreational venues. As noted, expect rain whenever you visit, and bring a good umbrella (or buy one from a vendor located at the exit of just about every Metro station when the weather turns inclement). Likewise, whatever the season, expect to do a lot of walking and pack comfortable, sturdy shoes; many D.C. women wear sneakers or other flats to and from the Metro, then change into their more fashionable pumps once they arrive at their final destination.

CRIME

Washington, D.C.'s reputation precedes it—but the problem is, when many people think of the capital city and its crime problems, they are imagining the city of decades past. Violent crime is mostly confined to neighborhoods that are plagued with drug trafficking and gangs. These aren't the areas most tourists will see. To minimize risks, in the evening keep to the Northwest quadrant of the city—where most attractions fall anyhow—and use caution wherever you travel during the day. Although petty crime is a real threat throughout the city, as with any large city, a little street smarts goes a long way. Avoid openly displaying cash, keep handbags and wallets secure, and be sure to keep vehicles locked. In addition, it's always wise to know where you're going before you set out, both to avoid getting sidetracked into a less desirable neighborhood and to avoid looking like a cash-laden tourist.

HANDICAP SERVICES

Washington, D.C., and Northern Virginia are well equipped to accommodate visitors with disabilities. Most restaurants, hotels, museums, and national monuments are handicap accessible, as are most cultural venues, including theaters, movie houses, and even historic properties, which have been retrofitted to allow wheelchair access.

Public transportation is also well designed for disabled patrons. All Metro stations have elevators, although they malfunction on a frustratingly regular basis. When detours are necessary to the next stop down the line, handicap-accessible Metro buses should be waiting to transport riders to the required station. Call Metrorail about current information regarding elevator and escalator malfunctions (202-637-7000 or TTY 202-638-3780).

There are Braille instructions posted in subway stops as well as on the subway cars themselves, and wheelchair-accessible entries at every station. Once on the train platforms, visually impaired visitors will find a raised rubber border to alert them to their proximity to the tracks, and there are chains strung between subway cars to protect guests from mistakenly stepping into the gaps between. Metrobuses have wheelchair lifts. Check the **Washington Metropolitan Transit Authority** (202-962-1245; TTY 202-638-3780; www.wmata .com) for the most current information on public transportation accessibility, and contact them to secure an I.D. card that entitles disabled individuals to transportation discounts. (Be sure to request this I.D. several weeks in advance of a visit.)

Rental car agencies at the three major airports have hand-controlled cars and vehicles with other specialized equipment, as well as accessible shuttle service from the terminals. Be sure to specify your needs in advance to ensure that a properly equipped rental is available.

Pedestrian travel is a slightly bigger obstacle within the city, thanks to ubiquitous renovation that often forces detours around sidewalks and restricts travel to one side of a street. In addition, the sidewalks themselves are sometimes hazardous, thanks to a continual freeze–thaw cycle that has left many byways cracked and pitted—although this is more of an issue in the business districts and less so in the heavily populated tourist areas of the National Mall and around major federal buildings, which are generally kept in better repair. Finally, traffic circles are a challenge even for able walkers, and allotted crossing times are often ridiculously short.

The Smithsonian Institution publishes a booklet titled "Smithsonian Access," which provides up-to-date information on accessibility for the museums throughout the city. These are available at the information desks of all museums. A limited number of wheelchairs are available at each museum. For the most comprehensive and up-to-date information on handicap accessibility throughout the area, check out **Access Information's** "Washington, DC, Access Guide" (301-528-8664; www.disabilityguide.org).

HOSPITALS

Arlington Hospital
703-558-5000
1701 N. George Mason Dr., Arlington

Children's Hospital National Medical Center
202-476-5000
111 Michigan Ave., N.W., Washington

George Washington University Hospital
202-715-4000
900 23rd St., N.W., Washington

Georgetown University Hospital
202-444-3111
4000 Reservoir Rd., N.W., Washington

Howard University Hospital
202-865-6100
2041 Georgia Ave., N.W., Washington

INOVA Alexandria Hospital
703-504-3000
4320 Seminary Rd., Alexandria

LOCAL MEDIA

Newspapers

Examiner	*Washington Blade*	*Washington Post*
Roll Call	*Washington City Paper*	*Washington Times*

Magazines

Metro Weekly *Washington Business Journal* *Washington Monthly*
On Tap Magazine *Washington Life Magazine* *Washingtonian*

Television

News Channel 8 (local news) WMDO, Channel 30 WRC, Channel 4 (NBC)
WETA, Channel 26 (PBS) *(Spanish language)* WUSA, Channel 9 (CBS)
WJLA, Channel 7 (ABC)

REAL ESTATE

Housing prices in Washington, D.C., are among the highest in the country. In 2005, the average selling price of a home in the District was more than $727,000. If you are looking to make D.C. your home, call the **Greater Capital Area Association of Realtors** (301-590-2000), which can refer you to licensed agents to help you buy or rent. You can also check out real estate Web sites for photographs and other specifics on current listings (a good source is www.realtor.com) or peruse the *Washington Post* real estate section in the Saturday paper, which is helpful in tracking new construction and finding existing properties for sale.

RELIGIOUS SERVICES

Because Washington, D.C., is such a multicultural city, you'll find just about every religion represented here, and many services are offered in languages other than English. To find particular religious services, check the USA Worship Here Directory (www.worshiphere.org) under Washington, D.C.

ROAD SERVICE

Getting stranded on the freeway is no one's idea of vacation fun. For emergency road service, members can call the American Automobile Association at 1-800-222-4357. Numerous local tow companies offer 24-hour assistance as well. Beware of tow trucks that come without being called first; such trucks troll the local highways and the Beltway for stranded motorists and often charge exorbitant towing rates. Get a quote in writing before you allow any company to move your vehicle.

SEASONAL EVENTS

Festivals are on a grand scale in D.C. and Northern Virginia, and it isn't unusual for the president of the U.S. to show up—along with tens of thousands of others. There are a plethora of free concerts and cultural events throughout the year, and regardless of weather, they are well attended. Plan to take public transportation and arrive as early as possible. Expect crowds, and be patient with the inevitable security measures that go along with them.

JANUARY: Kick off the year with events commemorating **Martin Luther King Jr.'s Birthday.** The official holiday is the third Monday in January, but observances begin the Friday before at the Department of the Interior (202-619-7222). Additional events are held

Beautifully restored town homes are among the most sought-after properties in the District.

Photo by Debbie K. Hardin.

at the Martin Luther King Jr. Memorial Library (202-727-0321). In Alexandria, check out the **Lee Birthday Celebrations** for Confederate General Robert E. Lee and Revolutionary War hero (and Robert E. Lee's dad) Harry Lee at the Lee-Fendall House (703-548-1789) on the third Sunday of the month. Festivities include tours of the house, music, and food. And, of course, every four years in late January, the **Presidential Inauguration** virtually shuts down the city, with an enormous parade of floats, bands, and (traditionally) the new president and spouse walking from Constitution Avenue down to Pennsylvania Avenue, from the U.S. Capitol to the White House.

FEBRUARY: In early February, **Chinese New Year** is celebrated for 10 or more days with street parades and fireworks throughout Chinatown, centering around the Friendship Arch at Seventh and H Streets, N.W. To blow off steam before the start of Lent, the wacky **Shrove Tuesday Pancake Race** is held the day before Ash Wednesday at the Washington National Cathedral (202-537-6200), continuing an odd yet hilarious English tradition of racing while flipping pancakes in a frying pan. Participants include local pastors as well as students from District parochial schools. **Abraham Lincoln's Birthday** on February 12 is observed at the Lincoln Memorial; the Gettysburg Address is read and a wreath is laid at noon. **George Washington's Birthday** is also commemorated with a wreath-laying this month, this time at the Washington Monument. Alexandria celebrates GW's birthday with the country's largest **Birthday Parade**, held in Old Town (703-991-4474; www.washington-birthday.com), along with a 10K race and a traditional Birthnight Banquet and Ball. February is also **Black History Month** throughout the country, and is celebrated in D.C. with special events at numerous Smithsonian museum sites as well as the Martin Luther King Jr. Library.

MARCH: Don your green garments and head to the festive **St. Patrick's Day Parade** (202-789-7000), which features exuberant marching bands and floats rolling down Constitution Avenue, N.W., from about Seventh through 17th Streets, on the Sunday immediately preceding March 17. Also this month on a Saturday (or sometimes on a weekend in early April), as part of the Cherry Blossom Festival, the very well-attended **Smithsonian Kite Festival** is held on the grounds surrounding the Washington Monument. Children of all ages are invited to show off their kite-making and kite-flying prowess at this annual event.

APRIL: There is probably no more photographed site in the city than the Tidal Basin at the Jefferson Memorial (as well as at Hains Point and scattered throughout the National Mall) during cherry blossom season, when the small flowers of thousands of Japanese cherry trees explode in delicate balloons of pale pink and white. Although the blooms come and go in a matter of days, the city celebrates for several weeks. (See the sidebar on page 300.) If you have young children, don't miss the **White House Easter Egg Roll** (202-208-1631), held the Saturday before Easter and again the Monday after. Kids aged 7 and younger are invited onto the South Lawn to hunt for wooden eggs, "roll" eggs with big wooden spoons, and enjoy costumed characters and special activities for youngsters. This tradition dates to 1878 and is extraordinarily popular; obtain timed tickets at the National Parks Service Ellipse Visitors Pavilion at 15th and E Streets starting at 7:30 AM (although expect to see lines forming for these tickets as early as the night before). Plan to arrive for the event as early as possible, because it takes longer to get through security than one would imagine, and generally the president makes an appearance early on in the festivities. **Sunrise Easter Service** is held at Arlington National Cemetery on Easter Sunday beginning at 6:15 AM in the Memorial Amphitheater; seating is first-come, first-served (703-607-8000). **Thomas**

Jefferson's Birthday on April 13 takes center stage at the Jefferson Memorial where—you guessed it—wreaths are laid and speeches are made. Also this month, movie-lovers will not want to miss the weeklong **Filmfest DC** (www.filmfestdc.org) at the end of April, a showcase of innovative cinema from some of the most talented filmmakers in the world. And since 2005, **Emancipation Day** is celebrated in the District on April 16 as a citywide holiday to commemorate the day in 1862 when President Abraham Lincoln signed the release of more than 3,000 slaves in D.C.—nearly a year before he signed the Emancipation Proclamation, which eventually led to the abolition of slavery throughout the U.S. In addition to a parade downtown, expect observances in venues throughout the city.

MAY: Get a peek into some of the city's loveliest private gardens during the **Georgetown Garden Tour** (202-789-7000) early this month; admission fees (about $30) include beverages and light snacks. Another great place to catch seasonal blooms is at the **National Cathedral Flower Mart** (www.nationalcathedral.org), a two-day festival at the beginning of the month that features floral displays, gardening hints, puppet shows, and other children's entertainment. At the end of the month, catch the **Memorial Day** ceremony at Arlington Cemetery (703-607-8000), where a wreath is placed at the Tomb of the Unknown Soldier. High-ranking government officials are on hand to make remarks, and this is often a good place to see the president. There's also a **National Memorial Day Parade** that runs along Constitution Avenue. You'll find services at the National World War II Memorial, the Vietnam Veterans Memorial, and the Korean War Veterans Memorial as well. A less somber observation of the official beginning of summer is held on the West Lawn of the Capitol, where the National Symphony Orchestra stages an **Annual Free Memorial Day Concert** beginning at 8 PM. And running from the end of this month through early June, the Shakespeare Theatre presents its annual **Free for All** (www.shakespearetheatre.org), with no-cost performances of Shakespeare plays at the Carter Barron Amphitheatre in Rock Creek Park.

Each year the patriotic National Memorial Day Parade rolls down Constitution Avenue, passing in front of the National Archives. Photo by Nathan Borchelt.

JUNE: Explore several eclectic neighborhoods in the **Dupont-Kalorama Museum Walk Day**, which highlights historic homes and museums and offers music, food, and crafts for children; this annual tradition is held on the first weekend of the month. The **Columbia Pike Blues Festival** kicks off in the middle of the month, with live music, food, and entertainment on South Walter Reed Drive in Arlington, Virginia. The **Juneteenth Celebration** (703-838-4356; www.alexblackhistory.org; 900 block of Wythe St.) is a family-oriented festival celebrating the day in African American history when slaves in Texas learned about their emancipation; this free event in Old Town Alexandria offers live music, food, and genealogists. Also starting this month is the **Smithsonian Festival of American Folklife**, an annual free event held on the National Mall that highlights the cultural traditions of a handful of select nations and states. This is a great event at which to enjoy authentic regional food, free music and dancing, and more crafts for the kids. This festival runs until the Sunday following the Fourth of July weekend. Also this month, celebrate girl power at the world's largest gathering of Girl Scouts, the **Girl Scout Sing-Along** (www.gscnc.org /singalong) held on the National Mall.

JULY: There is likely no better fireworks show on earth than the annual **Independence Day** show held on the National Mall each year on July 4. In addition, the day's festivities include the **National Independence Day Parade** down Constitution Avenue, a reading of the Declaration of Independence at the National Archives, and a truly fabulous evening concert on the west steps of the Capitol Building featuring the National Symphony Orchestra and many internationally recognized artists. There are also concerts on the open-air stage just east of the base of the Washington Monument. For more information on the day's events, call 202-789-7000. And if you miss the fireworks on the National Mall, never fear: The weekend after the Fourth celebration is the **USA and Alexandria Birthday Celebration** (703-883-4686; www.alexsym.org; held in Oronoco Bay Park at Union and Madison Sts. in Old Town), which offers entertainment by the Alexandria Symphony Orchestra and more fireworks—displayed in sync with Tchaikovsky's *1812 Overture*. If your musical tastes are slightly less classical, check out the **DC Hip-Hop Theater Festival** (www.hiphoptheaterfest.org), which includes live music from local and national artists, live theater, and dance performances. Catch a free classic movie every Monday this month and through August on a giant screen on the National Mall between Fourth and Seventh Streets at the annual **Screen on the Green** (www.nps.gov). And for about 10 days at the end of the month, catch the **Capitol Fringe Festival** (www.capitolfringe.org), an eclectic collection of performance art staged at a variety of venues throughout the District; ticket prices are kept low to keep the festival as accessible as possible.

AUGUST: Beat the high prices of D.C. dining early this month during **Washington DC Restaurant Week** (www.restaurantweekdc.com), when diners can enjoy three-course meals at select restaurants at substantial savings—a little more than $20 for lunch and $30 for dinner. In late August, catch the homespun fun of the **Arlington County Fair** (703-920-4556), held at the Thomas Jefferson Community Center (3501 S. Second St., Arlington) and featuring midway games, carnival rides, live entertainment, and plenty of food. And in Alexandria, don't miss costumed interpreters re-enacting history at the **Carlyle Housewarming** (www.carlylehouse.org).

SEPTEMBER: Another splendid opportunity to enjoy the talents of the National Symphony Orchestra, the **Labor Day Concert** is a free event held at 8 PM on the Sunday before Labor Day on the West Lawn of the Capitol. In the past, concerts have been moved to the Kennedy Center if the weather promises to be inclement. Call 202-619-7222 for details. In midmonth, the fun and inclusive **Black Family Reunion** (www.ncnw.org) comes to the National Mall. This free celebration of African American culture and tradition includes food, music, and performances, and all are welcome. Another party not to be missed this month is the **Adams-Morgan Day** celebration, running along 18th Street and Columbia Road, N.W. In addition to a bewildering display of international food from the neighborhood's cornucopia of excellent restaurants, visitors will find plenty of music and dancing—and plenty of fellow revelers. In Alexandria, check out some of the city's loveliest privately owned houses during the **Tour of Historic Alexandria Homes,** held the third Saturday of the month. And in Arlington this month, don't miss the **Rosslyn Jazz Festival** (703-696-3399), featuring numerous live performances in Gateway Park on North Lynn Street.

OCTOBER: This month closes with the fifth-largest marathon in the country: More than 30,000 participants take part in the annual **Marine Corps Marathon** (202-RUN-USMC) on the fourth Sunday of the month, starting at the Marine Corps Memorial in Arlington, Virginia, and winding over the Potomac and through more than 26 miles in the city. Even if you don't participate, it's fun to cheer on the brave souls who do. But remember that many of the city's streets will be closed for the race, so come early and take public transportation. Also this month, get ready for spooky fun in Alexandria on the **Halloween Walking Tour,** a lantern-guided stroll through graveyards and haunted sites, featuring some of the area's creepiest legends and myths.

NOVEMBER: The somber holiday of **Veterans Day** is observed with a wreath ceremony at 11 AM at the Tomb of the Unknown Soldier in Arlington National Cemetery (703-607-8000), followed by a memorial service at which a high-ranking government official (generally the president) speaks. At the end of the month, find unusual holiday gift items in Old Town Alexandria at the annual **Torpedo Factory Art Center Holiday Open House** (703-838-4565; www.torpedofactory.org). Guests can check out pieces created by the resident artists, as well as enjoy live music and refreshments.

DECEMBER: Celebrate the start of the holiday season at the **Christmas Pageant of Peace** (202-208-1631), which kicks off early this month with the annual **National Tree Lighting Ceremony** held on the Ellipse behind the White House, at which a high-ranking official from the administration (sometimes the president) ceremonially lights the National Christmas Tree. In addition, you'll also find a large National Menorah, smaller Christmas trees from every one of the country's states and territories, and a toasty yule log fire. The Pageant of Peace continues for four weeks and includes free musical performances nightly on the Ellipse. Note that even though the event is free, you must obtain advance tickets to attend the ceremony. Also early in the month, don't miss the stunning **Annual Holiday Parade of Boats** (703-838-5005; www.funside.com) in Old Town Alexandria; more than 50 boats decorated in twinkling lights illuminate the Potomac River waterfront while visitors enjoy live music and entertainment. During the second week in December, take part in the **Historic Alexandria Candlelight Tour,** which features Colonial dancing, madrigal singers, and visits to seasonally decorated historic homes. Wrap up the year with **First Night Alexandria** (703-838-5005; www.firstnightalexandria.org), an alcohol-free, family-oriented New Year's Eve celebration in Old Town that offers live performances and fireworks at midnight.

SECURITY MEASURES POST-SEPTEMBER 11

Gaining admission to Smithsonian museums takes longer than it did before the 9/11 terrorist attacks. Security measures are in place at every museum; expect to have your bags and

Crazy for Cherry Blossoms

The District of Columbia is known as the City of Trees, and every spring the city goes particularly wild over one blossoming variety. The pale pink cherry trees for which the city is famous inspire bartenders around D.C. to concoct new cocktails like the frozen cherry bellini at **Bangkok Joe's** (202-333-4422; 3000 K St., N.W.) and the Cherrypolitan at **Morton's** (202-342-6258; 3251 Prospect St., N.W.); pastry chefs to create new masterpieces like the white chocolate cherry cake with cherry blossom essence at **Café MoZU** at the Mandarin Oriental (202-787-6040; 1330 Maryland Ave., N.W.) and **Indebleu's** (202-333-2538; 707 G St., N.W.) saffron cardamom crème brûlée with vanilla braised cherries; and the city's finest chefs to whip up new entrées like crisp salmon with cherry butter at **The Oceanaire Seafood Room** (202-347-2277; 1201 F St., N.W.) or the wild cherry and wine braised short ribs at the Fairmont Hotel's **Juniper** (202-457-5020; 2400 M St., N.W.).

To *really* celebrate the cherry trees, the city also puts on a two-week party every year in late March/early April to coincide with the peak blossom period. Highlights of the **National Cherry Blossom Festival** include a colorful, eclectic parade down Constitution Avenue that features lively taiko drumming by corps from Japan and the U.S.; delicately decorated floats adorned with pretty girls; and oversized balloon characters to amuse the kids. Visitors can purchase grandstand seats and watch the parade from bleachers along the route or just show up early and watch from the sidewalk. Another standout of the festival is the *Sakura Matsuri*, a one-day exhibition of Japanese culture that includes multiple live performance venues, karate demonstrations, a Japanese beer garden, traditional Japanese arts like *ikebana* (flower arrangement), and *kamishibai* (Japanese folk tales) for children. Get daily schedules of the festival from www.nationalcherryblossomfestival.org.

Delicate cherry blossoms draw spring crowds to D.C. by the tens of thousands. Photo by Debbie K. Hardin.

purses hand-checked or X-rayed—which inevitably causes delays in gaining admittance. Some museums require that backpacks and large bags be left behind. It's a good idea to bring only what you need.

SERVICE EXPECTATIONS

John F. Kennedy once said, "Washington, D.C., has all the charm of the North and all the efficiency of the South." When it comes to service in the city, who are we to argue with the president? Although there are exceptions, of course—especially in fine dining establishments and four-star accommodations—visitors to D.C. are generally struck by the slow pace in restaurants, stores, and hotels, and the sometimes less-than-civil approach to customer service throughout all industries. Some have wondered if this can be explained by the low rate of unemployment in the city. Indeed, many of the finest establishments in the D.C. tourist industry regularly recruit employees from Europe and Asia, presumably to widen the net for the best qualified job candidates. Whatever the explanation, in the likely event that you encounter rude or inefficient service, try not to take it personally. Tourists in general are not treated any worse than locals—although this is cold comfort if you're on the receiving end of a snotty waiter! By all means, don't be shy about complaining when service is subpar. Restaurant and hotel managers are generally quite sensitive to this sort of criticism, and if they *can* ameliorate the situation, they will usually do so.

SMOKING LAWS

Smoking is prohibited in restaurants, bars, and most other public venues in the District of Columbia. However, cross the river into Virginia (an old tobacco state), and it's a different story. Despite recent legislative moves toward a ban on smoking in public areas in Virginia, the commonwealth still allows smoking in restaurants and bars, and leaves it up to individual establishments to create (or not) nonsmoking sections. When such divisions exist, they are often meaningless—for example, a partitionless room may be designated a nonsmoking dining area, but it may be located within a few feet of a very smoky bar.

TOURIST INFORMATION AND ONLINE ADDRESSES

Alexandria Visitors Center
703-838-4200
www.funside.com
221 King St., Alexandria, VA 22314

Arlington Visitors Center
703-228-5720
www.stayarlington.com
1301 Joyce St., Arlington, VA 22202

Cultural Tourism D.C.
www.culturaltourismdc.org

Washington, D.C., Convention and Tourism Corporation
202-789-7000 or 1-800-422-8644
www.washington.org
901 Seventh St., N.W., Washington, D.C. 20001

Washington Post (nightlife, restaurant reviews, weather)
www.washingtonpost.com

The U.S. Capitol from the southwest lawn. Photo by Debbie K. Hardin.

10

If Time Is Short

The Best of the Best

In a city as rich in culture, history, and entertainment possibilities as Washington, D.C., it isn't easy to narrow down the alternatives and come up with a "best of the best" list. What follows are our favorites, and we're confident they won't disappoint. We hope that you use this book to go out and find your own favorites as well.

CULTURAL AND HISTORICAL ATTRACTIONS

John F. Kennedy Center for the Performing Arts (202-467-4600; www.kennedy-center.org; 2700 F St., N.W., Washington). This elegant, expansive center located on the picturesque Potomac River is more than a venue: It's an homage to the American performing arts. You'll find the very best of the theater, opera, ballet, and symphonic music here. Ticket prices can be steep, but there are numerous free performances throughout the year that can help stretch your budget. Even if you aren't up for a show, come to see the incomparable vistas from the terrace (views of the Fourth of July fireworks are tops here); get a tour of the opulent Opera House; or just head to the rooftop **KC Cafeteria** for an oversized chocolate chip cookie or a glass of wine and watch the planes skim the Potomac River as they head into Reagan National Airport.

Lincoln Memorial (202-426-6841; www.nps.gov/linc; westernmost end of the Mall between Constitution and Independence Aves., N.W.). All memorials on the National Mall are must-sees, but the Lincoln remains our favorite. Whether you come to read the inscribed words of the Great Emancipator himself, stand on the exact spot where Martin Luther King Jr. delivered his historic "I Have a Dream" speech, or just remember film character Forrest Gump finding his beloved here, the Lincoln Memorial is a surprisingly moving experience. Come at dusk and watch the lights come up; or arrive late at night, sit on the steps, and enjoy the moonlight playing off the Reflecting Pool.

Mount Vernon (703-780-2000; www.mountvernon.org; 3200 Mount Vernon Memorial Hwy., Mount Vernon). Nowhere does history come alive more than Mount Vernon, the lovely home of our first president. Touring the meticulously restored mansion, expansive gardens, and poignant slave quarters allows visitors an intimate look at George and Martha Washington that goes beyond the pages of a textbook and provides a glimpse into what their genteel life must have been like. Don't miss the chance to sit on the old-fashioned wooden chairs lined up on the back porch and gaze out at the peaceful Potomac River beyond.

The Kennedy Center is the jewel in the crown of D.C.'s performing arts community. Photo courtesy of the Washington, D.C., Convention and Tourism Corporation. Used with permission.

National Air and Space Museum (202-633-1000; www.nasm.si.edu; Independence Ave. and Seventh St., S.W., Washington). The National Air and Space Museum is by far the most popular museum on the National Mall—and with good reason. Exhibits in this inspiring gallery capture the imagination of adults and children alike and pay tribute to the ambitious human spirit and the seemingly limitless possibilities that science and engineering make possible. If your time is limited—and the crowds are discouraging—be sure to take time to touch the moon rock near the security checkpoint and lift your eyes to the *Spirit of St. Louis,* suspended in a place of honor near the front door. And if you can squeeze in another hour, catch an entertaining and educational IMAX film.

LODGING

Hotel Monaco (202-628-7177 or 1-800-649-1202; www.monaco-dc.com; 700 F St., N.W., Washington). This fanciful and chic property offers the best of both worlds: Modern style and high design packaged in an elegant, historic structure. The prime location in the hot Penn Quarter puts guests within steps of fine dining, myriad cultural opportunities, and exciting nightlife. Hospitable, efficient service from staff with a keen sense of humor and whimsy makes staying at the Hotel Monaco a fun and relaxing respite from the stress and strife of the big city.

The River Inn (202-337-7600 or 1-800-424-2741; www.theriverinn.com; 924 25th St., N.W., Washington). Large suites with expansive picture windows; a convenient, quiet location between the sought-after neighborhoods of Foggy Bottom and Georgetown; and stylish and inviting decor make The River Inn a fantastic lodging choice, regardless of the price. Add to the mix the relatively low rates available throughout the year and this hotel rockets to the top of our list as one of the best values in the city. The stunning Dish, a jewel-box restaurant downstairs, is an added bonus.

Willard InterContinental Washington (202-628-9100 or 1-800-827-1747; www.washington.intercontinental.com; 1401 Pennsylvania Ave., N.W., Washington). Rooms without a view can fetch upwards of $1,000 a night here, but if money is no object, the iconic Willard is the place to stay in the District. There is no more historically relevant hotel in the city, and the Willard's guest list reads like a who's who of American politics, highbrow culture, and high society. Visitors are treated like royalty—in part because many visitors *are* royalty—and the opulent, Old World atmosphere and impeccably professional service make even us commoners feel worthy.

RESTAURANTS

Michel Richard Citronelle (202-625-2150; www.citronelledc.com; 3000 M St., N.W., Washington). You won't find a finer dining experience in Washington, D.C. Period. Chef Michel Richard is nothing short of a culinary genius, and his dishes are routinely exquisite—poetically imaginative, lusciously beautiful, and surprisingly fortifying as

Look for the Spirit of St. Louis *near the entrance of the National Air and Space Museum.*
Photo by Debbie K. Hardin.

If walls could talk: The renowned Willard is one of the finest historic accommodations in the world.
Photo by Debbie K. Hardin.

well. Service is warm, well orchestrated, and unobtrusive. Citronelle is not a well-kept secret, so come here and expect to rub elbows with political heavyweights, deep-pocket lobbyists, and the occasional Hollywood celebrity. The restaurant is an expensive indulgence, for sure, but well worth it for the gourmet experience of a lifetime.

The Reef (202-518-3800; www.thereefdc.com; 2446 18th St., N.W., Washington). This establishment elevates the genre of gastro-pub cuisine to dizzying levels of satisfaction and surprise, in part because they use only locally grown, all-organic ingredients. Fantastic beer, gourmet twists on the traditional, and sinful desserts—all without dropping half your paycheck on one meal. The restaurant has three levels, including an expansive, year-round roof deck; a small, jungle-themed, street-level lounge; and a large second-floor dining room—and the kitchen is open from brunch to late night.

Thai Square (703-685-7040; www.thaisquarerestaurant.com; 3217 Columbia Pike, Arlington). This hole-in-the-wall may not be much to look at, but the crowded dining room encourages a second glance. Simply put, this place dishes out our favorite Thai food in the city, with menu items familiar both to people who grew up on Bangkok street food and those exposed only to Americanized versions. Even better, it'll never put a dent in your wallet.

NIGHTLIFE

Nightclub 9:30 (202-393-0930; www.930.com; 815 V St., N.W., Washington). If you are a fan of live, loud music in a place with no chairs and a profusions of bars, then this place is destined to become the one venue to which you compare all others. Consistently rated as one of the best nightclubs in the country, among musicians the 9:30 holds near-iconic status. Why? How about a wraparound second-floor balcony, a basement-level bar, and a sound system so pure it makes your iPod headset sound like two cans tied together with a taut piece of string? This world-class venue is graced by artists whose styles range from hip-hop to D.C.'s own go-go, indie pop to alt-country, electronica to international lounge, roots music to funk.

One of PX's artful concoctions.
Photo by Meshelle Armstrong. Used with permission.

Russia House (202-234-9433; 1800 Connecticut Ave., N.W., Washington). To experience the international personality of D.C. at its best, travel north of Dupont Circle, climb the stone stairs at Connecticut and Florida Avenues, and slip into the sumptuous glories of this intimate lounge. The Old World decor; the perpetually buzzing vibe; and an unpredictable mixture of Russian ex-pats, locals, and diplomats tossing back shots of vodka like medicine might make you think you've stepped into D.C.'s version of Cold War Moscow.

PX (703-299-8384; www.eamonnsdublinchipper.com; 728 King St., Alexandria). The logistics of this Old Town Alexandria watering hole are a little pretentious (no sign, just a small blue light and a pirate flag flown by its downstairs neighbor, Eamonn's restaurant; you buzz to gain access; and a list of "rules" are posted in the stairway, including a request for respectable dress). But if you can snag one of the 30 or so seats at this 21st-century speakeasy, the little hassles will not detract from the overall charm. The intimate interior creates an inviting, turn-of-the-century feel, but it's the seasonal drinks that demand repeated visits. Each and every ingredient here (save the liquor itself) has been handcrafted in house, from the bitters to the soda water and cola to the kumquats fermented in liquor for more than a year. The cocktails themselves look *almost* too good to drink—and they taste even better.

Subject Index

Lodging Index by Price

Restaurant Index by Price

Restaurant Index by Cuisine

American

America, 176–177
Ardeo, 199–200
Ben's Chili Bowl, 216–217
Breadline, 211
Bus Boys and Poets, 217
Café Lombardy, 76
Café Promenade, 82
Café Saint Ex, 197–198
Cascade Café, 109
Cashion's Eat Place, 172–173
Castle Café and Coffee Bar, 115
CityZen, 170
Clyde's, 192–193
Diner, The, 213
Dish, 83
Evening Star Café, 207
Five Guys, 211
Garden Café, 109
Hard Times Café, 219–220
Indigo Landing, 208–209
Jack's Restaurant and Bar, 215
Little Fountain Café, 173
Love Café, 217–218
Luna Grill and Diner, 215
Majestic, The, 210
Market Lunch, 213
Morrison-Clark Inn Restaurant, 74
Occidental, 172
Old Ebbitt Grill, 171–172
Reef, The, 175–176
Restaurant Eve, 210–211
Restaurant Nora, 189–190
Seasons, 86
1789 Restaurant, 190–191
Source, The, 156
Spy City Café, 153
Tryst, 213
Urbana, 77
Vidalia, 190
Willard Grill, 70
Zola, 186–187

Asian Fusion

Mie N Yu, 194–195
Teaism, 214–215
TenPenh, 185–186

Barbeque

Capital Q, 214
Old Glory, 196
Rocklands BBQ and Grilling Company, 218–219

Cajun

Acadiana, 179–180

Chinese

Full Kee, 214

Colonial American

Christiana Campbell's Tavern (Williamsburg), 57
Gadsby's Tavern Restaurant, 207–208
King's Arms Tvern (Williamsburg), 56–57
Mt. Vernon Inn, 143

Continental

Astor International Cuisine, The, 212–213
Colonnade, The, 75
Grille, The, 208

Ethiopian

Meskerem, 173–174
Zed's, 196–197

French

Bastille, 206–207
Bistro, The, 75
Bistro Bis, 177
Bistro du Coin, 187